في ذكرى

مارك لينز

The Unfinished Arab Spring

Micro-Dynamics of Revolts between Change and Continuity

edited by
Fatima El-Issawi and Francesco Cavatorta

GINGKO

First published in 2020 by
Gingko
4 Molasses Row
London SW11 3UX

ISBN 978-1-909942-48-6
e-ISBN 978-1-909942-49-3

Typeset in Times by MacGuru Ltd
Printed in the United Kingdom

www.gingko.org.uk
@GingkoLibrary

Contents

Acknowledgements

This book is partly based on the research project 'Media and Transitions to Democracy – Journalistic Practices in Communicating Conflicts: the Arab Spring'. The editors are grateful to the British Academy for generously funding our research. We likewise acknowledge the contribution of all the external reviewers who took the time to go painstakingly through the chapters and provide invaluable comments and suggestions on how to improve them. Without their work, the book would not have been what it is. The personnel at Gingko have been a true pleasure to work with, spurring us on when required and being patient when needed. Last, but certainly not least, the editors are truly indebted to the contributors who were both patient and responsive to all the requests we made. They all demonstrated great commitment to the project and delivered outstanding fieldwork-based research that greatly enriches the scholarship on social and political changes in the Arab world. This book is a testament to their professionalism and intellectual abilities.

1

Introduction. The Arab Uprisings: Micro-Dynamics of Activism and Revolt between Change and Continuity

Fatima El-Issawi and Francesco Cavatorta

The Arab uprisings of 2011 have generated a significant amount of scholarship, as they represented a seemingly momentous shift in the politics of the Middle East and North Africa. Although the implications and future consequences of these uprisings have yet to be fully teased out, given the relatively short period of time that has since elapsed, the revolts and their immediate aftermath have been dissected and analysed from numerous perspectives and theoretical frameworks. Central to such debates on how to interpret the uprisings has been the theorised struggle between democratisation and authoritarian resilience. Flowing from that macro-debate, there have been numerous studies looking at specific aspects of the uprisings, ranging from the actors driving the protests to the responses of the military and security apparatuses, and from the rise of political parties and elections to the massive violence and instability that characterises the region, including renewed sectarian rivalries. In light of the absence of genuine democratisation across the region – with the exception of Tunisia – more recent studies have examined the 'desire' for democracy that Arabs might, or might not, have, and the meaning that they give to the term. These studies are usually based on survey research, which carries with it a number of potential pitfalls. Narratives of the uprisings and their developments usually focus, moreover, on national actors and institutions, marginalising micro-dynamics of struggle and dissent.

Following the uprisings, we have also witnessed diverging institutional trajectories between the different countries involved, and it has therefore become quite difficult to generalise about the region. With an intensive focus on mainstream politics and institutions, and on regional-level analyses, comes the risk of failing to explore what happens 'below the radar' of ruling elites and established opposition parties and movements, within countries that have experienced a revolt and those where seemingly no changes took place. In short, there is a danger of making the same mistake as was made in the 2000s, when the focus on authoritarian mechanisms of reproduction of power and elites made it impossible to gauge the level of change occurring in society, and that was to lead to the 2011 revolts. Little has been said thus far about the inner dynamics of protest movements – both peaceful and violent – and the impact that these have on the everyday life on citizens, with significant consequences for the regimes in place. Central to the preoccupations of this book is the notion that the consequences of the 2011 Arab revolts have still to be fully worked out, and that their shockwaves might be felt for much longer than one would have expected, as the anti-regime movements in Algeria and Sudan in 2019 demonstrated. What the 2019 protests in two seemingly stable authoritarian countries suggested is that there are various micro-dynamics operating at the local level that often go undetected, and that there is a need to pay greater attention to these. Among the factors that have permitted local and often marginal movements to impact broader politics has been the ability of non-elite agents to use social media platforms to challenge regime policies: an issue highlighted in this volume. From football fans chanting anti-regime slogans in stadiums to ordinary citizens using YouTube to express frustration at their poor living conditions, a number of previously marginal social and political actors managed to disrupt mainstream media and politics, giving more space and power to subaltern, as against dominant, publics;[1] and the same patterns still characterise the politics of the Arab world, demonstrating that the effects of the 2011 revolts have not yet faded. The highlighting or downplaying of specific social and political contentions is connected to the role played by institutional media in shaping the trajectories and sometimes the outcomes of movements' struggles and priorities, through the important processes of framing and agenda-setting, direct and indirect alliances between media and the institutions of power and the way in which these alliances contribute to the formation of both media narratives and political processes in complex, interdependent dynamics.

---

1 Mohamed Zayani, *Networked Publics and Digital Contention*, Oxford 2015.

Democratisation, Authoritarianism and the Uprisings

A recent survey by Di Peri of the literature on democratisation and authoritarianism in the Arab world summarises how the paradigms of democratisation and authoritarian resilience have come to dominate our understanding of Arab political developments.[2] During the heydays of the democratisation paradigm in the 1980s and 1990s, the liberalising steps that Arab regimes were undertaking at the time were interpreted as an indication that democratic mechanisms and genuine political pluralism were about to make their way to the region, just as they had done in Eastern Europe and Latin America.[3] Despite its failure, the process of democratisation in Algeria seemed to confirm that democracy had become a central issue, and setbacks were to be expected, just as had occurred elsewhere before democracy succeeded in establishing itself.[4] By the early 2000s, the democratisation paradigm began to demonstrate signs of intellectual fatigue, as processes of democratisation that had begun over the previous decades stalled or were reversed.[5] Furthermore, the democracies that had been set up seemed quite weak. In the Arab world, the liberalising reforms of the 1990s turned out to be largely cosmetic: no Arab country transitioned to democracy, and many could be considered at best 'liberalised autocracies'.[6] Following on from this, the debate on Arab political systems shifted away from the democratisation paradigm to explore the reasons behind the survival of authoritarianism. It was argued that there was no real point in looking for signs of democratisation in the region, and that scholars should instead focus on what was confronting them in reality: namely, the survival of authoritarian rule behind a façade of the espousal of certain democratic mechanisms and pseudo-liberal reforms.[7] Faced with the seemingly unchanging authoritarian nature of Arab regimes, the success of the paradigm of authoritarian survival became the dominant theme within the literature, with research exploring

2 Rosita Di Peri, 'Democracy and Authoritarianism in the Arab World. Evolution of a Long Debate', *Nuovi Autoritarismi e Democrazie* 1.1, 2019, pp. 124–43.
3 Bahgat Korany, Rex Brynen and Paul Noble, *Liberalization and Democratization in the Arab World, Vol. 2: Comparative Experiences*, Boulder 1998.
4 Francesco Cavatorta, *The International Dimension of the Failed Algerian Transition. Democracy Betrayed?*, Manchester 2009.
5 Thomas Carothers, 'The End of the Transition Paradigm', *Journal of Democracy* 13.1, 2002, pp. 5–21.
6 Daniel Brumberg,. 'The Trap of Liberalised Autocracy', *Journal of Democracy* 13.4, 2002, pp. 56–68.
7 Lisa Anderson, 'Searching Where the Light Shines: Studying Democratization in the Middle East', *Annual Review of Political Science* 9, 2006, pp. 189–214; Steven Heydemann, 'Upgrading Authoritarianism in the Arab World', Analysis Paper 13, Brookings Institution 2007, https://www.brookings.edu/wp-content/uploads/2016/06/10arabworld.pdf.

the different strategies that regimes applied to remain in power. The dominance of this paradigm went unchallenged, as the reality on the ground did not seem to shift, with the majority of authoritarian leaders, such as Mubarak, Ben Ali, Saleh and Qaddafi having been in power since the 1980s, while in monarchies power was simply passed on to the next generation. The Syrian regime, for its part, experienced a quasi-monarchical transfer of power with Hafez al-Assad's son Bashar taking over the presidency, and suggestions that a similar process could take place in a number of other republics seemed to confirm that Arab authoritarian regimes were secure.[8] The focus on the part of the vast majority of scholars of the Arab world upon authoritarian survival was not necessarily misplaced, as it reflected the level of analysis with which the literature was mostly concerned: namely, national actors and institutions. A few scholars did analyse politics 'under the radar',[9] and contended that Arab societies were in a state of mobilisation when one looked away from national politics and focused instead on local actors. Indeed, many voices for change were active and audible on the margins, but these did not receive much academic, political or media attention. Those who pointed to the relevance of the voices on the margins turned out to be correct, however, although surprise at the uprisings was still considerable.[10] The revolts modified the scholarly debate once more, with the democratisation paradigm returning to the forefront to explain the events and suggest how they might develop.[11] The paradigm is also highly prescriptive, and it was therefore offered as a guide to what actors should or should not do to make the transition to democracy successful. Enthusiasm for the uprisings – both scholarly and among policy-makers – ended quite quickly, as processes of transition to democracy failed and a number of countries descended into civil conflict. As for those countries that did not experience a civil conflict, authoritarianism retrenched. This led to the return of the authoritarian

---

8 Larbi Sadiki, 'Whither Arab "Republicanism"? The Rise of Family Rule and the "End of Democratization" in Egypt, Libya and Yemen', *Mediterranean Politics* 15.1, 2010, pp. 99–107.

9 Amin Allal, 'Réformes néolibérales, clientélismes et protestations en situation autoritaire. Les mouvements contestataires dans le bassin minier de Gafsa en Tunisie (2008)', *Politique africaine* 117, 2010, pp. 107–26; Ellen Lust, 'Why Now? Micro Transitions and the Arab Uprisings', The Monkey Cage, October 2011, https://themonkeycage.org/wp-content/uploads/2011/10/Ellen_Lust_final.pdf.

10 Gregory Gause, 'Why Middle East Studies Missed the Arab Spring', *Foreign Affairs* 90.4, 2011, pp. 81–90.

11 Mary Kaldor, 'Civil Society in 1989 and 2011', *openDemocracy* 7 February 2011, http://www.opendemocracy.net/mary-kaldor/civil-society-in-1989-and-2011; Alfred Stepan, 'Tunisia's Transition and the Twin Tolerations', *Journal of Democracy* 23.2, 2012, pp. 89–103.

resilience paradigm at the forefront of explanations for political events taking place in the region,[12] again sidelining the democratisation paradigm, the helpfulness of which, to an extent, was limited to the case of Tunisia. Although there have been calls to develop a more middle-of-the-road perspective, combining aspects of both paradigms to account for diverging trajectories, or moving beyond them altogether,[13] this has hardly happened.

In the wake of this meta-debate between paradigms, there has been a plethora of studies looking at specific aspects of the trajectories taken by the different countries and actors involved, with a specific focus on what worked – Tunisia – and what did not: everywhere else. Comparative work distinguishing between different countries has increased significantly, with scholars examining the role of militaries, trade unions, political parties, social movements and cross-ideological coalitions, the role of media and technology and the desire of ordinary Arab citizens for democracy.[14] This volume plays its part in contributing to this trend through micro-level analyses of how the return of authoritarian rule and the explosion of violence have of course modified how citizens relate to power, but have also been unable to 'turn the clock back', as practices of dissent remain strong below the surface, even in democratic Tunisia.

In short, the perception of authoritarian continuity and of a failure of contestation does not account for the many changes that have occurred or are in the making within Arab societies: the Arab uprisings of 2011 should not be considered a finite, time-limited event, as the extent of their shockwaves and genuine impact have yet to be fully appreciated. The idea that 'nothing has changed', and that the revolts were simply a blip that made Arab citizens reconsider the value and usefulness of open dissent, might be useful as a political device for Arab ruling elites and,

---

12 Steven Heydemann and Reinoud Leenders, 'Authoritarian Learning and Authoritarian Resilience: Regime Responses to the Arab Awakening', *Globalizations* 8.5, 2011, pp. 647–53.

13 Michelle Pace and Francesco Cavatorta, 'The Arab Uprisings in Theoretical Perspectives', *Mediterranean Politics* 17.2, 2012, pp. 125–38.

14 Respectively: Kevin Koehler, 'Political Militaries in Popular Uprisings: A Comparative Perspective on the Arab Spring', *International Political Science Review* 38.3, 2016, pp. 363–77; Joel Beinin, *Workers and Thieves: Labor Movements and Popular Uprisings in Tunisia and Egypt*, Stanford 2015; Francesco Cavatorta and Lise Storm, *Political Parties in the Arab world*, Edinburgh 2018; Yasmine Berriane and Marie Duboc, 'Allying beyond Social Divides: An Introduction to Contentious Politics and Coalitions in the Middle East and North Africa', *Mediterranean Politics* 24.4, 2019, pp. 399–419; Fatima El-Issawi, *Arab National Media and Political Change*, London 2016; and Niels Spierings, 'Democratic disillusionment? Desire for Democracy after the Arab Uprisings', *International Political Science Review* OnlineFirst, 10 September 2019, DOI: 10.1177/0192512119867011.

often, their international allies. However, it obscures the fact that behind a façade of retrenched authoritarianism and violent chaos, states and societies have indeed changed considerably since 2011, with the ripple effects of the uprisings still affecting the relationship between state and society, as the cases of Algeria and Sudan suggest, but also in Egypt, with a resurgence of protests despite stifling authoritarianism and heavy repression, and in Morocco, with the rise of protests claiming to be in continuity with the 20 February movement. Albrecht and Schlumberger had already made this point about the evolving nature of Arab regimes and societies well before the uprisings, when they argued that Arab societies had changed profoundly despite the apparent authoritarian sclerosis from which they were suffering.[15] It is even more the case today that no Arab polity has been left unaffected by the uprisings, even though they seemed to succeed only in Tunisia.

This book therefore aims to celebrate and give weight to the disruptive power of human agency when this agency is restricted by hegemonic power. In terms of Bourdieu's habitus,[16] the individual's embodiment of preconditioned social structures does not lead to a deterministic behaviour in which personal agency has no place. As individuals adopt into their practices the social conditions and structures in which they were formed, they tend to reproduce these structures in a process that is flexible and can lead to the modification and sometimes to the transformation of those practices. As Swartz puts it, practices 'are not to be reduced to either habitus or field but grow out of the "interrelationship" established at each point in time by the sets of relations represented by both'.[17] This volume provides solid evidence of this active agency in times of uncertainty driven by troubled transitions or attempted transitions to democracy. The late-2019 street protests in Egypt, taking place in an environment of acute repression, is a further testament to the vitality of such agency confronted by a dehumanising form of oppression. This agency contradicts assumptions of a passive Arab public sphere wherein civil society is co-opted or silenced through counter-revolutionary forces' clever use of stick-and-carrot tactics to quell dissent. These acts of rebellious agency, taking creative forms in several domains, are beautifully defined by Bayat as the 'art of presence':

15 Holger Albrecht and Oliver Schlumberger, 'Waiting for Godot: Regime Change without Democratization in the Middle East', *International Political Science Review* 35.4, 2004, pp. 371–92.
16 Pierre Bourdieu, 'The Political Field, the Social Science Field, and the Journalistic Field', *Bourdieu and the Journalistic Field*, eds. Rodney Benson and Erik Neveu, Cambridge 2005, pp. 29–47.
17 David Swartz, *Culture and Power: The Sociology of Pierre Bourdieu*, Chicago 1997, pp. 141–42.

... a way in which a society, through the practices of daily life, may regenerate itself by affirming the values that deject the authoritarian personality, get ahead of its elites, and become capable of enforcing its sensibilities on the state and its henchmen.[18]

A growing dynamic hybridity in the media and political spheres empowers such agency. Beyond dichotomies of old and new, online and offline, liberal and authoritarian, diversity and uncertainty define the hybrid media and political systems across the region. Power is exercised and understood as 'the use of resources of varying kinds that in any given context of dependence and interdependence to enable individuals or collectivities to pursue their values and interests, both with and within different but interrelated media'.[19] While media hybridity is fuelling political hybridity, it is increasing the levels of uncertainty. By so doing, it is enabling subaltern publics to form and even to thrive in certain contexts. As the contributors to this volume convincingly demonstrate, the relationship between various societal agents in 'the field' is governed by interdependence, rather than dependence or independence. This interconnectedness is an opportunity for creativity, including for dissenting agency, mainly through its ability to expand pluralism and to challenge restrictive mainstream media and political structures. In most of the countries of the 'Arab Spring', media structures and practices witnessed significant diversification mirroring nascent political pluralism. This diversification regressed with the collapse of the democratic experiment into conflicts or renewed autocracy,[20] but there is no linear progressive or regressive path that countries move along, as significant pockets of pluralistic engagement remain in authoritarian systems, and pockets of authoritarian practice remain in democratic ones.

The Book. State–Society Relations: Micro-Dynamics of Activism and Revolt between Change and Continuity

This book adopts an original analytical approach that gives voice to local dynamics and legacies rather than concentrating on debates about paradigms. It does so through two intertwined dimensions. It highlights micro-perspectives of change

---

18 Asef Bayat, *Life as Politics: How Ordinary People Change the Middle East*, Stanford 2013, p. 134.
19 Andrew Chadwick, *The Hybrid Media System. Politics and Power*, 2nd edn, Oxford 2017, p. 207.
20 Fatima El-Issawi, *Arab National Media and Political Change*, London 2016.

and resistance, as well of contentious politics that are often marginalised and left unexplored in favour of macro-analyses. First, the story of the uprisings in Tunisia, Egypt, Syria, Morocco and Algeria is told from different and novel perspectives, looking at factors that have not yet been sufficiently emphasised, but which carry explanatory power in terms of what has occurred. Second, rather than focusing on macro-comparative regional trends, however useful these might be, the contributors to the book prefer to focus on the particularities of each country, highlighting distinctive micro-dynamics of change and continuity.

Reflecting the above, the book is divided in two interconnected parts. The first looks at how a number of Arab countries dealt with the uprisings – or lack thereof. The analysis draws on the interplay between structure, agency and national specificities in depicting the major forces either pushing for change or maintaining the status quo. This analysis is important, in order to set the stage for the book's second part, where specific policy areas, fields or sectors are examined, to highlight how macro-level analyses might fail to capture significant social changes. Scholars from the countries selected provide descriptions and explanations of events in those countries, transmitting their deep and sophisticated expertise in the national context of each to Western audiences. The suggestion has been offered by Rivetti, among others, that in the aftermath of the Arab uprisings, the domestic politics of Arab states could be understood as going through a series of radical changes and stubborn continuities, rather than along a linear path either towards democracy or towards the return of authoritarian rule.[21] Building on this insight, the contributions to this volume demonstrate what such changes and continuities mean in the daily reality of a number of Arab societies that have experienced considerable upheaval over the last decade. A number of elements emerge from the analyses contained in the book.

First is the considerable political role hydrocarbons play in 'guiding' the actions and behaviour of local actors. While the theory of the rentier state and the effect that hydrocarbon rents have on the domestic politics of countries that rely heavily on them has been extensively examined both before and after the uprisings,[22] the

21 Paola Rivetti, 'Continuity and Change before and after the Uprisings in Tunisia, Egypt and Morocco: Regime Reconfiguration and Policymaking in North Africa', *British Journal of Middle Eastern Studies* 42.1, 2015, pp. 1–11.
22 Hazem Beblawi, 'The Rentier State in the Arab World', *Arab Studies Quarterly* 9.4, 1987, pp. 383–98; Camilla Sandbakken, 'The Limits to Democracy Posed by Oil Rentier States: The Cases of Algeria, Nigeria and Libya', *Democratization* 13.1, 2006, pp. 135–52; Rolf Schwarz, 'The Political Economy of State Formation in the Arab Middle East: Rentier States, Economic Reform, and Democratization', *Review of International Political Economy*

contributions here of Addi on Algeria and of Kamel on Libya look at rents from the perspective of social, rather than of state, institutions. The scholarship has a tendency to focus on the distribution of oil rents as mechanisms to pay off political dissent and seal off the political system, allowing the ruling elite to isolate itself from society and thereby avoid democratic input into policy-making. While Addi and Kamel both acknowledge the relevance of this approach, they prefer to examine how social actors have employed the issue of hydrocarbon rents to promote their own interests and vision of society. While in Libya this has meant the use of oil rents and their control through the progressive militarisation of the civil conflict among a plethora of militias competing for power and influence outside of the political system, in Algeria the discussions on rents, coming from below, took the regime by surprise, and they were crucial in the anti-Bouteflika demonstration that ousted the president in the spring of 2019. While the street protests were ostensibly against Bouteflika seeking a fifth mandate, the reality is that Algerian society had been mobilising for quite some time against the way in which the regime operated on the economic front. Yerkes, in her contribution here, highlights how the 2019 protests had long been incubating in Algeria.

Yerkes's study underlines a second theme emerging from the volume: namely, the relevance of alternative politics outside official institutions. For a long period, the literature on Arab politics emphasised the newly found relevance of political parties, parliamentary competition and elections,[23] with a focus on the widening of official political participation in state institutions, exemplified by the access to these of Islamists, for instance. While there is certainly the need to take political parties and participation in elections seriously, the post-uprising period across the Arab world also demonstrates the vitality of alternative contentious politics, something that has a long tradition in the region.[24] In addition to Yerkes's contribution, the book offers new empirical evidence of how social movements operate in Morocco, where the monarchy-led reforms implemented in 2011 and 2012

15.4, 2008, pp. 599–621; Benjamin Smith, 'Resource Wealth as Rent-Leverage: Rethinking the Oil–Stability Nexus', *Conflict Management and Peace Science* 34.6, 2017, pp. 597–617; Francesco Cavatorta and Belgacem Tahci, 'La politique économique de la résilience autoritaire en Algérie: L'énigme de la diversification économique', *Études internationales* 50.1, 2019, pp. 7–38.
23 Ellen Lust-Okar, 'Elections under Authoritarianism: Preliminary Lessons from Jordan', *Democratization* 13.3, 2006, pp. 456–71; Tarek Masoud, *Counting Islam*, Cambridge 2014; Eva Wegner and Francesco Cavatorta, 'Revisiting the Islamist-Secular divide: Parties and Voters in the Arab World', *International Political Science Review* 40.4, 2019, pp. 558–75.
24 John Chalcraft, *Popular Politics in the Making of the Modern Middle East*, Cambridge 2016.

have failed further to liberalise the country. Monjib's chapter focuses its attention on the Rif Hirak, a protest movement that arose in the Rif region against the arbitrary nature of the political and economic power of the regime and against the inability of the government to deal with the social and economic crisis in the country. Nor has the Rif Hirak been confined to the Rif area, because its demands resonate across the country and link it more or less directly with the 20 February movement that shook the country in 2011. In this respect, Monjib's analysis of the Rif Hirak speaks to both changes and continuities in Moroccan political life. The legacy of the 2011 protests is still alive and well in Morocco, pointing to the fact that the political reforms implemented after the new constitution was approved did not have the impact protesters and citizens more broadly desired. Meanwhile the Rif Hirak has been able to innovate as regards its protest strategies, and link them to other, more localised, protests, attempting to become a genuinely national movement for change. A crucial aspect of the Rif Hirak is the leading role women have played in it despite the conservative nature of Rifian society. This is a third theme that emerges forcefully from the contributions to this book.

While Monjiib touches only briefly on the role of women in the Rif Hirak, Mili's chapter focuses specifically on this point. Using Tunisia as a case study, Mili demonstrates quite clearly that the establishment of democratic institutions, although laudable and positive for the progress of the country, is far from being the endpoint in the creation of a more progressive society. Women's activism in favour of legal equality has found a new lease of life in Tunisia, where it battled on two fronts. First, it had to withstand a conservative backlash in the Constituent Assembly, with attempts to roll back equality legislation. This battle was ultimately won, and once more this points to the activism that takes place in society, which can influence what occurs in official institutions to a significant degree. Second, attacks on women's rights have come from a conservative judiciary, which seems more interested in upholding problematic regressive views than moving quickly to embrace the rights that are protected by the constitution and therefore interpret legislation more progressively. A recent analysis of the difficulties involved in enshrining equality in inheritance law confirms Mili's argument with regard the conservative nature of the judiciary.[25] Linked to Mili's chapter is Bonci's analysis of the struggle between religion (usually represented in the form of political Islam) and secularism. In her study of the commission charged by the Tunisian president to review personal status legislation, Bonci highlights the

25 Akram Belkaïd, 'Femmes et héritage en Tunisie, l'échec d'une réforme', *Le Monde diplomatique* 785, August 2019, pp. 10–11.

relevance of the secular–religious divide, particularly when it comes to women's rights and struggles for gender equality. This is an interesting contribution, in so far as it challenges a number of assumptions. First, it argues convincingly that denying the existence of such a rift or divide does not do justice to the way in which society mobilises and to the issues around which the intensity of the political debate is strongest. Second, like Mili's argument, it defies expectations that democracy would deal with such issues simply through parliamentary procedures. Thus, although there might be disenchantment with the way in which democracy has been operating in Tunisia since its establishment, it would not be possible for such intense discussions of fundamental importance for society to take place unrestrained in the public arena. Mekki's analysis of the constitutional process in Tunisia and its successes and setbacks largely confirms this point. More broadly, and despite its often negative connotations when it comes to the Arab world,[26] the role of civil society as a guardian of progressive values and political change seems to find renewed affirmation in the region, as Joffé proposes in his contribution to this volume. He argues that civil society and social movements were the essential catalysts of the transition processes in Egypt and Tunisia, but that the nature of the 'pacting' process influenced the outcome. While in Tunisia the elite compromised with social movements, this process did not take place in Egypt. The mobilisation strategies used by civil society groups have become more innovative and better suited to the current technological environment, as Farmanfarmaian illustrates in her chapter.

A fourth theme emerging strongly from the book comes from the contributions of scholars dealing with countries where authoritarianism has reasserted itself through violence, and how the latter development has modified social relations and political actors. Hamzawy's contribution on Egypt is critical of the inability of genuine liberal-democrats to find common ground against a regime that is by most accounts even more repressive and arbitrary than Mubarak's.[27] In addition, Hamzawy's argument about alliances beyond divides is particularly timely, because it is precisely upon the building of such cross-ideological and cross-class coalitions that the possibility of a more pluralistic future for the region hinges.[28] Such coalitions have been often dismissed, and rightly so, as temporary and tac-

---

26 Amaney Jamal, *Barriers to Democracy: The Other Side of Social Capital in Palestine and the Arab World*, Princeton 2007.
27 Joshua Stacher, 'Egypt Running on Empty', *MERIP* 8 March 2016, https://merip.org/2016/03/egypt-running-on-empty/.
28 Vincent Durac, 'Opposition Coalitions in the Middle East: Origins, Demise and Afterlife?', *Mediterranean Politics* 24.4, 2019, pp. 534–44.

tical in nature – and therefore destined ultimately to fail. However, opposition coalitions in society and informal political spaces are making a comeback, creating micro-dynamics of resistance to authoritarianism. This was in evidence, as Kawakibi illustrates in his contribution on Syria, in the way in which the Syrian opposition attempted to govern the territories that it was able to take from al-Assad's control. Although pressured by both government forces and violent radical Islamists, these spaces, first of contestation and later of self-government, provided an important insight on the possibilities of alternative modes of governance in Syria, demonstrating the genuine democratic effort of large sectors of the Syrian opposition. Kawakibi argues convincingly, however, that these efforts did not find any genuine international support, which has led to the success of the government's military campaign, and to the return of Syria to the fold of the international community, as states and international organisations alike prefer stability to so-called chaos, and are already lining up to gain reconstruction contracts in a shattered country.

Conclusion

As mentioned in the introduction of this chapter, it is still early to have an accurate assessment of the Arab uprisings. Certain trends can be identified, however, and can be useful for future research on the politics of the Arab world. First, there is the necessity to move beyond the paradigms of democratisation and authoritarian resilience. While these both carry some explanatory power, their prescriptive and normative traits can obstruct consideration of the possibilities that democratisation might take a different direction and not culminate in a 'traditional' liberal democracy, and that authoritarianism is very capable of renewing itself in its relation to society. Second, official institutions, high politics and elites should not be over-emphasised. There are numerous movements and types of activism taking place in society that should be accounted for and made central to the analysis, and it is these micro-dynamics that this volume sees as crucial. Finally, it is important not to discount the role of physical violence in moulding society, or the responses the latter provides to it, as the cases of Libya, Syria and Egypt make painfully clear.

Bibliography

Albrecht, Holger and Oliver Schlumberger, 'Waiting for Godot: Regime Change without Democratization in the Middle East', *International Political Science Review* 35.4, 2004, pp. 371–92.

Allal, Amin, 'Réformes néolibérales, clientélismes et protestations en situation autoritaire. Les mouvements contestataires dans le bassin minier de Gafsa en Tunisie (2008)', *Politique africaine* 117, 2010, pp. 107–26.

Anderson, Lisa, 'Searching Where the Light Shines: Studying Democratization in the Middle East', *Annual Review of Political Science* 9, 2006, pp. 189–214.

Bayat, Asef, *Life as Politics: How Ordinary People Change the Middle East*, Stanford 2013.

Beblawi, Hazem, 'The Rentier State in the Arab World', *Arab Studies Quarterly* 9.4, 1987, pp. 383–98.

Beinin, Joel, *Workers and Thieves: Labor Movements and Popular Uprisings in Tunisia and Egypt*, Stanford 2015.

Belkaïd, Akram, 'Femmes et héritage en Tunisie, l'échec d'une réforme', *Le Monde diplomatique* 785, August 2019, pp. 10–11.

Berriane, Yasmine and Marie Duboc, 'Allying beyond Social Divides: An Introduction to Contentious Politics and Coalitions in the Middle East and North Africa', *Mediterranean Politics* 24.4, 2019, pp. 399–419.

Bourdieu, Pierre, 'The Political Field, the Social Science Field, and the Journalistic Field', *Bourdieu and the Journalistic Field,* ed. Rodney Benson and Erik Neveu, Cambridge 2005, pp. 29–47.

Brumberg, Daniel, 'The Trap of Liberalised Autocracy', *Journal of Democracy* 13, 2002, pp. 56–68.

Carothers, Thomas, 'The End of the Transition Paradigm', *Journal of Democracy* 13.1, 2002, pp. 5–21.

Cavatorta, Francesco, *The International Dimension of the Failed Algerian Transition. Democracy Betrayed?*, Manchester 2009.

Cavatorta, Francesco and Lise Storm, *Political Parties in the Arab World*, Edinburgh 2018.

Cavatorta, Francesco and Belgacem Tahci, 'La politique économique de la résilience autoritaire en Algérie: L'énigme de la diversification économique', *Études internationales* 50.1, 2019, pp. 7–38.

Chadwick, Andrew, *The Hybrid Media System. Politics and Power*, 2nd edn, Oxford 2017.

Chalcraft, John, *Popular Politics in the Making of the Modern Middle East*, Cambridge 2016.

Di Peri, Rosita, 'Democracy and Authoritarianism in the Arab World: Evolution of a Long Debate', *Nuovi Autoritarismi e Democrazie* 1.1, 2019, pp. 124–43.

Durac, Vincent, 'Opposition Coalitions in the Middle East: Origins, Demise and Afterlife?', *Mediterranean Politics* 24.4, 2019, pp. 534–44.

El- Issawi, Fatima, 'Algerian National Media: Freedom at a Cost', paper presented at the Middle East Centre, London School of Economics, February 2017.

El-Issawi, Fatima, *Arab National Media and Political Change*, London 2016.

El-Issawi, Fatima, 'Moroccan National Media between Change and Status Quo', paper presented at the Middle East Centre, London School of Economics, April 2016.

Gause, Gregory, 'Why Middle East Studies Missed the Arab Spring', *Foreign Affairs* 90.4, 2011, pp. 81–90.

Heydemann, Steven, 'Upgrading Authoritarianism in the Arab World', Analysis Paper 13, Brookings Institution 2007, https://www.brookings.edu/wp-content/uploads/2016/06/10arabworld.pdf.

Heydemann, Steven and Reinoud Leenders, 'Authoritarian Learning and Authoritarian Resilience: Regime Responses to the Arab Awakening', *Globalizations* 8.5, 2011, pp. 647–53.

Jamal, Amaney, *Barriers to Democracy: The Other Side of Social Capital in Palestine and the Arab World*, Princeton 2007.

Kaldor, Mary, 'Civil Society in 1989 and 2011', *openDemocracy* 7 February 2011, http://www.opendemocracy.net/mary-kaldor/civil-society-in-1989-and-2011.

Koehler, Kevin, 'Political Militaries in Popular Uprisings: A Comparative Perspective on the Arab Spring', *International Political Science Review* 38.3, 2016, pp. 363–77.

Korany, Bahgat, Rex Brynen and Paul Noble, *Liberalization and Democratization in the Arab world, Vol. 2: Comparative Experiences*, Boulder 1998.

Lust, Ellen, 'Why Now? Micro Transitions and the Arab Uprisings', The Monkey Cage, October 2011, https://themonkeycage.org/wp-content/uploads/2011/10/Ellen_Lust_final.pdf.

Lust-Okar, Ellen, 'Elections under Authoritarianism: Preliminary Lessons from Jordan', *Democratization* 13.3, 2006, pp. 456–71.

Masoud, Tarek, *Counting Islam*, Cambridge 2014.

Pace, Michelle and Francesco Cavatorta,. 'The Arab Uprisings in Theoretical Perspectives', *Mediterranean Politics* 17.2, 2012, pp. 125–38.

Rivetti, Paola, 'Continuity and Change before and after the Uprisings in Tunisia, Egypt and Morocco: Regime Reconfiguration and Policymaking in North Africa', *British Journal of Middle Eastern Studies* 42.1, 2015, pp. 1–11.

Sadiki, Larbi, 'Whither Arab "Republicanism"? The Rise of Family Rule and the "End of Democratization" in Egypt, Libya and Yemen', *Mediterranean Politics* 15.1, 2010, pp. 99–107.

Sandbakken, Camilla, 'The Limits to Democracy Posed by Oil Rentier States: The Cases of Algeria, Nigeria and Libya', *Democratization* 13.1, 2006, pp. 135–52.

Schwarz, Rolf, 'The Political Economy of State Formation in the Arab Middle East: Rentier States, Economic Reform, and Democratization', *Review of International Political Economy* 15.4, 2008, pp. 599–621.

Smith, Benjamin, 'Resource Wealth as Rent-Leverage: Rethinking the Oil–Stability Nexus', *Conflict Management and Peace Science* 34.6, 2017, pp. 597–617.

Spierings, Niels, 'Democratic Disillusionment? Desire for Democracy after the Arab Uprisings', *International Political Science Review* OnlineFirst, 10 September 2019, DOI: 10.1177/0192512119867011.

Stacher, Joshua, 'Egypt Running on Empty', *MERIP* 8 March 2016, https://merip.org/2016/03/egypt-running-on-empty/.

Stepan, Alfred, 'Tunisia's Transition and the Twin Tolerations', *Journal of Democracy* 23.2, 2012, pp. 89–103.

Swartz, David, *Culture and Power: The Sociology of Pierre Bourdieu*, Chicago 1997.

Wegner, Eva and Francesco Cavatorta, 'Revisiting the Islamist–Secular Divide: Parties and Voters in the Arab World', *International Political Science Review* 40.4, 2019, pp. 558–75.

Zayani, Mohamed, *Networked Publics and Digital Contention*, Oxford 2015.

Part 1

PATHS TO SUCCESS, PATHS TO FAILURE: DEMOCRATIC TRANSITIONS AFTER THE ARAB UPRISINGS

2

The Democratic Transition in Tunisia: Three Keys to Understanding a Success Story

Nidhal Mekki[1]

It is not at all an exaggeration to say that the popular revolution that took place in Tunisia in December 2010–January 2011 is one of the most significant events of the early twenty-first century. This revolution has not only fundamentally changed the philosophy and the political practice in this small country,[2] but has had effects far beyond its borders.[3] It was at the origin of a regional political reshuffling without precedent, bringing down regimes in its wake, revealing ethnic and tribal fractures and triggering the most deadly and devastating wars of the first quarter-century. If the world looks at the MENA region today with considerable distress and disappointment, Tunisia is an exception, arousing feelings ranging from cautious admiration to overwhelming enthusiasm.[4] From whatever perspective, the Tunisian revolution and the democratic transition that followed it attracted major interest.

1 The author thanks Sana El Mekki for her assistance in translating this text.
2 Ibrahim Elbadawai and Samir Makdisi, *Democratic Transitions in the Arab World*, Cambridge 2017.
3 Housam Darwisheh, 'Trajectories and Outcomes of the Arab Spring: Comparing Tunisia, Egypt, Libya and Syria', IDE discussion paper, 2014, http://hdl.handle.net/2344/1318.
4 Elbadawi and Makdisi, *Democratic Transitions*, p. 2.

There are a number of reasons for this worldwide interest in the revolution that took place in this small country on the southern shore of the Mediterranean.[5] One is the fact that it was carried out in a broadly peaceful way in a country of the Arab world whose entire modern history has been dominated by violent dictatorships.[6] Traditionally, revolutions in the Middle East have been popular only in name, because they were the work of factions of the army, rather than coming from below. The domino effect triggered by the Tunisian revolution naturally attracted the attention of observers, as the phenomenon was unusual in this region of the world. In the Tunisian case, the army did not intervene, except to protect institutions and sensitive buildings.[7] In addition, despite many victims being shot and killed by police, the uprising remained largely peaceful, especially in comparison with the bloody events in neighbouring countries.

Another important reason for the interest in the Tunisian revolution is the fact that it served to deconstruct the prejudice to the effect that Arab peoples were not receptive to the idea of democracy,[8] and that dictatorship was the only type of regime suited to them. The Tunisian revolution put an end to this essentialist assumption, by proving that historical and political circumstances can pave the way for democratisation in any setting, and that democracy does not belong to a specific cultural area.

Finally, the Tunisian revolution was a beacon of hope for a whole region subject to some of the worst dictatorships in the world. While it inspired similar dynamics elsewhere in the Middle East and North Africa, only Tunisia itself began a genuine process of democratic transition, which was eventually successful, even if it still remains fragile today and faces many challenges.

How is the Tunisian success to be explained? Several authors agree that the old native constitutional traditions permeated the Tunisian transition and partly explain the happier fate the country experienced in comparison to other Arab

---

5 Raphaël Lefèvre, 'Tunisia: A Fragile Political Transition', *The Journal of North African Studies* 20.2, 2015, pp. 307–11.

6 A few hundred deaths did occur, but this is little compared to the tens or hundreds of thousands killed in other Arab countries, in addition to the total destruction of their infrastructures.

7 Darwisheh, 'Trajectories and Outcomes'; Ian Kelly, 'Regime Elites and Transitions from Authoritarian Rule: A Comparative Analysis of the Tunisian and Egyptian Uprisings', Ph.D. thesis, Dublin City University, 2016.

8 Yadh Ben Achour, 'La révolution, la Constitution et la démocratie participative', *Le Blog de Yadh Ben Achour* 15 May 2015, http://yadhba.blogspot.com/2015/05/.

nations.[9] This constitutional tradition dates back to the middle of the nineteenth century, with the first constitution of the Arab world drafted in 1861, and the Fundamental Pact (*Ahd al-Aman*) of 1857. Tunisia also benefited from the thinking of great national reformers such as Khayreddine and Ibn Abi Dhiaf.[10] The Tunisian national movement, in its quest for independence, called itself 'the Destourian party', literally 'the Constitutional party'. In 1938, during the 9 April massacre perpetrated by French soldiers in Tunis, demonstrators chanted, among other slogans, 'Tunisian parliament!' The constitutional idea is, therefore, embedded in the Tunisian political tradition, and there is no doubt that it was present in the minds of the Tunisian elites who were called upon to manage the early stages of the transition.

Moreover, the very structure of Tunisian society further helps to explain the tumultuous but never irreparably interrupted trajectory of the Tunisian transition. With the exception of certain tiny religious minorities, Tunisian society is ethnically and religiously homogeneous, and not built around tribal traditions, which distinguishes it decisively from other Arab societies such as those of Libya (where tribalism predominates), Syria (with its ethnic and religious fractures) or Yemen (with its tribal and religious fractures).

Further reasons have also been put forward to explain the Tunisian revolution and its success. Despite the total control over political life for more than two decades of Ben Ali's dictatorial regime, civil society had not completely disappeared. The Tunisian General Labour Union (UGTT), for instance, remained emblematic of the country and retained a degree of vitality despite decades of oppression and co-optation of its national leadership. It was therefore able to play a prominent role in mobilising and supervising protesters in the largest cities of the country during the final days of the revolution, dealing a deadly blow to the regime.[11] Tunisia has also remained a country open to the outside world, has a low rate of illiteracy compared to other countries of the region and possesses a comparatively large middle class.[12] The circulation of notions relating to democracy, human rights, the rule of law and pluralism in academic spheres and even

---

9 Slim Laghmani, 'La transition démocratique: une théorie ou une pratique?', *La transition démocratique à la lumière des expériences comparées*, eds. Hatem M'Rad and Fadhel Moussa, Tunis 2012, pp. 37–44.

10 Yadh Ben Achour, 'Le peuple origine du droit et interprète de la Constitution' (in Arabic), *Le Blog de Yadh Ben Achour* 16 February 2015, http://yadhba.blogspot.com/2015/02/.

11 Hela Yusfi, *Trade Unions and Arab Revolutions: The Tunisian Case of UGTT*, New York 2017.

12 Laghmani, 'La transition démocratique', p. 39.

in the media (though to a minimal extent only in the latter) was never completely suppressed. The conceptual knowledge that had accumulated among Tunisian citizens meant that politicians, intellectuals, trade unionists, journalists and students were very familiar with these concepts and aware of their importance in building a democratic state. The discourse of human rights, which was merely propaganda at the time of the dictatorship, came to represent a reality after the overthrow of the regime.

All of the above is essential to an understanding of why the revolution broke out in Tunisia, and why it managed to be institutionally successful. It does not in itself fully explain the success of the country's transitional process, however, even if it provides its historical, sociological, political and cultural context. There is, therefore, a need to look at the specific choices political and social actors made following the fall of the regime. An exclusively structural explanation has its limits, in as much as it does not necessarily take into account how actor-led decision-making can also influence structure to a creative extent. Among the choices that actors made during the transition are those linked to constitutional and institutional continuity, to ensure that the country would not be left in a legal 'limbo' or in the grip of some sort of revolutionary government.[13] Thus, the success of the Tunisian transition is the result of certain choices made by political and social actors, in which the historical and institutional context of Tunisia played a determining role.

The first phase of the transition was conducted though the institutions of the old regime, and employing the legal texts of the old regime. Moreover, no single voice or institution was allowed to prevail throughout the transitional process. Avoiding past errors, the actors of the Tunisian transition chose dialogue, negotiations, peaceful resolution of conflicts and compromise. Finally, there was no question of adopting a dogmatic stance by closing the country's doors to foreign assistance: on the contrary, Tunisia opted for openness, and utilised all the experience that the international community has accumulated in the field of democratic transition to sustain its own process. These three actor-led elements – institutional continuity, dialogue and openness to foreign assistance, addressed each in turn below – explain the success of the Tunisian transition as compared to the painful and dramatic failures observed in the other countries of the region after 2011. These are the three key factors that account for the Tunisian democratic transition and its success.

---

13 Yadh Ben Achour, 'Remédier aux dangers du vote et du gouvernement majoritaire: Le recours au *tawâfuq*', *Leaders* 12 December 2012, https://www.leaders.com.tn/article/10145-remedier-aux-dangers-du-vote-et-du-gouvernement-majoritaires-le-recours-au-tawafuq.

The Role of Institutions and the Legal Framework of the Transition

The role played by institutions is an outstanding feature of the Tunisian transition, and was evident from early on in the process. Even if the legitimacy of the institutions of the former regime was very weak, the fear of an institutional vacuum led the Tunisian elites (historical figures of the Tunisian opposition, jurists and even the politicians of the fallen regime) to entrust them with conducting the first moments of the transition. This was, after all, better than anarchy. These institutions, while complying with the will of the people and adopting a 'reserved and modest attitude',[14] continued to operate within the terms of the constitutional text that governed them, or at least those of its provisions that would be effective in making the transition successful. These first moments of the transition were decisive in so far as they created a precedent according to which it would always be necessary to act according to an institutional logic and in accordance with the legal rules to avoid improvisation, or worse, anarchy. This precedent has been perfectly followed and respected thereafter. This is how the Tunisian transition became institutionalised and legally regulated.

A very institutionalised transition

One of the features that distinguished the Tunisian transition is that institutions (whether those of the former regime or those created after its fall) played a crucial role. Observers pointed out that government administration did not collapse, and that services continued to be provided to citizens throughout the country. Hence, we can say that the regime collapsed, but not the state, and this facilitated the transition. It should be noted, however, that beyond the state administration, in the strict sense, it was the political institutions and the role they played that marked the Tunisian transition.

The revolution did not immediately affect the political institutions of the former regime (in particular the two parliamentary chambers and the constitutional court). Quite the contrary: these institutions, especially during the first days following the fall of the regime, played a leading role in ensuring an ultimately peaceful transition, and one that, as far as possible, took place within a constitutional and/or legal framework. Thus, it was Ben Ali's last prime minister, Mohammed Ghannouchi, who invoked article 56 of the Constitution of 1959 to declare the provisional vacancy of the presidency of the republic before article 57 on the

---

14 Yadh Ben Achour, 'La force du droit ou la naissance d'une constitution en temps de révolution', http://yadhba.blogspot.com/2015/01/.

definitive vacancy was implemented and before the Constitutional Council noted the vacancy. Fouad Mebazzaa, the last president of the Chamber of Deputies under Ben Ali, then assumed the functions of the president of the republic.[15] It was he who presided over the first phase of the transition, until the election of the National Constituent Assembly held in October 2011. Such a transition to a new era, carried out by and through the institutions of the former regime, may seem like a heresy in the history of revolutions, and it came in for criticism;[16] but it ensured a peaceful transfer of power, and was in the final analysis beneficial. This choice of strategy certainly impacted the continuation of the process, since an institutional logic dominated all the other phases of the transition, through a kind of path dependency whereby extra-institutional means to produce change were de-legitimised.

Thus, the political institutions created after the collapse of the regime also played a central role in the conduct of the transition and its success. At the head of these institutions was the Higher Authority for the Realisation of the Objectives of the Revolution (HAROR), which served as a platform channelling debates over how to conduct the transition. Even if these debates often overflowed on to the streets, they never reached a 'point of no return' or overwhelmed the institutional logic. The HAROR not only framed political debates, but also prepared the main texts of the Tunisian revolution, denominated by an authorised doctrine as 'the six laws of liberation'.[17] These comprise Decree-Law 27 of 10 April 2011, which established the Independent High Authority for Elections (ISIE), Decree-Law 35 of 10 May 2011, organising the elections of the National Constituent Assembly, Decree-Law 87 of 24 September 2011, regulating the legal regime of political parties, Decree-Law 88 of the same date, on the legal regime of associations and finally Decree-Laws 115 and 116 of 2 November 2011, establishing freedom of the press and media.

These texts created or allowed the establishment of, among others, two of the most important institutions of transition, namely the National Constituent Assembly (NCA), responsible for drafting the new constitution of the country, and the Independent High Authority for the Elections, whose role was to prepare and organise the first democratic elections in the history of the country. Of these, the NCA deserved the greater attention, because it was the key element of the

---

15 Rafâa Ben Achour and Sana Ben Achour, 'La transition démocratique en Tunisie: Entre légalité constitutionnelle et légitimité révolutionnaire', *Revue française de droit constitutionnel* 92, 2012, pp. 715–32.
16 'Le Point International' (last modified 20 January 2011), https://www.lepoint.fr/monde/le-president-tunisien-de-transition-fouad-mebazaa-appelle-au-calme-20-01-2011-130389_24.php.
17 Ben Achour, 'La force du droit'.

transition.[18] While considerable criticism surrounded it both before and after its creation,[19] it would be very difficult to deny that it was the main element in the success of the Tunisian democratic renewal. The NCA played the role previously assigned to the HAROR, but it also had democratic legitimacy, and therefore the power and popular mandate to take decisions under the terms of the texts creating it. The NCA had the most important mission in determining the success of the transition – namely, the drafting a new constitution for the country, which would determine the rules of the political game, speak to issues of identity and formalise the sources of legislation. It was a cornerstone of the transition because it also allowed the most important political sensitivities to express themselves and confront each other within an elected chamber, and not in the streets. By doing so, it reinforced the idea that political differences must be negotiated, debated and resolved within, not outside, institutions. This influenced the way in which political actors of conflicting ideological persuasions related to each other. This is not to say that 'street politics' did not occur, and the Tunisian transition was characterised by sit-ins, protests and marches; but sensitive issues were ultimately discussed and often resolved within the NCA. Thus, the NCA also played a historical pedagogical role, in that political parties, citizens and components of civil society, as well as the media, learned to engage in dialogue, to debate and to discover their differences and disputes, and realised that it is often unavoidable for both sides to make concessions in order to reach an agreement.

The NCA embodied to a large extent the participatory democracy whose establishment explains the success of the Tunisian transition, notwithstanding the criticisms that have been levelled at the institution, a number of which were substantiated.[20] The great lesson in constitutional law – the elaboration of the Constitution of 27 January 2014 and its collective appointment by the representatives of the people, civil society and the citizens through the National Dialogue on the Constitution – contributed to reinforcing the idea of the importance of going through institutions to solve political problems.[21] Paradoxically, by criticising the

---

18 Nidhal Mekki, 'L'Assemblée nationale constituante: Perspectives démocratiques', *La Tunisie réinvente l'histoire: Récits d'une révolution*, ed. Hedi Saidi, Paris 2012, pp. 181–198.
19 Criticism focused on the slowness of its work and the extension of its mandate through the passing of many laws.
20 The Carter Center, *The Constitution-Making Process in Tunisia. Final Report*, 2011–2014, https://www.cartercenter.org/resources/pdfs/news/peace_publications/democracy/tunisia-constitution-making-process.pdf.
21 Nidhal Mekki, 'Le processus constituant tunisien: quels enseignements pour les pays de la région?', *Arab Law Quarterly* 32.4, 2018, pp. 355–84.

NCA, and blaming it for all the ills besetting the country at that time, many Tunisians did not perceive that they were indirectly contributing to consolidation of the culture of institutions, whereby all responsibility must be placed on the NCA as a collegiate body and symbol *par excellence* of representative democracy, and not on individuals as such, regardless of their political affiliations.

A transition marked by legalism

A revolution is supposed to overthrow the existing order, whether it be political, economic, ideological or, of course, legal. Even if the rhetoric that accompanied the Tunisian revolution embraced this rationale, through calls for the abrogation of the 1959 Constitution, which to many was the symbol of the dictatorship, the reality was quite different, and revolutionary élan was channelled through a powerful and restraining legal framework. Indeed, following the flight of Ben Ali on 14 January 2011, the constitutional order in force did not collapse like a house of cards. Quite the contrary: it was this very order, and particularly its highest expression, namely the 1959 Constitution, which served to prepare the transition to a new constitutional order and consequently orchestrated its own demise. Thus article 56 (temporary vacancy of the presidency of the republic) was first invoked, before article 57 was applied to determine the permanent vacancy of the presidency. It was by yet another article of the defunct Constitution of 1959 (article 28) that the two chambers had delegated to the president of the republic the power to legislate by decree.[22]

Even Decree-Law 14 of 23 March 2011,[23] which dissolved the political institutions emanating from the 1959 Constitution, stated that (article 3) 'the Administrative Tribunal and the Court of Auditors shall exercise their prerogatives according to the laws and regulations in force'. A supreme manifestation of this attachment to the law is the judgement of the Court of Appeal of Tunis released on 5 February 2013. In this judgement, which dealt with the freedom of movement recognised by article 10 of the 1959 Constitution, 'the Court affirms that the latter remains in force in its provisions guaranteeing fundamental rights and freedoms, adding, however, that these rights and freedoms, by their very nature, as well as by the effect of article 12 of the International Covenant for Political and Civil Rights that Tunisia adhered to on 29 November 1968, were not eligible to be repealed'. Thus,

---

22 Ben Achour, 'La transition démocratique', p. 720.
23 Available at http://www.wipo.int/wipolex/fr/text.jsp?file_id=245405 (accessed 23 December 2019).

not only did certain institutions of the former order – the Administrative Court, the Court of Auditors, the entire judicial jurisdictional order – survive, but also the substantive rules relating to the rights and freedoms to which citizens were entitled under the principle of state continuity: which means that the legal *acquis* relating to human rights could not be revoked.

All this attests to the will of the actors conducting the transition through its first stages not to create a legal or constitutional loophole that would pave the way for 'de facto governments' and the potential abuses of 'revolutionary governments'. At each stage, the ruling authorities, institutions, political parties and the country's elite sought to rely on the law to legitimise their actions, such that politics remained framed in legal terms. It can hardly be doubted that this was a wise choice, which helped prevent excessive improvisation, trial and error and consequent lethal pitfalls.[24] There is no question that the country's long state and administrative (even constitutional) tradition played a role in this commitment to the law, but nor can it be ignored that the transition was conducted during its first hours by prominent figures of the former regime (the president of the Chamber of Deputies becoming the acting president of the republic, and the prime minister, who became president of the republic for a few hours, later leading two governments before stepping down from the political scene); and that their behaviour contributed to a successful regime change.

The policy resulting from this choice to avoid at all costs legal loopholes continued with the Provisional Regulations of public policies of 23 March 2011 (also known as the 'Small Constitution') which, without building on the former constitution, claimed revolutionary legitimacy and thus established a new constitutional order, albeit provisional and limited.[25] The country was governed under this Small Constitution until the election of the NCA. It would be followed by another Small Constitution (Provisional Regulation of the public policies of 16 December 2011[26]), to govern the third transitional phase, namely the period when elected deputies drafted the new constitution. The second Small Constitution exhausted its effects with the entry into force of the new Constitution of 2014. As can be seen, therefore, through the different transitional periods, the country was at no moment left in legal void. It must be admitted that those who led the Tunisian transition displayed considerable wisdom in emphasising that politics should be

---

24 Ben Achour, 'La force du droit'.
25 Ben Achour, 'La force du droit'.
26 Constituent Act 2011–2016 on the provisional organisation of public authorities. Available at http://mjp.univ-perp.fr/constit/tn2011.htm (accessed 23 December 2019).

governed by law, because in so doing they traced the limits of the political action of the various actors involved, and set out clearly the rules of the game along with the roles and responsibilities of its various players. This attachment among elites to legality spread throughout the country, though it also provoked incomprehension and aroused the wrath of people who (especially at the time of the HAROR) castigated what was labelled a 'government of jurists'. Indeed, there was at one point a diffuse feeling that jurists occupied an exaggeratedly prominent place in public debate and in the process of transition. While acknowledging this, it seems to us that the role they played was not a harmful one and helped to better regulate and pacify the national discussion.

The Search for Compromise

The term 'compromise' (*tawafuq*) is perhaps the one that has been most used, even misused, in post-revolutionary Tunisia. The reason for this is that compromise played a decisive role in the transition,[27] and in its culmination in the new Constitution and the 2014 legislative and presidential elections.[28] One might in fact argue that the transition was possible and successful only due to the willingness to compromise in the stances adopted by political and social actors over the course of the transitory phase, as this helped to defuse its most serious crises and contributed to the overcoming of political blockages and of the volatility inherent in any process of regime change. While the need for compromise was first felt in relation to the constitutional choices to be made, the principle was subsequently extended to political life more broadly, once the resolution of ideological and political conflicts through purely legal mechanisms had become impossible.

The search for compromise around the law

The drafting of the Tunisian Constitution of 2014 was an opportunity to implement the participatory approach to the elaboration of constitutions, the defining feature of the 'new constitutionalism'.[29] At a very early stage, the NCA expressed

---

27 Nadia Marzouki, 'La transition tunisienne: Du compromis démocratique à la réconciliation forcée', *Pouvoirs* 156, 2016, pp. 83–94.
28 President Béji Caid Essebsi determined that the configuration of the post-election political scene in 2014 was not fundamentally very different from that of 2011, and that it again dictated the compromise to avoid blockage and discord.
29 Democracy Reporting International, *Le nouveau constitutionnalisme: Une nouvelle forme du processus constituant*, November 2012, http://democracy-reporting.org/

its willingness to open up to civil society and citizens during the constituent process.[30] The parties represented within the NCA also emphasised the importance
of seeking a compromise at the decision-making level and avoiding as far as
possible the appeal to a majority vote which might crystallise contradictions and
lead to a stiffening of individual positions. Two essential processes were followed
in this regard: within the NCA, at the level of the commissions and the plenary
assembly, an attempt was made to reach the maximum achievable compromise
with regard to the articles of the new constitution. Outside the NCA, an initiative
was organised and received considerable public attention: namely, the National
Dialogue on the Constitution, which allowed civil society, citizens and parties not
represented in the NCA to participate in debates relating to the constitution and
to make their voices heard regarding the fundamental choices to be embodied in
the constitutional text.[31]

The compromise within the NCA regarding the wording of the articles of the
constitution took several forms and went through two stages. The first manifestation of compromise was at the level of the constituent committees,[32] particularly
at the beginning of their work. The members of the committees representing the
main groups of the NCA had agreed to adopt the purely technical articles, which
do not reflect significant political challenges, by consensus (without a vote). This
honeymoon did not last very long, however, because as soon as contentious issues
(the status of Islam and/or Shariah; the nature of the political regime) came to
be discussed, tension rose and the gaps between different positions became so
wide that it was impossible to reach a consensus. This led the Ennahdha party
and its allies to try to force matters by taking a vote, a process that certainly
allowed them to impose their preferences,[33] but was perceived by the opposing
parties as an attempt to exclude and marginalise them in the process of drafting
the constitution. The crisis became serious,[34] and it was at this time that the second

---

wp-content/uploads/2016/03/dri-rapport_fr_nouveau_constitutionnalisme_2012-11.pdf;
Xavier Philippe, 'Le rôle du constitutionnalisme dans la construction des nouveaux États de
droit', *Constitution et finances publiques. Études en l'honneur de Loïc Philip*, eds. Louis
Favoreu, André Roux and Robert Hertzog, Paris 2005, pp. 187–206.
30 Among other initiatives, the NCA held open days at the NCA in early 2012.
31 Mekki, 'Le processus constituant', p. 378.
32 Six in number, each commission was charged with drafting a chapter of the constitution.
33 The troika in power at the time enjoyed an absolute majority within the NCA.
34 The work of the 3rd Committee (Legislative and Executive Power) was suspended for
several weeks, for example, when they came up against the issue of the nature of the regime,
and specifically the mode of election, minimum age required for running and prerogatives of
the president of the republic.

stage of the search for compromise began, with a 'Compromises Commission', whose role was precisely to bring the views of the various actors closer together, to iron out any difficulties and to reach a consensual formulation in terms of the various proposals. Of course, the work of this Compromises Commission would not have been possible without outside party-to-party dialogue and negotiations, but it proved in itself to be a very effective means of overcoming a large number of disputes; the initiative allowed for the creation of a forum for the development of ideas and debate, more technical and therefore less directly influenced by political considerations. The work of this commission continued until the final hours of the adoption of the articles of the constitution in plenary, and to it we owe some great successes, such as article 46 (parity of the sexes), but also lower-key achievements such as article 6, which is riddled with contradictions aiming to satisfy everyone to the point of falling into a vague syncretism, bordering on the infelicitous. Some observers point out that this at times obsessive search for compromise explains the choice of a convoluted political regime with a high risk of blockages.[35]

The Compromise Commission's experience is indicative of the importance of entrusting certain tasks of a legal nature during a transition not to a representative and enlarged political body, but to technical commissions supported by experts and able to find, from the wide range of constitutional choices available, solutions which allow the overcoming of what seem at first glance insurmountable contradictions, before returning to seek the validation of these solutions by the institution that holds the political legitimacy.

The search for the compromise beyond the law

Beyond the search for a compromise on the constitution or some of its articles, the Tunisian transition involved a somewhat original experiment aimed at advancing the transitional process and preserving its democratic character beyond the compromises among political parties on the constitutional text. This was not a question of circumventing the NCA, but rather of working through a parallel and agreed political process among the principle political actors in order to reach political agreement on contentious issues, including points of constitutional discord. Actors outside the NCA were responsible for seeking compromise between political parties and it was on the initiative of such actors that compromise became the

---

35 Rafâa Ben Achour, 'Rafâa Ben Achour: La Constitution tunisienne, deux ans après (2014–2016)', *Leaders* 3 April 2016, http://www.leaders.com.tn/article/19290-rafaa-ben-achour-la-constitution-tunisienne-deux-ans-apres-2014-2016.

linchpin of the democratic transition. Since it began its work, blockages, political point-scoring and time-wasting had characterised the work of the NCA and
undermined its credibility. When the political and security climate in the country
significantly deteriorated following the political assassinations of Chokri Belaid
and Mohamed Brahmi and the rise of the Salafist movement, the NCA was seriously discredited and seemed to run out of steam, endangering the whole process
of regime change. In fact it seemed that the NCA had become part of the crisis,[36]
and it was at this juncture that a number of national organisations unconnected
to political parties got together and sponsored rounds of the National Dialogue,
bringing together about 20 of the parties.[37] In this new forum and with the mediation and contribution of national organisations, long months passed and painful
negotiations took place between political parties to unblock the situation and final-
ise the text of the constitution, as well as to agree on the setting up and adminisra-
tion of the first legislative and presidential elections after the approval of the new
constitution.

While it is true that this National Dialogue went through ups and downs, the
dispute settlement method that was put in place remains interesting and worthy
of closer scrutiny, because it allowed 'transfer' of what was discussed during the
dialogue to the NCA, where decision-making power formally belonged. A rigid
way of thinking would have dictated sticking solely with the NCA elected in
October 2011, which enjoyed democratic legitimacy following free and fair elections. Political actors agreed to also work with each other outside the institution,
however, and sectors of Tunisian civil society had the ingenious idea of circumventing the NCA to an extent and offering a platform for discussion, debate and
negotiation that would 'force' parties to listen to the concerns of broader society.
Without totally neutralising the NCA, but conscious of the fact that it had lost all
initiative and was itself a victim of the political deadlock, civil society offered to
parties an innovative forum wherein to settle ideological and political disputes.
The National Dialogue would not have been possible if the four national civil
society organisations involved had not been strong and firmly rooted in Tunisian
society, benefiting from several relays in the various centres of power and the

---

36 Nidhal Mekki, 'Tunisia's National Constituent Assembly: From Solution to Problem',
2013, http://www.constitutionnet.org/news/tunisias-national-constituent-assembly-solution-
problem.
37 Hatem M'rad, *Le dialogue national en Tunisie*, Tunis 2015. The unaffiliated organisations
concerned were the Tunisian General Labour Union (UGTT), the Tunisian Confederation of
Industry, Trade and Handicrafts (UTICA), the Tunisian Human Rights League (LTDH) and
the Tunisian Order of Lawyers (ONA).

regions. Rather than constituting an alternative centre of power to the NCA and therefore simply pursuing their own interests, the four organisations encouraged democratically elected representatives to find a solution to the institutional dead-lock. The level of confidence enjoyed by these four organisations made possible the role they played, but they were also acutely aware that they had to work with and around institutions, without replacing political parties, but instead promoting new dynamics for their actions at a time when parties were stuck in a zero-sum struggle for power and control of the NCA proceedings. The role of Tunisian civil society organisations in safeguarding the transition was recognised and welcomed by the international community, and the quartet of bodies sponsoring the National Dialogue won the Nobel Peace Prize in 2015.

International Accompaniment: Guaranteeing the Transition

Democratic transition is always an event and a process that is both national and international, despite the early focus of transitology being exclusively upon domestic dynamics and actors. Transitions are obviously national, because they lead to the gradual establishment of a democracy at the level of the nation state, with all the implications for its citizens in terms of rights and freedoms, the rule of law and political openness. It is also national because it is domestic actors who are formally in charge of designing the rules of the institutional game and who are endowed with the necessary legitimacy to do so. Transitions have an interna-tional dimension too, however, because a democratic transition does not occur in a vacuum, and because domestic processes of regime change more broadly affect external relations with other states of the region and even beyond.[38] For instance, the discourse and practice of human rights at the international level can strengthen the transitional national system for the protection of rights, making it more effective and efficient, as domestic actors rely on it to advance their objec-tives. Besides, foreign states and international organisations, first among them the United Nations, follow democratic transitions very closely. It is in the interest of the international democratic community that a new state should join it, and it must support that state in its transitional process, to foster a world where rights are more respected and friendly relations between countries are strengthened. It

---

38 Lars Berger, 'The Missing Link? US Policy and the International Dimensions of Failed Democratic Transitions in the Arab World', *Political Studies* 59.1, 2011, pp. 38–55; Laurence Whitehead, *The International Dimensions of Democratization: Europe and the Americas*, Oxford 2001.

is easy, therefore, to see the commitment of many countries, which, after a period of dictatorship, demonstrate their attachment and openness to international law in general and to international human rights law in particular. This was the case in the countries of Eastern Europe after the fall of the Berlin Wall and the wave of democratisation they experienced, and also in many Latin American countries and, more recently, Tunisia.[39] Contrary to other cases across the Arab region, where democratic powers have been more reluctant to support genuine democratisation – notably Egypt – the international community offered and provided considerable assistance to the Tunisian democratic transition. This was of utmost importance, and ensured that domestic actors struggling with how to build a new regime felt that they had support. This 'diligence' was a genuine case of partnership, in so far as it did not undermine the sovereignty of Tunisia. The partnership operated on two levels: at that of the constituent process, and at that of the political process. It should also be emphasised here that Tunisian domestic actors readily accepted such support.

Accompanying the constituent process

The United Nations and a number of other international and non-governmental organisations have historically demonstrated a keen interest in providing logistical and financial support for policies leading to democratisation. This support has primarily been aimed at the elaboration of new constitutions. The expertise accumulated by these organisations in this area has given rise to several publications and even 'guides' aimed at presenting to states and to internal and international actors in transitions the good practices and lessons learned through experience, in all their diversity and richness.[40]

The Tunisian constituent process was not immune to this phenomenon and the support was more systematic and significant.[41] Even if Tunisia did not display strong tribal, social, religious or linguistic divides, the schism which separated the

---

39 Geoffrey Weichselbaum and Xavier Philippe, 'Le processus constituant et la Constitution tunisienne du 27 janvier 2014: Un modèle à suivre?', *Maghreb Machrek* 223, 2015, pp. 49–69.
40 See for example: *The Constitution-Making Handbook* (developed by Interpeace and Women's Constitutional Voices in partnership with the United Nations United for Development), available at: https://constitutionmakingforpeace.org/the-constitution-making-handbook/.
41 The United Nations has a great deal of interest in supporting democratic transitions, given the links between democracy, peace and development, which are among the goals of the world organisation.

religious from the secular modernist sectors of society nevertheless posed serious risks to the cohesion of the social fabric and therefore to the success of the transition. Undoubtedly, for the international and non-governmental organisations that became involved in the Tunisian transitional process, particularly in its constituent phase, one of the main concerns was the risk that extremist Islamist movements might hijack the process of regime change. In particular, the pressure exerted by certain political parties with a religious ethos might have led to a constitutional text that would likely have widened the gap between the secular modernist and conservative camps. Such a text would have been especially prejudicial to universally recognised rights and freedoms, while one of the main aims of the international partnership of the constituent processes was to achieve the consecration of those rights and respect for them in the final constitutional text.[42] Another source of concern for international partners was the potential for a return to authoritarianism, through the accession to power or rehabilitation of figures from the former regime, and especially the rehabilitation of authoritarian practices and the 'system' of a dictatorship (police state, silenced media, flouted freedoms, widespread corruption).

The international actors actively involved in the Tunisian constituent process were diverse. First and foremost was the United Nations, particularly through the United Nations Development Programme (UNDP), which, in addition to logistical support for the NCA, organised and financed the National Dialogue on the Constitution, which led to deputies being 'on the road' throughout all regions of the country,[43] and travelling abroad to meet with the largest Tunisian diasporic communities (France and Italy). For its part, the United Nations High Commission for Human Rights was involved through the organisation of training and seminars for the members of the NCA as well as consulting on the chapter concerning rights and freedoms.[44]

International bodies such as the Council of Europe meanwhile became involved

---

42 Mekki, 'Le processus constituant', pp. 371–372.
43 Carter Center, *Constitution-Making Process in Tunisia*, Final Report, https://www. cartercenter.org/news/publications/peace/democracy_publications/tunisia-peace-reports. html.
44 Dimiter Chalev, Mazen Shaquoura and Abou Abbass, 'Rôle des Nations Unies dans le processus constitutionnel tunisien et résultat en termes de garanties relatives aux Droits de l'homme', https://www.tn.undp.org/content/dam/rbas/doc/Compendium/Part%203/39%20 R%C3%B4le%20des%20Nations%20Unies%20dans%20le%20processus%20 constitutionnel%20tunisien.pdf, *La Constitution de la Tunisie: Le contenu de la Constitution*, 2016, http://www.tn.undp.org/content/tunisia/fr/home/library/democratic_ governance/la-constitution-de-la-tunisie-.html.

through the Venice Commission.[45] The latter played a leading role in the Tunisian constituent process. In addition to a comprehensive and careful commentary on the final version of the draft constitution,[46] it sent many experts who participated in numerous round tables at the NCA on technical issues of constitutional law. International IDEA (International Institute for Democracy and Electoral Assistance) also closely followed the constituent process and published numerous legal and policy analyses on the constituent process and the various articles and chapters of the constitution.[47]

Contrary to what one might have expected from political parties finally liberated from authoritarian constraints and legitimately mandated to design a new political system, Tunisian parties, with the exception of a few small ones including Ettahrir,[48] were quite open to international support for the constituent process, whether at the level of logistics or scientific and constitutional expertise. The Islamist Ennahdha party, in particular, reacted very positively to the comments of the Venice Commission. This appears to be in contrast to the traditional attitude of political Islam, which opposes any form of 'Western' intervention, seeing it as suspicious and self-serving. Other parties too cooperated, and everyone seems to have seen the benefit they could gain from this assistance.

National actors knew that they were being closely observed by international ones, and were keen to demonstrate their democratic credentials and good faith. They knew that any drift away from democratic commitments would be penalised by the withdrawal of support (in particular financial). Withdrawal of such support would not have been beneficial to any of the domestic actors, and would have in fact been detrimental to the country and the democratic transition. However, it must be emphasised that if this partnership with international actors was successful, this was because it did not pose significant problems, in as much as they adopted an advisory role only, providing technical expertise and logistical support without interfering with the more political aspects of the transition. This allowed national actors to have the sense (real in many respects) that the constitution was

---

45 That is, the European Commission for Democracy through Law, advisory body of the Council of Europe.
46 The draft opinions of the Venice Commission on the different drafts of the Tunisian constitution are available at https://www.venice.coe.int/webforms/documents/default.aspx?country=127&year=all.
47 The author of this chapter has written extensively on these issues on the IDEA website: see http://www.constitutionnet.org/search2?query=nidhal%20mekki. We can also mention the important role played by NGOs such as The Carter Center (especially for the electoral process), Human Rights Watch and Amnesty International.
48 Laghmani, 'La transition démocratique', p. 40.

the product of their will, and not a diktat of international and regional organisations. The 'national ownership' of a constitution that all the international organisations had promoted is the secret of the success of the international accompaniment
of the constituent.[49] The international dimension therefore acted as a pledge and
guarantee of the success of the constituent process and as an element of appeasement between the different national protagonists. Evidence of the pacifying role of
such international mentoring is that international experts enjoyed greater credibility with certain Tunisian political parties (in particular the 'troika' parties) than did
national experts, given the presumption of neutrality they enjoyed.[50] This credibility allowed them to be considered as disinterested advisers, or even as trustworthy
intermediaries capable of bypassing domestic ideological and political squabbles.

Accompanying the political process

From the first days of the Tunisian revolution, demonstrations of support from
foreign states, the United Nations and other international organisations multiplied.
It is true that there was initially a very unpleasant note that rang false in the support
from France for Tunisian demonstrators, but broadly speaking, international
support could be felt domestically for the changes taking place. Thus, a few months
after the escape of Ben Ali, the United States stood as a guarantor for the Tunisian
debt, allowing the country to borrow on the international market and at least sustain
its economy at a time of political volatility.[51] In itself, this American commitment
constituted a breath of fresh air for the internal market and reassured the donor
organisations, thus preventing the collapse of the country's economy as a result
of the political earthquake that it was going through. The position of the United
Nations, also, was decisive, in that the organisation embraced the change and said
that it was ready to accompany and support it. Following from this, declarations of
support multiplied, as the world realised the significance of what had just happened.

When it comes to the direct political role and influence of Western democracies, it can be argued that they played a very shy role on the Tunisian scene
compared to the very active one played by those supportive of the Ben Ali authoritarian regime, particularly when one analyses how authoritarian regional powers
such as Saudi Arabia, United Arab Emirates, Turkey, Qatar and Algeria attempted

---

49 Mekki, 'Le processus constituant', pp. 364–365.
50 Mekki, 'Le processus constituant', p. 366.
51 https://www.espacemanager.com/les-usa-se-portent-garants-des-dettes-tunisiennes.html,
21 April 2012 (accessed 23 December 2019).

to interfere with the Tunisian transition.[52] At some stages during the transition, one could have been forgiven for having the impression that Western democracies had exposed a fledgling democracy to the direct influence of authoritarian regimes whose 'projects' for Tunisia were counter-revolutionary. On the one hand, some countries worked to undermine Ennahdha and promoted a policy of exclusion of the Islamist party that would have derailed the transition. On the other hand, some countries worked in the opposite direction, attempting to ensure Ennahdha dominance of the political system to the detriment of its secular counterparts. The point in common between these two projects is that they would have led eventually to an undemocratic regime, and thus to the failure of the transition. Tunisia became a real battlefield between these harmful influences, risking a return to authoritarianism. That Tunisian actors managed to rise above external pressures is to their credit, particularly when one factors in their enormous political, economic, social and security difficulties. We can obviously argue that some Western democracies have preferred to protect their economic interests in certain well-off but authoritarian countries than to support a country that had just embraced the values of democracy, the rule of law, pluralism and social justice. At the same time, however, it should be noted that Western democracies preferred to follow the path of indirect influence (through support for the transitional process in its constitutive and electoral components, by strengthening the capacities of civil society and contributing to the promotion of the values of the rule of law, democracy and human rights): work of the utmost importance and that was carried out by a wide range of foundations and NGOs.[53]

But if this 'soft' influence had the disadvantage of not directly impacting the political scene and, above all, having little or no quick positive effect on the economy, it had the enormous advantage of not appearing as an attempt to impose a model of political regime or democracy on Tunisia. This attitude on the part of Western democracies, which might be described as 'reserved', was a wise choice in terms of their relations with a developing country with a traumatic experience of colonisation. Indeed, by avoiding employing their full weight in the internal political game and limiting themselves to strengthening the capacity of civil society and providing platforms for dialogue between the various internal political

---

52 For a contrary opinion, see Pietro Marzo, 'Foreign Actors in Post-Revolutionary Tunisia: Enhancing Democracy and Lowering Political Tensions', available at http://www.mei.edu/publications/foreign-actors-post-revolutionary-tunisia-enhancing-Democratization-and-Lowering, 25 September 2018.
53 In this regard, we might mention the particularly important role played by German party foundations.

and social actors, Western countries led the protagonists of the Tunisian transition to talk to each other and negotiate; hence a culture of compromise was able to develop. It was by realising that there would be no externally imposed solution, and that Western countries had no real 'horse in the race', that political parties were obliged to talk to each other directly and come up with their own solutions to the blockages and disagreements the transition encountered. Local solutions had of necessity to arise from the so-called 'Tunisian genius'. It is this culture of compromise that is life-saving, and it is the belief in the possibilities of internal dialogue that will create the conditions for a healthy and stable political life in spite of the many problems the country still faces.

Conclusion

The Tunisian democratic transition has succeeded. This can be stated with a degree of certainty following the successful organisation of two delicate elections, the participatory elaboration of a new constitution and, especially, after a first changeover of power carried out calmly and in a spirit of compromise. This success is due in part to the specificity of the Tunisian case (historical, cultural, demographic and sociological factors) and the structural advantages Tunisia may have over other countries in the region. However, as this chapter has demonstrated, the choices made by social and political actors during the transition were also crucial.

It is this concomitance of structural and institutional factors on the one hand, and the choices of political actors on the other, that largely explains the success of the Tunisian transition. We would not go so far as to say that the Tunisian revolution was, in view of the country's political history, a historical necessity, but we can say that the Tunisians have not missed the historic opportunity to launch their country on the path of democracy. This success should not be taken to imply, however, that the young Tunisian democracy is immune to all dangers. On the contrary, the Tunisian transition might be secure institutionally, but it still suffers from the weaknesses and shortcomings that other democracies, even more established ones, experience.[54] In addition to the risks that come from outside because of the continuation of regional rivalries and their impact on the Tunisian scene, that scene is itself fragmented, and its political conflicts can at any time escalate into a serious institutional crisis. In part this is due to the absence of a genuine

---

54 The risks posed to some Western democracies by the rise of populism makes these amply clear.

democratic spirit that would allow Tunisian political actors fully to accept each other despite their differences within the framework laid down by the constitution. But Tunisia's saving grace might be that the rules put in place after the fall of Ben Ali seem set in stone. Developing a genuine democratic spirit is nevertheless the great challenge remaining for any effective democratic transition that would be capable of moving beyond institutional success and addressing the substantive aspects of democratic governance that citizens call for.

Bibliography

Ben Achour, Rafâa. 'Rafâa Ben Achour: La Constitution tunisienne, deux ans après (2014–2016)', *Leaders* 3 April 2016, http://www.leaders.com. tn/article/19290-rafaa-ben-achour-la-constitution-tunisienne-deux-ans-apres-2014-2016.

Ben Achour, Rafâa and Sana Ben Achour, 'La transition démocratique en Tunisie: Entre légalité constitutionnelle et légitimité révolutionnaire', *Revue française de droit constitutionnel* 92, 2012, pp. 715–32.

Ben Achour, Yadh, 'La révolution, la Constitution et la démocratie participative', *Le Blog de Yadh Ben Achour* 15 May 2015, http://yadhba. blogspot.com/2015/05/.

Ben Achour, Yadh, 'Le peuple origine du droit et interprète de la Constitution' (in Arabic), *Le Blog de Yadh Ben Achour* 16 February 2015, http://yadhba. blogspot.com/2015/02/.

Ben Achour, Yadh, 'Remédier aux dangers du vote et du gouvernement majoritaire: Le recours au *tawâfuq*', *Leaders* 12 December 2012, https:// www.leaders.com.tn/article/10145-remedier-aux-dangers-du-vote-et-du-gouvernement-majoritaires-le-recours-au-tawafuq.

Berger, Lars, 'The Missing Link? US Policy and the International Dimensions of Failed Democratic Transitions in the Arab World', *Political Studies* 59.1, 2011, pp. 38–55.

[The] Carter Center, *The Constitution-Making Process in Tunisia. Final Report*, 2011–2014, https://www.cartercenter.org/resources/pdfs/news/peace_ publications/democracy/tunisia-constitution-making-process.pdf.

Chalev, Dimiter, Mazen Shaquoura and Abou Abbass, 'Rôle des Nations Unies dans le processus constitutionnel tunisien et résultat en termes de garanties relatives aux Droits de l'homme', *La Constitution de la Tunisie: Le contenu de la Constitution*, 2016, http://www.tn.undp.org/content/tunisia/fr/home/ library/democratic_governance/la-constitution-de-la-tunisie-.html.

Darwisheh, Housam, 'Trajectories and Outcomes of the Arab Spring: Comparing Tunisia, Egypt, Libya and Syria', IDE discussion paper, 2014, http://hdl.handle.net/2344/1318.

Democracy Reporting International, 'Le nouveau constitutionnalisme: Une nouvelle forme du processus constituant', November 2012, http://democracy-reporting.org/wp-content/uploads/2016/03/dri-rapport_fr_nouveau_constitutionnalisme_2012-11.pdf.

Elbadawai, Ibrahim and Samir Makdisi, *Democratic Transitions in the Arab World*, Cambridge 2017.

Kelly, Ian, 'Regime Elites and Transitions from Authoritarian Rule: A Comparative Analysis of the Tunisian and Egyptian Uprisings', Ph.D. thesis, Dublin City University, 2016.

Laghmani, Slim, 'La transition démocratique: une théorie ou une pratique?', *La transition démocratique à la lumière des expériences comparées*, eds. Hatem M'Rad and Fadhel Moussa, Tunis 2012, pp. 37–44.

Lefèvre, Raphaël, 'Tunisia: A Fragile Political Transition', *The Journal of North African Studies* 20.2, 2015, pp. 307–11.

Marzo, Pietro, 'Foreign Actors in Post-Revolutionary Tunisia: Enhancing Democracy and Lowering Political Tensions', Middle East Institute 2018, http://www.mei.edu/publications/foreign-actors-post-revolutionary-tunisia-enhancing-Democratization-and-Lowering.

Marzouki, Nadia, 'La transition tunisienne: Du compromis démocratique à la réconciliation forcée', *Pouvoirs* 156, 2016, pp. 83–94.

Mekki, Nidhal, 'L'Assemblée nationale constituante: Perspectives démocratiques', *La Tunisie réinvente l'histoire: Récits d'une révolution*, ed. Hedi Saidi, Paris 2012, pp. 181–198.

Mekki, Nidhal, 'Le processus constituant tunisien: quels enseignements pour les pays de la région?', *Arab Law Quarterly* 32.4, 2018, pp. 355–84.

Mekki, Nidhal, 'Tunisia's National Constituent Assembly: From Solution to Problem', 2013, http://www.constitutionnet.org/news/tunisias-national-constituent-assembly-solution-problem.

M'rad, Hatem, *Le dialogue national en Tunisie*, Tunis 2015.

Philippe, Xavier, 'Le rôle du constitutionnalisme dans la construction des nouveaux États de droit', *Constitution et finances publiques. Études en l'honneur de Loïc Philip*, eds. Louis Favoreu, André Roux and Robert Hertzog, Paris 2005, pp. 187–206.

Weichselbaum, Geoffrey and Xavier Philippe, 'Le processus constituant et la Constitution tunisienne du 27 janvier 2014: Un modèle à suivre?', *Maghreb Machrek* 223, 2015, pp. 49–69.

Whitehead, Laurence, *The International Dimensions of Democratization: Europe and the Americas*, Oxford 2001.

Yusfi, Hela, *Trade Unions and Arab Revolutions: The Tunisian Case of UGTT*, New York 2017.

3

Post-2013 Egypt: On Delegitimising Democratic Demands

Amr Hamzawy

The year 2020 marks the ninth anniversary of the 25 January Revolution (2011) in Egypt. Still now, the military-led government continues to repeat the same assertion, that Egypt is not ready for democracy, and propagating an anti-democratic discourse to justify the lack of freedom in the public sphere. Government officials argue, for example, that to establish democracy, a set of social and political preconditions is required. Principal among these are the rule of law and the stability and neutrality of state institutions. Without these preconditions, Egyptian officials contend, processes such as regular elections and peaceful rotation of power become meaningless, and structures such as multi-party systems and pluralist civil societies irrelevant. They also claim that building a functioning democracy requires greater economic growth and an affluent middle class, arguing that undemocratic governments are more capable of ensuring rapid economic growth and developing important public institutions such as education, health, efficient social services and the fundamental assets the middle class needs to prosper.[1] Government officials make these claims, forgetting that the many challenges facing the rule of law in today's Egypt, deteriorating economic and social conditions and the fragility of the middle class are direct consequences of seated long-established authoritarianism and its continuous failures.[2] This chapter discusses some of the

---

1 Roberto Stefan Foa, 'Modernization and Authoritarianism', *Journal of Democracy* 29.3, 2018, pp. 129–140.
2 Steven Cook, 'Sisi Isn't Mubarak. He Is Much Worse', *Foreign Policy* 19 December 2018, https://foreignpolicy.com/2018/12/19/sisi-isnt-mubarak-hes-much-worse/.

factors that have enabled the Egyptian government effectively to propagate an authoritarian discourse after the popular uprising in 2011, and to rule undemocratically, at low cost, a society embattled by social, economic and political crises.

Vulnerable but Unthreatened Authoritarianism

The contemporary Egyptian scene reveals an important paradox: the lack of societal challenges facing the government despite its problematic economic and social track record.[3] The government has failed to drive back corruption, nepotism, misuse of public office and the almost complete absence of transparency and accountability in public and private institutions.[4] It has reinstated its control over society and citizens with an iron fist, curtailing freedom of information and banning freedom of expression. Civil society activism and peaceful political participation have been de facto outlawed by the adoption of an arsenal of undemocratically-spirited and restrictive laws.[5] Nevertheless, the military-led government has faced no significant challenges since 2013. Popular resistance to its repressive measures has been marginal. The government has hardly had to resort to wide-scale violence to dominate society and subjugate citizens.

Before the ninth anniversary of the January 2011 revolution, the Egyptian president repeated more than once his depiction of the popular uprisings that swept different Arab countries in 2011 as a 'wrong cure' that was based on a 'wrong diagnosis'.[6] Abdel Fattah al-Sisi claimed that the 'events of 2011' set Egypt back, because they offered the wrong treatment by insisting on 'bringing down the regime', exposing both state and society to great risks. Nor was Egypt's situation the only issue al-Sisi addressed. He asserted that 2011 has had devastating consequences in countries such as Syria, Libya and Yemen. These countries have witnessed, according to al-Sisi, the collapse of their stability, and it will take them years to rebuild state institutions, in addition to hundreds of billions of dollars to reconstruct their destroyed societies.[7] This presidential insistence on

---

3 World Economic Forum, *The Global Competitiveness Report* 2018, https://www.weforum. org/reports/the-global-competitveness-report-2018.
4 Transparency International 19 January 2019, 'Middle East and North Africa: Corruption Continues as Institutions and Political Rights Weaken', https://www.transparency.org/news/ feature/regional-analysis-MENA.
5 Joshua Stacher, 'Egypt Running on Empty', *Middle East Report* 8 March 2016, https:// merip.org/2016/03/egypt-running-on-empty/.
6 Masrawy 11 October 2018, 'Al-Sisi: 2011 Wrong Cure to Wrong Diagnosis' (in Arabic), https://www.masrawy.com/news/news_egypt/details/2018/10/11/1442477/.
7 Masrawy, 'Al-Sisi'.

equating the popular uprisings with high-risk and/or destructive 'events' lies at the heart of how, since 2013, the military-led government in Egypt has attempted to silence the demand for democracy by propagating an authoritarian discourse on politics.

On the one hand, the word '*ahdath*' replaces in the presidential discourse terms such as 'revolution', 'uprising', 'democratic movement' and 'Arab Spring'. These previously were used to describe how Egyptian citizens took to the streets in January 2011, calling for the end of then-President Mubarak's regime and for the establishment of a constitutional and political framework enabling the democratic transfer of power and safeguards for human rights and freedoms. The word 'events' disguises many meanings that the presidential discourse thus strips away from January 2011. By the same token, the use of 'events' forcibly associates the popular uprising with other meanings that distort its true democratic nature. The term eliminates the systematic and peaceful qualities of the popular demand for democracy, which millions of Egyptians had put forward before 2011, during the 18 days of the uprising (25 January to 11 February 2011) and between 2011 and 2013 – until the military took power on 3 July 2013. Linguistically, 'event' designates an unplanned, spontaneous or sudden act, without any pre-organised mobilisation or clear demands. The use of 'events' implicitly ascribes to January 2011 chaotic, criminal and violent contents. It parallels the labelling as 'events' of the uprising of 18–19 January 1977 – the bread uprising, a popular protest against high prices and economic policies that marginalised the low-income majority, which former president Sadat termed the 'uprising of thieves' and 'criminal events'.[8] It also parallels the description of the 1986 paramilitary riots as 'events' – riots of Egyptian conscripts, which involved some of the poor police recruits who demonstrated against the inhumane treatment they suffered.[9] January 2011 did witness violence in various places, but citizens did not incite it. Rather, violent acts during the 18 days of the uprising were initiated by the security services of the Mubarak regime, and aimed at undermining the popular demand for peaceful democratic change. The insistence of President al-Sisi upon using 'events' thus reflects an official desire on the part of the Egyptian government to criminalise January 2011 and to equate it in people's imaginations with chaos.

---

8 Misbah Qutb, '1977–2013: Bread Uprising and Hunger Revolution' (in Arabic), *Al-Masry al-Yawm* (The Egyptian Today) 16 January 2013 (special issue), https://www.almasryalyoum. com/news/details/282271.
9 Mohamed Atef, 'On the 30th Anniversary: Central Security Events Still Without Investigation', *Aswat Misriyya* (Egyptian Voices) 25 February 2016, http://www. aswatmasriya.com/news/details/59194.

On the other hand, the characterisation of the mobilisation that led to January 2011 and other popular uprisings as a 'wrong diagnosis' reveals a general conviction in the ruling establishment in Egypt that the demand for democracy is harmful, and that citizens' actions incorporating it are reprehensible. For the government, actions such as protesting and demonstrating for political purposes must be prevented by convincing the people that activism is useless, or by forcing the people to eschew them. In the speeches of President al-Sisi, the expression 'wrong diagnosis' supplements other formulations such as 'incomplete and false awareness is the real enemy',[10] or 'the countries that went through crises in the past years wouldn't have had to pay such high human, financial, and moral prices had the situation remained the same'; or still, 'What happened in 2011 was a reckless movement with good intentions … We opened the gates of hell in our country when we thought we could change our reality. This does not mean that we should silently endure our crises, but things can easily get out of control.'[11]

Taken together, these expressions reveal an official discourse that accuses democracy-demanding citizens in Egypt of false awareness and credulity, which resulted in careless actions and caused great harm to the country in 2011. In the terms of this discourse, 'well-intentioned' Egyptians who took to the streets in January 2011 are required to take a step back, to rely only on their government to deal with the existing social crises and to avoid inducing chaos (referred to in the presidential discourse as 'things spiralling out of control') by giving up their call for regime change and by refraining from interfering in politics altogether. Egyptian citizens are furthermore warned within the same discourse of the severe consequences of their 're-involvement in events similar to those of 2011', because the 'Egyptian state' – here the government is depicted as the sole embodiment of the state apparatus – will not tolerate their recurrence. It will inevitably punish those who ignore the warning, be it by protesting in the public sphere or by expressing dissenting opinions on social media networks. The repressive measures that met protesters in the autumn of 2019 are a clear indication that the regime follows through upon its warnings.

In characterising January 2011 in terms of a 'wrong diagnosis', the Egyptian

---

10 Hosni, Samir and Ibrahim Hassan, 'Al-Sisi: Lack of Awareness is the Real Enemy, 2011 Was the Wrong Cure to the Wrong Diagnosis' (in Arabic), *Al-Yawm al-Sabi* (The Seventh Day) 11 October 2018.
11 Nour Rashwan, 'Al-Sisi: We Opened the Gates of Hell to Our Country When We Imagined that We Are Capable of Changing the Reality', *Al-Shuruq* (The Sunrise), November 2018, https://www.shorouknews.com/news/view.aspx?cdate=04112018&id=e 2805369-dc4d-4776-be91-42548d7cedee.

government aims to reinstate a dominant political culture conducive to citizens' subjugation after a brief period of democratic mobilisation that began in the mid-2000s and culminated in the 2011 uprising and the political opening between 2011 and 2013. For the smooth functioning of authoritarian rule, citizens need to acknowledge the monopoly of the president, his government and the security services over politics and public matters. Egyptian authoritarianism has always been profoundly sceptical of the people and has systematically opted to silence them, regardless of how peacefully they may articulate their demands, or the real problems those demands may reveal.[12]

On an additional level, the characterisation of January 2011 as the result of a wrong diagnosis exposes the conviction of the Egyptian government that the country's situation in 2011 did not require a regime change. President al-Sisi has repeatedly referred to pre-2011 crises using the term 'quasi-state'. Labelling the Mubarak state of 1981 to 2011 a 'quasi-state' and characterising January 2011 as resulting from a wrong diagnosis imply that Egypt was headed in a troublesome political direction, but did not need a chaotic and destructive regime change. Rather, according to al-Sisi and other government officials, an 'organised change' at the highest level of authority, through a peaceful removal of President Mubarak would have been sufficient to avert Egypt's pre-2011 crises, without forcing both state and society to endure the 'hell' of January 2011. By claiming that organised change at the highest level of authority represents the safest way to get out of crises, the Egyptian government further attempts to silence the people: citizens should leave the fate of their country, even if it is collapsing, in the hands of mighty state institutions, especially the military. Only the generals can find safe solutions, thereby preventing the chaos and destruction that citizens cause with their false awareness and miscalculated demands. Thus, contemporary Egyptian authoritarianism propagates a discourse in which January 2011 is deprived of any positive content, and undemocratic governance is praised, in order to prevent citizens from articulating popular demands. This is by no means a vision limited to the current government.

Authoritarianism has been the only type of governance known to Egypt since the establishment of the republic in 1952, constantly reaffirmed in the wake of crises and uprisings, as was the case after January 2011. Since 1952, Egypt has only known the alliance of economic, financial, intellectual and media elites with authoritarian rulers. These elites have relied on the rulers to protect their benefits,

---

12 Maye Kassem, *Egyptian Politics: The Dynamics of Authoritarian Rule*, Boulder 2004; Lisa Blaydes, *Elections and Distributive Politics in Mubarak's Egypt*, Cambridge 2010.

and accepted the concomitant need constantly to justify official policies and decisions, regardless of content, implications and contradictions. Successive Egyptian
governments have systematically used repression, human rights violations and
co-optation to control society and keep citizens in check. The authoritarian barter
– 'bread and security for freedom' – has been widely disseminated, along with
the notion that the country was still not ready for democracy and amid fear tactics
claiming that chaos is the sole alternative to authoritarian rule: as former president
Mubarak put it, 'It is either me or chaos.'[13]

The result is the unlimited power Egyptian presidents and their ruling establishments have accumulated over time, the almost complete absence of checks and
balances between the overly dominant executive branch of government and weak
parliaments and judiciaries and the securitisation of politics, which, since 1952, has
come to be a domain of military, intelligence and police officers. Repeatedly, Egyptians have been forced to evacuate the public sphere, either persuaded by the authoritarian barter to give up on freedom in exchange for bread and security, or fearful
of prosecution if they expressed their opinions freely. Disseminating undemocratic
notions, threatening repression and restricting freedom of information, Egypt's
authoritarianism has always tried to distort people's collective awareness as well
as to impose fear on citizens in order to dissuade them from searching for freedom.

More than nine years after the democratic uprising in January 2011, the realities of governance in Egypt have not changed. The authoritarian contract per-
sists, as does the impasse of dissidents and human rights activists whose inability
to transcend secular–Islamists divisions, to provide viable policy alternatives to
societal crises and to build cross-ideological consensus contributed to the failure
of the short-lived democratisation process between 2011 and 2013.[14] Since 2013,
the interests of the majority of the population have shifted dramatically, with a
dwindling minority still believing that democracy matters and a clear majority
viewing economic and security concerns as the nation's top priority.[15] Egyptians
have largely refrained from challenging the military-led government, hoping that

---

13 See: https://www.youtube.com/watch?v=5F_aMapwz2c (in Arabic; accessed 4 January
2020).
14 Amr Hamzawy, 'Can Egypt's Hopes Be Revived?', *Journal of Democracy* 30.4, 2109,
pp. 157–68.
15 Gamal Abdel Soltan, Ahmed Nagui Qamha and Subhi Asilah, 'The Arab Barometer
Project – Arab Republic of Egypt, June 2011', www.arabbarometer.org/wpcontent/uploads/
Egypt_Public_Opinion_Survey_2011.pdf; Daniel Tavana, 'Egypt Five Years after the
Uprisings: Findings from the Arab Barometer', 20 July 2017, www.arabbarometer.org/
wp-content/uploads/Egypt_Public_Opinion_Survey_2016.pdf.

their living conditions would improve under the generals' administration despite a poverty rate of 33%, an inflation rate at 11%, and unemployment at 8% in 2019.[16] Popular faith in a democratic transition that can improve the living conditions of the majority has never been restored. In other words, after a short period of warming to the prospects of democratic transition, Egyptians are once more placing their hopes in an authoritarian government, and ready to tolerate the suppression of their personal freedoms and human rights.

Elements of Authoritarian Practice: Repression

The role of security services – state security, general intelligence and military intelligence – has increased over the few past years, and their financial allocations have come to represent one of the largest portions of the government budget.[17] The role of security officials is no longer limited to tracking opposition forces, nor to the use of repressive measures against those individuals that the government perceives as a source of immediate or potential threat. They have also assumed direct control of key arenas in society. For example, security officials have taken full charge of NGOs and trade unions, practically sidelining the ministries of Social Affairs and Labour respectively. They have acquired a leading role in delineating 'red lines' limiting the exercise of freedom of expression, be it in traditional media or on social media networks, which the government strongly surveils. Security officials have been managing elections and defining the legislative agenda of parliament since 2013.[18] Furthermore, retired state security and intelligence officers, along with retired army officers, have invaded the state bureaucracy, particularly increasing their presence in governorates and municipalities. This comprehensive and powerful security network controls key arenas in society and makes it difficult for citizens seeking the protection of their rights and freedoms to organise against the omnipresent authoritarianism.

---

16 *The Economist* 8 August 2019, 'Egypt Is Reforming Its Economy, but Poverty Is Rising', https://www.economist.com/middle-east-and-africa/2019/08/08/egypt-is-reforming-its-economy-but-poverty-is-rising; Reuters 15 May 2019, *The Economist* 8 August 2019, 'Egypt's Unemployment Rate Drops to 8.1% in Q1 2019 – Statistics Agency', https://www.reuters.com/article/egypt-economy-unemployment/egypts-unemployment-rate-drops-to-8-1-in-q1-2019-statistics-agency-idUSS8N1ZD022.
17 Yezid Sayigh, 'Owners of the republic – An anatomy of Egypt's military economy', Carnegie Endowment for International Peace, 2019, https://carnegieendowment.org/files/Sayigh-Egypt_full_final2.pdf.
18 Andrew Miller and Amy Hawthorne, 'Egypt's Sham Elections', *Foreign Affairs* 23 March 2018, https://www.foreignaffairs.com/articles/egypt/2018-03-23/egypts-sham-election.

Since 2013, the government has used repression as one of its main instruments to subordinate Egyptian citizens. Repressive measures have been employed systematically to ensure either the obedience or the silence of the majority, as well as to limit the outreach of opponents' voices. The government has worked to diminish the risk of losing the effectiveness of repression over time, primarily by combining it with the use of non-repressive measures geared to subjugating citizens to the official anti-democratic discourse of Egyptian authoritarianism.[19]

In propagating its discourse, the government has depended increasingly on the media. Along with its allies in the economic and financial elites, it considers the traditional media to be the easiest site from which to dominate the public sphere and to monopolise public debates utilising an anti-democratic discourse. Besides passing various laws that restrict media freedoms and subject journalists to the supervision of quasi-governmental bodies such as the Supreme Council of Media,[20] the government has extended direct ownership of traditional media outlets to the security services – especially television channels and newspapers. Either security-owned or security-controlled, traditional media outlets have sought to impose the government's discourse on Egyptians and to undermine voices of dissent by defaming them.[21] On social media networks, the security services have organised a strong pro-government presence and launched orchestrated campaigns to defame its opponents.

Since the summer of 2013, the security services have employed the expression 'either with us or against us' to accuse and demonise both secular and Islamist dissidents as enemies of the Egyptian state. In doing so, they have justified collective punishment of opponents without making any distinction between violent individuals, on the one hand, and peaceful citizens on the other. Pro-government intellectuals, writers and politicians have been brought to the forefront of the hysteria about purported treason, confusing the 'war on terror' and peaceful freedom of expression. This has stifled any possibility of dealing with the continuous violations of human rights and freedoms without falling into the trap of double standards. In the public sphere it has become impossible

---

19 Amr Hamzawy, 'Legislating Authoritarianism: Egypt's New Era of Repression', *Carnegie Endowment for International Peace* 16 March 2017, https://carnegieendowment. org/2017/03/16/legislating-authoritarianism-egypt-s-new-era-of-repression-pub-68285.
20 Hamzawy, 'Legislating Authoritarianism'.
21 Association for Freedom of Thought and Expression (AFTE), 'Oppression with a Taste of Emergency: The Sixth Annual Report on the Status of Freedom of Expression in Egypt – 2108', updated 23 January 2019, https://afteegypt.org/publications_org/2019/01/23/16998-afteegypt.html.

simultaneously to reject terrorism and state violence and demand accountability
for breaking the law.

It was in this climate of dehumanisation of opponents as enemies of the state
that the Rabaa massacre took place, in summer 2013. Nor was this killing of
nearly eight hundred Muslim Brothers the last attempt by the government to
violate citizens' right to life and to infringe the rule of law. On the contrary, it
marks the official start of a system of violence practised up to the present. The
victims' bodies piled on the streets and in mosques were a warning of forthcoming
illegal extrajudicial killings, forced disappearances, torture and incarceration for
political reasons. These acts have become instruments used regularly to liquidate
opponents, subjugate citizens, and control society.[22]

The public falsification of what really happened in Rabaa was hardly less catastrophic than the bloodshed itself: Egyptian authoritarianism mobilised its followers and those frightened of repression in the public sphere to deny the carnage. The
victims were accused of carrying arms and committing violence. They were all
classified as actual or potential terrorists. The killing was portrayed as 'legitimate
defence' by the security services; and whilst independent reports documenting
the massacre, refuted official claims of self-defence and the victims' violence,[23]
the security-owned and security-controlled media, habituated to undermining the
truth, deluding awareness and rejecting reason justified the massacre as a 'national
necessity' imposed by the 'war on terror', while being dismissive of the victims'
losses and their families' suffering.[24]

Since 2013, Egyptian authoritarianism has continued to exploit its control of
the media to legitimise repression. A set of interrelated statements, well known to
citizens since the 1950s, have been widely propagated: 'No voice above the voice
of the war on terror'; 'Saving society and the state and defending our national
security require gathering around the presidency and the executive power'; 'Governance in Egypt respects the rule of law and protects all the rights and freedoms,
including economic and social rights, and continues to build democracy'; 'Those

---

22 EIPR 2016; El-Nadeem 2018; Amnesty International 2017/2018.
23 *getty*images, 'Rabaa Massacre' (stock pictures), https://www.gettyimages.ca/photos/raba
amassacre?sort=mostpopular&mediatype=photography&phrase=rabaa%20massacre
(accessed 3 January 2020); Human Rights Watch, 13 August 2018, 'Egypt: No Justice for
Rabaa Victims 5 Years on', https://www.hrw.org/news/2018/08/13/egypt-no-justice-raba-
victims-5-years.
24 Bethan McKernan, 'Rabaa Massacre: Five Years On Egypt Struggles with Legacy of
Single Biggest Killing of Protesters in Modern History', *The Independent* 14 August 2018,
https://www.independent.co.uk/news/world/middle-east/egypt-rabaa-massacre-cairo-
muslim-brotherhood-abdel-fattah-al-sisi-ibrahim-halawa-a8491821.html.

who oppose the laws, regulations and procedures that enable the state to confront terrorism betray Egypt and conspire against the nation'; among others.

Elements of Authoritarian Discourse 1: Delegitimising the January 2011 Uprising

As mentioned earlier, President al-Sisi has consistently characterised the protests that swept across the Middle East in 2011 as 'a wrong cure, based on a wrong and misguided diagnosis, of the crises in Arab countries'.[25] The president's use of the term 'occurrences' (*ahdath*) serves to obscure the substantial democratic mobilisation that preceded the 2011 protests. In a political context, this word typically describes spontaneous or unexpected actions. Disparaging uses of the term have a long history in Egyptian official rhetoric, and Egypt's rulers once again aimed to delegitimise civic protests as violent, illicit acts that threaten the nation's stability. Of course, the 2011 protests were not without their share of violence. Islamist and other groupings carried out violent attacks on police stations, penitentiaries and other sites of state power. But the violence committed by segments of the population was a response to the violence of the state, which is believed to have claimed more than eight hundred civilian lives, while the number of deaths among the security forces was 26.[26] From any objective standpoint, participants in the 2011 democratic uprising were on the whole peaceful, while the word 'occurrences' misleadingly suggests otherwise.

Calling the uprising against Mubarak 'misguided', as al-Sisi does, also serves an additional purpose. It helps the regime to pin the blame for Egypt's current economic and security woes on the 2011 protesters. President al-Sisi recently asserted that the 'humanitarian, financial and moral price paid by Egypt' would not have been so high 'if the conditions reigning before 2011 had remained constant'. But the ill-considered 'movement of the populace', according to Egypt's current ruler, opened the 'gates of hell'.[27] Such statements not only betray al-Sisi's authoritarian understanding of politics, but also denigrate the citizenry. In the president's

---

25 Farah Tawfeek, '2011 Revolution "Was the Wrong Cure to the Wrong Diagnosis"', *Egypt Independent*11October2108,https://egyptindependent.com/2011-revolution-was-the-wrong-cure-to-the-wrong-diagnosis-sisi/.

26 BBC News 19 April 2011, 'Egypt Unrest: 846 Killed in Protests', http://bbc.com/news/world-middle-east-13134956.

27 Noha el-Tawil, 'Sisi Vows No Role for Muslim Brotherhood under His Rule', *Egypt Today* 13 October 2018, https://www.egypttoday.com/Article/2/58911/Sisi-vows-no-role-for-Muslim-Brotherhood-under-his-rule.

narrative, Egyptians are politically immature people who inflicted considerable damage on state and society with their unthinking demands for democracy. The president, in short, is charging his citizens with naïveté for having allowed themselves to believe that, by supporting democratisation, they could change their lives for the better. The authoritarian political understanding reflected in this charge demands that citizens be completely dependent on an omniscient regime, which it considers indistinguishable from the state. The regime, accordingly, has a monopoly on knowing what is good for Egyptians. Only those in power can introduce changes or enact reforms; only they know how to ensure the country's well-being. And this means that there can be no repeat of the 2011 democratic uprising. The president and his followers will protect Egyptians from the catastrophic outcomes that any renewed protests would invite; the populace, in turn, must be ready to accept the suppression of 'recalcitrant citizens'.[28]

Elements of Authoritarian Discourse 2: Ridiculing Politics

With the marked deterioration of economic conditions and the deepening of security challenges, the current government has failed to deliver on its long-standing promises of economic prosperity and stability. As signs of social discontent have grown, even in the face of brutal repression, the government has continued to blame its own failures on conspiracies and plots, allegedly led by external forces in collaboration with opposition groups and human rights advocates. It has also sought to pre-empt the emergence of any alternative to the political status quo through its repression, coupled with defamation campaigns that it has employed to slander and discredit dissident voices, often labelled as those of foreign agents. At the same time, the al-Sisi government has resorted to another influential strategy that can be described as 'ridiculing politics'. The latter term denotes a conscious attempt to discredit civilian political life in its entirety, while promoting the belief that only the generals are capable of governing the country.

Within this strategy of ridiculing politics, official rhetoric has reduced the state apparatus to its military and security components, which comprises the army, the security services and the intelligence community. It portrays civilian state institutions, especially national and local bureaucracies, as a set of benign bodies that are – and always have been – dependent on that military-security core. This same notion of a powerful, effective military-security core versus a weak, incompetent civilian community of public servants is also mirrored in the configuration

---

28 Tawfeek, '2011 Revolution'.

of power inside the government. Today the legislature, in effect, is beholden to the unchecked authority of the military-security establishment, represented in the institution of the presidency.[29] By operating under the full guardianship of the military, the state narrative goes, parliament is able to fulfil its national duties without falling prey to the inherent weakness of its civilian interlocutors. Thus, the current legislative assembly, also known as the House of Representatives, was essentially formed under the supervision of the office of the president, the military and the general intelligence and security agencies.

Furthermore, the regime adopted a parliamentary election law that gave the edge to independent candidates, and not political party lists, thereby undermining the role of party politics and national public policy debates. Traditionally, independent candidates have tended to eschew national policy issues in favour of local parochial interests. These interests have deepened these candidates' loyalties to the government, to familial and tribal networks and to the rich financiers supporting their campaigns. Thus, unlike parties, independent candidates usually have little incentive to adopt strong positions on salient public policy debates, or such issues as the representation of social groups and legislative oversight of the executive.

Prior to the 2015 parliamentary elections, moreover, the presidential office and the various security agencies structured the electoral contest in a manner that ensured a sweeping victory for their loyalists competing for the independent candidacy seats. They also formed a nationwide list, the infamous 'For Love of Egypt', and engineered an easy victory for it in the party list races. The military's approach to handpicking 'trusted' candidates (and would-be parliamentarians) reflected a deliberate effort to underscore the understanding that the role of parliament and its members is first and foremost to lend unequivocal support to the president's policies.

For their part, al-Sisi loyalists among parliamentary candidates proudly presented themselves as the political backbone of the president and his government. They often argued that support for the military-backed regime was a patriotic duty, to defend Egypt's national interests from external dangers. Their campaigns invoked the state's frequent portrayals of al-Sisi as a national (and perhaps the only possible) saviour, and simultaneously dismissing the possibility of any form of legislative scrutiny of his policies. In advancing such a narrative, these would-be parliamentarians were upholding the aforementioned notion that the generals

---

29 Jan Völkel, 'Sidelined by Design: Egypt's Parliament in Transition', *The Journal of North African Studies* 22.4, 2017, pp. 595–619.

alone are qualified to rule Egypt, and endorsing the dominance of the military-security core over civilian institutions, notably the legislature. Most importantly, they ridiculed parliamentary politics and, more generally, civilian political life in the eyes of wide segments of the Egyptian public.

The regime's choices of candidates, furthermore, implicitly conveyed the notion that the legislature would not function without the presence of military and security veterans. Retired officers, so the story goes, will guide and streamline the performance of gullible civilian legislators who do not have the experience necessary to comprehend the national security threats and external conspiracies supposedly confronting the Egyptian nation. It is no surprise, therefore, to find that almost one-sixth of elected members are former army or police officers. Like most independent candidates turned parliamentarians, retired army and police officers rarely make any substantive contributions to public policy debates or proposals. Instead, their increased presence in public life following the military takeover of 3 July 2013 has helped to reify the military's dominance over mainstream media. For instance, retired army and police officers would often appear on television to enlist public support for al-Sisi's autocratic ways and to defame his opponents, labelling them as enemies of the nation, and such officers' presence in parliament serves a similar purpose: they can be expected to employ their alleged 'security expertise' to advance the regime's fear-mongering conspiracy theories and to level accusations of treason against oppositionist voices. Key within this picture is the supposed mark of credibility that former affiliation with the military and security agencies affords these legislators. According to this reasoning, they are the logical choice for leading consensus inside parliament and keeping inadequate civilians in check.[30]

Not only does the military regime's narrative reduce civilian elites to the status of ineffective public servants in need of the supervision and control of the officers, they are also portrayed as misguided individuals who eschew attention to national problems and the basic needs of the Egyptian people in favour of personal interests. Ultimately, this all serves the purpose of ridiculing civilian politics, and undermining any effort to build an alternative to the rule of the generals. This narrative can be discerned in key phrases that allies of the ruling establishment have used systematically in the media to justify the superiority of the military-security core

---

30 The Conversation UK, 13 March 2109, 'Egypt: Hopes for Democratic Future Die as al-Sisi Marches Country towards Dictatorship – with Parliament's Blessing', http://theconversation.com/egypt-hopes-for-democratic-future-die-as-al-sisi-marches-country-towards-dictatorship-with-parliaments-blessing-113491.

over the state's civilian components. Examples include: 'The president is working singlehandedly, while other state institutions are undermining his achievements'; 'The president and the army are working hard to rescue the nation, while parliament and civil servants are busy with nonsensical debates and petty demands'; and 'The Egyptian state would have collapsed already if it were not for the army and the security institutions safeguarding its stability and unity.'

Within the framework of this strategy of ridiculing politics, the regime worked, in the lead-up to the 2015 legislative elections, to ensure that the prospective parliament would rubber-stamp the president's proposed policies. Chief among these are the several hundred laws that the executive decreed in the absence of a legislature between 3 July 2013 and 10 January 2016, when the House of Representatives finally convened. In a legislative environment devoid of political and salient public policy debate, the passing of these laws occurred within a brief period, and involved no meaningful discussion. In short, by generating an apolitical legislature, the regime has ruled out any possibility of the emergence of real policy debates and proposals. Thus it is that the regime's strategy of ridiculing politics has gone hand-in-hand with its abolition of freedom, of the right to meaningful representation and, in effect, of the very existence of the individual citizen in Egypt.[31]

In sum, the regime has structured the new political arena in a way that completely discredits civilian politics and that presents al-Sisi's as the only path for stability and survival. Egyptians are told to accept the president's authority and his guidance not only in the realm of politics, but also in how they lead their private lives, even down to their household consumption habits. Al-Sisi presents himself as a pious yet worldly head of the Egyptian nation, who advocates religious tolerance, works to better Egypt's economic and security situation and pushes for the social equality of women. On Islamic holidays, he holds forth on 'moderate Islam'. On Christian holidays, he opens new or restored cathedrals serving the minority Coptic community. He negotiates favourable trade agreements with representatives of major international corporations while the cameras roll, regularly meets with the defence and interior ministers to discuss the security situation and charges his cabinet – again in front of the cameras – with the strengthening of legal protections for women who experience domestic violence. In return for his comprehensive service in promoting Egypt's interests, al-Sisi demands that Egyptians stand behind him and accept restrictions on their political rights. They are called upon

---

31 Amr Hamzawy, 'Egypt after the 2013 Military Coup: Law-Making in Service of the New Authoritarianism', *Philosophy and Social Criticism* 43.4–5, 2017, pp. 392–405.

to work hard, stop protesting and give up their political rights and freedom for the sake of bread, security and stability. Finally, they are urged to unite behind their saviour and not flock around the evidently inadequate civilian elites and politicians who are incapable of meeting the basic needs of the Egyptian people.

Elements of Authoritarian Discourse 3: Populism

As a further significant stream of the contemporary authoritarian discourse, the government in Egypt has depended increasingly on religious and nationalistic populism. This allows the ruling establishment to tighten its grip on many aspects of life in the country, under the pretence that the president is governing on behalf of ordinary citizens, to whose needs he has been attentive.

Religious populism elevates the ruler to the level of a moral paragon who has the right to speak in the name of religion not just as regards the public and political spheres, but also in terms of its impact on private life and ethics. Nationalistic populism, in turn, is used to justify the ruling establishment's monopoly on power. It allows the ruling general, Abdel Fattah al-Sisi, to align himself with the national interest and national security, enabling him to undertake the role of 'protector of the masses'.[32]

Egypt's military and security generals use official Islamic and Christian institutions to impose their own interpretations of religion upon everyday life. These interpretations are manifested in three interrelated ways: first, by framing obedience to the ruler and the approval of government policies as a religious duty; second, by claiming that the government-promoted understanding of religion is moderate, so that anything that tends against it can be labelled 'extremist'; and third, by depicting the ruler as a protector of 'dignified morals and values', so that divergent moral conceptions can be denounced as 'inappropriate for Egypt'.[33]

Exploiting the nationalistic strain of populism, the ruling establishment depicts itself as the guarantor of stability and protector of ordinary citizens. Thus, nationalistic populism opens a door to the ridiculing of politics and civilian politicians, as shown above, and as politics and politicians are derided, the ruling establishment justifies filling the alleged void with military and security officers, as representatives of the only institutions capable of safeguarding the nation and providing for the basic needs of citizens. Furthermore, nationalistic populism

---

32 https://www.shorouknews.com/news/view.aspx?cdate=20092019&id=47c31ddf-cc11-40f0-94b4-44e6cdfea3d7 (in Arabic; accessed 4 January 2020).
33 http://gate.ahram.org.eg/News/2283158.aspx (in Arabic; accessed 4 January 2020).

creates a governing framework that is in clear contradiction to the rule of law and good governance. Military institutions benefit from such populism to obtain constitutional, legal and political immunity; their lack of any form of accountability undermines the power of the legislative and judicial branches of government, thereby limiting the checks and balances in the system, and neutralises monitoring agencies such as the Central Auditing Organisation.

The 2014 constitution, even prior to its 2019 amendments, enshrines a special status for the military. Its budget cannot be discussed in a transparent manner, mechanisms for oversight of the armed forces are eliminated and civilians are subject to military courts whensoever the generals may decide. In the past three years, thousands of Egyptians, including university students, young activists and workers, have faced trials before military tribunals. Capitalising on its special status enshrined in the constitution, the military has also increased its economic and social role. In 2015, for example, a presidential decree gave the armed forces the power to establish profit-seeking companies and investment firms with both Egyptian and foreign partners.[34]

In the public sphere, nationalistic populism silences the free voices that demand democratic change and the social movements that try to defend human rights and freedoms. The ruling establishment has sought to discredit those voices and movements and to break any conceptual link between democracy, human rights and the interests of ordinary people. Security-owned as well as security-controlled media have attacked pro-democracy activists and industrial workers demanding legitimate wage increases, accusing them, without any evidence, of corruption, treason and conspiring with the 'enemies of the nation'. Independent non-governmental organisations and professional associations, critical of widespread human rights abuses and of economic and social policies, have also been subjected to systematic defamation campaigns in media outlets. The government's aim is to create an environment that facilitates repressive measures and silencing tactics.

All of this has created an Orwellian paradox. In the name of the people, the Egyptian government has effectively engaged in behaviour directed primarily against the people. The ruling establishment uses nationalistic populism to dismantle any infrastructure that supports the rule of law. Today in Egypt, legal changes that contradict the principles of justice and equality have been introduced

---

34 Shana Marshall, 'The Egyptian Armed Forces and the Remaking of an Economic Empire', Carnegie Middle East Center, April 2105, https://carnegieendowment.org/files/egyptian_armed_forces.pdf.

under the guise of defending the nation and bolstering national security. Claiming to wage a 'war on terror', with the aim of restoring stability and defending the state's territorial integrity, the military and security forces have engaged in unlawful surveillance, while constantly threatening citizens' rights and freedoms.[35] A clear case of undemocratic legal measures is the amendment of article 78 of the penal code. This criminalises foreign funding for all purposes, and in so doing makes pro-democracy activists and independent non-governmental organisations liable to harsh government retribution.

Furthermore, nationalistic populism tends to create an environment that allows for the dismissal of universal standards of the rule of law, democracy and human rights as 'Western' practices that do not apply to Egypt and are not binding on the government. Indeed, in the worldview represented by nationalistic populism, the rule of law and democracy are Trojan horses pushed by internal and external 'enemies of the nation' to undermine its stability. Enforced disappearances, torture, extrajudicial killings and various abuses of rights are all committed under the banner of protecting the nation and defending the interests of ordinary Egyptians.

Nor has the military-led government implemented sound public policy, or laid the foundations for economic growth. Instead, it has exploited nationalistic populism to ignore facts, deny the free flow of information and belittle the value of knowledge and scientific thinking in public policy matters. Such hostility stems from the ruling establishment's tendency to deny crises, blame others for the negativity rampant in society today, suggest to citizens that their duty is only to obey and use its disdain for policy details to propagate haphazard solutions to Egypt's many hardships: as if the country could be saved while human rights violations, the excessive economic role of the military and the lukewarm fight against corruption continue.

Against a background of growing economic and social crises, rising political tensions, ineffective public policies and the dwindling approval ratings for the president, the use of both religious and nationalistic populism has thus become, along with the ridiculing of politics and fear tactics, a major stream in the authoritarian discourse propagated by the government to maintain its control over Egypt.

---

35 Alaa al-Aswany, 'Egypt's Phony War on Terror is Really about Silencing Dissent', *The Washington Post* 13 June 2109, https://www.washingtonpost.com/outlook/egypts-phony-war-on-terror-is-really-about-silencing-dissent/2019/06/12/8473f61a-70e6-11e9-9eb4-0828f5389013_story.html.

Elements of Authoritarian Discourse 4: Fear Tactics

Facing these different elements of the government's discourse, dissidents and pro-democracy activists have been demanding a return to the democratisation path of 2011–2013. They have been calling for a redressing of injustices, an end to violations of rights and freedoms and suspension of the repressive measures that have been inflicted on people over the past several years. Those dissidents and activists, in addition to the repression they endure every day, face the challenge of translating democratic principles into realistic visions, ideas and demands that can garner attention in the public sphere; of providing a clear alternative to the ruling authoritarianism, an alternative that can attract popular support. In the absence of such a positive engagement with public opinion, and a recapturing of the interest of the citizens who are reluctant to support democratic demands, the authoritarian onslaught will continue. The regime will keep on demonising democracy, pushing the people continuously to apologise for its experience between 2011 and 2013.

Thousands of young, middle-aged and elderly people are unjustly held behind Egyptian prison walls and in detention sites.[36] To this day, Egyptian authoritarianism maintains its repression against those who refused to abandon the democratic demands of 2011. It targets those who peacefully opposed practices and policies that infringed human rights and freedoms. Egyptian authoritarianism thus aims to silence its opponents' voices while inflicting unbearable suffering on them and their families.

The use of fear is an ancient strategy that Egyptian governments have come to master and to implement by mobilising a variety of formal and informal instruments. The existing laws have been the primary tool employed since 2013, supplemented by the enactment of repressive new laws such as the Protest Law, the Terrorism Lists and Terrorist Entities Law and the NGO laws. The regime has also passed legal amendments that violate the constitutional guarantees of the citizen's rights and freedoms, such as amendments to the penal code. In order to subordinate public authorities and government institutions that are not under the direct control of the executive power and the will of the president, the regime has been using legal tools systematically over recent years. For example, it implemented amendments to the laws governing the regulatory authorities (such as the Administrative Control Authority and the Central Auditing Organisation that monitor the power of the executive). It also imposed amendments to the power of the judiciary. This enabled the president of the republic alone to appoint and dismiss the

---

36 ANHRI (Arab Network for Human Rights Information), 'There is Room for Everyone: Egypt's Prisons before and after the 25 January Revolution' report, September 2016.

heads of the regulatory authorities and holders of higher positions in the courts (such as the presidents of the Court of Cassation and of the State Council). This legal tool is also manipulated to disrupt everyday Egyptian life and impose an unlimited and extendable state of emergency: the president reintroduced the state of emergency in 2017 and has been renewing it with the approval of parliament ever since. The Emergency Supreme State Security Courts continue to be held. Finally, the legal tools deprive citizens of their freedom by exploiting vague legal texts to allow long-term preventive detention and sometimes to enable the judicial authority illegally to extend dissidents' confinement. As for the informal tools deployed, there is a wide range of extrajudicial killings, enforced disappearances and torture in prisons and places of detention. These informal instruments encompass the inhumane treatment of dissidents, prohibiting their rights to treatment and health care, to communicate with their families and to legal defence.[37]

Whilst resisting any idealisation of the defenders of freedom by presenting them as existential heroes, it remains difficult to overcome the frustrations of their suffering, which would require the use of various resistance tools. In the absence of democracy, however, human rights defenders daily monitor new violations, while looking for legal, political, mediatic and awareness-raising means to confront impervious official institutions that deny and obscure the truth. There is a need for collective action and debate, professional support and human solidarity, while dismissing individuality and isolation and disregarding intra-group conflicts among the organisations defending human rights and freedoms. In the absence of democracy, human rights defenders must admit, to themselves individually and collectively, the psychological, human and societal impact of their inability to stop the violations or hold anyone accountable, as well as the impact of the distortion and rejection they face from public opinion.

Without democracy, and with the spread of fear, dissidents and human rights defenders are confronted with the silence and reluctance to be involved of the majority of citizens. Under difficult economic and social conditions, they witness the use of the media by the government and its allied elites to deny human rights violations and to flout the rule of law. Egyptians are thus faced with an unenviable choice: either they abstain from any participation in the public sphere, and abandon social and political affairs to protect their right to life and provide security and stability for their families; or else they resolve to demand change and peacefully oppose authoritarianism, but at huge personal risk.

Unsurprisingly, the majority opts for abstention. Peaceful opposition has

---

37 Hamzawy, 'Egypt after the 2013 Military Coup'.

become the choice of a scattered few. Dissidents and human rights defenders have been adamant in distancing themselves from, on the one hand, apologists for the current authoritarianism and all those who seek to replace it with another authoritarianism in the name of religion, and, the other hand, both intellectually and politically, from secular forces that endorsed the military takeover of politics in 2013. This double detachment affords dissidents and human rights defenders a small, distinct place in the Egyptian public sphere.

If we look beyond the silenced majority and the few scattered voices of dissent, independent political and media figures generally fail to demonstrate solidarity with victims of human rights violations. Various factors explain their attitude. Principally, they avoid criticism of authoritarianism from fear that state institutions and networks of economic and financial power will isolate them: for this reason, they are afraid to adopt opinions and positions that may contradict, fully or partially, government policies. Even before 2011, many independent political and media figures never openly criticised the president or the government. Such acquiescent behaviour has intensified since 2013 due to the widespread implementation of repressive measures as well as of direct media control by the government.

As a result of fear tactics, voices of dissent and advocates for democracy have been showing signs of fatigue. Their writings have become petitions of complaint, expressions of lamentation and despair, discourses full of anger and mocking of the other, lacking the intellectual depth that might be able to promote political change. Their collective suffering has been escalating due to the constant threat of repression, ceaseless accusations and the limited extent of popular solidarity.

Concluding Remarks

Repression imposes paranoid fear on the ruler and the ruling elite: fear of conspiracies and alleged conspirators, fear of latent or apparent public anger and fear of the societal repercussions of injustices and violations, which are difficult to estimate and predict. Authoritarian regimes have an insatiable will to hold a monopoly on information and to know all the details of every citizen's life. They have a tendency to keep citizens oblivious to the real situation of the state and society, and falsify people's awareness as an additional tool of control and oppression. Such governments and systems dread losing their control over their citizens, and constantly fear uprisings or revolutions.

There are two main reasons for this fear, and many disastrous consequences. The first reason lies in the constant oppression, the lack of justice and liberties and the continuous violations of human rights. Violations range from large-scale

eradication to torture and inhumane treatment of political prisoners and prisoners of conscience. Regardless of the extent to which liberty is curtailed, whether
targeting political opposition groups or affecting all segments of the populace and
social movements, the consequences of oppression, injustice and violations will
ultimately be the collapse of the government, the regression of society and civil
strife.[38] On another level, authoritarian regimes, and particularly their security services, recognise the limited long-term effectiveness of repression. No matter how
fierce and violent authoritarian regimes can be, oppression and injustice provide
impetus for some citizens to gradually shift from being supporters (of the cheering
or of the silent kind) to terrified retreaters, or from passive opponents of injustice
to active resisters seeking efficient alternatives.

It is perfectly clear today that authoritarianism was established in Egypt in
2013 on the ruins of a failed democratisation process. Its first political goal was
to remove the citizens from the public sphere, liquidate independent civil society,
suppress opposition, eliminate free media and seal off the public domain. The aim
was to restore the supposedly golden age of 'one leader, the symbol of the nation
and the heart of the state' that ended in 1967. To this day, successive governments
in Egypt have not overcome the legacy of this delusional era. Everyone is aware
today that the regime is controlled by the military and security forces, assisted by a
group of technocrats, university professors and Egyptian experts working in international financial institutions. In dealing with public affairs, these ruling circles
completely separate serving the nation through the management of economic,
social and service issues, on the one hand, from concern with human rights, conditions and liberties, on the other. The latter mean little to them and do not influence
them towards rejection of a government that accumulates violations daily. Since
2013, the regime has sought to consolidate the state's military, security and civil
institutions after the years of the uprising and the democratic revolution between
2011 and 2013. Supported by a great number of people, it seeks to confront terrorism and the major security challenges at both the national level (Sinai) and the
regional (the western border with Libya and the Grand Ethiopian Renaissance
Dam being the two main challenges). However, the regime's desire to annihilate
political life, stifle the opposition and restrict the public sphere have prompted it
to ignore the importance of ceasing to violate human rights and of safeguarding
public liberties.

---

38 Ahmad Abd al-Rahman, 'Al-Sisi: There is No Political Detainee in Egypt and Fair Tials
are Held Following the Law' (in Arabic), *Al-Yawm al-Sabi* (The Seventh Day) 23 October
2017.

An objective reading of Egypt's situation today shows that the government has managed to achieve several economic reforms, such as floating the national currency and recasting energy and food support policies; but the heaviest burden of these reforms falls on the poor and low-income citizens, who also lack social support. The government seeks to silence these social classes and uses political and media propaganda to diffuse the discourse of 'We all have to be patient to build the nation.' It also stifles them by means of violence and repression at the hands of the security services, restoring the walls of fear that had fallen during the years of revolution and the democratic uprising of 2011–2013. But this attitude towards the lower classes is extremely dangerous for community stability and national consensus. The poor should not carry the burden of building the nation alone. Moreover, walls of fear can be too fragile to endure. It is not surprising, therefore, that the new authoritarianism in Egypt denies the crisis caused by difficult economic and social conditions, which are mainly borne by the poor and low-income families. Official circles admit to no injustices and violations of rights and freedoms, or depict them as isolated cases. Some officials are also involved in inciting the collective punishment of opponents. It is, finally, of no surprise to anyone that limited public resources are drained between the inflation of the security and intelligence services budget and the high cost of 'major projects' presented without any serious preparatory scientific studies. Loans and debts continue, while sustainable development opportunities face severe decline.

It is plain that the government in Egypt will not renounce its authoritarian path, reduce control by military and security forces or explore political and societal requirements to strengthen the state. There is no way to comfort those who believe that the Egyptians have the right to protect their rights and freedoms and that their country has the right to a balanced economic, social and political development that does not replicate the situation of the 'single leader' era, but actually helps to avoid dangers to state and society – similar to those faced after the crushing 1967 defeat. Indeed, there has been an escalation in censorship of independent websites and newspapers in 2019, and one of the main objectives of these censorship policies is to prevent the circulation of information about the country's economic and social situation, as well as in relation to human rights violations.

There is very little in Egypt's current political landscape to suggest that, less than a decade ago, the country embarked upon an attempt at democratic transformation. President Abdel Fattah al-Sisi is now serving his second term. According to the 2014 constitution, this term was to end in 2022 and should have been al-Sisi's last. That changed on 16 April 2019, when the Egyptian parliament – whose majority consists of the president's acolytes and representatives of the security establishment – passed constitutional amendments that extend al-Sisi's current term into 2024 and enable him to once more seek re-election; al-Sisi could now remain in office until 2030.[39] The package of constitutional changes confirmed in a referendum on 20–22 April 2019 also expands presidential powers vis-à-vis the justice system, and confers a political role on the army.

Egypt is caught today between two evils: on the one hand, systemic corruption on the part of the new authoritarianism, involving official circles and economic, financial, media and party elites who accept submission to the regime in exchange for protection and benefits; and, on the other, the use of a variety of authoritarian narratives to impose submission on citizens. Egyptians are trapped by fear and intimidation and are thereby forced to ignore public matters. The war on freedom in Egypt comes at a high price. In order to fight corruption, it is necessary to allocate public and private resources fairly to the beneficiaries and to implement monitoring at both official and popular levels of the executive power responsible for assigning resources. To overcome the systemic waste of public and private resources, it is necessary to apply rules of transparency and accountability and foster a fearless public debate able to trace, document and expose negligence. Terrorism is, certainly, a criminal violation of the right to life and an absolute denial of liberty; but the only way to overcome it is to secure justice, rights and freedoms, to commit to a credible promise to stop all violations and to use military and security tools within the rule of law. Finally, violence, which results from the spread of inhumane extremism in unjust environments lacking sustainable development and social justice, can be overcome only by the exercise of liberty of thought, liberty of peaceful and public expression, liberty of public debate guaranteeing its objectivity and liberty to ask for justice and to activate its mechanisms vis-à-vis the individual, the community and the state.

The majority in Egypt seems to be headed in a different direction, however, largely thanks to the government's effective exploitation of authoritarian narratives. The voter turnout rate, which was close to 50% from 2011 to 2013, has sunk to about 25% over the subsequent years; and while sinking turnout rates might be understood as reflecting a lack of interest in participating in elections where the outcome is a foregone conclusion, opinion polls conducted by Princeton University's Arab Barometer Project indicate that a considerable segment of the Egyptian population has backed away from demands for democratic government

---

39 *The New York Times* 23 April 2019, 'Egypt Approves New Muscle for el-Sisi, Its Strongman Leader', www.nytimes.com/2019/04/23/world/middleeast/sisi-egypt-referendum. html.

altogether.[40] In June 2011, almost 80% of Egyptians surveyed considered democracy to be the optimal political system. By 2016, this had fallen to 53%. Egyptians' dwindling support for democracy is clearly linked to dramatic shifts in their perceptions of economic and security conditions, as well as to declining public confidence in political actors. Between June 2011 and the first half of 2013, the number of Egyptians who took a positive view of their economic and security situation plummeted. In both these areas, confidence in the current state of affairs has since bounced back. In 2013, only 7% of the population judged the economic situation to be good, down from 23% in 2011. In 2016, three years after the end of the democratic experiment, 30% of respondents were satisfied with the economy. As mentioned above, the number of Egyptians who regarded the economic situation as a top priority in 2016 dwarfed the number who prioritised the formation of a democratic government.

Still more dramatic changes have occurred in the public's assessment of the security situation. In 2011, a majority – 53% – had a generally positive outlook on this issue; in 2013, this figure had slipped to 20%; by 2016, it had risen again, dramatically, to almost 80%. Political parties in particular appear to have borne the brunt of popular discontent, as citizens' trust in parties sank from 58% in 2011 to 20% in 2016. Confidence in state institutions generally declined less precipitously, with trust in the armed forces remaining at 85% (compared to 99% in 2011).

The perceptions of the majority of the Egyptian population thus seem to be in many ways aligned with the current discourse of the authoritarian regime, which depicts the democratic uprising of 2011 and the ensuing political changes – or, in the regime's language, the 'occurrences' – as harmful events whose repetition would only inflict further damage on the country. In 2016, a majority of 82% of Egyptians opined that political reforms, if any, should be introduced very gradually, with the government closely supervising their introduction. In that same year, public confidence in the government was 65%.

In 2019, Egypt is an anxious nation, and Egyptians are uncertain with regard to the future course of their country.

---

40 Daniel Tavana, 'Egypt Five Years After the Uprisings: Findings from the Arab Barometer', 20 July 2017, www.arabbarometer.org/wp-content/uploads/Egypt_Public_ Opinion_Survey_2016.pdf.

Bibliography

Abd al-Rahman, Ahmad, 'Al-Sisi: There is No Political Detainee in Egypt and Fair Tials are Held Following the Law', *Al-Yawm al-Sabi* (The Seventh Day) 23 October 2017, https://www.youm7.com/story/2017/10/23/%D8%A8%D8%A7%D9%84%D9%81%D9%8A%D8%AF%D9%8A%D9%88%D8%A7%D9%84%D8%B3%D9%8A%D8%B3%D9%89-%D9%84%D8%A7-%D9%8A%D9%88%D8%AC%D8%AF %D9%85%D8%B9%D8%AA%D9%82%D9%84%D8%B3%D9%8A%D8%A7%D8%B3%D9%89-%D9%81%D9%89-%D9%85%D8%B5%D8%B1 %D9%88%D9%85%D8%AD%D8%A7%D9%83%D9%85%D8%A7%D8%AA-%D8%B9%D8%A7%D8%AF%D9%84%D8%A9/3477630.

Al-Aswany, Alaa, 'Egypt's Phony War on Terror is Really about Silencing Dissent', *The Washington Post* 13 June 2109, https://www.washingtonpost.com/outlook/egypts-phony-war-on-terror-is-really-about-silencing-dissent/2019/06/12/8473f61a-70e6-11e9-9eb4-0828f5389013_story.html.

ANHRI (Arab Network for Human Rights Information), 'There is Room for Everyone: Egypt's Prisons before and after the 25 January Revolution' report, September 2016, https://anhri.net/%D9%87%D9%86%D8%A7%D9%83%D9%85%D8%AA%D8%B3%D8%B9-%D9%84%D9%84%D8%AC%D9%85%D9%8A%D8%B9/.

Association for Freedom of Thought and Expression (AFTE), 'Oppression with a Taste of Emergency: The Sixth Annual Report on the Status of Freedom of Expression in Egypt – 2108', January 2109, https://afteegypt.org/publications_org/2019/01/23/16998-afteegypt.html.

Atef, Mohamed, 'On the 30th Anniversary: Central Security Events Still without Investigation', *Aswat Misriyya* (Egyptian Voices) 25 February 2016, http://www.aswatmasriya.com/news/details/59194.

BBC News 19 April 2011, 'Egypt Unrest: 846 Killed in Protests', http://bbc.com/news/world-middle-east-13134956.

Blaydes, Lisa, *Elections and Distributive Politics in Mubarak's Egypt*, Cambridge 2010.

The Conversation UK, 13 March 2109, 'Egypt: Hopes for Democratic Future Die as al-Sisi Marches Country towards Dictatorship – with Parliament's Blessing', http://theconversation.com/egypt-hopes-for-democratic-future-die-as-al-sisi-marches-country-towards-dictatorship-with-parliaments-blessing-113491.

Cook, Steven, 'Sisi Isn't Mubarak. He Is Much Worse', *Foreign Policy* 19
December 2018, https://foreignpolicy.com/2018/12/19/sisi-isnt-mubarak-
hes-much-worse/.

The Economist 8 August 2019, 'Egypt Is Reforming Its Economy, but Poverty
Is Rising', https://www.economist.com/middle-east-and-africa/2019/08/08/
egypt-is-reforming-its-economy-but-poverty-is-rising.

El-Tawil, Noha, 'Sisi Vows No Role for Muslim Brotherhood under His Rule',
Egypt Today 13 October 2018, https://www.egypttoday.com/Article/2/58911/
Sisi-vows-no-role-for-Muslim-Brotherhood-under-his-rule.

Foa, Roberto Stefan, 'Modernization and Authoritarianism', *Journal of
Democracy* 29.3, 2018, pp. 129–40.

gettyimages, 'Rabaa Massacre' (stock pictures), https://www.gettyimages.ca/
photos/rabaamassacre?sort=mostpopular&mediatype=photography&phrase=
rabaa%20massacre.

Hamzawy, Amr, 'Can Egypt's Hopes Be Revived?', *Journal of Democracy* 30.4,
2109, pp. 157–68.

Hamzawy, Amr, 'Egypt after the 2013 Military Coup: Law-Making in Service
of the New Authoritarianism', *Philosophy and Social Criticism* 43.4–5, 2017,
pp. 392–405.

Hamzawy, Amr, 'Legislating Authoritarianism: Egypt's New Era
of Repression', *Carnegie Endowment for International Peace*
16 March 2017, https://carnegieendowment.org/2017/03/16/
legislating-authoritarianism-egypt-s-new-era-of-repression-pub-68285.

Hosni, Samir and Ibrahim Hassan, 'Al-Sisi: Lack of Awareness is the
Real Enemy, 2011 Was the Wrong Cure to the Wrong Diagnosis'
(in Arabic), *Al-Yawm al-Sabi* (The Seventh Day), 11 October 2018,
https://www.youm7.com/story/2018/10/11/%D8%A7%D9%84%D
8%B3%D9%8A%D8%B3%D9%89-%D9%86%D9%82%D8%B5-
%D8%A7%D9%84%D9%88%D8%B9%D9%89-%D9%87%D9%88-
%D8%A7%D9%84%D8%B9%D8%AF%D9%88-%D8%
A7%D9%84%D8%AD%D9%82%D9%8A%D9%8
2%D9%89-%D9%88%D8%A3%D8%AD%D8%AF%D8%A7%D8%AB-
2011-%D8%B9%D9%84%D8%A7%D8%AC-%D8%AE%D8%A7%D8%B
7%D8%A6/3984859.

Human Rights Watch, 'Egypt: No Justice for Rabaa Victims 5 Years On', 13
August 2018, https://www.hrw.org/news/2018/08/13/egypt-no-justice-raba-
victims-5-years.

Kassem, Maye, *Egyptian Politics: The Dynamics of Authoritarian Rule*, Boulder 2004.

Marshall, Shana, 'The Egyptian Armed Forces and the Remaking of an Economic Empire', Carnegie Middle East Center, April 2105, https://carnegieendowment.org/files/egyptian_armed_forces.pdf.

McKernan, Bethan, 'Rabaa Massacre: Five Years On Egypt Struggles with Legacy of Single Biggest Killing of Protesters in Modern History', *The Independent* 14 August 2018, https://www.independent.co.uk/news/world/middle-east/egypt-rabaa-massacre-cairo-muslim-brotherhood-abdel-fattah-al-sisi-ibrahim-halawa-a8491821.html.

Miller, Andrew and Amy Hawthorne, 'Egypt's Sham Elections', *Foreign Affairs* 23 March 2018, https://www.foreignaffairs.com/articles/egypt/2018-03-23/egypts-sham-election.

Masrawy 11 October 2018, 'Al-Sisi: 2011 Wrong Cure to Wrong Diagnosis' (in Arabic), https://www.masrawy.com/news/news_egypt/details/2018/10/11/1442477/.

The New York Times 23 April 2019, 'Egypt Approves New Muscle for el-Sisi, Its Strongman Leader', www.nytimes.com/2019/04/23/world/middleeast/sisi-egypt-referendum.html.

Qutb, Misbah, '1977–2013: Bread Uprising and Hunger Revolution' (in Arabic), *Al-Masry al-Yawm* (The Egyptian Today) 16 January 2013 (special issue), https://www.almasryalyoum.com/news/details/282271.

Rashwan, Nour, 'Al-Sisi: We Opened the Gates of Hell to Our Country When We Imagined that We Are Capable of Changing the Reality', *Al-Shuruq* (The Sunrise) November 2018, https://www.shorouknews.com/news/view.aspx?cdate=04112018&id=e2805369-dc4d-4776-be91-42548d7cedee.

Reuters 15 May 2019, 'Egypt's Unemployment Rate Drops to 8.1% in Q1 2019 – Statistics Agency', https://www.reuters.com/article/egypt-economy-unemployment/egypts-unemployment-rate-drops-to-8-1-in-q1-2019-statistics-agency-idUSS8N1ZD022.

Sayigh, Yezid, 'Owners of the republic – An anatomy of Egypt's military economy', Carnegie Endowment for International Peace, 2019, https://carnegieendowment.org/files/Sayigh-Egypt_full_final2.pdf

Soltan, Gamal Abdel, Ahmed Nagui Qamha and Subhi Asilah, 'The Arab Barometer Project – Arab Republic of Egypt, June 2011', www.arabbarometer.org/wpcontent/uploads/Egypt_Public_Opinion_Survey_2011.pdf.

Stacher, Joshua, 'Egypt Running on Empty', *Middle East Report* 8 March 2016, https://merip.org/2016/03/egypt-running-on-empty/.

Tavana, Daniel, 'Egypt Five Years after the Uprisings: Findings from the Arab Barometer', 20 July 2017, www.arabbarometer.org/wp-content/uploads/ Egypt_Public_Opinion_Survey_2016.pdf.

Tawfeek, Farah, '2011 Revolution "Was the Wrong Cure to the Wrong Diagnosis" ', *Egypt Independent* 11 October 2108, https://egyptindependent. com/2011-revolution-was-the-wrong-cure-to-the-wrong-diagnosis-sisi/.

Transparency International 29 January 2019, 'Middle East and North Africa: Corruption Continues as Institutions and Political Rights Weaken', https:// www.transparency.org/news/feature/regional-analysis-MENA.

Völkel, Jan, 'Sidelined by Design: Egypt's Parliament in Transition', *The Journal of North African Studies* 22.4, 2107, pp. 595–619.

World Economic Forum, *The Global Competitiveness Report* 2018, https:// www.weforum.org/reports/the-global-competitveness-report-2018.

4

Syria: Causes and Consequences of the Popular Uprising

Salam Kawakibi

As of the spring of 2019, fighting continued in parts of Syria, but the outcome of conflict was by then favourable to the Assad regime and had been for quite some time, given its military support from Russia. Although the regime had been unable to recover the entirety of Syrian territory, it was increasingly focused on the reconstruction of the country and on the reassertion of its sovereign power. The international actors opposed to Assad had implicitly or explicitly recognised the survival of the regime, suggesting that fighting for and over Syria was for the moment finished. Despite the military, political and diplomatic victory of the regime, however, the conflict in Syria had demonstrated clearly that the very legitimacy of the state had been called into the question. This should be the starting point for any analysis of the Syrian uprising and its consequences. The civil war represents in fact the most significant questioning of the legitimacy of the Syrian state since its creation in 1920, and it is a particularly consequential issue that goes beyond the regime in place. The Arab uprisings destabilised not only regimes and governments across the region, but in some instances questioned the very legitimacy of the established states, weakening state structures and providing alternative political arrangements,[1] no matter how normatively unappealing, as the example of the Islamic State demonstrates.[2] Syria is only one such case.

---

1 Ariel Ahram and Ellen Lust, 'The Decline and Fall of the Arab State', *Survival* 58.2, 2016, pp. 7–34.
2 Quinn Mecham, 'How Much of a State is the Islamic State?', *POMEPS Studies* 12, 2015, pp. 20–24.

Despite the tormented political history of the country since the collapse of the Ottoman Empire, it is important to underline that there were periods in Syrian history when the collective construction of a genuine and legitimate nation state was not simply a 'delusion',[3] but a real political project, contributed to by elites and citizens alike. The years since the beginning of the uprising have to a large extent seen the dismantling of the idea of a collective national identity and the necessity for this identity to be expressed and legitimated through the Syrian state. For instance, the idea of a united nation that was Syrian first and Arab second dominated the thinking of the precursors of the Syrian renaissance at the end of the nineteenth century and the beginning of the twentieth.[4] This idea of a genuinely united Syrian nation has been undermined by the rise of two fundamentally opposed nationalisms with strong dogmatic certainties. The resulting struggle over and manipulation of ascriptive identities, which has been forged in armed conflict, is likely to endure and render the future of Syria politically problematic despite, or precisely because of, the survival of the regime. Religion and religious belonging feature prominently in the current conflict, but the emphasis on this religious dimension was not particularly strong in the early days of Syrian nationalism, and its reification today undermines both the regime and the state. To an extent, some scholars continued to argue initially that the conflict was not fully sectarian and that religious belonging did not yet trump other identities.[5] However, as conflict intensified, it became difficult to marginalise the religious/sectarian dimension. The historical absence of a rational management of diversity has compounded the problem.

This chapter emphasises the importance of history's *longue durée* to illustrate how the political and institutional choices of the past have influenced the current conflict, its outcome and its consequences. After revisiting the way in which Syrian history shaped and led to the 2011 uprising, the chapter focuses on one of its most important consequences: namely, the rebirth of civil society activism. While most of the literature focuses on the armed struggle and armed groups of

---

3 Raymond Hinnebusch, *Syria: Revolution from Above*, London 2002.
4 Adel Bishara, *The Origins of Syrian Nationhood: Histories, Pioneers, and Identity*, London 2011; Rana Issa, 'The Arabic Language and Syro-Lebanese National Identity Searching in Buṭrus Al-Bustānī's Muḥīṭ Al-Muḥīṭ', *Journal of Semitic Studies* 62.2, 2017, pp. 465–84; Daniel Pipes, *Greater Syria: The History of an Ambition*, New York 1990; Eliezer Tauber, 'Part I: Beginnings', *The Emergence of the Arab Movement*, ed. Eliezer Tauber, London 1996.
5 Christopher Philips, 'Sectarianism and Conflict in Syria', *Third World Quarterly* 36.2, 2015, pp. 357–76.

different ideological persuasions,[6] and on the Islamic State most particularly, it is important to note that the uprising also liberated citizens from fear, encouraging them to construct alternative ideas about how to govern a society.[7] While these experiments have failed to topple the regime and withstand the violence of armed groups, they nevertheless remain crucial as a demonstration of the 'energy' of Syrian society, and can aspire to be both an ethical inspiration and a concrete building block for the future of the country.

How Did Syria Get Here?

It is necessary to go back at least a century to understand how Syria got to this point. During the French mandate (1920–1946), there existed Western-style political parties, which were, at times, an emanation of, or strictly connected to, literary circles or civil society associations (*al-jamaiyyat al-ahliyya*), suggesting therefore that political pluralism was a reality in the country. Colonial authorities monitored and controlled political and intellectual life, but this did not impede its flourishing. The political debate at the time was structured around two main blocs: the National Bloc (al-Kutla al-Wataniyya) and the People's Party (Hizb al-Chab). Both political movements represented essentially the non-sectarian bourgeoisie of Aleppo and Damascus, which included feudal landowners, industrialists, financiers and intellectuals from the diverse religious sects present in the country. From an ideological point of view, both blocs can be considered very similar, emphasising nationalism and liberalism. The period also saw, together with the emergence of these two blocs, the rise of political parties more closely connected to the international environment: the Syrian-Lebanese Communist Party, with strong links to the Soviet Union; the Syrian Socialist-National Party, which drew inspiration from movements proliferating across Europe at the time; the Arab Baath Party (yet to embrace socialism); and the Muslim Brothers, closely connected to the Egyptian 'original' founded in 1928.

When Syria became formally independent in April 1946, all these parties became central actors in the new political system being set up. Contrary to the nascent authoritarianism that characterised the post-independence period elsewhere across the Arab world, Syrian political parties worked together in the newly

---

6 Thomas Pierret, 'Salafi Jihadism and the Syrian Civil War: National and International Repercussions', *Salafism after the Awakening*, eds. Francesco Cavatorta and Fabio Merone, Oxford 2017, pp. 137–54.
7 Gilles Dorronsoro, Adam Baczko and Arthur Quesnay, *Syrie: Anatomie d'une guerre civile*, Paris 2016.

elected parliament (1946–1949) irrespective of their ideological differences, in what was the first genuine expression of democratic political pluralism in the country. However, in March 1949, Colonel Hosni al-Zaim carried out a military coup against the elected representatives of the people, accusing the government of having skirted its obligation to stand against Israel in the 1948 war. From that point on, the 'Palestinian struggle' would become the trump card for all authoritarian leaders in Syria, although they did little or nothing actually to oppose Israeli foreign policy in the region or to 'free Palestine'. Indeed, apart from engaging in a vaguely pro-Palestinian rhetoric and the recurrent manipulation of Palestinian factions, Damascus did not implement any concrete political, diplomatic or military policy at any point to change in practice the political situation of the Palestinians in East Jerusalem, the West Bank and Gaza, or to establish a Palestinian state.

In any case, from 1949, and until 1954, a number of military dictatorships governed the country, although it should be underlined that in these military regimes civilians did play a role, in so far as they occupied the post of prime minister. What is also interesting to note is that many of these civilians quit their posts when popular revolts against the regime occurred. The current regime functions in a very similar way in this respect.[8] In 1954, Adib Shishakli, president of Syria from July 1953 until February 1954, was the last military leader of that period. He left office to avoid, in his words, 'a bloodbath' following anti-regime demonstrations across the country. In a way, historical experience demonstrates that Syrian society has been far from supine since independence, and that contentious politics managed to challenge the regime successfully at fairly regular intervals, highlighting the fact that perceived apathy under authoritarianism is often the product of outright repression rather than of acceptance of the status quo. Following Shishakli's departure, Syria went through four years of considerable political effervescence, with all sorts of political debates taking place coursing through society.

At the peak of Arab nationalism in the late 1950s, President Choukri al-Kouatli signed an act of unification with Nasser-led Egypt, leading to the creation of the United Arab Republic. This was the point at which the 'civilian' security services (*mukhabarat*) appeared in Syria for the first time, as they had not existed in the country since the end of the mandate. It is therefore the union with Egypt and the 'import' of Egyptian practices of governance that allowed for the setting up of a veritable police state, with its corollary of heavy-handed repression of opposition ranging from the dissolving in acid of leaders of the Communist Party to the arrest

---

8 Joshua Stacher, *Adaptable Autocrats: Regime Power in Egypt and Syria*, Stanford 2012.

and systematic torture of Muslim Brothers and the exclusion of Baathists from the army. Unsurprisingly, a military coup carried out in September 1961 ended the union with Egypt, re-establishing a vibrant political life in the Republic of Syria. Two years later, however, a further military coup carried out by the Baathists ended the pluralism of Syrian political life for good, until the 2011 uprising. While the usual contention is that political pluralism in the country ended with the creation of the United Arab Republic, the reality is that the period between 1961 and 1963 was a short democratic interlude that could have led to the establishment of a normalised political life. This was not to be; but it indicates that the vibrancy and ferment of Syrian political pluralism still bubbled in broader society. From 1963 until 1970, the country became the 'realm of a naïve utopian dictatorship', with the Syrian Baath radically engaged on a number of fronts: confrontation with Western powers, a precipitous and poorly managed agrarian reform and a programme of rapid nationalisations. All this had the effect of leading to the mass migration of the economic elites. The regime in power, however, was not yet systematically corrupt, and torture of dissenters had not yet become bureaucratised and routinised, although the use of repressive measures and the banning of political parties and press freedoms were put in place during this period.

In 1970, Hafez al-Assad came to power and set out to reconfigure the political system. Finding inspiration in the experience of the German Democratic Republic ('East Germany'), he introduced in 1972 a controlled form of political pluralism through the creation of the Progressive National Front (al-Jabha al-Wataniyya al-Taqaddumiyya). At the beginning, seven political parties were included in the Front, but its composition varied over time. Rather than providing an outlet for the different political persuasions in the country, the parties in the Front consisted in effect only of their representatives. In exchange for their co-optation into the apparatus of the authoritarian regime that Hafez was constructing, they received ministerial posts and material benefits. They did not have permission – or the inclination, for that matter – to exercise a genuinely autonomous political role, and for a time could not even publish their own dailies or magazines. Assad eventually reconsidered the latter ban and permitted the parties in the Front to have their own official publications, but there were no ordinary party members to speak of, and publication was therefore meaningless. Assad even managed to co-opt some of the leaders of the Communist Party, although the majority of these opted to resist his attempts to do so and remained in opposition. They eventually went on to create the Syrian Communist Party (Political Bureau) and were duly repressed, with their leader Riad al-Turk (who became known as 'the Syrian Mandela') spending eighteen years in jail (1980–1998).

It can be stated with fair accuracy that those who joined the Front in an attempt to provide some sort of legitimacy for the regime were not genuine political militants, but security agents tasked with 'managing' specific social constituencies. The real threats to Hafez's power were in fact the army and the Baath Party. He proceeded therefore to weaken the party and bend it to his will. When it came to the military, he developed a strategy of 'divide and rule', weakening the regular army units and the officer corps to the benefit of special units and intelligence services. This two-pronged strategy gave birth to the 'securitocracy' in Syria. In addition to the creation of the Front, Assad proceeded to the transformation of the Baath from a political party into a mechanism in the regime's repressive apparatus, as party members did not engage in political discussion and activities, but simply became the ears and eyes of the regime in society. In exchange for the smallest of benefits (a job, a scholarship, a permit) to improve their daily lives, they would denounce dissent within their families or in the workplace. In a way, again, the experience of East Germany was transported into Syria, which became a police state *par excellence*, counting on hundreds of thousands of official and non-official security personnel and informers.[9]

East Germany was not the only model that Hafez followed when reconfiguring political power in Syria. A visit to North Korea in 1973 provided the inspiration for the permanent pro-regime mobilisation of the whole of society, irrespective of age. In 1974 he created the Vanguard of the Baath Party (Talai al-Baath) for primary school children. The brainwashing at this early age of children, who now became the eyes and ears of the regime in the privacy of each household, provoked fear in their parents. In secondary school, children had to then join the Revolutionary Youth Union (Ittihad Shabibat al-Thawra). If their service in the Union was appreciated, their marks would be bumped up so as to allow them to enrol for the university programmes that were most in demand. This permanent mobilisation of society whereby the regime controlled individuals was not, as mentioned above, limited to young people. We find the same pattern in trade unions or women's associations. As in the 'people's democracies' of Eastern Europe, the regime referred to all these state-sanctioned associations as 'popular democratic organisations'. There could be no clearer misnomer, as in reality no broad collective autonomous public life was allowed to develop. In addition to these repressive measures to stifle any type of dissent and neutralise the party and the army, the regime continued to deploy the sectarian card to further divide the

---

9 Radwan Ziadeh, *Power and Policy in Syria: Intelligence Services, Foreign Relations and Democracy in the Middle East*, London 2012.

opposition and legitimise its rule. As Belhadj and Ruiz de Elvira Carrascal point out, 'since 1963 the Baathist regime has supervised and managed society in an authoritarian manner through sectarianism. Examples of such sectarian politics include the co-optation of certain minorities within the Baath party, the government and the state-controlled press [and] the selection of mostly Alawites and Sunnis for key positions in the intelligence services, the armed forces and the Baath national security office.'[10] In short the regime positioned itself as the guardian of national unity against what it labelled as sectarian demands and deviations.

Thus, through the promotion of a culture of fear, the regime was able to create a very individualistic and atomised politicisation. During the 1970s, the left and the Islamists – the latter having the possibility of employing their networks in Quranic schools and mosques – tried to set up initiatives to counter the regime's narrative and actions, but were unable to organise broadly and systematically. In the 1970s, the very concept of opposition in a way changed, in that there did not seem to be anything resembling an opposition movement, no matter how loosely organised, but simply dispersed individual opposition voices without the means to meet and organise. By 1976, demonstrations and opposition against the regime had grown somewhat, but in a move foreshadowing the way in which Bashar was to deal with the 2011 uprisings, Hafez's regime argued that radical Islamists were responsible for the social and political disturbance the country was experiencing. This provided the excuse for further clamping down, by playing up the secular nature of the regime. The widespread repression, which eventually led to military confrontation in Hama in 1982,[11] caused even any semblance of intellectual and political life to disappear. Syrian intellectuals were thus faced with three options: co-optation, corruption or exile.

The experience of exile is particularly important, as Syrians abroad were among the protagonists of the post-uprising period in 2011. It should be noted, however, that exile does not allow for the creation and sustenance of a well-structured opposition. Within the exile community it is very difficult to develop a meaningful political life beyond individual participation and mobilisation. The rare attempts to create more permanent and effective structures do not last long, as the example of the National Salvation Front (Jabhat al-Khalas al-Watani), set up by former vice-president Abdel Halim Khaddam and the Muslim Brothers

10 Souhaïl Belhadj and Laura Ruiz de Elvira Carrascal, 'Sectarianism and Civil Conflict in Syria: Reconfigurations of a Reluctant Issue', *Islamists and the Politics of the Arab Uprisings*, eds. Hendrik Kraetzschmar and Paola Rivetti, Edinburgh 2018, pp. 322–40.
11 Raphaël Lefèvre, *The Ashes of Hama: The Muslim Brotherhood in Syria*, Oxford 2013.

in 2005/2006, shows. In addition to logistical difficulties and ideological diver-
gences, exiled opponents have to contend with the ever-changing political agenda
of their host countries, particularly Arab ones.

A new impetus for political change in Syria seemed to come when Bashar al-
Assad ascended to power in 2000.[12] Soon after his appointment as president, the
country went through the so-called 'Damascus Spring', when the political opponents who had remained in Syria experienced a relative freedom of expression.
This spring did not last very long, and those intellectuals and opponents, such
Riad Seif, Michel Kilo, Aref Dalila and Yassin Haj Saleh, who had spoken up in
the name of reform and change became once more the victims of state repression.
It became clear that even under the rule of the 'cub of Damascus' the conditions
for the existence of a genuine and autonomous opposition did not exist, and Syria
embarked on what Wieland describes as a 'decade of lost chances' for the regime
genuinely to reform.[13]

The roots of the current crisis are thus to be found in the 1970s, when the
system of power – securitocracy – was put in place by Hafez al-Assad to suffo-
cate the aspirations of Syrian society and its plural identities and persuasions, but,
most of all, to control the Baath Party and the army, turning them eventually into
instruments of control and repression at the service of the security establishment.

Contentious Politics and Popular Uprising

Despite the overbearing presence of the security services, Syria did experience
contentious politics, particularly in the 1970s. Protest movements began, albeit
rather timidly, in the early years of the decade, to become then more widespread,
starting with the demands of trade unions and professional orders then extending
to other social and economic sectors of society. While there is a tendency, particular among Western analysts, to focus on the religious dimension of the protests,
this was not the only element that was present and that mattered. (As will be
illustrated below, a similar mistake was made in 2011 when analysing the nature
of the protest movement against Bashar al-Assad.) In any case, the successful
repression that ended the protests in the 1970s and early 1980s in Syria cemented
the wall of fear that had first been erected in 1958 when the United Arab Republic

---

12 Najib Ghadbian, 'The New Asad: Dynamics of Continuity and Change in Syria', *The
Middle East Journal* 55.4, 2001, pp. 624–41.
13 Cartsen Wieland, 'Syria, a Decade of Lost Chances', *openDemocracy* 29 August 2012,
https://www.opendemocracy.net/en/syria-decade-of-lost-chances/.

was set up and the intelligence and security services were given a prominent role in Syrian politics.

The country did not experience significant protest movements until 2011 when, in the wake of uprisings elsewhere in the region, ordinary Syrians also began to demand change, on the streets. The current Syrian conflict began in March 2011 with a peaceful popular movement that lasted for months, demanding political and socio-economic reforms. It should be noted, as it is often forgotten, that the protest movement did not have a clear political leadership and that protesters did not call into question the legitimacy of the state and its institutions. In fact, at the beginning they did not even call for the fall of the regime, and the movement was more in line with the demands made during the 2000 Damascus Spring, which had called for opening-up of the political system and greater respect for individual freedoms, without questioning the role of Assad or the legitimacy of the state institutions. That this attitude changed over time was the product of the repressive policies of the regime in line with what Bashar al-Assad had done following the end of the Damascus Spring.

Following the short-lived Damascus Spring, Assad had strengthened the security apparatus across all sectors of society, 'encouraging' Syrians to return to the time when they were subjects rather than citizens. In addition, the regime furthered its policy of 'divide and rule', as employed in the past by the colonial power, thus reviving tribal, ethnic, regional and religious allegiances, to the detriment of national identity. This was the deliberate object of the policies the regime put in place, and not simply an unintended consequence. Despite appearing as a secular regime, Assad-led Syria manipulated and instrumentalised religion and projected an image of being the protector of 'religious minorities' against extremism. This did not necessarily correspond to the reality on the ground, but religious belonging became increasingly relevant for ordinary citizens, further undermining national unity. This occurred as well due to the changing economic situation:[14] as the state retreated from economic management, market-economic reforms widened the gap between the few 'haves' connected to the regime and the many 'have-nots' living in growing poverty in a country, moreover, where severe droughts undermined the rural economy. In this context, religious charities and groups took up some of the slack, reinserting religion in the public sphere.[15]

14 Bassam Haddad, *Business Networks in Syria: The Political Economy of Authoritarian Resilience*, Stanford 2011.
15 Kjetil Selvik and Thomas Pierret, 'Limits if Authoritarian Upgrading in Syria: Private Welfare, Islamic Charities and the Rise of the Zayd Movement', *International Journal of Middle East Studies* 41.4, 2009, pp. 595–614.

A number of policies implemented by the regime over the course of the 2000s furthermore encouraged religious radicalism, which was to be used as a scare-monger for the rest of society. While Assad was busy repressing progressive intel-lectual life, whether secular or religious, he also contributed to the stoking of radicalism in a conservative society, with the aim of using it to justify his continu-ing hold on power: to save Syria from extremism. To this end, the regime toler-ated the diffusion of radical and obscurantist religious practices. As Khatib also demonstrates, the presence of radical religious ideologies and groups precedes the civil war and is the outcome of specific policies enacted by the regime.[16] The Assads had a long tradition of supporting radical movements in Lebanon, Pales-tine and Iraq, for instance, as instruments of foreign policy, and hoped that the same strategy would work at home.

Opposition Dynamics

As mentioned earlier, Hafez al-Assad was able to remain in power through the strength of his repressive apparatus and clever manipulation of religious identi-ties; but central to his survival was also the ability to appease the middle class through the distribution of government jobs and strategic economic openings that benefited crucial Sunni middle-class constituencies. By the time Bashar came to power, the old economic model had become untenable, and with his young eco-nomic advisers Bashar began inserting Syria into the global economy, promoting a host of market-oriented reforms that would attract foreign investment and, at the same time, allow Syrian entrepreneurship on both the domestic and inter-national markets to operate more freely. However, as in other countries across the region,[17] and due to the authoritarian and arbitrary nature of political power, which cannot be separated from the economic sphere, market-oriented reforms inevitably favoured those who were close to or an integral part of the regime. It is no surprise to find that the resulting disconnect from society more generally grew exponentially, as poorly executed economic reforms now combined with politi-cal and intellectual repression. As elsewhere in the region, the last vestiges of the post-independence social contract disappeared. In such a context, the opposition to the regime did not need to be politically coordinated, and emerged from Syrian

16 Line Khatib, *Islamic Revivalism in Syria: The Rise and Fall of Bathist Secularism*, London 2011.
17 Bradford Dillmann, 'Facing the Market in North Africa', *The Middle East Journal* 55.2, 2001, pp. 198–215.

cities and villages in a spontaneous manner, with local people-turned-activists at
the forefront. Indeed, historical opponents of the regime remained convinced for
quite some time that the regime would be able to manage the demonstrations in
the early months of 2011, and therefore kept a safe distance from them.

To be fair, it was difficult to see how protests would occur and endure, given
that there was no real 'civil society' to speak of, since the regime controlled all
mobilising organisations, as described above, and because the civil society domain
had been largely monopolised by the FLANGO (First Lady's Non-Governmental
Organisations) phenomenon.[18] In this situation, it is hardly surprising that the real
revolutionaries were young people without political affiliations, but who emerged
as leaders in local neighbourhoods, sport clubs and university campuses and both
energised and mobilised following the funerals of the early victims of the repression. In that respect, the Syrian revolution resembles very closely that of Tunisia,
where the younger generation, supposedly apolitical, disdaining activism as never
before and interested only in the internet and possibilities of emigration, became
the real protagonist. It would be a mistake to interpret the Syrian uprising simply
in terms of an armed struggle between the regime and armed rebel groups. This is
how it ultimately turned out, but the early daily experience of it was far from that.

Unlike in Tunisia, however, the protesters did not have, and were not able to
find, a political framework through which to channel their strength and demands.
Where Tunisian political parties, trade unions, professional associations and opposition personalities had been able over time to build bridges and present a coherent
alternative to the regime in place, nothing of the sort existed in Syria. Protesters in
Syria were willing to fill the streets to demand radical change and be done with the
hogra (contempt) that permeated their lives, but they did not have a clear political project, nor was one on offer. The local leaders who had emerged from the
spontaneous protests were critical of historical opposition figures, and the latter
were initially suspicious of the demonstrations. Mutual suspicions and criticism
prevented connections between the two sets of players, undermining the possibility of setting out a clear political path regarding how to deal with the regime and
its repressive measures. At the same time, the first Syrian National Council, built
on the template provided by the equivalent Libyan council, was formed abroad
in 2011 to oversee and guide the revolutionary process. This did not work either,
however, because many of the members of the Council had never been to Syria

18 Salam Kawakibi, 'The Paradox of Government-Organized Civil Activism in Syria', *Civil
Society in Syria and Iran: Activism in Authoritarian Contexts*, eds. Paul Aarts and Francesco
Cavatorta, Boulder 2013, pp. 169–86.

or had not been there in decades, which resulted in them and their views being out of kilter with local dynamics and leaders. The Council attempted to broaden its representativeness and created the National Coalition; but this turned out to be a mistake. It was too idealistic, and fell prey to regional and international interests, which further undermined efforts to present a coherent project for Syria. The existence of such an organ, so distant from the events on the ground shaping the uprising, undermined the communication between those inside and those outside the country.

For its part, the regime was able to take advantage of the problems affecting the opposition movement and targeted the young leaders of the uprising with systematic repression: arrests, torture, assassinations and exile. The local institutions created during the uprising and charged with coordinating it therefore lost a large part of their leadership very quickly. Furthermore, the local leaders who left Syria to collaborate with the opposition in exile did not manage to come back to the country, severing the links between the local groups – crucial to the uprising – and their leadership. It was within these local revolutionary committees and groups that the most crucial aspects of the uprising, both practical and political, were discussed: what action to take, what kinds of slogan should be put forth, what principles should be enunciated and committees set up and what points a political platform should privilege. As mentioned above, these local committees and the networks they created were exposed to the relentless repression initiated by the regime in response, and were unable to find sufficiently strong support either from the historical opposition or within the institutions established abroad.

On the ground, local committees were soon marginalised, falling victim first to the regime's repression and later to the militarisation of the conflict. When they were initially set up, the population did participate through elections in their success, but this quickly became quite meaningless. It should be noted, however, that civil society actors quickly stepped into the political and social void to guarantee essential services to the population, demonstrating the vitality of Syrian associational life despite decades of repression. This experiment was too short-lived to provide a template for an alternative type of governance that would attract those who had remained loyal to the regime. In the areas under regime control, the Patriotic Opposition (al-Muarada al-Wataniyya) was organised to demonstrate the legitimacy of the Syrian state.

The turning point for both the local revolutionary committees and the regime itself came with the militarisation of the conflict. The regime welcomed this, and effectively attempted to bring it about to shore up its legitimacy both domestically and abroad, promptly placing Syria in the camp of those fighting a 'war on terror'. Even if one considers the militarisation of the conflict inevitable, in view of the severe repression of peaceful protesters that the regime carried out, the direction of such militarisation could have been different. At the beginning of the revolution, the Free Syrian Army (FSA) – the first military outfit to grow out of the uprising, and composed of army deserters – asked the National Council to supervise it politically, thereby potentially providing the opposition with a coherent combined political and military strategy. The FSA was aware of the limitations of its purely military activities against the regime, and hoped for some sort of unified political backing; but the National Council refused, because it rejected the notion of a militarisation of the conflict. Once the FSA was denied such political role, the door was open to the proliferation of a variety of armed groups, with very specific allegiances, whether local, national or, as foreign powers began to meddle in the conflict, international. The largest military outfits did create their own political wings and co-opted civilians for that task, but their proliferation and subsequent inability to coordinate led to infighting, undermining attempts to present a common front – politically and militarily – against the regime.

The Syrian opposition has lost and, like the country itself, is in tatters. Irreconcilable ideological differences between communists, Islamists, and Arab nationalists prevented them from working effectively and from coordinating both political and military activities. Personal rivalries also undermined efforts at unity and consensus on a mutually agreed political vision for the country. Rather than attempting to find common ground over shared democratic practices that could later be implemented in Syria, upon the defeat of the regime, the leaders of opposition groups preferred to seek support – financial, political and military – from foreign states with a stake in the struggle for Syria and very little time for the interests of ordinary Syrians. Foreign meddling was therefore a factor contributing to the absence of unity and coordination among opposition groups, as regional and international powers privileged some groups over others, each striving meanwhile to see its own preferred outcome become reality. In short, the different political groups of the Syrian opposition failed in their mission because of the absence of a consensual political project and lack of a charismatic, selfless leadership, but also because of the lack of genuine support from the 'friends of Syria' in the Arab world and in the West.

It would, however, be a serious error to hold the opposition uniquely responsible for the resulting situation. The Syrian regime, in addition to its violent repressive measures, was able to manipulate opposition actors. Building on strategies that had been successful in Lebanon and Palestine, it was able to sow doubt and mistrust among opposition actors, weakening their resolve. Thus, by a powerful combination of military violence, external support from foreign powers and manipulation of identity politics, Assad and his regime survived.

New Political Practices

During the conflict, different areas of the country experienced diverging politi-cal practices, which are likely to have an impact on the process of political and physical reconstruction in Syria. In the areas under regime control, all groups and organisations are associated with the regime, with no real autonomy to speak of, suggesting that regime practices did not change during the conflict and are unlikely to change in the future. In the areas outside the control of the regime, the Islamists are by far the dominant actors, thanks to their organisational capabili-ties. The other groups are either too weak or under too much pressure from the Islamists to be effective. The term 'Islamists' does not here refer to the Syrian Muslim Brotherhood, which has been marginalised and overtaken by more radical groups. In the areas where they have an ascendancy, political life is considerably restricted and individual rights suppressed. Only in the Kurdish areas of Syria is there a degree of pluralism. A number of political parties exist, although it should be noted that the PYD (Partiya Yekitiya Demokratik: Democratic Union Party and Syrian branch of the Turkish PKK) also possesses sufficient military capacity to mobilise against other political groupings.

Broadly speaking, the revolution did not lead to the emergence of a clear politi-cal party structure, but it did lead to considerable civil society activism. The latter reflected and still reflects to an extent the diverse nature of Syrian society, and is therefore far from perfect and certainly not homogeneous, but has produced a collective political consciousness that anticipates 'the day after'. It has had to deal with distance from the official opposition, the reactivation of traditional ascrip-tive identities and repression, all of which will influence the future of Syria in its attempt at reconstruction.

Rushing towards Reconstruction

The legacy of the conflict is disastrous. The country is literally in ruins, the secu-rocratic state and its external supporters are the dominant political actors, the economy is moribund at best, at least seven million people are refugees outside the country and with no prospect of return, corruption is endemic and terror reigns in most areas, whether under regime control or not. In fact territorial control – if one can actually speak of veritable control – is the reserve of local non-state actors such as the pro-regime National Defence Forces or armed groups linked to influential local notables, rendering administration of civil affairs arbitrary.

In spite of this dramatic context, reconstruction seems to be the order of the day. It is of course not a 'political' reconstruction, as the regime has prevailed. After the successful repression of the opposition in the 1980s, Hafez al-Assad's regime had already adopted 'revenge' as the dominant attitude towards the political reconstruction of the country, punishing dissidents and further limiting political space. In addition, he adopted a new religious policy, whereby the regime intervened more seriously in religious affairs, developing a network of Quranic schools named after Assad and symbolising the control of the authorities over the religious sphere. A similar strategy is being replicated in the aftermath of the civil war, wherein a crucial aspect in the politics of the regime is again 'revenge'. Benefiting from the expertise of the Russian regime, which takes a very dim and unforgiving view of political dissent, the Assad regime is busy targeting opposition figures and areas where contestation of the regime was prominent. This has become clear through the ways in which the Damascus government has managed, economically and demographically, the areas it has reoccupied. For instance, legal measures such as Law 10/2018 have been applied to expropriate political opponents and their families. More specifically, this legislation forces refugees who left home to appear in person to reclaim their property before a certain date, and if they do not do so their property will be transferred to the state. Another factor that contributes to the demographic change of the country in favour of the regime has to do with the fact that the rebel-held areas the regime bombed from the air were and are considered 'pop-up neighbourhoods'. This means that there were no recognised sale or lease contracts. It follows that there is no way to know precisely who obtained what and how, leaving the door open to the regime to abuse this 'legal limbo' and reassign properties as it sees fit. Accordingly, it is difficult to see how refugees – even those who did not commit any hostile act against the regime – can actually go back and reclaim what they owned, thus ensuring that a number of localities are now completely different ethnically and religiously from how they looked before 2011. In the Aleppo area, as well as Der Ezzor, there are reports that Iranian investors together with pro-regime businessmen are trying to convert needy families before providing them with social housing.

While as a rule even the most despotic regimes partially open up the political sphere following a clear military victory in a civil war, if only to demonstrate their strength, the Syrian regime has not adopted a similar attitude. On the contrary, the regime continues to threaten its opponents through symbolic and effective means. For instance, during a talk show on Syrian state television, the grand Mufti of the

République, Ahmad Hassoun, invited refugees to come back to Syria, but made sure to let them know that there would be a price to pay. In addition, he stated that those Syrians who left the country to avoid military service will have to compensate the regime for their actions through an active engagement on its side once back in the country.[19]

When it comes to the physical and economic reconstruction of the country, a number of trends can be identified. The Russian patron is not entirely satisfied with how the economic reconstruction is proceeding and it is particularly critical of how the security forces and the pro-regime militias manage economic transactions and affairs on the ground. Indeed, Russia is now ready to reap the rewards for having saved the regime from collapse. Among the 'prizes' she is keen to claim are acquisition of the port of Tartous,[20] control of Damascus's international airport and the exploitation of phosphate mines.[21] More recently, Russia has also demanded that the Syrian regime pay considerable sums back to Moscow for its intervention, and Assad has begun to collect money from within his clan to meet this demand. In order to convince the wealthy members to pay up, he has reportedly used rather aggressive tactics, including some form of house arrest.[22] The potential bonanza from reconstruction exerts its appeal beyond Iran and Russia, and past rivalries are likely to be set aside. The European Union is highly unlikely to play an apolitical role that would reflect its core values of democracy and human rights. Rather, Europe will be told that it can 'pay and not play', in a scenario reminiscent of the way in which it operates in the context of the conflict between Israelis and Palestinians, whereby it subsidises the periodic reconstruction of the Palestinian infrastructure Israelis destroy, without having a say in the so-called peace process. At the time of writing, the envoys of European countries are already reviving their contacts with the Syrian regime to obtain the contracts that will underpin the reconstruction of Syria, implicitly legitimating Assad's political practices, with Italy, for instance, considering reopening its embassy. As a matter of fact, three European Union members – Romania, the Czech Republic and Bulgaria – never closed their embassies in Damascus, in violation of an EU

---

19 https://www.youtube.com/watch?v=n126Y0lwm1U (in Arabic; accessed 7 January 2020).
20 *The Syrian Observer* 30 April 2019, https://syrianobserver.com/EN/news/50098/ transport-minister-russian-investment-in-tartous-port-comes-with-high-economic-benefits. html.
21 *The Syrian Observer* 3 August 2018, https://syrianobserver.com/EN/features/19755/ russian_ambitions_syrian_phosphates.html.
22 *The Syrian Observer* 30 August 2019, https://syrianobserver.com/EN/features/52645/ whats-the-truth-of-the-rami-makhlouf-arrest-rumors.html.

consensus, and have been active in setting out their stalls to obtain a piece of the reconstruction project. Switzerland, similarly, has opened a 'humanitarian' bureau, which functions in reality as a project office examining opportunities for Swiss businesses to participate in the reconstruction of Syria. Much like European Union members, other regional and international actors such as China, Brazil and India are currently discussing how to obtain a prominent role in the reconstruction of the country.[23]

In an unstable international environment where authoritarian rule has become once more a lesser evil for Western countries – mired as they are in populism and seemingly unable to defend and promote the value of democracy and human rights – the Syrian regime's discourse about the necessity for stability is not unappealing. Material interests also drive Western policy to the extent that if dictators such as Haftar in Libya, al-Sisi in Egypt and Assad in Syria are seen as able to stem the flow of refugees and fight 'terrorism', their democratic credentials and respect for human rights are of lesser importance. If, in addition, they end up buying weapons manufactured in the West, then so much the better.

Nor, given this context, is it surprising that international organisations have also come on board when it is a matter of promoting the normalisation of relations with despotic regimes under the banner of security and stability. Failure to be directed by a 'moral compass' on the part of Western countries and the international organisations they dominate reflects a very pragmatic stance, and might even be acceptable were it not accompanied by a species of empty liberal rhetoric intended to compensate for the realism that in fact drives their foreign policies. In the case of Syria, Western liberal discourse focuses incessantly on the protection of religious minorities, albeit to the detriment of an excluded and repressed majority. This harmonises with the discourse emanating from Damascus, with the Syrian regime claiming to be the protector of minorities and therefore the only viable interlocutor for Western decision-makers. Accordingly, Syria runs the risk of becoming the graveyard of transitional justice, as Russia, with the silent complicity of the West, searches for an apolitical 'solution' to the conflict that would in fact be devoid of any justice for the victims of the regime. In the name of regional stability, the international community as a whole is ready to turn the page and ignore the values it previously purported to defend.

While stability and pacification might indeed be achieved, one can legitimately

---

23 Salam Said and Jihad Yazigi, *The Reconstruction of Syria: Socially Just Re-integration and Peace Building or Regime Re-consolidation?*, Friedrich Ebert Stiftung International Policy Analysis, December 2018, http://library.fes.de/pdf-files/iez/14939.pdf.

ask what kind of stability this is going to be, and for how long. Pacification without transitional justice will inevitably be precarious, and respect for the rights of minorities, assurances of which seem to satisfy Western decision-makers, cannot actually be separated from the issue of the broader rights that all citizens should be able to enjoy. After years of killing and suffering, with millions of refugees across the world and massive destruction of infrastructure, the Syrian 'file' is being closed in the most cynical manner: the page has been turned and the general attitude seems to be 'Move on, nothing here to see.'

Conclusion: Managing Defeat

The reforms the regime announced in 2000, which provided the incipit for the Damascus Spring, turned out to be a false hope, and for some an aborted hope. Ultimately, Bashar al-Assad turned out to be the son of the system, and his father imposed him on it. Bashar was never a reformer, and the security state that had been in place since 1970 could not tolerate any demonstration of dissent and opposition to the way in which the system was set up. While the regime did use co-optation to stem dissent, its most important instrument has always been violence. When Hafez repressed in blood the Islamist opposition in Hama, killing thousands of civilians at one blow with the tacit consent of the international community, he understood that violence produced results. When it was time for Bashar to decide between genuine reforms that would end up dismantling his regime and repression, he opted for violence, which, at least in the short term, has paid off. In 2011, Syrians experienced a sort of waiting period, and they had to 'manage hope'. In the following years of repression and violence against them, they had to 'manage the pain' of constant suffering. Finally, with the Russian intervention, Western indifference, the paralysis of the United Nations, the total impunity of the forces loyal to the regime, and the 'kidnapping' of the revolution by extremist groups and the rise of Daesh, Syrians found themselves 'managing defeat'. But something more insidious and sinister may now be in the works. Syria is the graveyard of the role of morality in politics, both domestic and international; and it has become the apex of the most cynical realpolitik. It is also the graveyard of the hopes of generations of Syrians. The problem is that from graveyards, what is often resuscitated is revenge.

Bibliography

Ahram, Ariel and Ellen Lust, 'The Decline and Fall of the Arab State', *Survival* 58.2, 2016, pp. 7–34.

Bishara, Adel, *The Origins of Syrian Nationhood: Histories, Pioneers, and Identity*, London 2011.

Dillmann, Bradford, 'Facing the Market in North Africa', *The Middle East Journal* 55.2, 2001, pp. 198–215.

Dorronsoro, Gilles, Adam Baczko and Arthur Quesnay, *Syrie: Anatomie d'une guerre civile*, Paris 2016.

Ghadbian, Najib, 'The New Asad: Dynamics of Continuity and Change in Syria', *The Middle East Journal* 55.4, 2001, pp. 624–41.

Haddad, Bassam, *Business Networks in Syria: The Political Economy of Authoritarian Resilience*, Stanford 2011.

Hinnebusch, Raymond, *Syria: Revolution from Above*, London 2002.

Issa, Rana, 'The Arabic Language and Syro-Lebanese National Identity Searching in Buṭrus Al-Bustānī's Muḥīṭ Al-Muḥīṭ', *Journal of Semitic Studies* 62.2, 2017, pp. 465–84.

Kawakibi, Salam, 'The Paradox of Government-Organized Civil Activism in Syria', *Civil Society in Syria and Iran: Activism in Authoritarian Contexts*, eds. Paul Aarts and Francesco Cavatorta, Boulder 2013, pp. 169–86.

Khatib, Line, *Islamic Revivalism in Syria: The Rise and Fall of Bathist Secularism*, London 2011.

Lefèvre, Raphaël, *The Ashes of Hama: The Muslim Brotherhood in Syria*, Oxford 2013.

Mecham, Quinn, 'How Much of a State is the Islamic State?', *POMEPS Studies* 12, 2015, pp. 20–24.

Philips, Christopher, 'Sectarianism and Conflict in Syria', *Third World Quarterly* 36.2, 2015, pp. 357–76.

Pierret, Thomas, 'Salafi Jihadism and the Syrian Civil War: National and International Repercussions', *Salafism after the Awakening*, eds. Francesco Cavatorta and Fabio Merone, Oxford 2017, pp. 137–54.

Pipes, Daniel, *Greater Syria: The History of an Ambition*, New York 1990.

Belhadj, Souhaïl and Laura Ruiz de Elvira Carrascal, , 'Sectarianism and Civil Conflict in Syria: Reconfigurations of a Reluctant Issue', *Islamists and the Politics of the Arab Uprisings*, eds. Hendrik Kraetzschmar and Paola Rivetti, Edinburgh 2018, pp. 322–40.

Said, Salam and Jihad Yazigi, *The Reconstruction of Syria: Socially Just Re-integration and Peace Building or Regime Re-consolidation?*, Friedrich

Ebert Stiftung International Policy Analysis, December 2018, http://library. fes.de/pdf-files/iez/14939.pdf.

Selvik, Kjetil and Thomas Pierret, 'Limits if Authoritarian Upgrading in Syria: Private Welfare, Islamic Charities and the Rise of the Zayd Movement', *International Journal of Middle East Studies* 41.4, 2009, pp. 595–614.

Stacher, Joshua, *Adaptable Autocrats: Regime Power in Egypt and Syria*, Stanford 2012.

Tauber, Eliezer, 'Part I: Beginnings', *The Emergence of the Arab Movement*, ed. Eliezer Tauber, London 1996.

Wieland, Cartsen, 'Syria, a Decade of Lost Chances', *openDemocracy* 29 August 2012, https://www.opendemocracy.net/en/syria-decade-of-lost-chances/.

Ziadeh, Radwan, *Power and Policy in Syria: Intelligence Services, Foreign Relations and Democracy in the Middle East*, London 2012.

5

Libya: The Altered Resource Competition

Amir Magdy Kamel

The 2011 Libyan uprisings liberated the country from the Muammar al-Gaddafi controlled regime, unleashing the potential for a new political system and inclusive economic growth in the country. This potential is underpinned by Libya's vast hydrocarbon reserves, discovered in the late 1950s, and more recently by its status as having the ninth largest proven oil reserves in the world in 2017, and the tenth largest gas reserves.[1] The actions of local forces and the contextual drivers (or dynamics) in the country has meant that the control of these resources became a source of political leverage and even conflict, rather than of cooperation and stability. In turn, this had a debilitating impact on the production and export of hydrocarbons, aggravating the situation further. This chapter aims to capture these domestic forces and dynamics, and highlights how integral they are to understanding post-2011 Libya.

Importantly, the domestic forces that influenced change resulted from a number of structures and trends in the country. These forces include tribal and regional rivalries, the impact of hydrocarbon discovery, production, and distribution processes and the legacy and influence of former governing actors (including the Ottomans, Italians, British, French, the King Idris al-Senussi monarchy and the Gaddafi regime). By evaluating how these domestic forces and dynamics affected the potential for change in Libya, this chapter demonstrates how the control of

---

1 Energy Information Administration (EIA), 'Libya's Key Energy Statistics', 2019, https://www.eia.gov/beta/international/country.php?iso=LBY.

hydrocarbon infrastructure became a source of, and accentuated, unrest in the country. In so doing, it unveils how these resources have the uncanny ability to cut through political institutional structures (or anything resembling such a thing in the country) and play to tribal and regional rivalries. By focusing on local forces and dynamics, this study pulls apart broad assumptions about countries in transition[2] and, importantly, pinpoints the role that resource infrastructure control plays in explaining developments in Libya. To put it differently, this chapter focuses on how local actors highlighted the importance of hydrocarbons as they sought to shape the political landscape in post-2011 Libya. This approach then underlines how capturing micro-perspectives (local actors) is essential to inform an understanding of countries in transition, in a way that macro-level analyses (broad theories) do not.

Before continuing it is important to make clear that this chapter by no means claims that hydrocarbons alone explain why and how Libya changed following the fall of the Gaddafi regime. Nor does it aim to determine that the analysis of the hydrocarbons 'variable' is the only way to provide a complete examination of post-2011 Libya. Instead, this chapter seeks to identify where, how and to what extent local actors used the control of hydrocarbons for political gains, and thereby undermined the political transition process and maintained the ongoing unrest (at the time of writing).

The focus on the idea of hydrocarbons having a restraining impact on economic growth or political performance is nothing new. The 'resource curse' hypothesis seeks to explain the way in which governments fail to benefit economically from their naturally provided gifts,[3] a notion that has been extended to include 'social or political well-being'.[4] This is closely aligned with the rentier state theory,[5] which focuses on how such resource-accrued wealth enables governments to suppress political opposition.[6] What these broad theoretical notions fail to take into account, however, is how micro-level forces leverage their control of domestic resource infrastructures for political and economic gain, providing a different

---

2 See Guillermo O'Donnell and Philippe C. Schmitter, *Transitions from Authoritarian Rule*, Baltimore 1986.

3 Richard M. Auty, *Sustaining Development in Mineral Economies: The Resource Curse Thesis*, London 1993.

4 Michael L. Ross, 'What Have We Learned about the Resource Curse?', *Annual Review of Political Science* 18, 2015, p. 240.

5 Hazem Beblawi and Giacomo Luciani, *The Rentier State*, Abingdon 2016 [1987].

6 Matthias Basedau and Jann Lay, 'Resource Curse or Rentier Peace? The Ambiguous Effects of Oil Wealth and Oil Dependence on Violent Conflict', *Journal of Peace Research* 46.6, 2009, p. 758.

explanation as to how countries may move towards change or transition. The case of Libya, particularly since the 2011 uprisings, illustrates this point in a clear and convincing manner.

The point is further reinforced by the value and trajectory of the country's hydrocarbon resources up until 2019. To quantify this and make its point, this chapter tracks the trend and proportion of wealth accrued from hydrocarbons, alongside the political developments that took place in Libya. In order to max-imise data availability and reliability, statistics were collected from a range of sources, including the International Monetary Fund (IMF), the World Bank, the Organisation of the Petroleum Exporting Countries (OPEC), the United States Energy Information Administration (EIA), the British Petroleum (BP) Statistical Review of World Energy and Trading Economics. These data were then analysed alongside the empirical evidence (collected from a range of official and secondary sources), whilst engaging with the scholarly debates on the topic.

To make its argument, this chapter first focuses on the literature that links resources and the control of their infrastructure with the performance of a country in political and economic terms. By engaging with this scholarship, the chapter articulates where and how these broad theoretical ideas fail to take into account the contextual forces that drive that same performance. From there, the focus shifts to Libya specifically, and identifies the local dynamics that were in play in the country before 2011. In this section, the analysis pinpoints how historical legacies in Libya fomented an unstable environment that made the competition to control the country's resource infrastructures inevitable. Then, through an exami-nation of the 2011 uprisings and post-2011 developments, the chapter uncovers how the economic underpinnings of the country drove competition and instability between local forces. In other words, it evaluates how tribal, regional and exter-nal actors played into the competition over resource infrastructure control for political and economic gain – a process that in turn undermined any attempt at bolstering political pluralism and democratic institutional structures. The chapter concludes by emphasising how the Libyan context and local forces feed into such a competition-laden environment. This demonstrates the need for a more nuanced analysis than can be afforded by the arguments associated more broadly with resource-dependency, rentier states and countries in transition.

Resource Frameworks Unravelled

One of the fundamental problems arising from the use of the transition paradigm in examining states going through change is the lack of attention given to contextual dynamics.[7] In our case, these dynamics concern the various actors and forces that impacted developments pre- and post-2011 in Libya. In a departure from O'Donnell and Schmitter's line, Anderson highlights 'the historical significance of corporate, lineage, and tribal groups in exercising political authority alongside – and sometimes within – centralised bureaucratic administrations'.[8] Meijer and Butenschøn focus meanwhile on how the relationship between Middle East and North African (MENA) states and citizens has changed post-2011;[9] and in a complimentary effort, this chapter investigates how the control of resource infrastructures plays out in political terms in a specific MENA state: that is, Libya. In doing so, it highlights the importance of capturing local dynamics and forces in formulating an understanding of the country and the triggers for unrest and change.

Within this realm of scholarship, Auty's resource curse argument is generated through an empirical analysis of rentier states that rely on minerals or natural resources for the majority of their income (as compared to otherwise similar non-rentier states). He finds that rentier states underachieve in economic performance terms relative to their non-rentier counterparts. This finding is attributed to the fact that wealth accrued from resources has enabled rentier states to delay economic development initiatives, such as opening up various sectors to international competition.[10] Auty concludes that the greater the rentier nature of states, the more the following four consequences are in evidence: first, poor economic policies are tolerated for a longer period; second, there is less pressure to develop the country's industries; third, those groups who control rents become more entrenched; and finally, there is an increased potential for unstable economic growth.[11] Atkinson and Hamilton corroborate this, and determine that the quantity of resources and the proportion of a country's Gross Domestic Product (GDP) that they constitute are negatively correlated with the country's GDP per capita growth levels.[12] Ross notes, in addition, that this negative correlation can be expanded to include social

---

7 For the paradigm, see O'Donnell and Schmitter, *Transitions from Authoritarian Rule*.
8 Lisa Anderson, 'The State in the Middle East and North Africa', *Comparative Politics* 20.2, 1987, p. 14.
9 Roel Meijer and Nils Butenschøn, *The Crisis of Citizenship in the Arab World*, Boston, MA 2017, p. 3.
10 Richard Auty, 'Industrial Policy Reform in Six Large Newly Industrializing Countries: The Resource Curse Thesis', *World Development* 22.1, 1994, p. 12.
11 Auty, 'Industrial Policy Reform', p. 24.
12 Giles Atkinson and Kirk Hamilton, 'Savings, Growth and the Resource Curse Hypothesis', *World Development* 31.11, 2003, p. 1804.

or political well-being along with economic health.[13] A concern regarding the resource curse literature, however, is the assumption that the state or government is the resource-controlling actor. Thus the resource curse theory fails to account for environments where this is not necessarily the case, or indeed neglects to consider how other local actors might impact the control or trajectory of those same resources. The Libyan context, particularly post-2011, provides a striking example of how local forces and dynamics have led to such a situation. The resource curse hypothesis clearly fails to provide for an apt understanding of at least this particular MENA state.

A related strand of scholarship, rentier state theory, evokes similar concerns in terms of fundamental assumptions that ignore the domestic context. Basedau and Lay note that the theory links rentier states directly to 'economic stagnation, corruption and authoritarianism … [as well as the ability of these states to] use abundant resources to buy off opposition or suppress armed rebellion, thereby contributing to political stability and preventing armed conflict'.[14] While they do recognise the existence of non-state local forces, this is dealt with, once again, under the assumption that rentier governments hold the monopoly over power and control of resource infrastructures in their respective states.

Along overlapping lines, Collier and Hoeffle find that the level of a rentier state's economic development from the outset is what determines the potential for conflict, and specifically civil war. Their work notes that the higher 'per capita income on an internationally comparable measure, the lower is the risk of civil war', and they explain that the level of this risk changes over time. In the first instance, 'increased natural resources increase the risk of war … due to the taxable base of the economy constituting an attraction for rebels wishing to capture the state'. They go on to clarify that in the longer term the opposite is true, 'due to the enhanced financial capacity of the government, and hence its ability to defend itself through military expenditure, gradually coming to dominate'.[15] Similarly, Bjorvatn and Naghavi find that the way rents are distributed determines whether a state's stability is compromised. Their findings demonstrate that distribution 'at a low level can destabilize a regime, as opposition groups find it profitable to challenge the dictator's monopoly on the rents'; and so it must be carried out in a way that ensures the cost of conflict is greater than that of the status quo, in order

---

13 Ross, 'What Have We Learned', p. 240.
14 Basedau and Lay, 'Resource Curse or Rentier Peace?', p. 758.
15 Paul Collier and Anke Hoeffle, 'On Economic Causes of Civil War', *Oxford Economic Papers* 50, 1998, p. 751.

to ensure stability.[16] Such transaction-focused studies, however, divert attention from the role that domestic forces have in explaining the relationship between resource rents and stability. Collier and Hoeffle's study, as well as Bjorvatn and Naghavi's work operate under the assumption that regime survival is paramount, whilst not explicitly capturing the domestic context that drives instability over resource control. This chapter therefore focuses on precisely this point, in order more comprehensively to explain this relationship, citing Libya as a case in point.

Finally, the literature on African states is also captured in this chapter's content. Jensen and Wantchekon find that between 1970 and 1995 countries 'with higher levels of natural resource dependence tended to be more authoritarian than their less resource dependent counterparts', whilst making the point that those African countries that have become more democratic came to be so through external pressure.[17] Wright, Frantz and Geddes go one step further, and note that following the Second World War, rentier states – specifically those that depend on oil – have largely moved to autocratic models.[18] They do reflect, however, that differences between rentier state performances may be due to 'circumstances that predate the discovery of oil', and therefore do not rule out the impact this can have on stability.[19] Once more, however, this scholarly focus and its conclusions are heavily dependent on the notion of a specified regime type (autocratic or otherwise). This chapter, by contrast, points to how the focus on a regime (for example, Gaddafi's government) fails to reveal how important other local forces (for example, the House of Representatives, the General National Congress or the Libyan National Army, among others detailed below) may be when it comes to impacting the country's stability.

In sum, by examining a rentier state in Libya, this chapter highlights how the control of resource infrastructure impacts stability in the country; and this focus distinguishes it from other work concerned with whether poor economic policies are pursued, whether the economic status of a country explains stability levels, whether an autocratic regime is in place or whether the rents are distributed at a high or low level. Perhaps the most salient feature of these strands of the literature is that they all make the assumption, in the course of their argument, that the

---

16 Kjetil Bjorvatn and Alireza Naghavi, 'Rent Seeking and Regime Stability in Rentier States', *European Journal of Political Economy* 27, 2011, p. 748.
17 Nathan Jensen and Leonard Wantchekon, 'Resource Wealth and Political Regimes in Africa', *Comparative Political Studies* 37.7, 2004, p. 836.
18 Joseph Wright, Erica Frantz and Barbara Geddes, 'Oil and Autocratic Regime Survival', *British Journal of Political Science* 45.2, 2011, p. 287.
19 Wright, Frantz and Geddes, 'Oil', p. 305.

government or regime holds a monopoly over resources – something that was not the case in post-2011 Libya. Indeed, this case study demonstrates the full extent to which domestic dynamics and actors sought to control hydrocarbon infrastructure for political and economic gain, thereby affecting the trajectory of change in Libya.

Pre-2011 Dynamics

As noted in previous work,[20] one of the fundamental underpinnings for an understanding of Libya lies in the priority given to tribal, regional and strategic or elitist loyalties over those of a conventional 'state'. This was something that was recognised by the Ottoman Empire, which left domestic actors to govern themselves, provided they remained under the 'umbrella' of the Empire itself. This was in contrast to the way in which Italian forces, from 1911 to 1943, and then, until 1951, British and French (or Allied) forces tried to exert more direct control in the country.[21] During that period, domestic infighting (as well as conflict with the occupying forces) characterised a population that was resistant to conforming to a state-based entity. Then, in 1951, the UN oversaw the establishment of the United Kingdom of Libya under Senussi of the Cyrenaica region in the east of the country.[22]

Importantly, Senussi himself was reluctant to represent a 'united Libya' that included the rival regions of Tripolitania (north-west) and the Fezzan (south-west), having himself previously fought tribes from these regions as well as the Allied forces. Further, Senussi's biased policies towards his regional tribesmen and foreign oil companies that provided the finance to cement his regime. These were cited by the Gaddafi-led 1969 revolutionaries as the rationale for deposing the king.[23] What followed, however, was a Gaddafi regime that in seeking to undo Senussi's pro-Cyrenaica policies ended up replicating the same conditions in the form of pro-Tripolitania policies (Gaddafi was Tripolitanian), to the detriment

---

20 Alia Brahimi, 'Libya's Revolution', *North Africa's Arab Spring*, ed. George Joffé, Abingdon 2013, pp. 101–20; Amir Magdy Kamel, 'Post-Gaddafi Libya: Rejecting a Political Party System', *Political Parties in the Arab World: Continuity and Change*, eds. Francesco Cavatorta and Lise Storm, Edinburgh 2018, pp. 184–203; Dirk Vandewalle, *A History of Modern Libya*, Cambridge 2012.
21 Vandewalle, *A History of Modern Libya*, p. 18.
22 UN, 'Summary of AG-051 United Nations Commissioner in Libya (1949–1952)', UN Archives and Records Management Section, https://search.archives.un.org/downloads/united-nations-commissioner-in-libya-1949-1952.pdf, p. 1.
23 Camilla Sandbakken, 'The Limits to Democracy Posed by Oil Rentier States: The Cases of Algeria, Nigeria and Libya', *Democratization* 13.1, 2006, p. 145.

of Cyrenaica and the Fezzan.[24] These preferential practices included providing privileged terms for foreign oil companies to operate in the country in return for propping up the Gaddafi regime.[25] This was despite a number of developments taking place that had the potential to alter this approach to governing the country. Examples include: Gaddafi's 1975 Green Book, which produced the *Jamahiriya* system under the auspices of the Third Universal Theory; involvement in the 1988 Lockerbie (PanAm flight 103) and 1989 Niger (UTA flight 772) attacks, and subsequent sanctions; the pursuit, and then abandonment in 2003, of a Weapons of Mass Destruction (WMD) programme; and efforts to liberalise the Libyan economy in the 2000s, involving attempts to privatise banks – with six out of 16 banks having foreign involvement.[26] Each of these developments highlights how the political landscape in Libya was prone to change; and yet this change did not result in an end to the preferential treatment of Gaddafi's allies. This meant that his rivals were continually maltreated, and tensions being bottled up until his removal in 2011.

Each of these developments moreover took place in the wake of the oil-sector discovery and boom in the late 1950s thanks to the 1955 Libyan Petroleum Law that set favourable conditions for foreign companies (who took home 87.5% of the profits, with the state taking the rest). This law remained in place for six years until it was repealed to ensure that profits were distributed equally between the state and the oil companies.[27] This value of hydrocarbons from 1965 onwards is demonstrated in Figure 1, and in particular with regard to oil, a production level peak of 3.36 million barrels per day (bpd) being reached in 1969.[28]

The second peak in oil production, following the 2003 dismantling of the Libyan WMD programme, aligns with the subsequent jump from 1.38 million bpd in 2002 to 1.82 million bpd five years later, and the highest level – 15.97 billion cubic meters – of natural gas production in 2010.[29] This was enabled by the lifting of UN Security Council (UNSC) sanctions which had been imposed following the

---

24 Tariq Ali, *The Obama Syndrome: Surrender at Home, War Abroad*, New York 2011, pp. 142–43.

25 F. Gregory Gause III, 'Why Middle East Studies Missed the Arab Spring: The Myth of Authoritarian Stability', *Foreign Affairs* 90.4, 2011, p. 85.

26 IMF, 'Libya beyond the Revolution: Challenges and Opportunities', Middle East and Central Asia Department, IMF Publication Services, 2012, https://www.imf.org/external/pubs/ft/dp/2012/1201mcd.pdf, p. 7.

27 John I. Clarke, 'Oil in Libya: Some Implications', *Economic Geography* 39.1, 1963, pp. 41–42.

28 BP, 'BP Statistical Review of World Energy', *Data Download*, 2019, https://www.bp.com/en/global/corporate/energy-economics/statistical-review-of-world-energy.html.

29 BP, 'Statistical Review'.

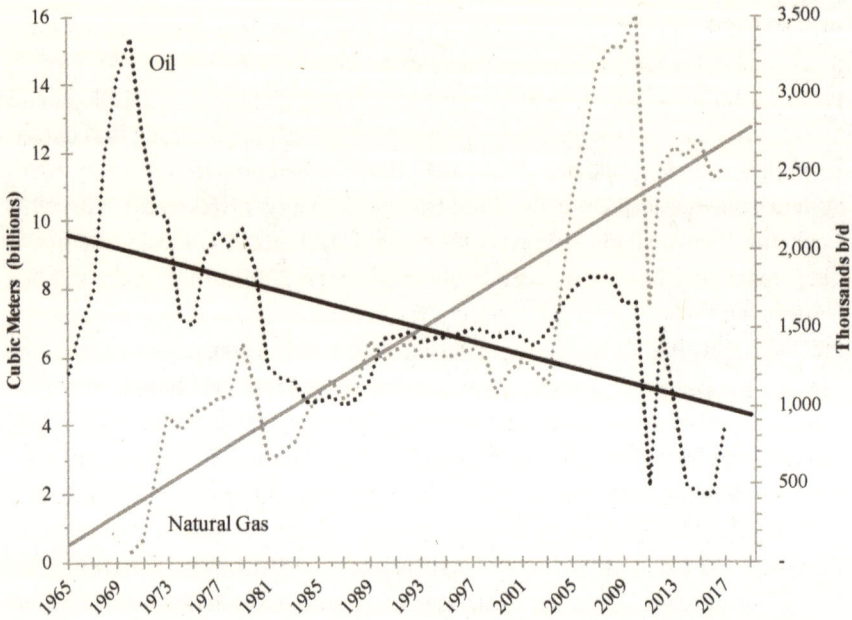

Figure 1: Libyan natural gas and oil production 1965–2019 (with trend lines)

Source: BP Statistical Review of World Energy

flight 103 and flight 772 incidents,[30] and led to a steady economic performance up until the 2011 uprisings. As real GDP growth averaged 5%, inflation averaged just under 4%, and the implementation of liberal economic policies enabled some headway to be made in diversifying the economy, albeit with concerns remaining over the fact that 'social and governance indicators remained poor, job creation was lackluster, and dependence on expatriate workers increased'.[31] The fact that the peaks and troughs in Figure 1 align with periods of conflict, instability, sanctions and the 2011 uprisings demonstrates the importance of resources when analysing Libya. This in turn conveys the value that local actors attach to controlling oil and gas infrastructure (examined in more detail below).

The legacies of tribal and regional fidelities, and of Italian, British and French

---

30 UN, 'Resolution 1506 (2003)', UN Security Council S/RES/1506 (2003), 12 September 2003, https://www.undocs.org/S/RES/1506(2003).
31 IMF, 'Libya beyond the Revolution', p. 2.

dominion, meanwhile, as well as the Senussi and Gaddafi regimes, accentuated still further the desire of local forces to resist cooperation and to compete for the leverage that could be gained from the control of hydrocarbon facilities. The 2011 uprisings and their aftermath did not alter this notion: the reliance on fossil fuels continued, and provided political and economic leverage incentives for local actors to battle for their control. Thus the contextual dynamics in Libya prior to the post-2011 era provide an explanation for the continued embroilment of domestic forces in a competition for resource control to benefit their tribal and regional affinities.

The 2011 Uprisings Incite Competition

17 February 2011 – the Day of Rage – marked the beginning of mass protests, violence and instability in Libya that further accentuated divisions between local actors and highlighted the domestic dynamics in the state. This instability was heightened by the country's dependence on hydrocarbons (detailed below), which became a natural target for rival forces to disrupt, control and ultimately leverage for political and economic benefit in the wake of the UNSC Resolution 1970, nine days after the Day of Rage, restricting access to arms, finance and travel for government and state officials.[32] These sanctions were expanded under Resolution 1973, less than a month later, which strengthened the arms embargo, implemented a no-fly zone, froze government assets and forced weapons inspections on the country,[33] resulting in the largest dip in hydrocarbon production levels to date (see Figure 1), as oil production fell by 71.14% from its 2010 level to reach 478.77 thousand bpd a year later, and natural gas falling by 53.3% to 7.46 billion cubic meters over the same period.[34] This had a debilitating impact on the Libyan economy, leading local actors to seek control over hydrocarbon facilities as political and economic leverage, intensifying rivalries in the process.

This is corroborated by Lewis, who establishes that during and after the 2011 uprisings, tribal and regional rivals sought to control oil and gas terminals for

---

32 UN, 'Resolution 1970 (2011)', UN Security Council S/RES/1970, 26 February 2011, https://undocs.org/S/RES/1970(2011).
33 UN, 'Resolution 1973 (2011)', UN Security Council S/RES/1973, 17 March 2011, https://undocs.org/S/RES/1973(2011).
34 BP, 'Statistical Review'.

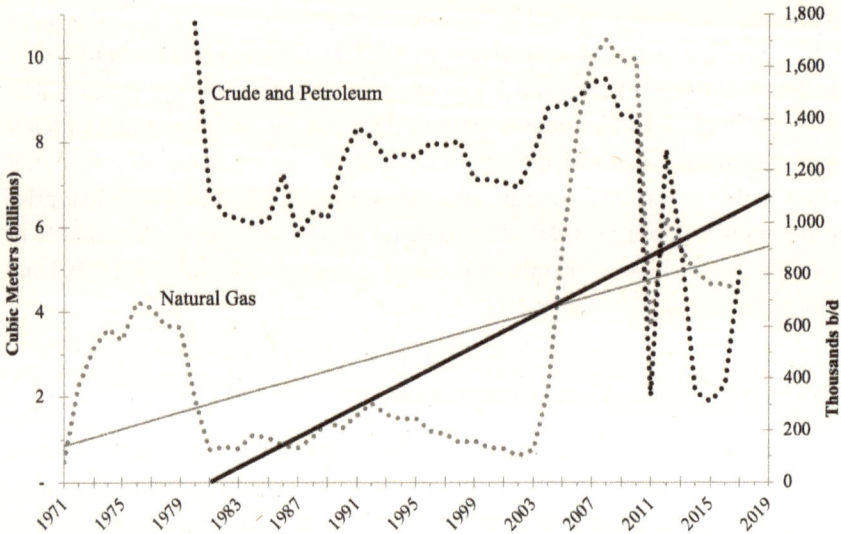

Figure 2: Libyan natural gas, crude oil and petroleum exports 1971–2019 (with trend lines)

Source: OPEC

political and financial gain.[35] It is no surprise that the immediate aftermath of the uprisings saw violence increase, to differing degrees, across the country. As depicted in Figure 2, the ability of any local actor in Libya to gain financially from the hydrocarbon sector was severely impacted, with crude oil and petroleum exports falling from 1.4 million bpd to 333.35 thousand bpd between 2010 and 2011, and natural gas exports falling from 9.97 to 3.67 billion cubic meters in the same period.[36] For the non-hydrocarbon sector, the impact was equally detrimental, as destruction of production facilities, disruption of the banking sector, limitations of access to foreign assets and exchange and a brain-drain of workers abroad all ensued during the violence, leading to a 50% fall in non-hydrocarbon real GDP terms from 2010 to 2011.[37]

It was precisely during this period that the fall and subsequent removal of the

---

35 Aidan Lewis, 'How Unstable is Libya's Oil Production?', *Reuters* 16 July 2018, https://www.reuters.com/article/us-libya-oil-explainer/how-unstable-is-libyas-oil-production-idUSKBN1K61Y6.
36 OPEC, 'Data Download', 2019, https://asb.opec.org/index.php/data-download.
37 IMF, 'Libya beyond the Revolution', pp 2–3.

Gaddafi regime led to rival local forces behaving with little to no restraint, as they sought to capitalise on the absence of a functioning government. In this situation, competition between the various domestic factions was given a new impetus,[38] and the country's hydrocarbon infrastructure was targeted to leverage and fund their respective political agendas.

The instability in Libya following the uprisings once more highlighted the dependence upon and importance of hydrocarbons in the country, not just in economic terms, but also with respect to political stability and change. The fact that rival local forces prioritised their narrow allegiances over increased hydrocarbon production and export levels makes this point emphatically. This was, moreover, something that continued through the 2010s, as the competition for resource control determined the trajectory of Libya, which became increasingly subject to infighting and interactions between domestic forces.

Resource Competition Confounding Libya's Arab Spring

Following on from the 2011 uprisings, Libya entered a period of ongoing instability, marked by numerous failed attempts at fostering a unified government. It was within this context that the country's pre-Arab Spring local structures and dynamics continued to drive domestic forces into a competition for control of Libya's hydrocarbon infrastructure. Naturally, this had an impact on political stability. These destabilising forces were entrenched in the domestic dynamics that pre-date the modern Libyan state, and it is therefore imperative to take these into account when examining the country, particularly post-2011.

Previously, the link between the Gaddafi regime's security and the country's stability has been explicitly connected to increasing oil production and the building of the associated oil facilities, rather than conventional security measures such as barriers, armed forces or police presence.[39] Following the removal of the regime, this importance placed on hydrocarbons continued, as they provided rival domestic forces, and in particular militias, with the leverage and financial capacity to safeguard their own interests.[40] Taking into account that in 2013 an estimated 8% of Libya's workforce was under militia employment,[41] these points highlight

---

38 Ronald Bruce St John, *Libya: Continuity and Change*, Abingdon 2015, p. 77.
39 John Davis, *Libyan Politics: Tribe and Revolution*, Berkeley 1987, pp. 7–8.
40 Ricardo René Larémont, 'After the Fall of Qaddafi: Political, Economic, and Security Consequences for Libya, Mali, Niger, and Algeria', *Stability: International Journal of Security and Development* 2.2, 2013, p. 2.
41 Maggie Michael, 'Libya's Militarized Youth Feed into Economic Woes', *The Daily Star*

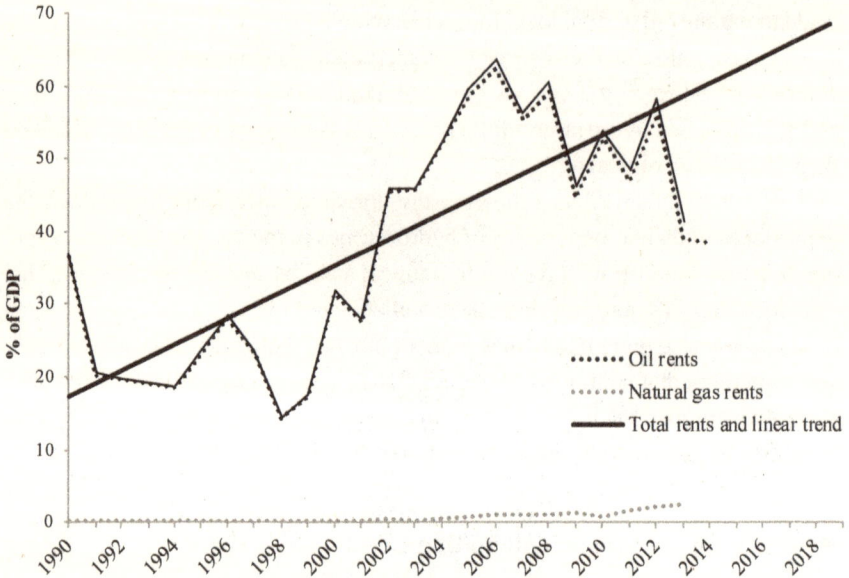

Figure 3: Libyan natural gas, oil, and total rents share of GDP 1990–2019 (with total trend line)

Sources: World Bank, IMF, and Trading Economics

just how integral the control of hydrocarbon facilities was to political leverage, and thus the stability of the country post-2011.

This point was reflected further by the value and trajectory of hydrocarbons as a share of Libya's GDP, both before and after the ousting of Gaddafi. The data show total hydrocarbon rents hitting their third highest point of 58.10% of GDP in 2012, with the previous peaks coming in 2006 (63.46%) and 2008 (60.39%), following the Gaddafi-era economic reforms and before the 2008–2009 global recession,[42] as demonstrated in Figure 3.

The upward and increasing trajectory of hydrocarbon rents as a share of Libya's GDP quantifies their full importance as a source of wealth in the country,

13 March 2013, http://www.dailystar.com.lb/Business/Middle-East/2013/Mar-13/209972-libyas-militarized-youth-feed-into-economic-woes.ashx.
42 Trading Economics, 'Gas', 2019, https://tradingeconomics.com/libya/natural-gas-rents-percent-of-gdp-wb-data.html; Trading Economics, 'Oil', 2019, https://tradingeconomics.com/libya/oil-rents-percent-of-gdp-wb-data.html.

in particular with regard to natural gas, which hit its highest level of 2.36% of GDP in 2013.[43] Further, as Figure 2 above demonstrates, the quantity of hydrocarbon exports bounced back following the 2011 uprisings, and was subject to an intermittent growth pattern as a result of ongoing instability until 2017. That said, the overall growth trajectory in terms of quantity of crude oil, petroleum and natural gas exports (albeit with the former two having a more exponential growth tendency, as demonstrated by the trend lines in Figure 2) has been positive, even taking into account the available data for the entire period from 1971 to 2017. This once more points to the importance of hydrocarbons when it comes to accruing wealth and leverage in the country, and thereby confirms why there has been such competition for the control of oil, petroleum and natural gas terminals and their associated production levels.

This was something that was not taken into account, however, in the course of the international community's efforts to promote stability in the country following Gaddafi's fall from power. The UN itself maintained the line that it was 'reaffirming its strong commitment to the sovereignty, independence, territorial integrity and national unity of Libya' following Gaddafi's removal,[44] as it had done repeatedly beforehand. This once again did not take into account local dynamics and forces resisting such unity.[45] These same forces moreover began and continued to seek and control hydrocarbon production facilities as a means to bargain for political and financial gain, through such practices as cutting off field and port production processes and blocking oil terminals.[46] It was during this period that efforts towards a transition to a formalised political structure, through the National Transition Council (NTC), came to be seen as illegitimate by local forces, and rejected for the very notion of trying to forge a 'united Libya'.[47]

At the national level, two sides, both of which had tribal, regional and even external actor support following the end of the Gaddafi regime, competed for political gains. The first came under the remit of the General National Congress (GNC), which was elected to take over the governance of Libya from the NTC following the 2012 elections, and became increasingly driven by a supposedly Islamically inspired majority. The GNC was dissolved in 2016, and its members were elected to the High Council of State (HCS) that same year. The second was

43 Trading Economics, 'Gas'.
44 UN, 'Resolution 2009 (2011)', UN Security Council S/RES/2009 16 September 2011, https://undocs.org/S/RES/2009(2011).
45 Kamel, 'Post-Gaddafi Libya'.
46 Lewis, 'How Unstable is Libya's Oil Production?'.
47 Brahimi, 'Libya's Revolution', p. 115.

the House of Representatives (HoR), elected to replace the GNC following the disputed 2014 elections. After the repeated failure of the UN-backed Government of National Accord (GNA) to forge unity between the HoR and rival forces (including remnants of the former GNC), there were a number of conflicts, violent and otherwise, between these domestic forces from 2012 and into 2019. It is to be noted that the GNC was, and the HCS is, based in Tripoli (Tripolitania), whilst the HoR is backed by and aligned with the notable former Gaddafi-loyalist turned exile Field-Marshal Khalifa Belqasim Haftar and his Libyan National Army (LNA) in Tobruk, to the east (Cyrenaica). Both sides have disputed the authority and legitimacy of the GNA (with only some GNC members recognising the body), led by Prime Minister Fayez Mustafa al-Sarraj. This dispute has been most evident in the battle for hydrocarbon infrastructure control.

An example of this struggle occurred on 6 July 2012, when the Cyrenaica Federalists halted oil production in Ras Lanuf, Sidra, Brega, Zuweitina and Al Hreigaarea in Libya's 'oil crescent' for 48 hours, and blocked the main highway separating the region from neighbouring Tripolitania to demand representation equal to that of their neighbours and the Fezzan in the NTC.[48] The move led to their demands being met, and demonstrated the political leverage that hydrocarbon infrastructure control had over other dynamics in the country. Meanwhile, the blockade made it difficult for public institutions (particularly the central bank) to function, with reports that only half of the 2012 budget was spent, due to instability and armed conflict in the country.[49] This was replicated soon afterwards, when the Petroleum Facilities Guard (PFG) took control of terminals in the oil crescent, crippling national production levels and providing the precedent for over four years of competition (violent and otherwise) for the control of the facilities. This was as a result of the area becoming 'the zone in Libya where armed conflict and insecurity most affected the oil industry, causing volatility in output, particularly in 2014–17'.[50]

The 2014 elections sought to end the impasse and usher in an era of elected and representative government. This was not to be the case, however. Continuing

---

48 Ebtissam El Kailani and Zuhair Saleh, 'Extractive Industry and Conflict Risk in Libya', Civil Society Dialogue Network (CSDN), private sector and conflict meeting, Brussels, 2012, http://eplo.org/wp-content/uploads/2017/02/CSDN_Policy-meeting_Private-Sector_Libya.pdf, pp. 11–12.
49 Edward Randall, 'After Qadhafi: Development and Democratization in Libya', *The Middle East Journal* 69.2, 2015, p. 212.
50 Richard Barltrop, 'Oil and Gas in a New Libyan Era: Conflict and Continuity', OIES (Oxford Institute for Energy Studies) paper MEP 22, 2019, p. 16.

disputes between the HoR and the GNA (including the GNC and then HCS elements that supported it) led to public institutions competing with one another,[51] which became particularly problematic for the National Oil Corporation (NOC) – the public body charged with managing oil production and distribution in the country and externally. The sustained violence made it difficult for the NOC to attract and protect foreign company operations and investments in the country. This problem became even more acute as tribal militias began to take protective control over oil and gas terminals in their own areas.[52] This resulted in hydrocarbon exports in this period becoming sporadic, as demonstrated in Figure 2 above, and led to the lowest recorded crude oil and petroleum export level of 310.22 thousand bpd in 2015 with low export levels also being recorded for 2014, at 346.63 thousand bpd, and 2016, at 373.28 thousand bpd.[53]

Further, the competition between the domestic forces made it clear just how important the control of hydrocarbon facilities, and particularly oil facilities, was when it came to domestic drivers of fragmentation. The NOC, along with the central bank, was left with the difficult task of straddling alliances with both the HoR and the GNC (and then the HCS) in order to ensure continued access to the public budget and to be able to service public sector requirements. As a result, a situation was created in which the NOC and central bank were contributing to the functioning of the state (which had the de facto duty to ensure stability and security) as well as to the domestic forces that were perpetuating violence and instability in the country.[54] Predictably, this further fuelled the competition for the control of hydrocarbon facilities themselves, as both sides sought political leverage and funds for their activities.

Indeed, the HoR and the GNC (later the HCS) continuously fought for recognised and formalised control of the NOC between 2014 and 2017. Following the signing of the 2015 Libyan Political Agreement seeking to form a unified government through the setting up of the GNA, this competition involved the HoR, GNA and HCS.[55] Despite this development, it became clear that the two non-GNA sides were continuing to engage in a contest over hydrocarbons as a means to achieve political gains. This was something that was explicitly embodied (and later identified) by the NOC chairman Mustafa Sanalla.

---

51 Randall, 'After Qadhafi', p. 213.
52 El Kailani and Saleh, 'Extractive Industry', pp. 12–13.
53 OPEC, 'Data Download'.
54 Irene Costantini, 'Conflict Dynamics in Post-2011 Libya: A Political Economy Perspective', *Conflict, Security and Development* 16.5, 2016, p. 415.
55 Barltrop, 'Oil and Gas in a New Libyan Era', p. 18.

The specific actions of the Sanalla-headed NOC demonstrated just how entrenched the competition between local forces was. This was exemplified in January 2017, when the eastern arm of the NOC awarded some 29 contracts to foreign states without the consent of the NOC headquarters in Tripoli. In response, the HoR supported Haftar's LNA in forcibly taking control of the Sirte oil terminals, and ended its support for unifying the eastern and western arms of the NOC, a stalemate that continued into 2018.[56] This demonstrated the varying degree of NOC control over hydrocarbon facilities in Libya during this period. Sanalla himself penned an op-ed in *The New York Times* reflecting these concerns,[57] noting that

[s]ince the revolution of 2011, the country's oil and gas resources have been held hostage to both its fractious politics and power struggles in the Middle East … The PFG, which is charged with protecting Libya's oil infrastructure, has devolved into local fiefs. Between 2013 and last September [2016], these blockaded nearly all of Libya's main oil ports and tried to leverage that chokehold into ransom money and political power.

Amidst UN-sponsored efforts to forge an alignment between the HoR and the HCS, the competition for control of hydrocarbons continued into 2018, as domestic actors established and maintained power over their territorial oil and central bank bodies.[58] Each side operated in a different manner in this contest, with GNA-led Tripolitania (north-west) seeing micro-level groups and individuals seeking as much control of national level revenue streams as possible as allies, while in the south (the Fezzan, which came under forced control of the LNA in 2019), a lack of conventional security forces meant the region fell prey to an illicit and smuggling market culture, whilst the HoR and LNA in Cyrenaica (east) were subject to more conventional military rule under Haftar. This accentuated the features of a situation in which the overlap of interests and alliances between state, regional and militia groups meant that state actors were able to profit from the informal war economy despite their nominally public mandate.[59] In addition, this

56 Barltrop, 'Oil and Gas in a New Libyan Era', pp. 19–20.
57 Mustafa Sanalla, 'How to Save Libya From Itself? Protect Its Oil from Its Politics', *The New York Times* 19 June 2017, https://www.nytimes.com/2017/06/19/opinion/libya-and-another-oil-curse.
58 Council on Foreign Relations (CFR), 'Civil War in Libya', *Global Conflict Tracker* 18 April 2019, https://www.cfr.org/interactive/global-conflict-tracker/conflict/civil-war-libya.
59 Tim Eaton, 'Libya's War Economy Predation, Profiteering and State Weakness', Chatham

led once more to domestic actors continuing to use the control of these resources as a bargaining chip in political negotiations. An example occurred in December 2018: the al-Sharara oil field, capable of producing some 33% of the country's output, was closed when local tribes seized the facility and demanded that the GNA address their poor economic conditions.[60] This continued the trend of local actors destabilising the country as they sought political gains.

Such security issues represented a crippling impact on production levels, leading to a continuing downward trajectory in oil production, as the trend line in Figure 1 above shows. This, along with continued instability within the country, took place moreover against a wider backdrop of increased global oil production levels and energy alternatives post-2014 – largely attributed to the 2015 Joint Comprehensive Plan of Action (JCPOA) lifting oil sanctions on Iran over its nuclear programme, and the US (as well as other states) implementing fracking technologies to increase energy production from gas resources. That said, such developments also reinforce the very rationale behind the warring domestic actors' concern for controlling hydrocarbons more broadly: that is, their awareness of the value of these resources at a global level. It becomes clearer than ever that the competition for control of hydrocarbon facilities represented a rallying force for local actors to channel their efforts in Libya. This in turn led to increased instability in the country, and significantly undermined transition efforts.

Concluding Thoughts

The events that took place in Libya following the 2011 uprisings demonstrate just how integral a contextual understanding is to the formation of any comprehensive picture of the trajectories for change in the country. The importance of hydrocarbons, not just in terms of proven reserves, production levels and performance, but also in terms of future trajectories and the amount of political leverage they capture, highlights how domestic dynamics and forces perceive their value. This in turn illustrates why they sought to control these resources for political and economic gain. In light of this, this chapter has tried to convey the full extent to which such local drivers impacted the MENA state's post-Gaddafi trajectory: something

---

House research paper, April 2018, https://www.chathamhouse.org/sites/default/files/publications/research/2018-04-12-libyas-war-economy-eaton-final.pdf, p. 6.
60 Wintour, Patrick, 'Conflict Erupts for Control of Libya's Largest Oil Field', *The Guardian* 8 February 2019, https://www.theguardian.com/world/2019/feb/08/conflict-erupts-for-control-of-libyas-largest-oil-field.

that is not afforded as much attention in broader approaches towards examining countries in transition.[61]

Furthermore, it is clear that the interplay between the various local actors has been determined to a degree by the particular historical dynamics of Libya, exemplified in the practices of Italian and Allied forces in the earlier twentieth century, the reluctant Senussi monarchy and the more or less equally discriminatory approach of the Gaddafi regime. What is also interesting in the case of Libya is that domestic forces are driven by the desire to further their own local interests at the expense of the concept of a unified country. Eaton makes this point in noting that this tactic is deployed in an attempt to achieve the highest status possible in preparation for the post-political transition regime[62] – a perception corroborated by Vandewalle's prediction some 20 years previously, to the effect that 'few Libyans are likely to have accumulated enough of a fortune to pursue an exit option … [and post-Gaddafi regimes] will undoubtedly want to jettison Qadhafi's [sic] internal political experiments'.[63] In this context, and given the high value of hydrocarbon resources for the country's economy, it is clear that domestic forces are primarily concerned with ensuring their tribal and regional interests are furthered in pursuit of an 'exit option', as demonstrated by continued infighting and an entrenched reluctance to forge a unity government. The focus on the control of resources as a form of political leverage to assess this point makes the argument that much more telling. Indeed, this highlights how the domestic forces continue to compete with one another, despite the fact that there exists enough hydrocarbon-related wealth to incentivise a settlement.

Reflecting on the Libyan case more broadly, it is clear that the importance of domestic dynamics weighs heavily upon the decision-making of local actors, at the tribal, regional or rival government level. As such, it is clear that despite the broader potential for financial gain and power deriving from the country's vast hydrocarbon reserves and the GDP make-up of those reserves, differences between rival groups are so entrenched that they take precedence over all else. This in itself reveals not only how central these domestic dynamics are to an understanding of Libya, but also the impact hydrocarbons (in terms of infrastructure control) have on violence, conflict and instability, and thus the potential trajectories for change in the country.

---

61 O'Donnell and Scmitter, *Transitions from Authoritarian Rule*.
62 Eaton, 'Libya's War Economy Predation, Profiteering and State Weakness', pp. 5–6.
63 Dirk Vandewalle, *Libya since Independence: Oil and State-Building*, Ithaca, NY 1998, p. 186.

Bibliography

Ali, Tariq, *The Obama Syndrome: Surrender at Home, War Abroad*, New York 2011.

Anderson, Lisa, 'The State in the Middle East and North Africa', *Comparative Politics* 20.2, 1987, pp. 1–18.

Atkinson, Giles and Kirk Hamilton, 'Savings, Growth and the Resource Curse Hypothesis', *World Development* 31.11, 2003, pp. 1793–807.

Auty, Richard, 'Industrial Policy Reform in Six Large Newly Industrializing Countries: The Resource Curse Thesis', *World Development* 22.1, 1994, pp. 11–26.

Auty, Richard M., *Sustaining Development in Mineral Economies: The Resource Curse Thesis*, London 1993.

Barltrop, Richard, 'Oil and Gas in a New Libyan Era: Conflict and Continuity', OIES (Oxford Institute for Energy Studies) paper MEP 22, 2019, https://www.oxfordenergy.org/wpcms/wp-content/uploads/2019/02/Oil-and-Gas-in-a-New-Libyan-Era-Conflict-and-Continuity-MEP-22.pdf.

Basedau, Matthias and Jann Lay, 'Resource Curse or Rentier Peace? The Ambiguous Effects of Oil Wealth and Oil Dependence on Violent Conflict', *Journal of Peace Research* 46.6, 2009, pp. 757–76.

Beblawi, Hazem and Giacomo Luciani, *The Rentier State*, Abingdon 2016 [1987].

Bjorvatn, Kjetil and Alireza Naghavi, 'Rent Seeking and Regime Stability in Rentier States', *European Journal of Political Economy* 27, 2011, pp. 740–48.

British Petroleum (BP), 'BP Statistical Review of World Energy', *Data Download*, 2019, https://www.bp.com/en/global/corporate/energy-economics/statistical-review-of-world-energy.html.

Brahimi, Alia, 'Libya's Revolution', *North Africa's Arab Spring*, ed. George Joffé, Abingdon 2013. pp. 101–20

Council on Foreign Relations (CFR), 'Civil War in Libya', *Global Conflict Tracker* 18 April 2019, https://www.cfr.org/interactive/global-conflict-tracker/conflict/civil-war-libya.

Clarke, John I., 'Oil in Libya: Some Implications', *Economic Geography* 39.1, 1963, pp. 40–59.

Collier, Paul and Anke Hoeffle, 'On Economic Causes of Civil War', *Oxford Economic Papers* 50, 1998, pp. 743–53.

Costantini, Irene, 'Conflict Dynamics in Post-2011 Libya: A Political Economy Perspective', *Conflict, Security and Development* 16.5, 2016, pp. 405–22.

Davis, John, *Libyan Politics: Tribe and Revolution*, Berkeley 1987.

Eaton, Tim, 'Libya's War Economy Predation, Profiteering and State Weakness', Chatham House research paper, April 2018, https://www.chathamhouse.org/sites/default/files/publications/research/2018-04-12-libyas-war-economy-eaton-final.pdf.

Energy Information Administration (EIA), 'Libya's Key Energy Statistics', 2019, https://www.eia.gov/beta/international/country.php?iso=LBY.

El Kailani, Ebtissam and Zuhair Saleh, 'Extractive Industry and Conflict Risk in Libya', Civil Society Dialogue Network (CSDN), private sector and conflict meeting, Brussels, 2012, http://eplo.org/wp-content/uploads/2017/02/CSDN_Policy-meeting_Private-Sector_Libya.pdf.

Gause, F. Gregory, III, 'Why Middle East Studies Missed the Arab Spring: The Myth of Authoritarian Stability', *Foreign Affairs* 90.4, 2011, pp. 81–90.

International Monetary Fund (IMF), 'Libya beyond the Revolution: Challenges and Opportunities', Middle East and Central Asia Department, IMF Publication Services, 2012, https://www.imf.org/external/pubs/ft/dp/2012/1201mcd.pdf.

Jensen, Nathan and Leonard Wantchekon, 'Resource Wealth and Political Regimes in Africa', *Comparative Political Studies* 37.7, 2004, pp. 816–41.

Kamel, Amir Magdy, 'Post-Gaddafi Libya: Rejecting a Political Party System', *Political Parties in the Arab World: Continuity and Change*, eds. Francesco Cavatorta and Lise Storm, Edinburgh 2018, pp. 184–203.

Larémont, Ricardo René, 'After the Fall of Qaddafi: Political, Economic, and Security Consequences for Libya, Mali, Niger, and Algeria', *Stability: International Journal of Security and Development* 2.2, 2013, pp. 1–8.

Lewis, Aidan, 'How Unstable is Libya's Oil Production?', Reuters 16 July 2018, https://www.reuters.com/article/us-libya-oil-explainer/how-unstable-is-libyas-oil-production-idUSKBN1K61Y6.

Meijer, Roel and Nils Butenschøn, *The Crisis of Citizenship in the Arab World*, Boston, MA 2017.

Michael, Maggie, 'Libya's Militarized Youth Feed into Economic Woes', *The Daily Star* 13 March 2013, http://www.dailystar.com.lb/Business/Middle-East/2013/Mar-13/209972-libyas-militarized-youth-feed-into-economic-woes.ashx.

O'Donnell, Guillermo and Philippe C. Schmitter, *Transitions from Authoritarian Rule*, Baltimore 1986.

OPEC (Organisation of the Petroleum Exporting Countries), 'Data Download', 2019, https://asb.opec.org/index.php/data-download.

Randall, Edward, 'After Qadhafi: Development and Democratization in Libya', *The Middle East Journal* 69.2, 2015, pp. 199–221.

Ross, Michael L., 'What Have We Learned about the Resource Curse?', *Annual Review of Political Science* 18, 2015, pp. 239–59.

Sanalla, Mustafa, 'How to Save Libya From Itself? Protect Its Oil from Its Politics', *The New York Times* 19 June 2017, https://www.nytimes.com/2017/06/19/opinion/libya-and-another-oil-curse.

Sandbakken, Camilla, 'The Limits to Democracy Posed by Oil Rentier States: The Cases of Algeria, Nigeria and Libya', *Democratization* 13.1, 2006, pp. 135–52.

St John, Ronald Bruce, *Libya: Continuity and Change*, Abingdon 2015.

Trading Economics, 'Gas', 2019, https://tradingeconomics.com/libya/natural-gas-rents-percent-of-gdp-wb-data.html.

Trading Economics, 'Oil', 2019, https://tradingeconomics.com/libya/oil-rents-percent-of-gdp-wb-data.html.

United Nations (UN), 'Resolution 1506 (2003)', UN Security Council S/RES/1506 (2003), 12 September 2003, https://www.undocs.org/S/RES/1506(2003).

United Nations (UN), 'Resolution 1970 (2011)', UN Security Council S/RES/1970, 26 February 2011, https://undocs.org/S/RES/1970(2011).

United Nations (UN), 'Resolution 1973 (2011)', UN Security Council S/RES/1973, 17 March 2011, https://undocs.org/S/RES/1973(2011).

United Nations (UN), 'Resolution 2009 (2011)', UN Security Council S/RES/2009 16 September 2011, https://undocs.org/S/RES/2009(2011).

United Nations (UN), 'Summary of AG-051 United Nations Commissioner in Libya (1949–1952)', UN Archives and Records Management Section, https://search.archives.un.org/downloads/united-nations-commissioner-in-libya-1949-1952.pdf.

Vandewalle, Dirk, *A History of Modern Libya*, Cambridge 2012.

Vandewalle, Dirk, *Libya since Independence: Oil and State-Building*, Ithaca, NY 1998.

Wintour, Patrick, 'Conflict Erupts for Control of Libya's Largest Oil Field', *The Guardian* 8 February 2019, https://www.theguardian.com/world/2019/feb/08/conflict-erupts-for-control-of-libyas-largest-oil-field.

World Bank, 'World Development Indicators', 21 March 2019, https://data.worldbank.org/.

Wright, Joseph, Erica Frantz and Barbara Geddes, 'Oil and Autocratic Regime Survival', *British Journal of Political Science* 45.2, 2011, pp. 287–306.

6

The Moroccan Spring is Back: The Rif Hirak

Maati Monjib

The purpose of this chapter is to show, with the aid of a field survey, that the Moroccan Spring did not come to an end with the constitutional and political reforms King Mohammed VI put in place in 2011. The superficial nature of these reforms and their partial as well as temporary implementation in fact provided fertile ground for various social movements in the country. The new mind-set created by the Mouvement du 20 Février (M20F), as well as diminished public fear of confrontation, are at the root of new social movements such as the Rif Hirak. While these new movements are often local, and less political than M20F, they express the same fundamental desire for change.

Adil Benhamza is a moderate political personality and an informed observer of Morocco's current affairs. Yet, he uses alarming terms when it comes to describing the situation in Morocco in 2019: 'there's a trend emanating from accumulating tensions', illustrated by the proliferation of social movements. According to Benhamza, if the state does not take this reality into account, and does not respond by adapting its public policies and revamping the management of politics in the country, the result could be a 'big explosion'.[1] Prominent sociologist Mohamed A. Chaabani agrees: 'If the state doesn't positively address the claims of these social movements ... if the only answer is informed by security concerns, it will result

---

1 Adil Benhamza, 'Tarakoum al-Ihtiqan' (in Arabic), *Akhbar Alyaoum* 18 March 2019, p. 20.

in the return of the Mouvement du 20 Février, but stronger and more violent.'[2] Finally, John Waterbury argues that M20F could return in a more radicalised form, affecting deprived populations directly, as the regime's 'democratic transitions' come and go, but seem to have no effect.[3]

The regression of civil liberties and strong royal resurgence, with the monarchy's men dominating every aspect of the decision-making process, are the clearest manifestations of the end of the reform process since 2013.[4] Essentially, this regression favoured the involvement of the intelligence services in managing politics, and reinforced the political role of businessmen who benefit from the rentier economy.[5] Furthermore, it amplified the stagnation of social conditions for middle- and low-income sectors of the population, resulting in a stagnant wealth gap and significant income inequality.[6] According to the UNDP Human Development Index, Morocco ranks 123rd in the world, below Algeria (95th), Libya, Egypt and Iraq. Even compared to Sub-Saharan Africa, Morocco's situation is deplorable, as it is ranked far behind Mauritius, Botswana and Gabon, among others.[7]

We ought to remember that through its slogans and protests, M20F had defined

2 Mohamed Ali Chaabani, 'Sociology warns of the possibility that the protests might escalate beyond the government's control' (in Arabic), *Hespress* 1 April 2019, https://www.hespress.com/societe/427194.html.
3 John Waterbury, 'Introduction' (in Arabic), *February 20, and the Outcomes of Democratization in Morocco*, ed. Arab Center for Research and Policy Studies, Doha 2018, pp. 55–66.
4 Maati Monjib, 'Morocco's Illiberal Regime and Fragmented Political Society', *Arab Citizenship Review* 10, 2015, https://warwick.ac.uk/fac/soc/pais/research/researchcentres/irs/euspring/publications/arab_citizenship_review_n10.pdf.
5 In the parliamentary elections of 7 October 2016, the moderate Islamist party won a relative majority of seats. Benkirane, the party's popular leader, was unconstitutionally dismissed from his position as head of government. Meanwhile, the palace and state media propelled Aziz Akhannouch, a leading billionaire, to the leadership of a coalition of four small parties against Benkirane. The government included three powerful personalities whose fortunes each exceed 800 million dollars. The head of the DGST (domestic and political intelligence) has since 2015 become the director of national security while keeping his initial position. The security apparatus has since participated in the management of partisan politics, the elaboration of the content of state media and pro-regime media, and is very present on social media.
6 Abdelkader Berrada, 'Constitution de 2011, dépenses publiques et exigences du développement durable: cas du Maroc', *La nouvelle constitution marocaine à l'épreuve de la pratique*, eds. Omar Bendourou, Rkia El Mossadeq and Mohammed Madani, Casablanca 2014, pp. 283–338.
7 UNDP (United Nations Development Programme), 'Human Development Index Classification', http://hdr.undp.org/sites/default/files/2018_human_development_statistical_update.pdf.

its main goals as follows: first, the end of 'despotism' and 'corruption' (*isqat alfas-sad wal istibdad*); second, the establishment of a parliamentary democracy based on the will of the people through an elected constituent assembly; and third, a social and geographical democracy prioritising middle- and low-income families and marginalised areas in public development policies.[8] M20F also expressed a collective and individual need for cultural changes through the state's – and society's – recognition of various individual, artistic and religious freedoms. As one participant in the study reported here put it, 'It concerns an urgent need to fully breathe and to reject the iron fist, which promotes collectivity and suppresses individuality. It is the rejection of the normative and the omnipresent culture which crushes any aspiration towards individual liberties and suppresses the distinction of each and everyone, in favour of particularism.'[9] A young activist from M20F explained the liberating impact that the movement had on him in these terms: 'M20F allowed me, among other things, to break free from this silence which was turning me into this passive subject, without a voice and without a life.'[10]

Although the street movement was relatively potent and popular and expressed a strong need for change, the regime was able to defeat it through three initiatives. First was the regime's quick and, on the surface, positive reaction to M20F's claims. The king's speech of 9 March 2011, 17 days after the beginning of the demonstrations, promised radical constitutional and political reforms. Second, the most popular leader of the most popular party in Morocco was appointed as head of government. The third initiative was of a socio-economic nature: salary increases for state and 'semi-public' employees and the direct recruitment – in other words, without competitive examination – of a large proportion of the unemployed graduates who had been demonstrating for years in the streets. As soon as the street calmed down, authoritarian practices returned in force. The political security apparatus, for instance, vindictively cracked down on activists and groups which had played a key role in the 2011 protests. One needs to recall here briefly that the failure of the first so-called 'democratic transition' (Gouvernement d'Alternance I: 1998–2002)[11] followed by the second one (Gouvernement d'Alternance II:

---

8 Mohammed el-Assry, *The Legitimacy of the Demands of the February 20 Movement* (in Arabic), Tangier 2012.

9 Participant 2018/19 (author's research). Participants' quotations will be identified as shown here. See also Dounia Benqassem, *Né(e) un 20 Février 2011: Témoignages des 20Févriéristes*, Casablanca 2014.

10 Benqassem, *Né(e) un 20 Février 2011*.

11 Hassan Aourid, 'Democratic Transition in Morocco: Origins and Obstacles' (in Arabic), *February 20*, ed. Arab Center for Research and Policy Studies, pp. 307–309.

2012–2016)[12] played an important role in reinforcing anti-regime feelings. This aggregated failure to reform the political and social system radically, with the result that neither power nor wealth switched hands, allowed for deeper distrust between society and regime to set in. This is at the root of the rise of diverse contentious social movements across Morocco between 2013 and 2019.[13]

Before analysing the impact of M20F on current dynamics and their possible future perspectives, we need to introduce certain important elements of the methodology of the study discussed in this chapter. First, the author conducted qualitative field research in Rabat and in the surrounding urban areas, along with six other regions in Morocco, from November 2018 to January 2019. This material largely informs the study. A short questionnaire with seven questions was sent to 40 activists. Of those 40, 32 filled out the questionnaire entirely. The research participants were selected on the basis of their knowledge of current affairs and Moroccan politics – their reading of at least one newspaper per day (print or online) and participation in M20F or any subsequent social movement. Out of the 32 respondents, 19 were aged between 21 and 35 years, and the remaining were above 36. The group consisted of 14 women and 18 men. Each one was in a somewhat 'intellectual' career, or at least possessed formal academic education. The group included teachers, lawyers, journalists and students, either employed or unemployed. The 32 respondents represented the various currents of society active during Moroccan Spring – especially the main Islamist factions ('oppositionist, such as al-Adl wal-Ihssan group, and 'legitimist', such as the PJD) and the main secularist trends (leftist groups, whether radical or reformist, and independent democrats).

The second element of the research consisted of five in-depth interviews with expert observers of Morocco's political or socio-cultural evolution.[14] These interviews, conducted by the author, were semi-structured, with open questions on social movements in Morocco and about issues that emerged from the analysis of the questionnaire data. Finally, the research also drew upon a collection of

---

12 Mohamed Sassi, 'M20F Aftermath on the Moroccan Political Regime' (in Arabic), *February 20*, ed. Arab Center for Research and Policy Studies, pp. 69–105.

13 According to the Arab Barometer 2018–2019, unlike the majority of Arab populations, who would prefer a gradual political evolution of their country, very many Moroccans (49%) appear to desire immediate political change. In 2011, the situation was quite the opposite from today: the slogans of M20F very rarely called for the fall of the regime. See https://www.arabbarometer.org/.

14 Observer 2018/19 (author's research). Resource individuals who agreed to participate in this research are Abdelaziz Nouaydi, Rochdi Bouyebri, Fouad Abdelmouni, Saïda El Kamel and Rachid Tarik. Their quotations will be identified as shown here.

actors' and activists' testimonies, statements and stances, and organisations' pro-grammes from the government, political groups, citizens and social movements, either heard in the street (slogans) through observant participation and collected by the author with the help of a research assistant, or published in the print press or online, and on social media.

The Legacy of the Mouvement du 20 Février

M20F is a pro-democracy street movement, which arose in Morocco during the 2011 Arab Spring. It builds, however, on preceding social events in Morocco such as the 2008 popular protest in Sidi Ifni.[15] As to the legacy of M20F, of the 32 respondents to the questionnaire, 26 asserted that the 2011 pro-democracy move-ment influenced, or at the very least inspired, the Rif Hirak, the Jerada protests (2017–2018), the Zagora Thirst Revolt (*Thawrat Alâtach* in 2017) and the 2018 Boycott movement (*Almoqatâa*, against three commercial brands)[16] as well as the 2018 student protests opposing timetable change. In Morocco, these movements combined result in what Mohamed Sassi called 'fragile stability [promoted by the regime as] an alternative to democracy'.[17]

The reform 'programme' of M20F was a compromise between radical and moderate activists from the movement – Islamists and secularists – and this con-vergence only occurred partially and briefly during 2011. Ironically, the mixed success of the movement was encouraging for activists, because they can claim that it was neither a complete failure nor such a real and complete success as to dissuade people from further activism. This mixed feeling can also be explained by the hybrid nature of the Moroccan regime. One of our respondents asserted that 'if our M20F movement (had) succeeded in bringing about democracy, I would have left activism to focus on my career, on my life. If it had led to civil war like elsewhere, may Allah's mercy be upon us, I would have left the country, but we almost succeeded. Thus, we must try again. We'll get to it [government] by wearing them down.'[18] An essential motivating element for current and future

---

15 Amin Allal and Karine Bennafla, 'Les mouvements protestataires de Gafsa (Tunisie) et Sidi Ifni (Maroc) de 2005 à 2009. Des mobilisations en faveur du réengagement de l'État ou contre l'ordre politique?', *Revue Tiers Monde* 5, 2011, pp. 27–45.
16 Damien Liccia, 'Astroturfing et fake activism: La dynamique cachée du boycott au Maroc', SlideShare presentation, September 2018, https://fr.slideshare.net/mobile/DamienLiccia/astroturfing-et-fake-activism-la-dynamique-cachee-du-Boycott-au-maroc.
17 Sassi, 'M20F Aftermath', pp. 69–105.
18 Participant 2018/19.

social movements is this overwhelming feeling of moral success,[19] due to the high level of citizens' participation in M20F and to the regime's reaction, which was relatively positive.[20]

M20F had a number of political, cultural and psychological outcomes, which are likely to affect the political and social future of Morocco, 'producing pro-reforms activism'.[21] A number of these are discussed below.

Escaping fear and the emancipation of freedom of speech

Among respondents, 21 out of the 32 pointed out that breaking out of fear was one of M20F's most important legacies. Hence, liberation was intertwined with the fear the Makhzen (traditional state) inspired. However, this liberation was relative and sectorial, as young, educated citizens living in urban centres tend to be less fearful than other groups.[22] 'Sacred' fear (*heyba*) of the Makhzen, which was weakened in 2011, still haunts people's minds. This is a hard sociological reality, deeply rooted in the collective political imaginary. Yet, fear as a reality is aging, and mainly derives from the traditional concept of *heybat el-makhzen*, with its variant *heybat sultan*.

Politicisation of the social

There is a growing politicisation of social activism in Morocco.[23] This has allowed

---

19 'Moral success' is here simply a personal expression that I used previously only in Arabic (*najah manaui*). It does not denote a sociological concept close to James Jasper's concept of 'moral shock'. According to Jasper, moral shock derives from 'an unexpected event [... that] raises such a sense of outrage in a person that it becomes inclined toward political action' (*The Art of Moral Protest*, Chicago 1997). 'Moral success' as used here refers rather to the feeling experienced by the activists of having succeeded in making a significant impact on the country (in this case Morocco), whether at the popular level (several hundred thousand demonstrators in a hundred cities throughout the national territory) or at the state level, since the king delivered an important speech in which he promised political and constitutional reforms. In Morocco, the Makhzen (traditional state of divine right) very rarely reacts to a street movement.
20 Malika Zakhnini, 'Le bilan de la lutte contre la corruption et le despotisme dans le Maroc d'après le mouvement du M20F' (in Arabic), *Le Maroc après le mouvement de 2011: Qu'est-ce qui a changé?*, Casablanca 2016, pp 124–147.
21 Observer 2018/19.
22 Paradoxically perhaps, some 'intellectual' and well-informed groups such as journalists are much more fearful than young unemployed people.
23 I use the term 'politicisation' in this sense: a politicised social movement means a movement having a political character and/or making political demands.

for groups of young citizens, usually non-political ones such as football supporters (the Ultras, found especially in Casablanca), to shout slogans and songs against oppression, *hogra* (contempt) and *dholm* (tyranny), and against what is seen as the regime's contempt for citizens. For example, *Fi Bladi Dhalmouni* was a protest song initiated in Moroccan stadiums that spread across the Arab world. These slogans express the profound social malaise of youth. Sometimes, these songs resemble an argumentative, anti-regime political manifesto.[24]

A social movement looking into the future

In reality, the official promises of the past and the unfulfilled 'democratic transition' initiated decades ago, which seems never truly to succeed, are very disappointing for the pioneers of the movement as well as for politicised Moroccans in general. This is illustrated in one M20F activist's statement: 'As opposed to my father and brother [members of the USFP], I didn't believe Morocco had moved on, that we were in a new era. I grew up with the repetitive song of "democratic transition", which we would hear over and over again after Mohammed VI's inauguration and the Government of Change ... But I couldn't see any transition. The king continued to rule the country's politics and economy. For me, the only thing that has changed with this so-called Government of Change is the monarchy's new alliances with old opposition parties such as my father's.'[25]

The recent decades of Moroccan political life show that the regime has used various political crises to integrate the oppositional elite, yet not as part of a programme for social change, but, on the contrary, as individuals with political credibility who can provide short-term legitimacy. Once their credibility has worn thin because of co-optation, and depending on the political context and partisan interests, the regime then shifts to new alliances.[26] This Makhzen tactic can be perceived as a form of *usure du pouvoir sans pouvoir.*

Many M20F pioneers, either young or older, have lost trust in the regime's promises and its 'amicable settlement' between the pro-democracy opposition

---

24 *Maghreb Voices* 20 December 2017, 'You Don't Want Us to Get Educated! ... Political Slogans of Raja Ultras of Casablanca', https://www.maghrebvoices.com/a/409276.html; Aida Alami, 'The Soccer Politics of Morocco', *The New York Review of Books* 20 December 2018, https://www.nybooks.com/daily/2018/12/20/the-soccer-politics-of-morocco/.
25 Cédric Baylocq and Jacopo Granci, '"20 février": Discours et portraits d'un mouvement de révolte au Maroc', *Un printemps arabe?*, OpenEdition Dossier VIII, 2102, https://journals.openedition.org/anneemaghreb/1483?lang=ar.
26 Mohamed Kably, *Histoire du Maroc, réactualisation et synthèse*, Rabat 2011.

and the ruling monarchy. Indeed, as 23 of our 32 respondents believe, there was deeper respect for civil liberties at the beginning of the Benkirane government. Greater freedom still seemed to be the outcome of the 2011 street pressure, rather than of any proactive decision on the part of the executive. It did not signal a truly new governmental public policy. Time eventually revealed it as little more than a tactical effort to defuse public anger.

The argument behind this claim is that once citizens dispersed and protests slowly dissipated, there was a rapid return of the iron fist in Morocco, as other Arab countries fell into civil wars and political instability. Activists and associations who took part in the Moroccan Spring, or helped to bring different ideological trends closer, were repressed as of 2013 by a number of methods, ranging from arrests and prosecutions to bans on demonstrations, sit-ins and protests, as well as libel and smear campaigns (Human Rights Watch, 2014). The interior minister even stated before the House of Representatives that human rights organisations in Morocco accepted foreign money, thus benefiting a foreign political agenda and impeding the fight against terrorism.[27] This was actually a pretext for mobilising the political intelligence apparatus against the opposition and human rights defenders. Of our respondents 24 out of 32 label this reality as a serious political regression. Three observers of this study think that only a wide coalition of opposition parties and civil society organisations, along with ad hoc social movement committees, can help to change the balance of power between society and the regime. Such a coalition would mobilise the population and might put Morocco on the road to political change. Fouad Abdelmoumni declared to the author that 'there is a real need for change, but it cannot get stronger as long as there is no convincing political offer. This imposes a realistic and plural offer with an acceptable level of risk for the majority of citizens (most of all, no civil war). Until the FGD [three-party left-wing political alliance], al-Adl wal-Ihssan [Islamists] and the Democratic Path [radical left] … try to put together a coalition for change, I don't see how we can move forward and peacefully impose, still through struggle and solidarity, a democratic shift. A coalition of corporate interests is incapable of producing the desired democratic change'.[28] Rochdi Boueybri thinks likewise, arguing that the subjective element of change is lacking: 'Anti-system social movements arose in Morocco as a result of the

---

27 FIDH (International Federation for Human Rights) 29 July 2014, 'Un ministre accuse les ONG de répondre à un agenda étranger et d'entraver la lutte contre le terrorisme', https://www.fidh.org/fr/regions/maghreb-moyen-orient/
maroc/15831-maroc-un-ministre-accuse-les-ong-de-repondre-a-un-agenda-etranger-et-d.
28 Observer 2108/19.

economic and social crisis, mainly caused by a struggling economy, corruption and authoritarianism. These protest movements provide hope for change. Yet, influencing the balance of power such as to favour changes actually requires the union (*istifaf*) of the forces of change through a charter which would bring their points of view closer and would synergise efforts to produce a joint effect. There is an existing front "in itself" aspiring to change, but that still does not live "for itself". It needs permanent national coordination. It has to reunite all the active forces while respecting ideological political diversity and mixing them within the national political "melting pot" that would lead Morocco towards a historic change, with as few risks as possible.'[29]

Autonomisation of social movements and the emergence of local leaderships

M20F's impact was as powerful as it was because it was the most important movement to emerge from the streets since the protests organised by opposition parties on 3 February 1991 to denounce Morocco's involvement in the US-led first Gulf War against Iraq.[30] The street protests organised by M20F were entirely independent of institutional organisations. Nevertheless, the interior minister acknowledged the importance of the movement, as he stated that 53 provinces and prefectures saw protesting crowds that day.[31] Thus, in terms of the numbers of communities and territories the movement was active in, it was, geographically speaking, the widest in MENA countries affected during the 2011 uprisings. The autonomy of M20F was obvious: the calls to protest were broadcast by young activists without partisan attachment. M20F decisions were taken locally, moreover, during general assemblies, which would lead to local *tansiqyat* (coordinators committees) These latter coordinated nationally, and a few survived M20F. They participated in organising protests such as those of the summer of 2013 concerning the so-called Danielgate scandal.[32] Additionally, this dissociation from political parties and civil associations would greatly impact subsequent social movements, which tended to manage their actions and decision-making process through ad-hoc local committees, without interference from pre-existing organisations, as witnessed in Jerada

---

29 Observer 2108/19.

30 Maati Monjib, 'The "Democratization" Process in Morocco: Progress, Obstacles and the Impact of the Islamist–Secularist Divide', Brookings Institution Working Paper 5, 2011.

31 Tayeb Cherkaoui, 'The Minister of Interior's statement' (in Arabic), *Hespress* 20 February 2011, https://m.hespress.com/videos/28299.html.

32 This street protest took place after the royal pardon of Daniel Galvin, who had been sentenced to 30 years in prison for sexual abuse of 11 children.

and Al-Hoceima. The Rif Hirak, considered in detail below, is a clear example of the emergence of local leaderships.

The Rif Hirak

Undeniably, the Rif Hirak was the most important social movement since the 2011 demonstrations,[33] and the one that has lasted the longest. Paradoxically, it was both a demand for more state investment in the region and a rejection of the political regime. The first Hirak protests erupted in the autumn of 2016, following the death of Mohsin Fikri, a young man who died in a garbage truck while trying to save his goods from being destroyed on the order of the authorities. This incident marked the beginning of the Rif Spring or Hirak. Nasser Zefzafi, aged 38, with no permanent work and no university degree, took the lead from from the beginning. The demonstrations, taking place mainly in the city of Al-Hoceima and its surroundings, lasted for nine months (October 2016–July 2017). They brought together thousands of people, whose demands were both socio-economic and political. As one can clearly see, the Rif Spring was set off by an incident similar to that which triggered the Arab Spring: in that case, the horrible death of Mohamed Bouazizi.[34] Mohsin Fikri's death, however, did not in itself cause the population to reclaim the public space over several months; it was the *casus belli*. The state, which feared unrest in the Rif, took advantage of the momentarily peaceful days after the Arab Spring and of the November 2011 legislative elections to clamp down on any protest movement in the region. Thus, social protests in Beni Bouayach and Imzourn, near Al-Hoceima, were strongly suppressed in 2012, with protest leaders arrested and sentenced to up to five years in prison.[35] These repressive measures created profound tensions and widespread popular resentment, which was finally released after Fikri's tragic death. This appalling accident affected the local balance of power for many months, as the authorities left control of the streets in the hands of Hirak leaders. 'A true feeling of freedom seized us. A feeling similar to the one imposed in 2011 by M20F on the Makhzen,' said Faissal, one of our respondents and a Hirak activist.

---

33 Raphaël Lefèvre, '"No to *hoghra!*": Morocco's Protest Movement and Its Prospects', *The Journal of North African Studies* 22.1, 2016, pp. 1–5.
34 Nadia el-Awady, 'Arab Spring or Long Desolate Arab Winter?', Institut d'Estudis Catalans, Barcelona, 2016, available at https://publicacions.iec.cat/repository/pdf/00000245/00000001.pdf.
35 Alyaoum24 2017. Mohamed Jelloul, a leader of the 2012 social protest in the Rif, was jailed for five years (2012–2017). A month and a half after his release, he was arrested again and sentenced to ten years as a Hirak activist.

The protest movement solidified over time and climaxed in May 2017, with tens of thousands of protestors gathering in Al-Hoceima. The government was forced to send a committee consisting of seven ministers, whose mandate was to reinstate peace in the region through negotiations with local leaders. Yet, the negotiations seemed useless for many reasons. First of all, there exists considerable mistrust in the relationship between the central authorities and Rifians. Second, the authorities negotiated with local elected officials and other elements of political and civil society – largely unrepresentative of the protest movement – and tried to weaken Hirak leadership, which strongly controlled the field. The regime refused to negotiate directly with the protest leaders, considering them to be dissidents. It also did not want to recognise their legitimacy, for fear that other regions would follow the same course. Negotiating with locally elected representatives was problematic, however, because they lacked legitimacy having been elected with very low voter turnout in the 2015 municipal and 2016 legislative elections. The Authenticity and Modernity Party (PAM), close to the monarch and dominant in the region, seemed totally unable to influence the situation, even if its main officials are from the region and the party's secretary general even chaired the regional council of Tangier-Tetouan-Al-Hoceima. Finally, a national political crisis (*le blocage*) occurred at the same time as Hirak, preventing more effective engagement. The PJD, the most legitimate party at national level, lived in a kind of political paralysis because of the lengthy *blocage* crisis, and suffered from the anti-constitutional decision to dismiss Abdelilah Benkirane as head of government on 15 March 2017,[36] fuelling deep anger within the party. The secretary general of the PJD, who at the beginning of the protest had asked supporters of his own party to abstain from participating in the demonstrations occurring in the north, changed his position and no longer made such demands. These mixed messages confused an already tense situation. For its part, the Istiqlal Party, which had been authoritatively excluded, under monarchical pressure, from the pro-government coalition, took an anti-regime stance, and this arrangement meant that local Istiqlalians eventually came to support Hirak. Similarly, party members participated in pro-Hirak protests all over the kingdom. Ultimately, Istiqlal officially endorsed Hirak.[37] As we will see below, the majority of opposition parties (La Voie démocratique, FGD, al-Adl wal-Ihssan) supported Hirak even more strongly

---

36 Kamal Kassir, 'The Failure to Form a Government in Morocco: Political Engineering or an Experience Sabotaged?' (in Arabic), Aljazeera Centre for Studies, Doha 2017, https://bit. ly/2Uh03M5.
37 Alyaoum24 2017.

than the local PJD or Istiqlal. Opposition party members participated actively in the protests.

Overall, the months-long *blocage* opposing the monarchy and the principal party (PJD) contributed to worsening the situation in the north. After the repression, the regime's isolation was so conspicuous that sectors of the still credible civil and political class independent from the palace were called into action by the regime, hoping to secure peace in the Rif region. The palace was so keen to re-establish order in the Rif that, following the tension arising from the arrest and the detention of Hirak leadership, it resorted to calling upon Benkirane for help, despite the former prime minister having fallen out of favour with the monarchy. Thus, while the leader of the leading parliamentary party disapproved of Hirak activists' arrest,[38] he nevertheless acted as a mediator by meeting the parents of Nasser Zefzafi, the Hirak leader.

Between Hirak and M20F

Hirak slogans and general demands revolved around the issues of respect, dignity and civil rights – economic, social and cultural – for the Rif citizens.[39] They also called for the end of 'corruption' and 'tyranny' (*alfassad wal istibdad*), as had M20F. General demands from Hirak strongly mirrored those that had been put forth in 2011 across the MENA.[40] As a matter of fact, 'many of the grievances which had prompted the birth of the 20th February protest movement in 2011 still resonate'; thus 'the sense of social despair and political disenfranchisement resulting from it was key in mobilizing protesters beyond Fikri's hometown of Al-Hoceima'.[41]

In fact, there are many connections and similarities between Hirak and M20F. Symbolically, Hirak leaders called significant protests for 20 July 2017, as this date represents both the anti-colonial battle of Anoual, which began on 22 July 1921, and the monthly national protest that M20F organised on each 20th of the month, or on the Sunday closest to it. In addition, Nasser Zefzafi, Hirak leader,

---

38 Lakome2.com, 5 June 2017, 'Benkirane Receives Zefzafi's Parents at His Home and Deplores Arrests in the Rif' (in Arabic), https://bit.ly/2Hi3Q5G.
39 For these and further details on Hirak's demands, see Abdellatif el-Hamamouchi, 'The Moroccan Rifi Hirak: Repression is the Primary Choice' (in Arabic), *openDemocracy* 21 September 2017, https://bit.ly/2TgGoaC.
40 Aman, M. Mohammed, 'The Rise and Demise of the Middle East Quest for Reforms, 2011–2017', *Digest of Middle East Studies* 26.1, 2017, pp. 170–86.
41 Lefèvre, '"No to hoghra!": Morocco's Protest Movement and Its Prospects'.

had participated in the 2011 M20F protests. In order to highlight the connection between the two movements, Zefzafi requested, from the very beginning of Hirak, an independent investigation into the death of Fikri, and also into those of five young people found dead in a bank in Al-Hoceima shortly after the end of the first day of M20F protests.

State media and the 'governing' coalition parties propagated the narrative of separatists controlling Hirak, accusing it of 'having destructive ideas' and being manipulated, and financed from abroad.[42] The same sort of propaganda had targeted M20F in 2011. Rabat also sent a significant number of security reinforcements, including the royal gendarmerie and the auxiliary and national security forces.[43] Parallel to this physical presence, a psychological and political campaign was directed against the activists of the movement, especially Nasser Zefzafi, Cilia Zayani and Nawal Benaissa. Electronic newspapers known to have ties to the regime's security apparatus led a vigorous defamation campaign against the three leaders and others. Le360, a media outlet founded by the king's private secretary and with close ties to the monarchy, accused Zefzafi of accepting money from abroad.[44] Another website, Cawalisse, which reports directly to regime's security services (colloquially named *srabs*), also accused him of collusion with 'foreign traitors'.[45] This propaganda was so defamatory that even the Istiqlal, usually a pro-regime nationalist party, demanded the 'end of the media campaign' against Hirak.[46] There was also an attempt to limit the access of Hirak leaders to the media, and local authorities prevented several media and journalists from reaching Al-Hoceima.[47] Moreover, a Zefzafi interview on the website Lakome2. com, which was viewed by a record number of people, was eventually 'neutralised' and disappeared from its Facebook page.

Hirak's leadership reacted to the official accusation of separatism and the smear campaign with a general strike and a demonstration on 18 May 2017. Slogans

42 Tarik Benhenda, 'The Rif Hirak is Heading Towards a General Strike in Response to the Government' (in Arabic), *Hespress* 16 May 2017, https://bit.ly/2KaCRe3.
43 Ismail al-Adarissi, 'Huge Reinforcements have Arrived in Al Hoceima. The Military Are in the Suburbs' (in Arabic), *Al3omq.com*, Rabat, May 2017, https://bit.ly/2J8qjnu.
44 Jawad el-Kabboury, 'Foreign Funds Embarrass Zefzafi' (in Arabic), *le360.ma* 1 June 2017, https://bit.ly/2HVbaDH.
45 Cawalisse Alyaoum, 10 April 2018, 'Breaking: Zefzafi Admits to Intelligence Sharing with Traitors outside of Morocco' (in Arabic), https://bit.ly/2FvazpB.
46 Press release of the Istiqlal Party Executive Committee, June 2017, https://m.alyaoum24. com/890624.html.
47 Anadolu Agency, 30 May 2017, 'Morocco Expelled an Algerian Journalist Covering the Rif Hirak' (in Arabic), https://bit.ly/2uyRU79; https://bit.ly/2JYelgS.

became at the same time more political, more radical and less local. It now seemed that if 'the state wants to solve the problem of the Rif, it must solve the problem of lack of democracy facing the country as a whole'. Indeed the leader of Hirak declared in the interview mentioned above that 'under no circumstances can the regime divide us ... We affirm that our demands are almost the same as those of all towns in Morocco. The solidarity of other towns will give us more strength ... The Rif Hirak is the *hirak* of all the Moroccan people against *hogra*, contempt, marginalisation and poverty'.

Nasser Zefzafi represents the average Moroccan. In a few months in 2016–2017, he became a leading political actor for a large part of Moroccan society. What explains his meteoric rise? It is a rare political phenomenon in Morocco. The cause seems to lie in a climate of fear and repression that gradually gathered sway over Morocco from the summer of 2013 and intensified from 2016. Silence had reigned among politicians since that date. Zefzafi was one of the rare exceptions: he spoke freely. 'He is boldly outspoken. He seems to ignore that he has a wolf by the ear. He says loudly what others whisper or say just to family. He thus, thanks to YouTube, invites himself imperceptibly into the intimate sphere of people. He becomes like a member of the family. He speaks without fear or mistrust, like a parent who speaks to you between four walls.'[48] Hence the attachment to him of a large part of the younger generation, who call him by his first name. 'He's a big mouth. It looks like he's wearing a shroud all the time. He airs all the political dirty laundry in the open. He is afraid of nothing and nobody. Imagine! He has treated the region's most powerful politician – a regime security figure – as "the biggest traitor to the Rif!" He attacked the head of the regional administration and called him corrupt. He gave public evidence of this. He says "*Abdelkrim radya Allahu anh* [God favour him]". But he does not use this honorary formula, of course, for the king or his royal ancestors. Unbelievable!'[49]

Indeed, Zefzafi attacked the strongmen of the regime head-on despite the fear they instilled in Moroccan politicians, including a large number of opponents. Sometimes he did not even spare the palace and the entourage of the king.[50] He became a 'true hero for the youth who had been already excited by the slogans of M20F'.[51] This popularity, the mistreatment he suffered during his arrest and the

---

48 Observer 2018/19.
49 Observer 2018/19.
50 Nasser Zefzafi, 'El-Himma and Majidi are Using the Hirak as a Battlefield in Their Struggle for Influence vis-à-vis the King' (in Arabic), Lakome2.com 18 May 2017, https://bit.ly/2HJX4Gf.
51 Participant 2018/19.

'relevance' and moderate and peaceful aspect of Hirak socio-economic demands resulted in strong popular reaction to the arrest and subsequent political trial of the Hirak leadership. Thus a local movement sparked a national solidarity movement that would last for about two years. Several important initiatives of solidarity with Hirak and Zefzafi were thus launched.

First, al-Adl wal-Ihssan (AWI), the most powerful opposition group in Morocco, called for 'a national and popular march' in support of the movement led by Zefzafi, on 11 June 2017.[52] The event brought together tens of thousands of people in Rabat. It was symbolically organised at noon in hot weather and during Ramadan. It is very rare to demonstrate during the day in Ramadan. There are precedents only in the popular memory of the colonial era. The following year, on 15 July 2018, and in protest at the heavy sentences for the Hirak leadership – 20 years in prison for Zefzafi and three of his comrades – the AWI, in coordination with other civil society groups, called for a protest that brought together 150,000 people from all over Morocco. The AWI's statement declared that the purpose of the march was 'to protest against the contempt, arbitrariness and oppression of the state against the movement of those who claim their just and legitimate rights'. The organisers decided to put Zefzafi's parents at the head of the demonstration. Just behind them walked left-wing personalities such as the anthropologist Abdellah Hammoudi, Ahmed El Haij, chairperson of the main human rights association in Morocco, AMDH and the secretary general of the Socialist Vanguard Party (PADS), as well as the leaders of AWI and civil society leaders and trade unionists. This meant that a good part of the opposition supported Hirak. It should be noted that the AWI had not called for protests devoted to a national issue for six years – that is, since its dispute with leftist opposition and its withdrawal from M20F at the end of 2011. This means that the Rif Hirak has facilitated the resumption of collaboration between leftist groups and the AWI and independent pro-change activists. All this fuels the development of the social movement in Morocco.

Second, parties and leftist groups in coordination also called for protest marches, for the same goals and across the country, on 20 June 2017 and 8 July 2018.[53] The 20 June protest coincided with the 36th anniversary of the 1981 anti-regime uprising in Casablanca.

Finally, it should also be remembered that there are about ten cities, including

---

52 Al-Adl wal-Ihssan, 'AWI Political Daïra Calls for Participation in the National March of 11 June' (in Arabic), June 2017, https://bit.ly/2VYagtR.
53 Anwalpress June 2017, 'The National Committee for the Support of the Rif Hirak Calls for Participation in the Marches of the CDT on June 20th' (in Arabic), https://bit.ly/2VVjyXN.

Rabat, Casablanca, Tangier and Oujda, where former M20F activists and some left-wing political actors came out to demonstrate at least once a week for several weeks in 2016–2017. Several social movements, moreover, even very sectorial ones such as the movement of high school students at the end of 2018, at times shouted the slogans of Hirak and held up photos of Zefzafi.[54]

In fact, Zefzafi's discourse brings him closer to 'the average angry man of the street' and the grassroots activists of M20F than to its rather liberal-democratic leadership. He is neither explicitly Islamic nor secular, nor exclusively leftist or rightist. As he said on 20 May 2017, a few days before his arrest, 'Hirak is popular, everyone can relate to it, all ideologies and religions. This (Hirak) is for the secularist, the person of the left, the Islamist and the irreligious. That's why our discourse is unifying and simple. In our discourse we use religious formulas that are an integral part of us and our culture. We also use expressions of Marx and Lenin, so that everyone recognises himself in our wording. We do not want anyone to feel excluded, whoever he is.'[55] What makes for the cohesion of Zefzafi's discourse and the unity of the movement he leads is not ideological, but political: the dignity of the population through the recognition of its socio-economic rights, the end of the 'oppressive Makhzen' and its moral defeat.[56] Zefzafi argues that he aspires to 'the end of injustice and corruption', to 'change of the socio-economic system' and to 'the just distribution of national resources and an end of militarisation'.[57] These were also the demands of the so-called *massirat al-akfan* march organised by Hirak in early April 2017.[58]

The Hirak leadership wanted to achieve all this through peaceful means.[59] Thus

---

54 Jamal Figuigui, 'Hirak's Slogans Heard in Student Marches in The Rif' (in Arabic), *Assabah* 16 November 2018, https://bit.ly/2JKZ4zG.

55 Nasser Zefzafi, 'Interview: Zefzafi Says It All' (in Arabic), Alaoual.com, 20 May 2017, https://bit.ly/2V0OsOd.

56 Zefzafi often uses the expression '*Makhzen ghashim*' (*ghashim* means 'oppressive, inequitable, wrongful').

57 Zefzafi, 'Interview'.

58 Lakome2.com, 9 April 2017, 'The Rif Boils before a Visit of Laftit ... "March of Shrouds" Demanding an Equitable Distribution of Wealth and the End of Militarization' (in Arabic), https://bit.ly/2Ox5Yrd. *Massirat al-akfan* (march of shrouds) is a march during which protesters carried shrouds.

59 Nasser Zefzafi, 'An Appeal to the Rif and Alhoceima's Population: Keep it Always Peaceful!' (in Arabic), YouTube, 26 May 2017, https://www.youtube.com/watch?v=fNUtxmjnAXo.

the legendary physical bravery of the Rifians seems to have adapted.[60] It becomes peaceful and defensive in line with an evolution in the system of values of Moroccan society. The fact that Zefzafi declared himself a pacifist, the fact that he spoke 'true' and 'clear', brought him to the pinnacle of idolisation, notably in his own region. His popularity so disturbed the regime that the latter resorted to religion in an attempt to discredit him. Thus, media close to the regime accuse him of being 'the master mind of a Shiite project that has taken control of a social and economic movement'.[61] He was also arrested and prosecuted on the pretext that he disturbed Friday's prayer in a mosque in Al-Hoceima. In fact, the imam of the mosque had delivered a *khotba* (sermon) that sounded much like a hate speech. This *khotba*, written by the Ministry of Religious Affairs, is outrageously accusatory against Hirak and its leaders. The imam harangued the worshippers in the mosque where Zefzafi was present, and the loudspeakers spread his words throughout the neighbourhood. The imam accused Hirak people of 'inciting disobedience and disorder, using lies, deception, deceit and manipulation of the media for unworthy motives and dishonest purposes'.[62]

Conclusion

If we examine Hirak from a sociological standpoint, it clearly reveals four major developments that are crystallising in Moroccan society in general and the Rifian community in particular. First, the level of collective violence seems to have significantly decreased, reflecting a change in the value system of Moroccan society. There were numerous potential triggers for violent protests, but none of them elicited violence. The initial triggering event had been extremely shocking: a young fish vendor was crushed along with his confiscated goods, in a garbage truck. 'Information' spread that someone had given the criminal order '*T-han mmu!* (Crush him!)'.[63] A large part of the population of Al-Hoceima had understood in the early hours that 'someone of the Makhzen' may have ordered the deliberate killing of the young man in such a hideous manner. Despite this unfortunate event and the alarmist interpretations given to it, the initial and subsequent popular reac-

---

60 Célian Macé, 'Protests. Maroc: On a montré que les Rifains n'ont pas peur', *Libération* 21 July 2017, https://www.liberation.fr/planete/2017/07/21/maroc-on-a-montre-que-les-rifains-n-ont-pas-peur_1585465.

61 Manar Slimi, 'Zefzafi is the Mastermind of a Shiite Project that has Taken Control of a Social Movement' (in Arabic), *rue20.com* 30 May 2017, https://bit.ly/2urxYDl.

62 Rédaction de *Contretemps*, 'Maroc, la révolution qui vient' (pdf), 2017, available at https://www.contretemps.eu/read-offline/15499/maroc-revolte-rif-Hirak.pdf.

63 *T-han mmu* is a rude, insulting expression in Moroccan Arabic.

tion was so peaceful that no one, not even the family of the deceased, attempted to take revenge on the person or group considered responsible for the murder of Fikri; yet given the historical legacies and the Rifian memory of suffering,[64] the majority seemed to have no doubt: the crime for them was proven, and was additional evidence of persistent hostility of the Makhzen towards Rifians. In the same way, the Rifian population remained calm when riot police killed the young activist Imad Attabi in July 2017,[65] notwithstanding the fact that avenging a murdered loved one, violently opposing injustice and cleansing one's honour with blood were known practices in many parts of Morocco, including the north, at least until the last decades of the twentieth century. It should be noted here that as leader of Hirak, Nasser Zefzafi called on the population to be calm and peaceful, whatever the behaviour of the state. The information published on the violent manner in which the police arrested him, and his lawyer's statement that he was mistreated and beaten by security agents and that he suffered a fairly deep head injury and bruises to his face, resulted in no violent reaction.[66] The official National Council for Human Rights confirmed later that cases of torture did indeed occur.[67] Even Zefzafi's statement to the judge, widely reported in the media, that he had been subjected to sexual humiliation by police officers during his arrest did not provoke any violent reprisal.[68] Schwarz comments on the peaceful nature of the protests: 'Hirak leadership had cautiously sought to prevent the protests from turning into a riot, apparently adopting certain experiences of the open and peaceful approach of M20F.'[69]

Second, advances in gender equality should be noted. The organisational and political role that young women have played in Hirak has been remarkable since its inception. After the arrest of the first leadership, a group of young women took over. Several names emerged, including Nawal Benaissa and Cilia Zayani.

---

64 Maati Monjib, 'Maroc: le Hirak ou la révolte dans le Rif', *Orient XXI*, June 2017, https://orientxxi.info/magazine/maroc-le-hirak-ou-la-revolte-dans-le-rif,1898. The cultural component and the identity dimension of Hirak 'express both a memory malaise and a regional pride that are obvious to all Moroccans'.
65 Alyaoum24 2017.
66 Amnesty International, August 2017, 'Maroc. Des dizaines de personnes arrêtées dans le cadre de la contestation qui secoue le Rif dénoncent des actes de torture en detention', https://www.amnesty.org/fr/latest/news/2017/08/morocco-dozens-arrested-over-mass-protests-in-rif-report-torture-in-custody/.
67 Arabi21, 4 July 2017, https://arabi21.com/story/1018583/.
68 Arabi21, 12 April 2018, https://arabi21.com/story/1085972/.
69 Christoph Schwarz, 'Morocco's Social Protests across Time and Space', *openDemocracy* 13 June 2018, https://www.opendemocracy.net/north-africa-west-asia/christoph-h-schwarz/moroccos-social-protests-across-time-and-space.

Female leaders organised events even at night.[70] Thus patriarchal conservatism showed signs of weakening. It might be surmised that the decline in the status of violence on the scale of values permitted too a decline in male domination of the public space.

The third notable element to emerge from the Rifian social movement and its demands is the progress that seems to have been made in the process of national integration in Morocco. The Rif is an Amazigh region proud of its identity, but the appointment in March 2017 of a cabinet led for the first time in the history of independent Morocco by an Amazigh, Saadeddine el-Othmani, who put forth the idea of political autonomy for the Rif,[71] did not serve to lessen tension or mistrust between Hirak and the government. In addition, the second and third strongmen in the Othmani government, Aziz Akhannouch, minister of agriculture and fisheries, and Abdel Wafie Laftit, minister of interior, are also Amazigh. The latter is even a Rifian; but both were received with total indifference during their visit to the region. It should be recalled here that one of the fundamental demands of the 1958–1959 Rif uprising had been the appointment of a Rifian personality to the central government, but the region has moved on since that particularistic demand. Thus, despite an Amazigh and Rifian presence in the government, the leaders of Hirak continued to refuse to engage in dialogue with the cabinet, and demanded the presence of representatives of the king, who is the only genuine holder of power in the country. In the same vein, it is to be noted that the discourse of Hirak leaders since the beginning of events was often addressed to all Moroccans, not only Rifians. It follows that the non-Rifian inhabitants of Al-Hoceima and other Hirak locations also participated in the protests.[72]

Finally, the research reported here highlights various feelings shared by the overwhelming majority of social-movement activists. These can be formulated in the following terms: if the repressive approach continues to predominate, if Morocco cannot resolve three burning questions – the legitimacy of political

---

70 Mourad Mimouni, 'Women Shouting in Solidarity with the Rif Hirak' (in Arabic), *Hespress* 4 June 2017, https://m.hespress.com/regions/352795.html.

71 Nadhour Bellouss, 'Saadeddine El Othmani: The Rif Should Become Self-Governing' (in Arabic), *Hespress* 9 October 2011, https://www.hespress.com/politique/39166.html. Saadeddine el-Othmani, secretary general of the PJD and head of government, claims to be an activist in the Amazigh cause. He wrote, for instance, an article defending the Amazigh cause in the official online publication of the PJD: https://bit.ly/2CUkDIr (accessed 24 March 2019).

72 Mohamed Saadi, 'Hirak Rif: Baina Alhaja li Dawlawa Riba minha, Joruh Tarikhwa Tassaddoat Alhadir' (in Arabic), *Addawla wa Hirak Rif: Assolta, AssoltaAlmodaddawaAzmatAlwassata*, ed. Mohamed Radouani, Rabat 2018, pp. 75–86.

power, expansion of civil liberties and genuine national development – and if the government continues to ignore the political and socio-economic claims of the population, the regime runs the risk of a serious confrontation with 'the diverse oppositional dynamics, where small water streams would merge all together to form a great river'.[73]

Bibliography

Al-Adarissi, Ismail, 'Huge Reinforcements have Arrived in Al Hoceima. The Military Are in the Suburbs' (in Arabic), *Al3omq.com* May 2017, https://bit.ly/2J8qjnu.

Al-Adl wal-Ihssan, 'AWI Political Bureau Calls for Participation in the National March of 11 June' (in Arabic), June 2017, https://bit.ly/2VYagtR.

Alami, Aida, 'The Soccer Politics of Morocco', *The New York Review of Books* 20 December 2018, https://www.nybooks.com/daily/2018/12/20/the-soccer-politics-of-morocco/.

Allal, Amin and Karine Bennafla, 'Les mouvements protestataires de Gafsa (Tunisie) et Sidi Ifni (Maroc) de 2005 à 2009. Des mobilisations en faveur du réengagement de l'État ou contre l'ordre politique?', *Revue Tiers Monde* 5, 2011, pp. 27–45.

Alyaoum24.com, Casablanca, January 2017 (in Arabic), https://www.maghress.com/alyaoum24/811876.

Alyaoum24.com, Casablanca, May 2017 (in Arabic), http://www.alyaoum24.com/884459.html.

Alyaoum24.com, Casablanca, June 2017 (in Arabic), https://bit.ly/2TzMs2T.

Aman, M. Mohammed, 'The Rise and Demise of the Middle East Quest for Reforms, 2011–2017', *Digest of Middle East Studies* 26.1, 2017, pp. 170–86.

Amnesty International, August 2017, 'Maroc. Des dizaines de personnes arrêtées dans le cadre de la contestation qui secoue le Rif dénoncent des actes de torture en detention', https://www.amnesty.org/fr/latest/news/2017/08/morocco-dozens-arrested-over-mass-protests-in-rif-report-torture-in-custody/.

Anadolu Agency, 30 May 2017, 'Morocco Expelled an Algerian Journalist Covering the Rif Hirak' (in Arabic), https://bit.ly/2uyRU79; https://bit.ly/2JYelgS.

---

73 Observer 2108/19.

Anwalpress June 2017, 'The National Committee for the Support of the Rif Hirak Calls for Participation in the Marches of the CDT on June 20th' (in Arabic), https://bit.ly/2VVjyXN.

Aourid, Hassan, 'Democratic Transition in Morocco: Origins and Obstacles' (in Arabic), *February 20, and the Outcomes of Democratization in Morocco*, ed. Arab Center for Research and Policy Studies, Doha 2018, pp. 307–309.

Arabi21, 4 July 2017, https://arabi21.com/story/1018583/.

Arabi21, 12 April 2018, https://arabi21.com/story/1085972/.

Baylocq, Cédric and Jacopo Granci, '"20 février": Discours et portraits d'un mouvement de révolte au Maroc', *Un printemps arabe?*, OpenEdition Dossier VIII, 2102, https://journals.openedition.org/anneemaghreb/1483?lang=ar.

Bellouss, Nadhour, 'Saadeddine El Othmani: The Rif Should Become Self-Governing' (in Arabic), *Hespress* 9 October 2011, https://www.hespress.com/politique/39166.html.

Benhamza, Adil, 'Tarakoum al-Ihtiqan' (in Arabic), *Akhbar Alyaoum* 18 March 2019.

Benhenda, Tarik, 'The Rif Hirak is Heading Towards a General Strike in Response to the Government' (in Arabic), *Hespress* 16 May 2017, https://bit.ly/2KaCRe3.

Benqassem, Dounia, *Né(e) un 20 Février 2011: Témoignages des 20Févriéristes*, Casablanca 2014.

Berrada, Abdelkader, 'Constitution de 2011, dépenses publiques et exigences du développement durable: cas du Maroc', *La nouvelle constitution marocaine à l'épreuve de la pratique*, eds. Omar Bendourou, Rkia El Mossadeq and Mohammed Madani, Casablanca 2014, pp. 283–338.

Cawalisse Alyaoum, 10 April 2018, 'Breaking: Zefzafi Admits to Intelligence Sharing with Traitors outside of Morocco' (in Arabic), https://bit.ly/2FvazpB.

Chaabani, Mohamed Ali, … (in Arabic), *Hespress* 1 April 2019, https://www.hespress.com/societe/427194.html.

Cherkaoui, Tayeb, … (in Arabic), *Hespress* 20 February 2011, https://m.hespress.com/videos/28299.html.

El-Assry, Mohammed, *The Legitimacy of the Demands of the February 20 Movement* (in Arabic), Tangier 2012.

El-Awady, Nadia, 'Arab Spring or Long Desolate Arab Winter?', Institut d'Estudis Catalans, Barcelona, 2016, available at https://publicacions.iec.cat/repository/pdf/00000245/00000001.pdf.

El-Hamamouchi, Abdellatif, 'The Moroccan Rifi Hirak: Repression is the Primary Choice' (in Arabic), *openDemocracy* 21 September 2017, https://bit.ly/2TgGoaC.

El-Kabboury, Jawad, 'Foreign Funds Embarrass Zefzafi' (in Arabic), *le360.ma* 1 June 2017, https://bit.ly/2HVbaDH.

FIDH (International Federation for Human Rights) 29 July 2014, 'Un ministre accuse les ONG de répondre à un agenda étranger et d'entraver la lutte contre le terrorisme', https://www.fidh.org/fr/regions/maghreb-moyen-orient/maroc/15831-maroc-un-ministre-accuse-les-ong-de-repondre-a-un-agenda-etranger-et-d.

Figuigui, Jamal, 'Hirak's Slogans Heard in Student Marches in The Rif' (in Arabic), *Assabah* 16 November 2018, https://bit.ly/2JKZ4zG.

Human Rights Watch 7 November 2014, 'Maroc: Obstacles aux activités en faveur de droits humains', https://www.hrw.org/fr/news/2014/11/07/maroc-obstacles-aux-activites-en-faveur-des-droits-humains.

Kably, Mohamed, *Histoire du Maroc, réactualisation et synthèse*, Rabat 2011.

Kassir, Kamal, 'The Failure to Form a Government in Morocco: Political Engineering or an Experience Sabotaged?' (in Arabic), Aljazeera Centre for Studies, Doha 2017, https://bit.ly/2Uh03M5.

Lakome2.com, 5 June 2017, 'Benkirane Receives Zefzafi's Parents at His Home and Deplores Arrests in the Rif' (in Arabic), https://bit.ly/2Hi3Q5G.

Lakome2.com, 9 April 2017, 'The Rif Boils before a Visit of Laftit ... "March of Shrouds" Demanding an Equitable Distribution of Wealth and the End of Militarization' (in Arabic), https://bit.ly/2Ox5Yrd.

Lefèvre, Raphaël, '"No to *hoghra*!": Morocco's Protest Movement and Its Prospects', *The Journal of North African Studies* 22.1, 2016, pp. 1–5.

Liccia, Damien, 'Astroturfing et fake activism: La dynamique cachée du boycott au Maroc', SlideShare presentation, September 2018, https://fr.slideshare.net/mobile/DamienLiccia/astroturfing-et-fake-activism-la-dynamique-cachee-du-Boycott-au-maroc.

Macé, Célian, 'Protests. Maroc: On a montré que les Rifains n'ont pas peur', *Libération* 21 July 2017, https://www.liberation.fr/planete/2017/07/21/maroc-on-a-montre-que-les-rifains-n-ont-pas-peur_1585465.

Maghreb Voices 20 December 2017, 'You Don't Want Us to Get Educated! ... Political Slogans of Raja Ultras of Casablanca', https://www.maghrebvoices.com/a/409276.html.

Mimouni, Mourad, 'Women Shouting in Solidarity with the Rif Hirak' (in Arabic), *Hespress* 4 June 2017, https://m.hespress.com/regions/352795.html.

Monjib, Maati, 'The "Democratization" Process in Morocco: Progress, Obstacles and the Impact of the Islamist–Secularist Divide', Brookings Institution Working Paper 5, 2011.

Monjib, Maati, 'Maroc: le Hirak ou la révolte dans le Rif' *Orient XXI*, June 2017, https://orientxxi.info/magazine/maroc-le-hirak-ou-la-revolte-dans-le-rif,1898.

Monjib, Maati, 'Morocco's Illiberal Regime and Fragmented Political Society', *Arab Citizenship Review* 10, 2015, https://warwick.ac.uk/fac/soc/pais/research/researchcentres/irs/euspring/publications/arab_citizenship_review_n10.pdf.

Press release of the Istiqlal Party Executive Committee, June 2017, https://m.alyaoum24.com/890624.html.

Rédaction de *Contretemps*, 'Maroc, la révolution qui vient' (pdf), 2017, available at https://www.contretemps.eu/read-offline/15499/maroc-revolte-rif-Hirak.pdf.

Saadi, Mohamed, 'Hirak Rif: Baina Alhaja li Dawlawa Riba minha, Joruh Tarikhwa Tassaddoat Alhadir' (in Arabic), *Addawla wa Hirak Rif: Assolta, AssoltaAlmodaddawaAzmatAlwassata*, ed. Mohamed Radouani, Rabat 2018, pp. 75–86.

Sassi, Mohamed, 'M20F Aftermath on the Moroccan Political Regime' (in Arabic), *February 20, and the Outcomes of Democratization in Morocco*, ed. Arab Center for Research and Policy Studies, Doha 2018, pp. 69–105.

Schwarz, Christoph, 'Morocco's Social Protests across Time and Space', *openDemocracy* 13 June 2018, https://www.opendemocracy.net/north-africa-west-asia/christoph-h-schwarz/moroccos-social-protests-across-time-and-space.

Slimi, Manar, 'Zefzafi is the Mastermind of a Shiite Project that has Taken Control of a Social Movement' (in Arabic), *rue20.com* 30 May 2017, https://bit.ly/2urxYDl.

UNDP (United Nations Development Programme), 'Human Development Index Classification', http://hdr.undp.org/sites/default/files/2018_human_development_statistical_update.pdf.

Waterbury, John, 'Introduction' (in Arabic), *February 20, and the Outcomes of Democratization in Morocco*, ed. Arab Center for Research and Policy Studies, Doha 2018, pp. 55–66.

Zakhnini, Malika, 'Le bilan de la lutte contre la corruption et le despotisme dans le Maroc d'après le mouvement du M20F' (in Arabic), *Le Maroc après le mouvement de 2011: Qu'est-ce qui a changé?*, Casablanca 2016, pp. 124–147.

Zefzafi, Nasser, 'An Appeal to the Rif and Alhoceima's Population: Keep it Always Peaceful!' (in Arabic), YouTube, 26 May 2017, https://www.youtube.com/watch?v=fNUtxmjnAXo.

Zefzafi, Nasser, 'El-Himma and Majidi are Using the Hirak as a Battlefield in Their Struggle for Influence vis-à-vis the King' (in Arabic), Lakome2.com, 18 May 2017, https://bit.ly/2HJX4Gf.

Zefzafi, Nasser, 'Interview: Zefzafi Says It All' (in Arabic), Alaoual.com, 20 May 2017, https://bit.ly/2V0OsOd.

Zefzafi, Nasser, 'We Are Expecting the Participation of One Hundred Thousand People. We Are Ready to Negotiate' (in Arabic), Lakome2.com, 18 May 2017, https://bit.ly/2WwEggG.

7

Algeria; or, The Limits of the Democratic Facade

Lahouari Addi

The popular protest which began on 22 February 2019 in Algeria surprised many observers of North Africa. Massive demonstrations comprising hundreds of thousands of individuals occurred throughout the country, demanding that the ailing president Abdelaziz Bouteflika, in bad health since 2013, be prevented from running for a fifth term. After weeks of protests, demonstrators became increasingly 'radicalised' and began demanding changes to the regime itself.[1] To understand this unprecedented protest movement, one must be aware that the regime fuelled increasing social unrest by failing to reform the country's economy, mired as it is in the practices of rentierism,[2] and by its obstinacy in continuing to hold fraudulent elections. The contradictions of the rentier economy and a refusal to allow meaningful political participation were the main factors behind the rupture between the population and the regime.

More broadly, the massive protests of February 2019 were an expression of a crisis of the state born after independence in 1962. Having once centralised power and secured national unity, the military is perceived by post-independence generations as an obstacle to the rule of law. The military missed the opportunity to withdraw from the political field when multi-party politics was introduced

---

1 Lahouari Addi, 'Algeria's Joyful Revolution', *The Nation* 28 March 2019.
2 Francesco Cavatorta and Belgacem Tahchi, 'La politique économique de la résilience autoritaire en Algérie: l'énigme de la diversification économique', *Études Internationales* 50.1, 2019, pp. 7–38.

through a constitutional reform in 1989 and, by holding fraudulent elections, kept co-opting a civilian elite to run state institutions without genuinely relinquishing its own power. Feeling that they are not heard, citizens periodically resort to riots. Underestimating the political nature of these riots, the regime routinely tries to deal with them by increasing distribution of the oil rent, or by using force. In a telling instance, former prime minister Ahmed Ouyahya told a newspaper that the riots were the result 'of a manipulation of our youth's real grievances by mafia-like interests who feel threatened by the progress and transparency of the legal system'.[3] This type of political discourse suggests that the administration has no real intention of opening up the political system and allowing opposition forces to win elections.

The contradictions of the political system addressed in this chapter led to the collapse of a regime that for a long time ignored the legitimate expectations of the population. As soon as Abdelaziz Bouteflika declared that he was running for a fifth consecutive presidential term despite his age and his illness, hundreds of thousands of people poured on to the streets to express their anger on Friday 22 February 2019. Millions of citizens then protested peacefully each Friday, demanding not only that Bouteflika be removed from office but also a radical regime change. Surprised by the scale of the protest, the military forced the sitting president to step down and promised to implement a transition towards a new regime resting on article 7 of the constitution, which states that the people are the only source of power. This chapter shows that riots are a trait of the Algerian authoritarian political system, in which popular participation in the institutions of the state is weak. The chapter argues, furthermore, that the democratic facade in place for nearly three decades benefited only a rather small social group that profited from its links to military officers and their ability to disburse hydrocarbon rents.

Riots and the Rentier Economy

The 2011 Arab Spring did not affect Algeria, because it had recently experienced a bloody civil war which lasted from 1992 to 2002 and claimed the lives of 200,000 people.[4] During the war, state authorities had forbidden demonstrations and pro-

---

3 Quoted in Lakhdar Benchiba, 'Du bon usage des émeutes en Algérie', *Orient XXI* 9 January 2017.

4 Gianni Del Panta, 'Weathering the Storm: Why Was There No Arab Uprising in Algeria?', *Democratization* 24.6, 2017, pp. 1085–102; Frédéric Volpi, 'Algeria versus the Arab Spring', *Journal of Democracy* 24.3, 2013, pp. 104–15.

tests in the capital. Following the enactment of reconciliation legislation that put an end to the civil war between the military and the Islamists, popular demands for greater economic growth and increased purchasing power came on the public scene in the form of strikes and demonstrations.[5] The government was able to satisfy this demand thanks to the increasing price of oil on world markets. The price per barrel went from $18.48 (USD) in 1998 to $107.05 in 2008,[6] which permitted generous economic and social policies, mainly directed towards the remuneration of public servants and the construction of housing. The government's raising of salaries certainly satisfied one part of the population. Meanwhile, according to the financial expert Ferhat Aï Ali, 'between 2000 and 2014, Algeria's exports amounted to $727.9 billion, of which only $14 billion were non-hydrocarbon products, with a trade surplus of $271.5 billion'.[7] Indeed, during the period 2000–2014, the state was able not only to pay off its external debt (Table 1), but also to accumulate financial reserves of nearly $200 billion.

Table 1: Evolution of Algeria's external debt 2000–2011 (billions of USD)

2000	2003	2006	2009	2011
30	21.6	19.45	2.7	4.14

Source: Annual Report of the World Bank.

The population, both the well-off and the not so well-off, benefited from the state's financial largesse, which created numerous revenue streams and jobs, with investments in housing and infrastructure projects (an east–west highway, tramways and dams). To solve the housing crisis, the government began to eradicate the slums which had risen around large urban centres, as these festered with social discontent that was increasingly difficult to contain. By building hundreds of thousands of housing units for slum residents, state authorities lowered both social discontent and potential threats to social peace.[8] Moreover, the government authorised banks to issue loans for the purchase of fixed and movable property,

5 Lakhdar Benchiba, 'Alger: une capitale interdite de manifestations', *Orient XXI* 15 January 2018.
6 Annual average domestic crude oil prices ($/barrel), inflation-adjusted to February 2019.
7 Interview, *el-Watan* 31 January 2016.
8 Salima Mellah, 'Crise du logement en Algérie: du bidonville au ghetto', *Essafir al-Arabi* 15 February 2016.

which inflated the money supply, enabling access to – often imported – consumer goods. Demand pulled the economy, and the rentier logic fed such demand (both public and private). Rentier logic served as a means to bridge expanding national demand and the international market. With the price of a barrel of oil oscillating between $80 and $100 through much of the 2000s, the economy appeared to flourish, benefiting even the poor, who had access to new housing and subsidised goods. The effects of this public expenditure irrigated redistribution, which although inequitable, nonetheless benefited the population as a whole. The services sector created the most jobs (albeit most of them informal), relieving the pressure caused by unemployment. The data in Tables 2–7 illustrate relevant aspects of the Algerian economy in the post-civil war period.

Table 2: Algeria: international reserves (USD) 2105 and 2019

2015	2019
144.9 billion	80 billion

Source: Annual Report of the World Bank.

Table 3: Algeria: real GDP growth (%) 2006–2017 (* = estimate)

2006	2007	2008	2009	2010	2011	2012	2013	2014	2015	2016	2017
1.7	3.4	2.4	1.6	3.6	2.8	3.3	2.8	3.8	3.9	3.6*	2.9*

Note: 2017 total GDP = USD 178.4 billion*; GDP per capita (current prices) = USD 4,295.7*
Source: Annual Report of the World Bank.

Table 4: Algeria: GDP, composition by sector (%)...

Agriculture	Industry	Services
13.1	38.7	48.2

Source: Annual Report of the World Bank.

Table 5: Algeria: Inflation (%) 2013–2017 (= estimate)*

2013	2014	2015	2016	2017
3.3	2.9	4.8	5.9*	4.8*

Source: Annual Report of the World Bank.

Table 6: Algeria: Unemployment (%)2013–2017 (= estimate)*

2013	2014	2015	2016	2017
9.8	10.6	11.2	9.9*	10.4*

Source: Annual Report of the World Bank.

Table 7: Algeria: Public debt (general government gross debt as % of GDP) 2013–2017 (= estimate)*

2013	2014	2015	2016	2017
7.7	8.0	9.1	13.0*	17.1*

Source: Annual Report of the World Bank.

The government also established an agency called ANSEJ (Agence Nationale de Soutien à l'Emploi des Jeunes), which made bank loans to hundreds of thousands of unemployed youths, thus allowing them to create their own opportunities across a number of sectors ranging from transport to construction firms to services.[9] The period from the beginning of the 2000s up to 2014 was one of financial euphoria, during which the middle class reclaimed part of its purchasing power, which had degraded during the preceding years. It was also a period during which numerous private fortunes were built through import firms, a hectic estate market, the trafficking of privatised real estate ceded to regime cronies and widespread corruption. The media highlighted a number of high-profile cases of corruption involving high-ranking public officials, although it should be underlined

---

9 Since its foundation, the ANSEJ has at time of writing financed 367,980 projects for a total of $50 million, which has led to the creation of 900,000 jobs. According to data provided by the agency, 10% of projects go bankrupt, but debts are paid by the state. See 'L'ANSEJ à l'heure des bilans', *el-Watan* 28 February 2017; 'ANSEJ: les dettes épongées', *Liberté* 27 June 2017.

that networks and clans inimical to the regime and with knowledge of its workings leaked such stories. The increase in hydrocarbon rents allowed for the signing of massive contacts with foreign firms engaged in the exploration of oil and gas and construction of infrastructure and housing. Upon signing such contracts, high-ranking officers and ministers receive significant commissions, which were deposited in offshore bank accounts or transferred to accounts in tax havens. The press has focused, for instance, on the financial affairs of former minister Chakib Khelil and his involvement in the construction of the east–west highway – the budget for which ended up being twice the cost initially forecast – and in the signing of contracts between SONATRACH and US oil firms. It should be noted that the Algerian justice system did not prosecute Khelil, who was in fact found guilty of corruption in Italy, due to his involvement in facilitating a contract for an Italian firm who paid him bribes. The NGO Transparency International possesses numerous documents that provide accounts of these financial improprieties.[10]

This distribution of rents corresponded to the state's financial capacity, which began to fall in 2014 when the price of oil started sinking. Indeed, between 2014 and 2017, the price of oil fell by well over half (Table 8), thus saddling the state budget with deficits that could only be paid with foreign currency reserve. During these three years, these reserves shrank by $60 billion, according to official data.[11]

Table 8: Oil price per barrel 2014–2019 (USD)

2014	2015	2016	2017	2018	2019
96.29	49.49	40.68	51.85	69.52	62.08

Source: Annual Report of the World Bank.

Having initially hoped for the price of oil to rise again, the government needed to find alternative sources of funding. It did this by raising taxes, both direct and indirect, notably VAT, on all products with the exception of those already subsidised.[12] In doing so, the government ruptured the equilibrium of redistribution that had upheld social peace for a decade. Indeed, the state's 2000–2014 political

10 Djillali Hadjadj, 'Algeria: A Future Hijacked by Corruption', *Mediterranean Politics* 12.2, 2007, pp. 263–77; *Corruption et Démocratie en Algérie*, Paris 2001.
11 See 'Réserves de change: forte contraction en 2016: elles ont atteint $114,1 milliards', *Liberté* 30 January 2017. In January 2019, the amount was $80 billion.
12 'Loi de Finances 2017: ce qui attend les consommateurs', *el-Watan* 7 December 2016.

economy was only possible because of the oil price. Without this income stream, redistribution dried up, leading to a systemic crisis. Recurrent riots reveal this structure and illustrate the political weakness of Algeria's socio-economic system. In effect, the government is caught in a pincer by two intertwined constraints over which it has no control: the price of oil and pressure from the street.

In December 2016, on the initiative of Prime Minister Abdelmalek Sellal, the National Assembly levied new taxes to balance the state budget, thus provoking public anger, which manifested itself through numerous violent demonstrations in various parts of the country. In June 2017, Abdelmajid Tebboune replaced Sellal, promising to lower taxes and raise tariffs on imported products. Importers mobilised their networks and had the new prime minister sacked after only three months in office. His successor, Ahmed Ouyahya, proposed to solve the deficit problem by printing more money, which, naturally, led to inflation and the devaluation of the Algerian dinar against the US dollar (Table 9). Printing more money became the weapon used by successive governments to balance the state budget, to the detriment of the people's purchasing power: according to official data, inflation was 21.7% between 2013 and 2017.

Table 9: Evolution of the Algerian dinar's parity with the US dollar 1995–2019

1995	2000	2005	2010	2013	2014	2015	2016	2017	2018	2019
8.96	47.66	75.26	77.28	101.36	102.28	107.46	116.43	109.4	115.2	119.30

Source: Annual Report of the World Bank.

The policy of printing money meant that 2015 salaries needed to be multiplied by 14 to achieve the same purchasing power in 2017. Wages did increase between these two years, but not sufficiently to maintain the same purchasing power. The government's priority was to alleviate immediate constraints, applying short-term, partial solutions to address the crisis. The case of the January 2017 riots is illustrative: these began as a reaction to financial measures adopted by the National Assembly, which increased the VAT on goods and services – with some exceptions – by two percentage points. This raising of VAT was not implemented in the context of any five- or ten-year economic development project intended to reinforce the national market's potentialities; it was intended merely to raise the funds necessary to lower the state's budget deficit. The priority in this case was to alleviate the pressure brought about by the decrease in the price of oil, with the government fearing that this could be a long-term issue. This is why Sellal's government raised VAT without considering its potential effects on local competitiveness or purchasing power. The priority was to lower the deficit through a technically 'neutral' assessment of governmental accounting: all that was needed, it was thought, was to tinker with certain variables to adjust the budget in response to falling oil prices.

Of course, care had been taken to exempt from this tax-hike subsidised products such as cereals, sugar or coffee. The government's hope was to prevent the lower classes from taking to the streets in protest. Whatever tax is imposed on a merchant, however, will automatically affect consumers and will have far-reaching effects on the system of prices. Any tax rise affects the structure of prices, because the latter are linked to a logic that transfers value in the search for market equilibrium. Taxing the purchase of a luxury car will raise, one way or another, the price of a bottle of bleach, which is not a luxury. Consequently, to protect the revenue of the poor from a rise in VAT, it would have been necessary to raise their wages by the same proportion. However, neither the state nor private employers would have accepted such a solution, which would have been too much of a financial burden. Long dependent on its energy rents, the government is thus incapable of imagining an alternative whereby internal creation of wealth could replace the rent. Government policies have always focused on demand instead of incentives for local wealth-generation, which could act as a substitute for imports. The government has effectively painted itself into a corner of zero-sum thinking, and strives to find an optimal solution for its redistribution parameters. Sometimes, it changes tax rates, as Sellal and Tebboune did, while at other times it alters the dinar's parity to obtain more of its currency for the same amount of US dollars, as Ouyahya did. In both cases, the plan to reduce the deficit results in a diminishing of the public's purchasing power. By acting thus, the regime exposes itself to riots in the streets, which indicate that a point of equilibrium has been lost. If the new equilibrium favoured by the government had been negotiated with representatives of different socio-professional groups (workers, the unemployed, entrepreneurs, merchants), such riots could have been avoided. However, the government does not wish to negotiate with representatives that it does not control, and hence does not consider as legitimate spokesmen of various social groups. The formulation of the authoritarian regime's economic system has not changed despite political reforms that have legalised multi-party politics.

The State's Refusal to Recognise Representatives of Various Social Groups

The widespread riots that occurred before 22 February 2019 suggest that the country has yet to offer a definitive institutional answer to social demands made on the streets. Periodic local demonstrations in a village, a city or sometimes a whole region shake the country regularly, and the security services' arbitrary use of coercion, the shortage of housing, blackouts, lack of water or police blunders stoke these riots and protests. In 2001, Kabylie saw the outbreak of violent demonstrations following the assassination of a young student by the police. The city of Béchar is often the locus of riots, even during the summer, when the temperature reaches 40°C and blackouts shut down refrigerators and ventilators. Southern cities have witnessed numerous violent demonstrations against employment policies, which are skewed against the region's youth. Security service statistics record hundreds of demonstrations per week across the country. As large-scale protests by teachers' and doctors' unions, post office employees, taxi drivers, bakers and other professions are often held without the state's permission, Algeria can be said to be a country in which violent and non-violent protest amounts to a permanent state of affairs.[13] This is linked to the rentier structure of the economy and to the regime's inability and unwillingness to enter into a constructive dialogue with popular representatives.

Multi-party politics, introduced after the October 1988 riots, was meant to integrate into state institutions the voices of different social groups in order for politics to be non-violent and functional. There was at the time widespread agreement that the single-party regime of the 1960s and 1970s had reached its limits and needed to be opened up. Indeed, October 1988 appears to have been the most important political event in Algerian post-independence history, because it put an end to a political model that had failed to gain the long-term confidence of the ruled.[14] Thus, political reforms were enacted to let various social groups and ideological movements express themselves. Numerous parties sprouted from these reforms, and their activities were reported in the newly free press. Between 1989 and 1992, the country experienced political life as never before, characterised by open debates in which various public policies were proposed, and of which citizens could approve or disapprove.[15] The cancellation of the January 1992 election

---

13 Smail Goumeziane, 'Corporatisme, syndicalisme et mouvements sociaux en Algérie', *el-Watan* 29 April 2018.

14 John Reudy, *Modern Algeria*, Bloomington 2005.

15 Lahouari Addi, *L'Algérie et la démocratie*, Paris 1994; *Algérie: une expérience de modernisation postcoloniale*, Algiers 2012.

did not end formal multi-party politics. With the exception of the Islamic Salvation Front (FIS), which was dissolved, political parties participated in many subsequent elections. However, after 25 years and several elections, there has yet to be a genuine transition of power. Indeed, the post-independence 1962 regime still wields power, and the democratic transition appears to have failed. Thus, there has yet to occur a renewal of the ruling class, and the population remains largely excluded from political participation. The question here is, why did the transition to democracy fail despite the shift to multi-party politics? The answer is that multipartism did not function as an intermediate organ that would prompt the state to become receptive to the country's various social groups.

An appropriate analysis of politics and the relations between different centres of authority can provide an explanation for this failure, taking into account the ability of the regime to absorb and co-opt multi-party politics. Formally, the legitimacy of the regime rests on multipartism politics and electoral competition, but the reality is that opposition parties had to accept the rigging of elections on the part of the regime in order simply to take part in the electoral process. This therefore prevents a genuine changeover through elections. The political police (DRS) filters candidates before electoral contests, ridding the lists of all candidates who are suspected of disloyalty towards the regime, and this neutralises the ability of political parties in opposition to present a genuine alternative. Elected representatives thus do not take major political decisions, and are but an institutional facade for an opaque political structure; which suggests that the system's historical legitimacy is still anchored in the military, rather than in the sovereignty of the electorate. The regime's regular tactics of election fraud and the manipulation and infiltration of political parties has had the effect of neutralising opposition parties and co-opting them into a purely formal and sterile institutional arrangement. This strategy has alienated the population from state institutions, however, and is what led to the popular revolt which occurred when President Bouteflika stated his intention to run for a fifth term.

In effect, the regime proscribes political activity: that is, the institutional process through which the executive can be criticised and controlled through legal means. In these conditions, opposition parties lose their credibility, and are unable to act as intermediaries between state institutions and the population. Although political parties are permitted to speak relatively freely, they cannot criticise the role of the army as the ultimate source of power and defender of the regime. Moreover, various social groups are not permitted to have their own representatives, which could relay the grievances of workers, the unemployed or business people. In short, the regime refuses to deal with political actors it does not control, preferring instead to renew its elites strictly from within.[16] It is revealing, indeed, that political parties are allowed, whereas independent trade unions are not. The state deems it easier to manipulate and control party leaders, whilst autonomous trade unions, to maintain their legitimacy, must credibly represent the interests of their members. It is much easier to bribe party leaders than trade union heads who have to be accountable to their unionised workers on a daily basis.

There are thus no legal pathways through which workers, the unemployed, merchants and entrepreneurs can express their grievances – a state of affairs feeding frustration, which is in turn expressed through riots whenever the state's decisions are perceived as unjust. Despite multi-party politics and a relatively free press, violent protests, be they local or national, are therefore part and parcel of the political system, highlighting the ruptures between the government and ordinary citizens when the price of oil diminishes and social crises develop. These crises involve crucial issues such as purchasing power, unemployment, housing and pensions, all of which the government treats as bureaucratic matters, without con- sulting legitimate representatives of the social groups concerned: a state of affairs which results in direct and violent confrontations with local or corporate demands. In these situations, the government employs repressive measures to quell riots. To ensure its survival, the regime depends on the oil rent when the price of oil is sufficiently high. When it is not, the regime uses repression to contain civil strife. In such conditions, legitimate representation is impossible, and both government and opposition parties are powerless to act.

Thus, the February 1989 constitutional reform legalising multipartism was not implemented to allow the peaceful transfer of power, but rather to establish a facade democracy in which opposition parties have no real opportunity to form a government. The issue at hand was to lend some political credibility to the representatives of regime-affiliated political parties (FLN and RND), who could thereafter claim to form a legitimate government representing the electorate's interests, while the opposition parties could not. Indeed, multipartism has to some extent actually strengthened the regime, instead of allowing for its opening-up. The country's rigged elections allow the regime to claim an electoral legitimacy that was absent at the time of the single-party rule. The regime's legitimacy is

---

16 Rafael Bustos García de Castro and Aurèlia Mañé, 'Algeria: Post-Colonial Power Structure and Reproduction of Elites without Renewal', *Political Regimes in the Arab World: Society and the Exercise of Power*, ed. Ferran Izquierdo Brichs, London 2012, pp. 38–64; Isabelle Werenfels, *Managing Instability in Algeria. Elites and Political Change since 1995*, New York 2007; Lahouari Addi, *Radical Arab Nationalism and Political Islam*, Washington, DC 2017.

based in fact on two elements: elections and military power. The former is purely formal, and is used to co-opt docile elected representatives, while the latter is real, and remains in the hands of a few high-ranking officers. These officers' prerogatives comprise the designation of presidential candidates (which the administration will elect), the determination of quotas given to various political parties in the legislature and the distribution of the oil rent to the various ministries. The military establishes a general framework for governmental action, leaving the various ideological and economic interest groups just some latitude for negotiations and compromises. A number of authors claim that Bouteflika was able to reduce the power and influence of the military over political decisions;[17] but high-ranking officers remained the real wielders of power even under Bouteflika, although they found it convenient to appear to be operating under the president's orders. The actual political supremacy of the military over the political system was clearly demonstrated in 2019, however, when General Gaid Salah, the army's chief of staff, demanded that Bouteflika resign following street protests across the country. The president did so 48 hours later.

There are therefore three elements sustaining the political system: the directly elected presidency, the military and the two pro-regime political parties (FLN and RND), which always form a majority in the National Assembly. Through non-institutional channels, the military leadership sends instructions to the presidency, which translates the instructions into policies for the ministries to execute, and which the FLN and the RND adopt in parliament. The institutional process appears to give elected representatives the liberty to adopt laws, but the reality is that sovereign authority resides in the military and not in the electorate. In such a system, opposition parties play the role of lending credibility. In the National Assembly, members of the opposition often vote against legislation the government proposes, but these opposition representatives wield no real power; nor do they wish to do so, because they might fall out of favour with the genuine wielders of power. Thus, these representatives seek the privileges that come with their jobs, accepting whole-heartedly the fact that the military, not the electorate, pulls the strings. (Ellen Lust observes a similar situation in Jordan, where elections constitute a kind of selection for posts that allow personal advancement and the possibility of redistributing some resources to a clientelistic network.[18]) Press reports

17 Hugh Roberts, 'Demilitarizing Algeria', Carnegie Endowment for International Peace 2007, https://carnegieendowment.org/files/cp_86_final1.pdf.
18 Ellen Lust, 'Jordan Votes: Election or Selection?', *Journal of Democracy* 22.2, 2011, pp. 119–29.

indicate that before elections, many individuals pay significant sums of money to add their names to the lists for various elected positions.[19] Indeed, becoming a member of parliament allows one to access semi-official channels of corruption. In any case, opposition parties, which are mainly present in cities, are politically weak and are unable to impose any sort of neutrality upon local or national ballots. Without political neutrality and an independent judiciary, multi-party politics has no legitimate purpose. In a case of ballot-stuffing, no judge would dare rule in favour of a plaintiff and thus displease the Ministry of Justice, which only executes policies issuing from the presidency. The subordinate position of the judiciary and the civil service more broadly suggests that the regime has no intention of leading the country to an electoral transfer of power, and that its structure is incompatible with autonomous political parties seeking to do more than simply maintaining a democratic facade. The regime expects opposition parties to participate in state institutions, and even to criticise government policies, but it also expects them to refrain from attempting to win national elections, acting as a sort of loyal opposition with little to no input in policy-making.[20] For the military, the opposition's role is not to create a new regime or to claim some form of electoral legitimacy, because the regime, and more precisely the military itself, retains real, 'historical' legitimacy. As long as the regime has sufficient resources to impose itself on its adversaries, there will be no democratic transmission of power.

The Democratic Facade and the Power of Money

The democratic-facade model reached its limits during President Bouteflika's last term (2014–2019). Corruption had spread everywhere, purchasing power had degraded and some Algerians had found ways of greatly profiting from the situation. These factors led to the 22 February 2019 revolt, which produced the collapse of the regime's civilian facade. Under pressure from the population, the military asked Bouteflika to resign, which he promptly did, and the senate president Abdelkader Bensalah replaced him for three months. However, demonstrations continued, and people demanded that regime officials refrain from managing the upcoming government. Indeed, people demanded that there be a period of

---

19 Algerian political jargon has invented a new word, which surfaces at every election: the *chkara*, or the overflowing moneybag needed to be a candidate. See 'La campagne de collecte des signatures bat son plein. Les contraintes administratives et la chkara se mettent de la partie', *el-Watan* 13 February 2014.
20 Holger Albrecht, 'How Can Opposition Support Authoritarianism? Lessons from Egypt', *Democratization* 12.3, 2005, pp. 378–97.

transition similar to that which Tunisia had gone through after the fall of Ben Ali. What happened in Algeria in 2019 was a mutation of the interactions between state and society, with the latter demanding that elected institutions represent various social groups.

The interesting question, from a political science perspective, is why the middle class, with the support of lower classes, led the 'democratic revolution', rather than the business bourgeoisie, which appears indifferent to the said revolution. The problem is how to define the middle class in Arab countries.[21] According to orthodox European political science, it is the bourgeoisie which, in its defence of liberal economics, should lead a country to political liberalism and the rule of law. Why then does Algeria's bourgeoisie support the authoritarian regime rather than the democratic movement? The Algerian press has often spoken of the power of money, which was thought to have an important influence on the military, thus insinuating that the latter was subordinate to the business class. Well-known businessmen were believed to have an important role in the political decision-making process, as if they dominated the country. The press reported that during an economic Algerian–African forum, Ali Haddad, a representative of Algerian businessmen, began to speak before Prime Minister Abdelmalek Sellal, who was supposed to be the keynote speaker.[22] In their commentaries, journalists highlighted the important role businessmen had acquired, to the point that the role of the head of the government seemed to have been rendered marginal. The owner of a construction firm, Ali Haddad is the representative of a new business class that emerged following the liberal economic reforms introduced once the state had abandoned its monopoly on foreign trade. These reforms permitted some businessmen to amass vast fortunes in the construction business, as well as in speculative activities linked to imports. Some businessmen overtly funded political campaigns during elections, thus supporting regime-friendly political parties. For them, such an investment represented an opportunity to ask favours from the administration and thus obtain privileges for their businesses: for the

---

21 Benoît Challand, 'The False Question of the Middle Class', *Middle East – Topics & Arguments* 2, 2014, pp. 17–21; Rachid Ouaissa, 'The Misunderstanding about the Role of the Middle Classes', *Middle East – Topics & Arguments* 2, 2014, pp. 12–16.
22 On this incident, see 'Incident au Forum africain: Sellal quitte la salle en plein discours de Ali Haddad', Dia-Algerie.com, http://dia-algerie.com/incident-forum-africain-sellal-quitte-salle-plein-discours-de-ali-haddad/. 'The protocol incident which occurred during last week's opening of the African investment forum shocked even the highest levels of the government. The FCE president, who instigated this incident, will be held responsible.' Ali Haddad is still the president of the FCE.

rich, this is often necessary, to tame the regime's natural hostility to all initiatives that might escape its control. The state's neo-patrimonialism does indeed
restrict membership of the club for mass-profit activities. To join it, one must
either have the patronage of an influential official or be a member of such an
official's family. Capturing a part of the rent depends on clientelistic protection,
without which the arms of the state (taxes, tariffs, the police) would be insurmountable obstacles to the import of goods or to cornering some of the market for
public infrastructure projects. Although there has been a notable privatisation of
certain economic sectors, access to these markets is limited. As in politics, there
is a filter, which selects candidates for public tender offers, customs' authori-
sations permitting the import of goods, and credit on offer from public banks.
Recent fortunes are linked to the rentier nature of the Algerian economy, within
which oil represents 98% of all exports. These fortunes do not, however, represent
the generation of new wealth: they are the result of a redistribution of the rent,
thus respecting the regime's political logic of hostility towards any autonomous
economic power. Private enterprises' contribution to the export market is minus-
cule, with the notable exception of the Cevital company. The economic reforms
established after the end of the single-party system in 1989 were not intended to
create a vibrant private sector. They were limited to commerce and services, thus
encouraging imports, to the detriment of local production.[23] Numerous small and
medium-sized businesses were unable to compete with products originating from
Turkey, China or Vietnam. Artisans and small entrepreneurs producing clothing,
shoes and other consumer goods were forced to adapt their business towards commerce and informal activities, where profits are much higher.

Proximity to state officials means that businessmen can only prosper with the
help of the regime, to whom they are loyal because of the nature of their activities. Their political emancipation is unthinkable, as it would be contrary to their
interests, especially in the case of those who are, for example, partners with a general's son or brother-in-law. (The journalist Hichem Abboud wrote a book about
what he called '*la mafia des généraux*', illustrating precisely such dynamics.[24])
Understandably, these businessmen are far from willing to free themselves from
the regime and demand democratic reforms. This explains why they refrain from
associating with opposition parties. When businessmen do contribute to political

23 Prime Minister Mouloud Hamrouche was sacked in 1991 by President Chadli Bendjedid,
who was under pressure from importers whose interests lay in keeping Algeria a rich market
for imports.
24 Hicham Abboud, *La mafia des généraux*, Paris 2002.

campaigns, it is always to those of the FLN and the RND. Dependent as they are upon the state's resources, they are aware of their fragility, which has led them to opportunism. Indeed, businessmen do not have much political influence. As soon as the 2019 demonstrations began, the state began rounding up businessmen and charging them with corruption. The regime wanted to show the public that it was combating corruption, by sacrificing the very businessmen it had itself allowed to amass fortunes.

The various components of the private sector made their voices heard through an employers' association, the Forum des Chefs d'Entreprises (FCE), expressing interests divergent from those of the state. The FCE has witnessed severe internal struggles when importers and construction companies clashed with manufacturers. Importers are against tariffs, and are pushing the government to enter into an agreement with the IMF, whereas small and medium-sized businesses and manufacturers are pushing for protectionist policies. In the current situation, the latter have the upper hand, because of their access to state officials. The minister of industry even threatened Issad Rabrab, boss of Cevital, the number two exporter in Algeria after Sonatrach, suggesting that the government is more comfortable dealing with speculators than with private firms employing thousands of people.[25] This struggle between Issad Rebrab and the minister of industry, Abdeslam Bouchouareb (who, according to the 'Panama papers', has an offshore bank account) illustrates what happens when a group representing the accumulation of wealth through speculative activities linked to the oil rent clashes with entrepreneurs who believe that the oil rent should feed national and not international capitalism.

The regime does see the benefits of both sides, but it supports importers. The official discourse changes as the price of oil does. When it goes up, the balance of power goes to the importers, but when it goes down, the state stresses the importance of local manufacturing as a substitute for imports. These are but circumstantial declarations, however, as they do not translate into policy changes. The press often highlights the contrast between the state discourse and its actions, as was the case in an *el-Watan* editorial published on 18 January 2017: '[After] fifteen years the government, despite expenditure of over 800 billion dollars, has yet to find a way to diversify the Algerian economy, which remains dangerously anchored to oil exports.'

---

25 Issad Rabrab is head of Cevital, which has 3,000 employees and exports 200 million worth of goods, making it the second exporter after Sonatrach. On this dispute, see La Tribune des Lecteurs 29 September 2015, 'Rabrab réplique aux accusations du ministre de l'industrie: la guerre est ouverte.'

Conclusion

The Algerian experience highlights the relationships between politics and economics in neo-patrimonial regimes, where the economy is a political resource mobilised for regime survival. In such a context, the regime's implicit rule is that no civil society organisation (unions or employers) can have sufficient autonomous power to rival the executive branch. Between speculative commercial capital and wealth generation capital, the regime prefers the latter, as it is does not then have the burden of negotiating with social groups whose wealth does not depend on the state. Indeed, wealth-producing capital would lead to demands for the rule of law, competitive domestic markets, monetary parity and other reforms that would undermine the current system. The neo-patrimonial state fears the growth of an autonomous domestic economy uncoupled from hydrocarbon rents, because it would lead to demands from entrepreneurs for more political openness and legal clarity. It is, in short, much more difficult to subdue politically a businessman who contributes to GDP with exports, employs hundreds of workers and contributes to the state's coffers through taxes.

Algeria's leaders thrive on a paradox: they pretend to have electoral legitimacy, but are adamantly opposed to an independent judiciary, which could guarantee free and fair elections. By continuous recourse to ballot-stuffing, they have become accustomed to profound social discontent, which exists because of the contradictory nature of the authoritarian rentier state. Thus, the February 2019 revolt can be explained by a paradox that the regime was unable to hide. On one hand, the single-party system was abolished in 1989, but on the other, only the former ruling party, the FLN, wins national elections. At the time of writing, the situation on the ground in Algeria was still unfolding. Will the military yield to the protesters, or will they stand firm to keep the same regime with some superficial reforms? In contemporary Algerian history, three dates need to be remembered: 1962 was the year the country obtained its independence; 1992 was the year of the failure of the transition from the single-party system; 2019 was the year of the collapse of the Bouteflika regime. Will it also be the year of the end of the military's control over the state?

Bibliography

Abboud, Hicham, *La mafia des généraux*, Paris 2002.
Addi, Lahouari, 'Algeria's Joyful Revolution', *The Nation* 28 March 2019.
Addi, Lahouari, *L'Algérie et la démocratie*, Paris 1994.

Addi, Lahouari, *Algérie: une expérience de modernisation postcoloniale*, Algiers 2012.

Addi, Lahouari, *Radical Arab Nationalism and Political Islam*, Washington, DC 2017.

Albrecht, Holger, 'How Can Opposition Support Authoritarianism? Lessons from Egypt', *Democratization* 12.3, 2005, pp. 378–97.

Benchiba, Lakhdar, 'Alger: une capitale interdite de manifestations', *Orient XXI* 15 January 2018.

Benchiba, Lakhdar, 'Du bon usage des émeutes en Algérie', *Orient XXI* 9 January 2017.

Bustos García de Castro, Rafael and Aurèlia Mañé, 'Algeria: Post-Colonial Power Structure and Reproduction of Elites without Renewal', *Political Regimes in the Arab World: Society and the Exercise of Power*, ed. Ferran Izquierdo Brichs, London 2012, pp. 38–64.

Cavatorta, Francesco and Belgacem Tahchi, 'La politique économique de la résilience autoritaire en Algérie: l'énigme de la diversification économique', *Études Internationales* 50.1, 2019, pp. 7–38.

Challand, Benoît, 'The False Question of the Middle Class', *Middle East – Topics & Arguments* 2, 2014, pp. 17–21.

Del Panta, Gianni, 'Weathering the Storm: Why Was There No Arab Uprising in Algeria?', *Democratization* 24.6, 2017, pp. 1085–102.

Goumeziane, Smail, 'Corporatisme, syndicalisme et mouvements sociaux en Algérie', *el-Watan* 29 April 2018.

Hadjadj, Djillali, *Corruption et Démocratie en Algérie*, Paris 2001.

Hadjadj, Djillali, 'Algeria: A Future Hijacked by Corruption', *Mediterranean Politics* 12.2, 2007, pp. 263–77.

Lust, Ellen, 'Jordan Votes: Election or Selection?', *Journal of Democracy* 22.2, 2011, pp. 119–29.

Mellah, Salima, 'Crise du logement en Algérie: du bidonville au ghetto', *Essafir al-Arabi* 15 February 2016.

Ouaissa, Rachid, 'The Misunderstanding about the Role of the Middle Classes', *Middle East – Topics & Arguments* 2, 2014, pp. 12–16.

Reudy, John, *Modern Algeria* (2nd edn), Bloomington 2005.

Roberts, Hugh, 'Demilitarizing Algeria', Carnegie Endowment for International Peace 2007, https://carnegieendowment.org/files/cp_86_final1.pdf.

Volpi, Frédéric, 'Algeria versus the Arab Spring', *Journal of Democracy* 24.3, 2013, pp. 104–15.

Werenfels, Isabelle, *Managing Instability in Algeria. Elites and Political Change since 1995*, New York 2007.

Part 2

DYNAMICS OF CHANGE AND DYNAMICS OF CONTINUITY: SOCIAL TRANSFORMATIONS AFTER THE UPRISINGS

8

Guardians of Change

George Joffé

The great conundrum of the Arab Awakening Movement in 2011, in North Africa at least, has been why it was that the dramatic and virtually simultaneous demands for political participation voiced in nearly every country were so quickly neutralised or reversed, often with considerable violence, except in Tunisia. After all, the previous decade had presided over the apparent weakening of autocratic political systems in most countries in the Arab world, which had been accompanied by new social movements articulating expanded roles for civil society there, as the 'Guardians of Change' in regional politics. That, in turn, should have ensured the survival of the gains realised then, according to conventional modernisation and political transition theories. This, however, has not proved to be the case and this chapter suggests that the reasons for this may lie in conventional academic interpretation of the nature of social movements and civil society in the Arab world, alongside the relative importance to be accorded to the specificity of structure, process and agency in their evolution.

Conventional academic views of the way in which formal political systems evolve away from autocratic and dictatorial governance towards political participation have – even before Samuel Huntington's 'third democratic wave'[1] – implicitly or explicitly depended on teleological unicity. Mainstream modernisation theory, for example, concludes that the ineluctable political outcome of the process of economic development is inevitably democratic. Thus it defines principles of liberal

---

1 Samuel Huntington, *The Third Wave: Democratisation in the Late Twentieth Century*, Norman, OK 1991.

democracy as integral to the developmental process.[2] In short, political principles emerging uniquely from the European experience of the Enlightenment and
endowed with a sense of Whig historiographical optimism should have been the
ultimate outcome of political transition processes.[3] Yet the actual experience of the
modernisation process has not necessarily produced such results, with autocratic
governance proving to be an equally possible alternative – as the Chinese experience, for example, has demonstrated, with its successful combination of economic
development alongside the persistence of single-party authoritarian politics.

The modernisation experience of the Arab world, too, has been treated as para-
digmatic in this sense, as an exception to the general rule; so much so that it had
been seen as exceptional only in terms of the apparently popular toleration of
autocratic governance and of the rigidity of its resistance to democratic political
change.[4] Indeed, it has only been with the events of 2011 – the so-called 'Arab
Awakening'[5] – that these assumptions have been actively challenged, although
questions about their validity had been raised on rare occasions before. Indeed, the
underlying assumptions regarding democratic evolution described above had also
originally been expected to be the inevitable concomitants of theories of political
transition which emerged in the wake of modernisation theory.

When, however, this had proved not to be the case, political transition came
to be seen as the outcome of negotiation between centralised political authority
and alienated dissident elites, which would satisfy the essential interests of both
sides by facilitating collective political action without endangering the individual

---

2 W.W. Rostow, *The Stages of Economic Growth: A Non-Communist Manifesto*, Cambridge
1960; Jeffrey Sachs, *The End of Poverty: Economic Possibilities for Our Time*, New York
2005.
3 Herbert Butterfield, *The Whig Interpretation of History*, London 1931; William Cronon,
'Two Cheers for the Whig Interpretation of History', *Perspectives on History*, American
Historical Association, 1 September 2012, www.historians.org/publications-and-directories/
perspectives-on-history/september-2012-x41643; Nicolas Guilhot, 'Portrait of the Realist as a
Historian: On Anti-Whiggism in the History of International Relations', *European Journal
of International Relations* 21.1, 2015, pp. 3–26.
4 Ofira Seliktar, *The Politics of Intelligence and American Wars with Iraq*, New York 2008,
pp. 7–26.
5 This is the term generally used in the Arab world to refer to the events of 2011 which are
more conventionally referred to in Western countries as the 'Arab Spring'. The latter term is
generally disliked in the Arab world because it is felt to diminish indigenous Arab
ownership of the process and to subordinate it to prior Western paradigms, such as the
Prague Spring of 1968. Such concerns, however, overlook an authentic regional precursor
which, however, is not Arab: the 'Berber Spring' (*Tafsut Imazighen*) in Algeria in April 1980.
Nevertheless, the term 'Arab Awakening' will be used in this chapter.

interests of the parties involved. This was to be achieved by the joint recognition of the legitimacy, whether bounded or unbounded, of separate collective interests of sub-state actors and, thereby, the grant to them all of a stake within a shared political process through the definition of a 'pact' of shared interests between the two sides. The degree to which such processes would be restricted by the intrinsic interests of one side or the other would itself be part of the negotiating process, to be accepted or rejected in terms of the essential concerns of each and the autonomous power either could project into the process itself. Yet those disjunctures, in turn, were expected to be reduced through iterative experience over time and eventually transmute – for lack of any better alternative – into a generalised system of what would be, in effect, legitimised democratic governance. This process, which was first described with reference to the democratic transitions in South America in the 1960s and 1970s and then applied to political transition in Eastern Europe, has come to be known as 'pacting': the construction of political pacts to defuse the tensions that such concessions by central political authority to domestic entities that contest its political status might produce.[6]

However, these assumptions, in turn, have raised further questions that have acquired peculiar salience in the wake of the Arab Awakening, not least over how the legitimacy and the survival of individual interests, once recognised, could be determined, restricted or ensured. Was the alleged 'exceptionalism' of the Arab world really the mechanism by which resistance to political change there was both empowered and enforced? Would the legitimacy of the interests involved in political transition in the Arab world be universal or particularistic in nature and, if the latter, on what basis could their particularism be established? And who or what would be the gatekeepers of the political processes that would emerge there? This chapter is directed towards responding to such questions as part of an attempt to contribute to the expansion of the scope of current theories of political transition. In attempting to do so, it will draw on the experiences of the political transitions in Egypt and Tunisia.

As such, it will have to incorporate not only the initial Whig vision of inevitable democratic outcomes, inherent in modernisation theory, but also the more hybrid notions of 'illiberal democracy',[7] 'authoritarian resilience' and 'liberalised autocracy' that have undermined the original idealistic vision. These alternatives,

---

6 Guillermo O'Donnell and Philippe Schmitter, *Transitions from Authoritarian Rule: Tentative Conclusions about Uncertain Democracies*, Baltimore 1986, p. 37.
7 This is the democratic process freed from the constraints of the rule of law and accountability, as described by Fareed Zakaria, 'The Rise of Illiberal Democracy', *Foreign Affairs* 7.6, 1997, pp. 22–43.

in turn, depend on the role of elites inside processes of change, for they have determined the paths that those processes have followed and the outcomes that they have achieved. Thus, the pre-existence of a civil society and social movements in Tunisia has much to say about the outcomes there, despite the slow return subsequently of the pre-revolutionary hegemonic political party and the elites that it represented; whereas the dominance of the military in Egypt eventually undermined the role that either the dominant elites or the opposition to them could play in the aftermath of the 'Tahrir Revolution'. Nor has the role of elites substantially altered since 2011, except, perhaps, in Egypt, where an unstable autocracy has been reinstalled. Thus, despite the role of subalterns in Algeria today in challenging the consequences of 'facade democracy' (Algeria's version of 'illiberal democracy'), ultimate authority appears to remain with the country's 'shame-faced sovereign' – the army command.[8] And in Morocco, the Makhzen is still the hegemonic power, despite the constitutional reforms of July 2011;[9] whilst in Libya, the destruction of the personalised elite around the figure of Muammar Gaddafi himself at the end of the civil war has prevented any effective transition from occurring there.[10]

Political Transitions

Before turning to the specificities of these case studies in North Africa, however, it is perhaps necessary to determine the current status of the theoretical analysis of political transition.[11] The early version of this analysis was deeply embrocated with the unicity of theory and praxis which, it assumed, lay behind the key concept of the pacting process. In essence, this meant that the interests of isolated political leaderships anxious to escape their isolation were preserved by their grant of a degree of political autonomy to dissident elites. This, in turn, allowed the institutions of civil society, in so far as they existed, to become the guarantors of the process and to be aided and abetted in achieving it through social movements.[12]

---

8 Hugh Roberts, 'The Struggle for Constitutional Rule in Algeria', *Journal of Algerian Studies* 3.1, 1998, pp. 22–23.
9 Driss Maghraoui, 'Constitutional Reforms in Morocco: Between Consensus and Subaltern Politics', *The Journal of North African Studies* 16.1, 2011, pp. 679–99.
10 George Joffé, 'Civil Resistance in Libya during the Arab Spring', *Civil Resistance in the Arab Spring: Triumphs and Disasters*, ed. Adam Roberts et al., Oxford 2016, p. 138.
11 Daniel Brumberg, 'Theories of Transition', *The Arab Uprisings Explained*, ed. Marc Lynch, New York 2014, pp. 29–54.
12 Sidney Tarrow, *Power in Movement: Social Movements and Contentious Politics*, Cambridge 1998, p. 10; Quintan Wiktorowicz, 'Introduction: Islamic Activism and Social

Contemporary notions of civil society derive from paradigms established by Hegel, De Tocqueville and Gramsci '... as the sphere of intermediary organizations standing between the individual and the state'.[13] This was De Tocqueville's definition of civil society as separate from the state, and derived from Hegel's vision of *bürgerliche Gesellschaft*, an essentially economic concept, although also linked to Hegel's view of individual freedom as internalised and legitimised within and through the collective concept of the state.[14] It should be contrasted with Gramsci's view of civil society as a fragmented entity, inextricably intermeshed with the state ('political society') and as simultaneously a potential competitor and/or collaborator, but subject, too, to international pressures, from outside the state.[15] Social movements, in this context, become the agentic vehicles by which civil society articulates its new-found autonomy from political leaderships, by framing the demands of organised non-state actors contesting the discourses of political leaderships within the confines defined by the pacting process.[16]

In the Arab and Muslim worlds, such functions were traditionally discharged by predominantly urban institutions of considerable antiquity that sought to mediate between unitary political authority and the individual, which represented both civic and civil society (*al-mujtama al-madani* and *al-mujtama al-ahli*) respectively and which contributed towards the role of social justice within the political culture of the region, as derived from Islamic paradigms.[17] In contrast to the inherently competitive and agonistic nature of the Western paradigms, these represented a consensual vision of the formal requirements of social order (*hisba*: 'accountability') in accordance with sharia law and the principles of the *baya* (the contractual relationship between ruler and community over social consensus in the context of *hisba*), *maqasid al-sharia* (the innate hermeneutic significance of sharia law), *maslaha* (public interest) and *siyassia shariyya* (political jurisdiction

Movement Theory', *Islamic Activism: A Social Movement Theory Approach*, ed. Quintan Wiktorowicz, Bloomington 2008, p. 8.

13 D. Villa, 'Tocqueville and Civil Society', *Cambridge Companion to De Tocqueville*, ed. C.B. Welch, Cambridge 2006, p. 216.

14 P.G. Stillman, 'Hegel's Civil Society: A Locus of Freedom', *Polity* 12.4, 1980, p. 623.

15 Bob Jessop, 'Gramsci as a Spatial Theorist', *Contemporary Review of International Social and Political Philosophy* 8.4, 2005, pp. 421–37.

16 George Joffé, 'Antiphonal Responses, Social Movements and Networks', *Islamist Radicalisation in North Africa: Politics and Process*, ed. George Joffé, London 2012, pp. 2–3.

17 J. Schwedler, ed., *Toward a Civil Society in the Middle East? A Primer*, Boulder 1995, pp. 9–11, 26 (fn. 2).

in accordance with sharia law).[18] These principles reflected a flexible and pragmatic imperative towards the provision of social justice, and thus an implicit challenge to autocratic rule. They also, of course, reflected the same objectives of civil
society and social movements within the Western paradigm which was to seek to
replace them in the modern era.

Within transition theory, civil society and social movements, in turn, would
acquire an autonomous existence hitherto denied them, within the limits set by
the leadership, through the process of pacting and their similarity to traditional
Islamic constraint on political choice. Both types of institution acted on behalf of,
primarily, the middle classes as the alleged drivers of dissidence because of their
prior political and economic interests in the political and economic system organised by the state and their sense of exclusion from it resulting from their exclusion from the dominant elites within the regime. In many respects, this process
paralleled that described by Daniel Brumberg in his argument over the role of
'liberalised autocracies' in which regimes tolerated autonomous civil societies and
even social movements provided they were subject to close regime supervision,
thus apparently depriving them of autonomous agency, as part of the process of
'authoritarian resilience'.[19] The difference, of course, was that 'pacting' implied
a restoration of agency which would progressively liberate both civil society and
social movements from regime constraint – precisely the opposite objective from
that of liberalised autocracies.

The problems with the 'pacting' approach, however, were manifold. It assumed,
for example, that the pathway towards political transition was unidirectional,
linear, unique and uniformly inevitable, in that democratic governance was the

---

18 Anthony Shadid, *Legacy of the Prophet: Despots, Democrats and the New Politics of
Islam*, Boulder 2001, p. 323; David Warren, 'Doha – the Center of Reform in Islam?
Considering Radical Reform in the Qatar Context: Tariq Ramadan and the Research Center
for Islamic Legislation and Ethics', *Maqasid al-Sharia and Contemporary Reformist Muslim
Thought. An Examination*, ed. Adis Duderija, Basingstoke 2014, pp. 73–99. See also
al-Mawardi, *Ordinances of Government*, trans. Wafaa Wahba, Reading 2000. It should also
be noted that the ideas expressed here are very close to the political thought of Abdelkarim
Soroush, an Iranian political philosopher (Amir Sheikhzadegan, 'The Trajectory of the 1953
Military Coup and the Course of Liberal Islam in Iran', *Beyond the Islamic Revolution:
Perceptions of Modernity and Tradition in Iran before and after 1979*, eds. Amir
Sheikhzaegan and Astrid Meier, Berlin 2017, p. 53) concerning what he calls the
'accidentals' and the 'essentials' of Islamic belief and practice.
19 Daniel Brumberg, 'The Trap of Liberalized Autocracy', *Journal of Democracy* 13.4,
2002, pp. 56–68. For a critical discussion of 'authoritarian resilience', see Michelle Pace and
Francesco Cavatorta, 'The Arab Uprisings in Theoretical Perspective: An Introduction',
Mediterranean Politics 17.2, 2012, pp. 127–9.

unavoidable outcome of the transition process. This was not because of its intrinsic superiority as a form of governance – that was, in a sense, irrelevant to the argument – but because it was the lowest common political denominator acceptable to all sides in practice. It would be, in short, the outcome of an iterative and agonistic process of trial and error, of repeated conflict and compromise, based on the assumption that those involved were ultimately 'rational actors', concerned only with pragmatic outcomes. As such, of course, it ignored all components of the democratic process outside the issue of popular choice, thus tolerating the illiberality inherent in authoritarian resilience and the concept of liberalised autocracy, not to speak of the complex interplay of economic interest, elite behaviour and legal constraint.

The problem with this approach was that, by its unicity and its reliance on the 'rational actor' hypothesis, it excluded any consideration of regional, historical and cultural specificities, or of political models which did not correspond – both in structure and in outcomes – to the liberal democratic paradigm. In the Muslim world, and in the Arab world in particular, such alternative theoretical models did exist, and offered an increasingly potent challenge to the universalist democratic alternative. In fact, within traditional Muslim and Arab societies, the idea of political participation had long been established, even if articulated in terms very different from the universalist democratic alternative.[20] Although the initial, formally secular version – the holistic and unitarian vision of Arab nationalism, whether in its Baathist or Nasirist variants – was soon to fade away, despite its persistence as a theoretical legitimisation of autocracy in Syria and Iraq, its successor has not done so. Political Islam continues to offer a powerful challenge to democratic universalism as a cultural and regional alternative to it.

In essence, however, both were essentially specifically cultural in nature, despite their claims to universalism – one (secular and Islamic holism: Arab nationalism and political Islam) overtly so, and the other (democracy) by implication. Yet it was not clear, initially at least, that these two competing visions could be elided, the one into the other, thus resolving the apparent theoretical contradiction between them. After all, political transition dominated by a political Islamic perspective would have a very different mode of legitimisation and purpose from its liberal democratic parallel. Holism does not recognise the agonistic principles innate to the democratic alternative,[21] nor does it formally tolerate pragmatic

---

20 George Joffé, 'Traditions of Governance in North Africa', *The Journal of North African Studies* 20.5, 2015, pp. 722–34.
21 Chantal Mouffe, *Deliberative Democracy or Agonistic Pluralism*, Vienna 2000.

compromise. Its concept of 'good governance' is based on what it regards as the immutable practices of consultation and consensus in order to preserve social order within a community committed to Islamic principle, in which sovereign authority is an aspect of divinity, not of popular consent. Nor is this a second-best pragmatic outcome of iterative and antiphonal clashes of political authority; it is, rather, a moral obligation. In short, it is what Waterbury has described as 'mission-oriented', and thus apparently not open to compromise over its ultimate objectives.[22] We shall see below, however, the degree to which this absolutist vision has stood the test of time and experience.

Furthermore, such overtly cultural models of the political process could also influence the ways in which concepts such as 'civil society' and 'social movements', as gate-keepers of political liberalisation, might be articulated and understood. Firstly, although the components and structures of civil society may remain unchanged from those enunciated above, the purpose to which they were ideally directed would now be the maintenance of an apparently invariant and immutable Islamic social order. Rather than preserving pluralist class and elite interests against overweening political authority, civil society's duty would be to ensure consensually-established and religiously-authenticated social justice against morally deficient political authority. The same would also be true of the political frames adopted by the social movements mobilised to articulate and support these generalised objectives, as they sought to contest the policies and discourse of dominant regimes militating against them or seeking to undermine progress towards political liberalisation.[23]

There is, however, a fundamental problem with this analysis. If 'mission-oriented' concepts are as absolutist as it suggests, why should societies contesting the political narrative of a dominant state, whether as social movements or through the institutions of civil society, seek to compromise by 'pacting' with it at all? Surely, in such circumstances, the only appropriate response would be to challenge and, if possible, eliminate it? If that is not a viable alternative, then the absolutism of the 'mission-oriented' approach has to be compromised, and part of any response

---

22 John Waterbury, 'Democracy without Democrats?', *Democracy without Democrats? The Renewal of Politics in the Muslim World*, ed. Ghassam Salamé, London 1994, p. 39.
23 Wiktorowicz, 'Islamic Activism', p. 8. 'We can think of the way social movements make meanings through three broad mechanisms. They frame contentious politics by creating an interpretative scheme of the outside world for their followers. They construct collective identities, which includes setting boundaries between "us" and "them". They reflect, capture and shape emotions.' (Rory McCarthy, *Inside Tunisia's Al-Nahda: Between Politics and Meaning*, Cambridge 2018, pp. 157–58.)

to such a conundrum is bound to reproduce the drivers of classic transition theory. If neither side has the power to enforce its objectives, then compromise, however reluctantly endorsed, is the inevitable outcome. However, normative objectives do not necessarily reflect the real drivers of processes which may require such compromises for the actual interests of the groups concerned to be preserved. In short, the drivers for 'pacting' in these circumstances are not so different from those described within the classical view of political transition. The question then is, 'How can those objectives best be expressed in mission-oriented political systems, if liberal democracy is not ultimately a viable or pragmatic response to the difficulty of guaranteeing the essential interests of each side?'

Survival Strategies

The response to this also seems to lie in the fact that few of the regimes in the Arab world have proved to be as unwilling to accommodate to political demand as they are conventionally seen to have been. In the contemporary world, they have become semi-authoritarian and liberalised autocracies, rather than preserving themselves as full autocracies governed solely by holistic definitions of their political status. Before 2011, this had been true of North Africa, for instance, except for Libya, whilst in the Middle East, it had certainly been the case with Jordan and Lebanon. At the same time, their opponents within the state have demonstrated much greater flexibility in the ways in which their normative demands and their contestation of the narrative of the state are expressed and, in practice, compensated. Indeed, it has been this double-sided bargain that has permitted the so-called 'Arab exception' to survive, for it has really been an exception only by degree, not in kind. Three strategies for avoiding political liberalisation seem to have evolved, which had survived up to the challenge offered to them in 2011 and which will help to elucidate the outcomes that emerged in the wake of the events of that year: neo-patrimonialism,[24] liberalised autocracy and full autocracy.

---

24 This has been defined by Christopher Clapham, drawing on Weber's concepts of patrimonial and legal-rational authority as, 'a form of organization in which relationships of a broadly patrimonial type pervade a political and administrative system which is formally constructed on rational-legal lines. Officials hold positions in bureaucratic organizations with powers which are formally defined, but exercise those powers ... as a form of private property...' (Christopher Clapham, *Third World Politics: An Introduction*, London 1985, p. 48), where 'patrimonialism' is defined by Richard Pipes as a personalised regime '... where rights of sovereignty and rights of ownership blend to the point of being indistinguishable ...' (Richard Pipes, *Russia under the Old Regime*, Harmondsworth 1995, p. 22). It is to be contrasted with the concept of the state as a disinterested provider of goods

The neo-patrimonial option is, perhaps, the oldest means by which regimes in the Middle East and North Africa have sought to compound with potential opposition, rather than through simple repression of political dissidence. It is a mechanism typically adopted by the Arab Gulf states and, in that context, obviates the need for any kind of formal 'pacting' between government and opposition. It has the advantage that it reflects much older, instinctive practices over social management and incorporates principles of identity and linked social relationships that have provided long-term social and political stability in traditional society. In its most extreme form, neo-patrimonialism consists of an unspoken and informal bargain whereby political loyalty is purchased through the provision of economic services, employment or income in what has become known as an 'authoritarian bargain'.[25] It is thus generally only available to states, such as those in the Gulf, with significant rent flows available to them (usually from hydrocarbons); primarily states which, furthermore, are 'low capital absorbers', in that they have relatively small populations so that significant fluctuations in such revenue flows, given the volatility of the global oil and gas markets, do not adversely affect economic benefit.

States with large populations, as 'high capital absorbers', usually cannot rely on such economic bargains alone to ensure political quiescence, on account of market volatility. They must instead mobilise other techniques to ensure political peace, typically personalised concepts of patronage and clientage whereby individuals, in return for access to a patron's influence over the exploitation of the services of the state, offer loyalty in return. Such a relationship is, however, inherently corrupt, because it advantages those with access to it. It thus contributes to the delegitimisation of the state, rather than the reinforcement of its authority, because it is the patron, rather than the state, which is seen as the primary source of beneficial access. It is, therefore, with the patron, not the state, that ties of loyalty are reinforced, although the patron treats the state itself as a prebend.[26]

---

and services to its citizens on a basis of equality of treatment under a codified constitutional and legal system – an idealised liberal vision.

25 Raj Desai, Anders Olofsgard and Tarik Yousef, 'The Logic of Authoritarian Bargains', *Economics and Politics* 21.1, 2009, pp. 93–125.

26 'According to the theory of prebendalism, state offices are regarded as prebends that can be appropriated by officeholders, who use them to generate material benefits for themselves and their constituents and kin groups …' (Richard Joseph, 'Nigeria: Inside the Dismal Tunnel', *Current History* 95, 1996, pp. 193–200.) where traditionally the clergy were entitled to appropriate for personal use portions of tithes and benefits paid to the church itself. See also Richard Joseph, *Democracy and Prebendal Politics in Nigeria: The Rise and Fall of the Second Republic*, Cambridge 1987, pp. 56–57.

The official response tends to be for the regime leadership to identity groups, classes and elites which have sufficient political influence and special interests to encourage the creation of political pacts – not as part of an iterative process leading to the adoption of democratic governance to ensure state stability, but as a means of avoiding such an outcome by creating elites committed to the ruling group through its coincidence of common interest and differential access to the resources of the state.

However, this is hardly a viable long-term solution to the problem of regime security, especially as corrupt politico-economic systems easily create socially unstable outcomes, especially if they generate disaffection amongst the groups and elites to whom concessions have been made to persuade them to accept the existing dispensation of power structures within the state. This proved to be a real concern in Tunisia, where the Ben Ali regime increasingly tolerated (and indeed was part of) the creation of a kleptocracy within the ruling circles of the regime which marginalised entrepreneurial elites competing for the same benefits,[27] ultimately contributing thereby to its own destruction. Neo-patrimonialism, in short, is no lasting solution to the problem of political transition and liberalisation, even if it can mimic the principles of 'pacting' behind universalist theories of transition.

An alternative approach to the problem of delaying political liberalisation is through the creation of the 'liberalised autocracies' mentioned earlier. As pointed out above, Daniel Brumberg suggests that these are semi-authoritarian political systems where a formerly autocratic government concedes political space to elements of civil society or social movements provided they, in return, do not fundamentally challenge the legitimacy of its authority. Brumberg argued that, from the 1980s to the 2000s, there had been a transition away from authoritarianism and then back again in the Middle East and North Africa, based on such tactical political openings designed to sustain, rather than transform, autocracies there. This development was initially mistaken by opposition actors in the region and by external powers as an inherently unstable equilibrium which would have to lead to competitive democracy. In fact, the liberalised autocracies that were thereby created, unlike full autocracies that made no concession to political sensitivities, were far more durable than had been imagined. In fact, the combination of guided pluralism, controlled elections and selective repression was '[not] just a survival

27 Alexander Cooley, John Heathershaw and J.C. Sharman, 'The Rise of Kleptocracy: Laundering Cash, Whitewashing Reputations', *Journal of Democracy* 29.1, 2018, pp. 39–53.

strategy by authoritarian regimes but a type of political system whose institutions, rule and logic defy any linear model of democratization'.[28]

In effect, this response to demands for political liberalisation and participation created a parallel to the economic outcomes of neo-patrimonialism, in that civil society, as expressed through its associated social movements, acquired limited, albeit real, benefits in return for its acquiescence in the legitimisation of the authority of the regime and its leadership. In so doing, it supported an apparent long-term stability in return for benefits that became, over time because of the restrictions upon them, largely illusory. Of course, regimes can seek to bolster such stability by laying claim to shared identities, of both ideology and history, with their potential opponents, as happens with the mission-oriented oppositions mentioned above,[29] Morocco being an example of a successful attempt to do this through its appeal to the traditional ideology of the state as a caliphate,[30] and Algeria another, through the maintenance of an illusion of democratic governance as a *démocratie de façade*.[31] Such techniques, however, shade into the third variant of holding political liberalisation at bay: the maintenance of a so-called full autocracy.

Full autocracies remained a strategy to obviate the need for political liberalisation because, since the beginning of the so-called 'third wave of democratisation' in the late 1980s, the 'full autocracies' of the Middle East and North Africa – Saudi Arabia, Syria and Libya, in particular – did indeed seek to make concessions so as to defuse potential opposition by means other than outright repression, provided that the political integrity of their regimes would not be challenged, with popular awareness of outright repression remaining the ultimate backstop if all else failed. Political pacts were not involved, however, as the concessions were usually made in response to international pressure rather than to domestic challenge. In such circumstances, however, both civil society and its associated social movements, in so far as they existed, could be and were ignored as partners in regime adjustment, but – and this, perhaps, marked a distinct change from the past – they were not necessarily subject to deliberate and active repression. Thus, in Saudi Arabia, for example, the committee for legitimate rights survived the regime's displeasure at its opposition to the presence of non-Muslim forces in the Kingdom after 1990

---

28 Brumberg, 'The Trap', p. 56.

29 Waterbury, 'Democracy without Democrats?', p. 39.

30 Richard Pennell, 'What is the Significance of the Title "Amīr al-muminīn?"', *The Journal of North African Studies* 21.1, 2016, p. 640.

31 George Joffé, 'Have Algerians Seized Back the Initiative?', *The Journal of North African Studies* 24.3, 2019, p. 350.

to such an extent that, first, American forces moved from eastern Saudi Arabia to the King Khalid military city and then, in 2003, to Qatar. In Syria, the advent of the Damascus Spring did not immediately provoke a reaction comparable to the ferocious response of the Hafez al-Assad regime to the Hama uprising in 1982. And, in Libya, the regime's responses to protest in Cyrenaica at the beginning of the twenty-first century were remarkably timid and, indeed, contributed to the restoration of a skeletal civil society by the end of the decade.[32]

Outcomes

However, these minimal responses to popular pressure sufficed to delay political transitions in the Arab world until the end of the first decade of the twenty-first century, and thus contributed to the illusion of 'Arab exceptionalism'. Yet even if theoretical responses to analyses of political transition there failed to identify the role of universalist approaches in obscuring what was really taking place, the events at the end of 2010 and their sequelae the following year threw these practical and theoretical challenges into sharp relief. The pattern of events is by now well known, but their evolution raises questions over their timing, causes and failure, even in the case of Tunisia. Furthermore, what do these events tell us about the process of political transition and liberation and of the role of civil society and social movements within them?

Timing

The first issue is why the events of 2010–2011 occurred when they did. There is little doubt about the timing and the general cause of the events of 2011: they were primarily the result of profound economic frustration felt throughout the region in the aftermath of the 2008 global financial crisis. The crisis itself took some time to affect developing regions such as the Middle East and North Africa, despite its immediate effects on Western states as early as 2007, for they had benefited from the redirection of Gulf investment to the region. Thus net direct private foreign investment had dramatically increased from $6,531 billion in 2000 to $47,096 billion five years later, and remained at similar levels up to 2010 ($48,007 billion) until dropping away to as little as $5,260 billion in 2015.[33] Since all Middle East

---

32 Joffé, 'Civil Resistance'.
33 The fall was quite dramatic, from inflows of $126,454 billion in 2007 compared to only $12,186 billion seven years earlier or $37 billion seven years later. (IBRD (International

and North African states are to a greater or lesser extent rent dependent and, with the exception of the Gulf states, high capital absorbers, their abilities to resist such financial volatility was very limited.

This shock compounded other, more secular effects that indicated that, whatever macro-economic indicators suggested, the micro-economic reality had been one of stasis and decline for many years. The general view had been that neoliberal globalisation reforms – the so-called Washington Consensus – promoted by the major international financial institutions, such as the World Bank and the IMF, and their supporters in the developed world, such as the United States and the European Union, had belatedly benefited the region. Quite apart from theoretical and methodological considerations connected with concepts of neoliberal development, such views ignored some key realities that profoundly conditioned the economic environment in which the vast majority of the region's population lived. Demographic growth was one obvious indicator: between 2000 and 2015, the populations of the Middle Eastern and North African region rose by 128 million to a total of 426 million, at an annual rate of 4.25%, but GDP growth declined from 4.9% to 2.4% over the same period, particularly after 2007.

The consequences were clear; thus, by 2010, in Egypt, for example, the proportion of the population in extreme poverty had reached 3.8%, with a further 19.6% being rated as 'poor', with an income of less than $2 per day, although only 8% were unemployed. The country's GINI coefficient was static at 0.32, with the top 10% of the population controlling 27% of the nation's wealth. In Tunisia – regarded by the European Union at the time as a 'model' of economic development – 7.4% were rated as poverty-stricken, with unemployment running at 14% in 2007. Tunisia's GINI coefficient had declined slightly from 0.417 in 1995 to 0.4 in 2005, but the top 10% of the population controlled 31.5% of national wealth.[34] Much of this wealth, furthermore, was reflected in both countries by the habits of 'conspicuous consumption' by the newly empowered middle classes. This was rendered even more intolerable, especially in Tunisia, by the kleptocratic behaviour of the ruling elites close to the presidential family, which powerfully inflamed resentment amongst those elites who were not included, not to speak of massive popular resentment as well. And, quite apart from the resentment caused by these factors, there was also the popular irritation caused by constant Western rhetorical

Bank for Reconstruction and Development) 2019, 'MENA, direct private investment flows net', https://data.worldbank.org/indicator/BX.KLT.DINV.CD.WD?locations=ZQ.)
34 George Joffé, 'The Arab Spring in North Africa: Origins and Prospects', *The Journal of North African Studies* 16.1, 2011, p. 509.

admonition over human rights, undermined by Western preferences for regional regimes that ensured political stability instead.

There was thus an economic and social environment within the region that would prove to be propitious for a parallel political challenge, were it to be appropriately stimulated. This, in combination with some quite specific developments in the international sphere, was to provide the concatenation of circumstances that were to mature into the region-wide Awakening movement in 2010. The specific circumstances were also economic in nature and were twofold, involving energy and food prices, which rose during 2010 to quite unprecedented heights, with international oil prices reaching $91 per barrel in December 2010 and $109 per barrel three months later. As far as food prices were concerned, the United Nations Food and Agriculture Organisation in Rome noted dramatic rises in global cereal prices from July 2010 onwards and it reported that, by January 2011, its global food price index had risen to 230 from its base in 1990 when it had begun to index them. This was the highest level the index had ever reached, it noted.[35]

Given the ongoing rapid growth of regional populations, despite a notable decline in birth rates from 1990 onwards,[36] North African and Middle Eastern states had become import dependent in terms of food supply and, outside oil-and-gas producers, the energy their populations increasingly require. They were, furthermore, relatively inelastic in their demand for such imports and their populations were therefore very sensitive to price increases. The result has generally been major bouts of unrest whenever world prices suddenly increase or when economic reform forces up domestic prices instead. This was, after all, a major cause for massive demonstrations in Tunisia and Morocco in 1984, in Algeria in 1988, as a precursor to the Algerian civil war four years later, and in Morocco in late 1990. Not surprisingly, then, the economic situation at the end of 2010 had preconditioned North Africa and, indeed, the wider Arab region for protest as economic conditions suddenly and markedly worsened. However, only in Algeria were economic circumstances the primary cause and objective of the protests that erupted in December 2010. Elsewhere, quite different drivers appear to have provoked the protests that ended in attempts at regime change. Nevertheless, the generalised economic circumstances in which the region found itself certainly seem to have set the scene for what was to follow and thus provide an

---

35 FAO (United Nations Food and Agriculture Organisation) 2011, www.fao.org/news/story/en/item/50519/icode.
36 These declined from 7 per person in 1960 to 5 in 1990 and to 3 in 2000 – the level at which they have remained since (IBRD 2019, 'MENA').

explanation as to why the general movement for political change occurred when it did.

Actors

The second consideration regards who was responsible for carrying through the social revolutions that occurred. The subsequent demonstrations that set the scene for the Awakening movement did not follow some general plan, however. Instead, each national experience was unique, in terms both of the actual pattern of events and of the socio-political characteristics that informed them, suggesting that, even if the timing of such events could be explained in universalist terms, their actual evolution cannot. Furthermore, with the possible exception of Egypt, the role of political Islam as a cultural 'mission-oriented' driver of political transition seems to have been irrelevant to the actual process of transition itself, even if society throughout the region had been an Islamic socio-cultural domain, steeped in Islamic political archetypes and social practices. Political Islam may well have played a leading role subsequently in the organisation of a new system of political order in 2011 and 2012, but it did not play a determining role in creating the conditions upon which that could be constructed. Thus, although history, cultural conditioning and social structure were certainly key factors in the transition process, the actual roles they may have played in the way in which that process occurred seem to have been unique in each country where it did take place. The same was to prove to be true of the subsequent histories of the countries concerned.

Thus, in Morocco – the last of the North African states in which the Awakening took place – the Royal Palace (Makhzen) exploited its innate traditional legitimacy, derived from its religious status, to neutralise the demands of demonstrators for political change and to minimise the concessions it finally made through a pact it effectively imposed because its opponents lacked effective organised popular support to enforce their demands.[37] The concessions that it made were marginal, because none touched on the real issue of how the monarchy itself was to be constitutionalised or constrained into reigning – presiding over a constitutional system and, thereby guaranteeing its sovereign legitimacy – rather than ruling – directing and controlling the way in which the system operated. It thereby ensured that it alone, as the sovereign embodiment of the political system, should continue to determine what its legitimate actions should be. It was a discourse which Morocco's social movements and political parties either acquiesced in or would

---

37 Maghraoui, 'Constitutional Reforms', pp. 679–99.

not effectively challenge. Nor did it challenge the country's civil society, which thus kept its distance from formal and informal politics.[38]

In Algeria, on the other hand, the government was able to defuse popular tensions by its adroit consumer subsidy policy of reducing the prices of essential foodstuffs.[39] It was, no doubt, aided by popular memories of the horrors of the recent civil war, which made concerted contestation of government policy with the attendant dangers of resuscitating the conflict difficult, if not impossible, to contemplate. There was thus little popular demand to challenge the regime elite politically, despite widespread scepticism over Algeria's 'facade democracy' and the pact that its regime had made in 1988, before the outbreak of the civil war, itself one of the drivers of the subsequent conflict. That was to be delayed for a further eight years, only erupting into the domestic political arena in early 2019.[40]

Both countries, furthermore, had been 'liberalised autocracies' for more than a decade, in which actors in civil society had had recognised roles. This had been the case since 1988 in Algeria, despite the horrific interlude of the civil war between 1992 and 2000 and the frequent abuse by the army-backed regime of the pacting that had originally accompanied the liberalisation process. In Morocco this had been the case since 1996, given the constitutional changes introduced by the monarchy in that year. As a result, for largely historical reasons, social movements able to contest the hegemonic narrative of the dominant political elites in the regimes of either country were not capable of acquiring sufficient popular purchase to challenge elite control, nor could they embed themselves effectively within civil society to do so. There were cultural factors at play as well, not least the innate conservatism of society in both Morocco and Algeria, provided that corruption was not too severe a social burden. This was compounded by the fact that society in both was innately conditioned by historic precept towards a concept of social order imbued with an Islamic tradition, although not explicitly Islamic

---

38 Thus the PJD (Parti de la Justice et du Développement), a formal political party then in government, acquiesced, whereas Al-Adl wal-Ihssan (a social movement, not a formal political party, and outside government) lacked the support base to contest the Makhzen's narrative. See A. Benchemsi, 'Feb 20's Rise and Fall – a Moroccan Story', http://ahmedbenchemsi.com/feb20s-rise-and-fall-a-moroccan-story, reproduced as Ahmed Benchemsi, 'Morocco's Makhzen and the Haphazard Activists', *Taking to the Streets: Activism, Arab Uprisings and Democratization*, eds. Lina Khatib and Ellen Lust, Baltimore 2014, pp. 199–235.

39 John Entelis, 'Algeria: Democracy Denied, and Revived?', *The Journal of North African Studies* 16.1, 2011, 673–6.

40 Joffé, 'Have Algerians', pp. 349–55.

in expression. Thus considerations of consultation, consensus and social justice, rather than explicit principles of Western libertarianism or Islamic concepts of unicity and submission, reduced the appeal of political Islam.

Libya, however, was to be another matter. Unlike Morocco and Algeria, it had remained an absolute autocracy, in which, in theory, no compromise could be made with civil society. Indeed, formally at least, there were no institutions outside the compass of the state that could form a civil society. Nor, in fact, was there any structure that could approximate to a state in any of the commonly accepted definitions of what such an entity would be.[41] The Libyan reality was supposedly the 'stateless state' – which in its self-perception was a perfect democracy, but which became a perfect autocracy instead, dominated by a small clique around the personality of Colonel Gaddafi himself which tolerated no sharing of power with any other entity or institution.[42] Yet, quite apart from the inherent fragility of such a system, the Gaddafi regime was and knew itself to be weak, particularly in Cyrenaica, so that when it was challenged there by three separate political crises during the first decade of the twenty-first century, the collapse of the state was ineluctable. There were, however, no institutions available to replace it, either from civil society or through social movements. The result has been the fragmentation and chaos that characterise Libya today, in which multiple power centres now exist, each contesting the other for recovery of the state itself.[43]

The experiences of Egypt and Tunisia, meanwhile, were to be very different from those of the other three states in the Maghrib, for reasons that reflect directly on the inner dynamics of political transition and on the actual complexity of the process. Although both states were liberalised autocracies, the natures of their social movements and their civil societies were profoundly different, both from each other and from the states that surrounded them; hence the very different outcomes that each state experienced. Indeed, in both cases, the social movements involved elites that were very different in nature: in Tunisia corporatist and economic, whereas in Egypt they were essentially political and autocratic. It

---

41 Either in its Weberian or its Hegelian variant, as Hegel's 'actuality of the ethical idea' (Georg Wilhelm Friedrich Hegel, *The Philosophy of Right*, trans. T.M. Knox, Cambridge 1991, p. 257), or Weber's 'A state is a human community that (successfully) claims the monopoly of the legitimate use of physical force within a given territory' (Max Weber, 'Politics as a Vocation: Lecture to the Free Students Society at Munich University, January 1919', *From Max Weber: Essays in Sociology*, eds. Hans Gerth and C. Wright Mills, Oxford 1946, p. 77).
42 Alia Brahimi, 'Libya's Revolution', *The Journal of North African Studies* 16.4, 2011, p. 619.
43 Joffé, 'Civil Resistance', pp. 116–40.

is important to note at the outset that in neither state was the transitional process 'revolutionary' with respect to normal definitions of the term.[44] They did not involve the transformation of the basic structures of society alongside political change. Instead, they were what Goldstone has called 'colour revolutions',[45] in imitation of the political transformations that had occurred in Eastern Europe after the 1980s and had involved, with greater or lesser success, a pacting process whereby ruling elites had preserved their political control by being prepared to make concessions (if only temporarily) to other interest groups within their societies.

Process

The final question, then, is why, in the cases of Tunisia and Egypt, the outcomes were so different. In the former, after all, the pacting process has resulted, as transition theory predicts, in relative success, whilst in the latter it has not. The answer appears to lie in the differing natures of civil society and the social movements that were able to act as interlocutors between the demonstrators, seeking political change, and their ruling elites, determined to protect their power and privileges. This, however, requires some knowledge of the actual process by which transition can occur and of the ways in which reactive demonstrations against ruling elites and their policies are transformed into political projects that can be mobilised to contest the dominant narratives of those elites. In effect, such transformational processes need, in turn, a 'potentiating' event that allows the often inchoate discourse of the demonstrators to be focused upon a coherent discourse of contestation voiced by a social movement that the demonstrators can endorse. They also need coherent structures – leaderships, in short – in order to engage with, contest or confront the elites that potentially oppose them.

In the Tunisian case, such an event occurred through the self-immolation of Mohamed Bouazzizi in Sidi Bouzid on 17 December 2010. It was an event that

---

44 'Social revolutions are rapid, basic transformations of a society's state and class structures and they are accompanied and in part carried through by class-based revolts from below' (Theda Skocpol, *States and Social Revolutions: A Comparative Analysis of France, Russia and China*, Cambridge 1979, p. 4). An alternative definition could be '... an effort to transform the political institutions and the justifications for political authority in a society, accompanied by formal or informal mass mobilization and non-institutionalized actions that undermine existing authorities' (Jack Goldstone, 'Toward a Fourth Generation of Revolutionary Theory', *Annual Review of Political Science* 4, 2001, p. 150).
45 Jack Goldstone, 'Rethinking Revolutions: Integrating Origins, Process and Outcomes', *Comparative Studies of South Asia, Africa and the Middle East* 29.1, 2009, p. 31.

symbolised and focused the disparate anti-regime sentiments of the demonstrators on their antipathy towards the Ben Ali regime. This allowed social movements in Tunisia to articulate their project of removing the regime from power. Given the fact that Tunisia had long been a liberalised autocracy, in which autonomous power centres had either been intimidated or co-opted, the widespread demonstrations soon found vehicles to articulate a coherent narrative of grievance and to engage with the key elites inside Tunisia's hegemonic political party, the Rassemblement Constitutionnel Démocratique (RCD), over the ways in which political power was to be expressed in future.[46] Three such movements existed, each of which had created a discursive frame that reinforced the others.

Mabrouk has argued that one of these, which was less cohesive than the others but very widely represented in Tunisian society, was composed of rural elites: the rural notability that formed the rural backbone of Tunisia's hegemonic political movement, the RCD. That elite had originally supported Ben Youssef against Habib Bourguiba at the start of Tunisian independence, and had later sympathised with the major Islamist movement in Tunisia, Ennahdha, until this was suppressed by the Ben Ali regime. Its marginalisation in 1990 and 1992 had also marginalised, and thus alienated, the rural elite to advantage the regime's own kleptocratic interests. Another movement, Mabrouk suggests, was formed by the legal community which had long disliked the immorality of the regime and some of whose members had spoken out against its innate criminality. A less highly organised movement of journalists supported this position. The third movement was made up of local officials of the venerable trade union movement, the Union Générale des Travailleurs Tunisiens (the UGTT) which, since the colonial period, had had an existence autonomous from the national liberation movement, the néo-Destour, and which, since January 1978, had resisted regime attempts to take it over.

There were others, too, such as Tunisia's long-standing human rights bodies, but they did not have the populist reach of these three movements or their hegemonic control of the generalised discourse of contestation with the state. Tunisia, too, was to benefit from an early decision made by the Bourguiba regime in the 1960s, namely to ensure that Tunisia's military would be denied political ambition and would be kept under central, civilian control. This is indeed what occurred, and it was the Presidential Guard that facilitated President Ben Ali's departure

---

46 Mehdi Mabrouk, 'A Revolution for Dignity and Freedom: Preliminary Observations on the Social and Cultural Background to the Tunisian Revolution', *The Journal of North African Studies* 16.4, 2011, pp. 631–2.

from Tunisia on 17 January 2011.[47] The UGTT, lawyers, journalists and human rights activists, as representatives of social movements sanctioned by civil society, had been able to transform protest and public disgust at the regime engendered by its understanding of what had happened to Mohamed Bouazzizi into a political project to eliminate the regime and to order demonstrations to this end. In this movement, however, Ennahdha, largely excluded from the country by the repression of the previous 20 years, played little active part, even though Tunisian society had become notably more religiously observant at the start of the twenty-first century, partly in response to the behaviour of the regime.[48] The role of Ennahdha, however, was to change dramatically thereafter.

Events in Egypt were to unfurl in a similar way, although the eventual outcome was to be very different. Egypt had been, in effect, a liberalised autocracy since the end of the Nasserist era in 1970, primarily to accommodate the socio-political ambitions of the Muslim Brotherhood (al-Ikhwan al-Muslimun), although its role within the state had regularly fluctuated in rhythm with the ruling elite's perceptions, under President Anwar Sadat and his successor Hosni Mubarak, of the threat it might offer to its own control of the state. That elite, in turn, was essentially military and, after the privatisation of the economy began with the advent of the lengthy Mubarak era in 1981, became entwined as well with a new entrepreneurial economic elite. Interestingly enough, however, despite their apparently agonistic relationship, the Brotherhood, as a social movement, and the military-economic elite in charge of the state implicitly shared common interests, values and objectives, even if their political ambitions and discourses were to differ. An implicit, unstable pact which was repeatedly broken and then reforged was effectively to govern their relations thereafter.[49]

By the end of the 1990s, however, as more radical Islamists began to challenge both the Brotherhood's position and that of the ruling elite, other groups began to articulate their own senses of exclusion and to challenge the dominant discourse of the Egyptian state. Two groups, in particular, created social movements critical of the ruling elite around the Mubarak presidency: workers in the Delta, in the form of unofficial trade unions, and the secular intelligentsia in Cairo, through movements of socio-political protest such as 'Kifaya' and the 'Ghad' movement.

---

47 Noureddine Jebnoun, 'In the Shadow of Power: Civil–Military Relations and the Tunisian Popular Uprising', *The Journal of North African Studies* 19.1, 2014, pp. 296–316.
48 McCarthy, *Inside Tunisia's Al-Nahda*, p. 105; Anne Wolf, *Political Islam in Tunisia: The History of Ennahda*, London 2017, p. 130.
49 Anne Alexander, 'Brothers in Arms? The Egyptian Military, the *Ikhwan* and the Revolutions of 1952 and 2011', *The Journal of North African Studies* 16.4, 2011, pp. 547–8.

By the end of the first decade of the twenty-first century, these were joined by a
burgeoning youth movement (the 'Remember Khaled Mohamed Saeed Movement'), united through its increasing use of social media, and by individual,
younger elements of the Brotherhood who rejected the idea of an implicit com-
monality of purpose between itself and the ruling elite.[50]

By the start of 2011, therefore, a coalition of secular intelligentsia and working-
class social movements, backed up by elements of Egypt's youth and moderate
Islamists, had emerged, energised by both the consequences of the global financial
crisis and the example of populist success in Tunisia with the removal of the Ben
Ali regime there. That coalition found sufficient common ground to produce a
coherent narrative that could effectively challenge that of the state itself, once
the appropriate moment had arrived, as it soon did. The coalition, too, had found
a symbolic leader in the person of Mohammed el-Baradai, the former director
of the International Atomic Energy Authority (IAEA) who had just retired. The
'potentiating event' was to prove to be a demonstration in Tahrir Square in the
centre of Cairo, organised on National Police Day, 25 January 2011, where the
demonstrators held their own against police repression.[51] Three days later, after
Friday prayers and with the tacit encouragement of dissident members of the
Muslim Brotherhood, vast crowds of demonstrators filled the square, thus gaining
the momentum that was eventually to sweep the Mubarak regime from power two
weeks later.

Both the above examples of political transition suggest that, in reality, the transition process is far more complex than the basic theory suggests, whether it is
based on a universalist pragmatic model of pacting or on the culturalist model of
'mission orientation'. Timing, process and the actors involved also play a crucial
part, and the attribution to 'mission' of intransigence, which is said to interfere
with the pragmatism associated with pacting, may well be misplaced. In both
cases, the social movements that would have voiced such opposition were either
in part co-opted or had been excluded from the process itself, as was the case
elsewhere in North Africa and, indeed, in the Middle East as well. Furthermore,
both cases illustrate the primordial importance of social movements in controlling a narrative which contests the formally dominant alternative, put forward by
states and their ruling elites once it has been released into the popular imaginary
by some kind of potentiating event. And, of course, civil society provides the

---

50 Joffé, 'The Arab Spring', pp. 520–1.
51 This commemorates the deaths of 50 Egyptian policemen at the hands of British
occupation forces in Ismailiyya in the Canal Zone in 1952.

background and the sub-stratum upon which social movements can construct the legitimacy they need amongst the public at large to play their crucial central role in guiding the transition process itself.

The Aftermath

If civil society and social movements were indeed the essential catalysts of the transition processes in Egypt and Tunisia, it seems appropriate to pose the question as to why transition ultimately failed in Egypt but appears to have been successful in Tunisia. The nature of the pacting process involved may be part of the answer, in that, in Tunisia, the elite compromised with social movements contesting its discourse, whereas in Egypt, the Muslim Brotherhood never appreciated that it should have embraced the wider concerns of the population and avoided antagonising the army command. However, it is proposed here that the answer is really related to the phenomenon, discussed above, of 'mission orientation'. Originally, it was suggested that transitions in which social movements were mission-oriented were characterised by the unwillingness of such movements to compromise on their objectives for the sake of engaging in pragmatic pacting which would eventually lead to a liberalising process. Failure, then, was a consequence of moral rigidity and principle. However, neither Ennahdha nor the Muslim Brotherhood demonstrated such rigidity of purpose and, interestingly enough, both were effectively excluded from the construction of the coalitions that were actually engaged in the transitions that did occur.

That is not to say, however, that neither movement played an essential role in conditioning the intellectual and political environment in which social movements were eventually constructed inside the limited spheres allocated to autonomous political organisations within liberalised autocracies. Both did; the Muslim Brotherhood from 1970 onwards in Egypt, and Ennahdha since the 1980s in Tunisia until it was suppressed a decade later.[52] There is no doubt that both movements, as social movements, had been successful in achieving this before revolution occurred in 2011, for the societies in both countries became markedly more observant during the period in which they were active, no doubt from conviction, but also as a statement of overt opposition to the ruling elites in both countries. Each was thus legitimised within the context of civil society. However, in the construction of the social movement coalitions in both countries which actually contributed towards the transition process, neither had a direct role to play. In Tunisia,

---

52 Wolf, *Political Islam*, pp. 11–76.

the ongoing exclusion of Ennahdha as a discrete organisation from society at large, and in Egypt the unwillingness of the Brotherhood's leadership to become engaged with the emerging social movements, ensured that that would be the case.

Nevertheless, once the transition was completed, the way both movements responded affected the way the process evolved in each country. Ennahdha, after its lengthy exile in Britain and France, with its base in Tunisia imprisoned and marginalised, adopted a strategy of democratic participation and was prepared for the principle of electoral success or failure within a constitutional framework. In economic terms, it sought to pact with the indigenous Tunisian elite which had been alienated from the kleptocratic regime elite. This was to prove vital when it returned to Tunisia: it was able to resuscitate its political framework, and to weather the hostility of the fragmented political opposition that emerged as its principal antagonist in the post-coup legislative elections, with significant elite support. It was also able to compromise on its political dominance in 2014 and step down from power to make way for a technocratic government. Since then, it has continued to support the democratic process, thus helping to ensure that political liberalisation and constitutionalism have become entrenched despite the very real problems that Tunisia still faces.[53]

Political structures in Egypt, on the other hand, have been dominated by the country's experience of holistic Arab nationalism and a hegemonic executive presidency ever since 1952. The Muslim Brotherhood, even after it opted as an organisation for peaceful coexistence with government, also operates within the context of hegemonic structures of power. Thus, after the Tahrir Revolution in 2011 and the subsequent presidential and legislative elections, which it won, it instinctively looked towards a similar hegemonic outcome, forgetting its objective interests as a partner with the Egyptian army command. Thus, as early as mid-2012, the SCAF (Supreme Command of the Armed Forces) had determined that the Morsi regime was not an adequate partner in power and was determined to remove it from office. Since the Brotherhood government had managed to

---

53 Tunisia, too, has had a long-established belief in constitutionalism, as the name of its formerly dominant political party makes clear. The country had the first constitution in the Arab world, which was granted by the Bey – admittedly at European insistence – in 1857 and revised in 1861. Even though the constitution was subsequently abrogated by the Bey, in 1864, the fact of its existence has served as a symbol of legitimate governance ever since, appearing in the names of its two national liberation movements (the Destour and the néo-Destour) and then reappearing in the names and the discourse of the two single-party movements that dominated political life until the Ben Ali regime collapsed (Le Parti Socialiste Destourien and the Rassemblement Constitutionnel Démocratique).

antagonise virtually every element of the country's political structures by its absolutist control of political power, it proved very easy for the SCAF to find grounds
for its ultimate isolation and removal from power in mid-2013. In short, it was the
Brotherhood's inexperience in the democratic option that has allowed the army to
take over the totality of power, a hold that it will seek to retain without even the
concession of liberalised autocratic behaviour. Given its success in demonising its
erstwhile partner in power as a movement committed to violence justified by an
aberrant interpretation of Islam, it has also been able to exclude the Brotherhood
from civil society as a legitimate and integral component of the country's historical socio-political institutions.

It seems, therefore, that any meaningful comment on political transition must
also consider its aftermath as an integral part of the transition process itself. It also
seems to be the case that there really is no generalised theoretical guide that would
allow us to predict the outcomes of political transition processes or the principles
upon which they are based. It seems clear, in short, that historical experience plays
a far greater role than the early theorists were prepared to allow, as do cultural
factors, although political Islam in itself, rather than practical political experience,
is probably not as powerful a factor as they may have thought.

Bibliography

Alexander, Anne, 'Brothers in Arms? The Egyptian Military, the *Ikhwan* and the
    Revolutions of 1952 and 2011', *The Journal of North African Studies* 16.4,
    2011, pp. 533–54.

Al-Mawardi, *Ordinances of Government*, trans. Wafaa Wahba, Reading 2000.

Benchemsi, Ahmed, 'Morocco's Makhzen and the Haphazard Activists', *Taking
    to the Streets: Activism, Arab Uprisings and Democratization*, eds. Lina
    Khatib and Ellen Lust, Baltimore 2014, pp. 199–235.

Brahimi, Alia, 'Libya's Revolution', *The Journal of North African Studies* 16.4,
    2011, pp. 605–24.

Brumberg, Daniel, 'Theories of Transition', *The Arab Uprisings Explained*, ed.
    Marc Lynch, New York 2014.

Brumberg, Daniel, 'The Trap of Liberalized Autocracy', *Journal of Democracy*
    13.4, 2002, pp. 56–68.

Butterfield, Herbert, *The Whig Interpretation of History*, London 1931.

Clapham, Christopher, *Third World Politics: An Introduction*, London 1985.

Cooley, Alexander, John Heathershaw and J.C. Sharman, 'The Rise of Kleptocracy: Laundering Cash, Whitewashing Reputations', *Journal of Democracy* 29.1, 2018, pp. 39–53.

Cronon, William, 'Two Cheers for the Whig Interpretation of History', *Perspectives on History*, American Historical Association, 1 September 2012, www.historians.org/publications-and-directories/perspectives-on-history/september-2012-x41643.

Desai, Raj, Anders Olofsgard and Tarik Yousef, 'The Logic of Authoritarian Bargains', *Economics and Politics* 21.1, 2009, pp. 93–125.

Entelis, John, 'Algeria: Democracy Denied, and Revived?', *The Journal of North African Studies* 16.1, 2011, pp. 653–78.

FAO (United Nations Food and Agriculture Organisation) 2011, www.fao.org/news/story/en/item/50519/icode.

Goldstone, Jack, 'Rethinking Revolutions: Integrating Origins, Process and Outcomes', *Comparative Studies of South Asia, Africa and the Middle East* 29.1, 2009, pp. 19–32.

Goldstone, Jack, 'Toward a Fourth Generation of Revolutionary Theory', *Annual Review of Political Science* 4, 2001, pp. 139–87.

Guilhot, Nicolas, 'Portrait of the Realist as a Historian: On Anti-Whiggism in the History of International Relations', *European Journal of International Relations* 21.1, 2015, pp. 3–26.

Hegel, Georg Wilhelm Friedrich, *The Philosophy of Right*, trans. T.M. Knox, Cambridge 1991.

Huntington, Samuel, *The Third Wave: Democratisation in the Late Twentieth Century*, Norman, OK 1991.

IBRD (International Bank for Reconstruction and Development) 2019, 'MENA, direct private investment flows net', https://data.worldbank.org/indicator/BX.KLT.DINV.CD.WD?locations=ZQ.

Jebnoun, Noureddine, 'In the Shadow of Power: Civil–Military Relations and the Tunisian Popular Uprising', *The Journal of North African Studies* 19.1, 2014, pp. 296–316.

Jessop, Bob, 'Gramsci as a Spatial Theorist', *Contemporary Review of International Social and Political Philosophy* 8.4, 2005, pp. 421–37.

Joffé, George, 'Antiphonal Responses, Social Movements and Networks', *Islamist Radicalisation in North Africa: Politics and Process*, ed. George Joffé, London 2012.

Joffé, George, 'The Arab Spring in North Africa: Origins and Prospects', *The Journal of North African Studies* 16.1, 2011, pp. 507–32.

Joffé, George, 'Civil Resistance in Libya during the Arab Spring', *Civil Resistance in the Arab Spring: Triumphs and Disasters*, ed. Adam Roberts et al., Oxford 2016.

Joffé, George, 'Have Algerians Seized Back the Initiative?', *The Journal of North African Studies* 24.3, 2019, pp. 349–55.

Joffé, George, 'Traditions of Governance in North Africa', *The Journal of North African Studies* 20.5, 2015, pp. 722–34.

Joseph, Richard, 'Nigeria: Inside the Dismal Tunnel', *Current History* 95, 1996, pp. 193–200.

Joseph, Richard, *Democracy and Prebendal Politics in Nigeria: The Rise and Fall of the Second Republic*, Cambridge 1987.

Mabrouk, Mehdi, 'A Revolution for Dignity and Freedom: Preliminary Observations on the Social and Cultural Background to the Tunisian Revolution', *The Journal of North African Studies* 16.4, 2011, pp. 625–36.

Maghraoui, Driss, 'Constitutional Reforms in Morocco: Between Consensus and Subaltern Politics', *The Journal of North African Studies* 16.1, 2011, pp. 679–99.

McCarthy, Rory, *Inside Tunisia's Al-Nahda: Between Politics and Meaning*, Cambridge 2018.

Mouffe, Chantal, *Deliberative Democracy or Agonistic Pluralism*, Vienna 2000.

O'Donnell, Guillermo and Philippe Schmitter, *Transitions from Authoritarian Rule: Tentative Conclusions about Uncertain Democracies*, Baltimore 1986.

Pace, Michelle and Francesco Cavatorta, 'The Arab Uprisings in Theoretical Perspective An Introduction', *Mediterranean Politics* 17.2, 2012, pp. 125–38.

Pennell, Richard, 'What is the Significance of the Title "Amīr al-muminīn?"', *The Journal of North African Studies* 21.1, 2016, pp. 623–44.

Pipes, Richard, *Russia under the Old Regime*, Harmondsworth 1995.

Roberts, Hugh, 'The Struggle for Constitutional Rule in Algeria', *Journal of Algerian Studies* 3.1, 1998, pp. 19–30.

Rostow, W.W., *The Stages of Economic Growth: A Non-Communist Manifesto*, Cambridge 1960.

Sachs, Jeffrey, *The End of Poverty: Economic Possibilities for Our Time*, New York 2005.

Schwedler, J., ed., *Toward a Civil Society in the Middle East? A Primer*, Boulder 1995.

Shadid, Anthony, *Legacy of the Prophet: Despots, Democrats and the New Politics of Islam*, Boulder 2001.

Sheikhzadegan, Amir, 'The Trajectory of the 1953 Military Coup and the Course of Liberal Islam in Iran', *Beyond the Islamic Revolution: Perceptions of Modernity and Tradition in Iran before and after 1979*, eds. Amir Sheikhzaegan and Astrid Meier, Berlin 2017.

Skocpol, Theda, *States and Social Revolutions: A Comparative Analysis of France, Russia and China*, Cambridge 1979.

Seliktar, Ofira, *The Politics of Intelligence and American Wars with Iraq*, New York 2008.

Stillman, P.G., 'Hegel's Civil Society: A Locus of Freedom', *Polity* 12.4, 1980, pp. 622–46.

Tarrow, Sidney, *Power in Movement: Social Movements and Contentious Politics*, Cambridge 1998.

Villa D., 'Tocqueville and Civil Society', *Cambridge Companion to De Tocqueville*, ed. C.B. Welch, Cambridge 2006.

Warren, David, 'Doha – the Center of Reform in Islam? Considering Radical Reform in the Qatar Context: Tariq Ramadan and the Research Center for Islamic Legislation and Ethics', *Maqasid al-Sharia and Contemporary Reformist Muslim Thought. An Examination*, ed. Adis Duderija, Basingstoke 2014.

Waterbury, John, 'Democracy without Democrats?', *Democracy without Democrats? The Renewal of Politics in the Muslim World*, ed. Ghassam Salamé, London 1994.

Weber, Max, 'Politics as a Vocation: Lecture to the Free Students Society at Munich University, January 1919', *From Max Weber: Essays in Sociology*, eds. Hans Gerth and C. Wright Mills, Oxford 1946.

Wiktorowicz, Quintan, 'Introduction: Islamic Activism and Social Movement Theory', *Islamic Activism: A Social Movement Theory Approach*, ed. Quintan Wiktorowicz, Bloomington 2008.

Wolf, Anne, *Political Islam in Tunisia: The History of Ennahda*, London 2017.

Zakaria, Fareed, 'The Rise of Illiberal Democracy', *Foreign Affairs* 7.6, 1997, pp. 22–43.

9

Politics: The Mainstream, the Marginal and the Alternative

Sarah Yerkes

The Arab Spring fundamentally altered the relationship between citizens and the state in the Middle East and North Africa. In most cases, with the notable exception of Tunisia, the protests that took place across the MENA region in 2010–2011 did not lead to meaningful democratic reform. However, the success of protesters in ousting Tunisian president Zine el-Abidine Ben Ali and Egyptian president Hosni Mubarak inspired people across the region to believe in the power of protest to bring about change. The idea that the street – not the ballot box – is the most effective modality for change has strengthened the appeal of alternative politics, and the concomitant decline of traditional or formal politics, throughout the Arab world.[1]

Alternative Politics

What is 'alternative politics'?

The term 'alternative politics' refers to non-traditional modes of political participation, from protest to cyber activism to graffiti. Peter Dahlgren describes this phenomenon as 'the process whereby citizens, in various constellations, exercise

---

1 Sarah Yerkes, *Where Have All the Revolutionaries Gone?*, Center for Middle East Policy at Brookings, Washington, DC, March 2017, https://www.brookings.edu/wp-content/uploads/2017/03/cmep_20160317_where_have_revolutionaries_gone.pdf.

Table 1: Trust gap between people and institutions, 2007–2016

Percentage of people who trust the government (cabinet) to a great/medium extent	Algeria	Palestine	Iraq	Jordan	Lebanon	Morocco	Tunisia	Egypt	Yemen
Wave 1 (2007)	42.4	68.0		68.6	30.9	38.9			32.6
Wave 2 (2011)	29.3	51.7	40.6	71.5	22.0		62.2	78.6	29.6
Wave 3 (2013)	69.7	50.7	46.6	64.4	14.0	42.0	38.5	20.3	41.2
Wave 4 (2016)	32.1	31.7		53.6	8.4	43.3	33.4	64.8	

Percentage of people who trust the parliament to a great/medium extent	Algeria	Palestine	Iraq	Jordan	Lebanon	Morocco	Tunisia	Egypt	Yemen
Wave 1 (2007)	24.3	67.9		57.1	39.4	25.8			24.1
Wave 2 (2011)	18.7	42.9	28.0	48.0	25.8				26.0
Wave 3 (2013)	40.5	46.0	24.9	43.6	19.9	28.3	30.5	18.1	33.8
Wave 4 (2016)	17.1	26.6		26.1	10.5	25.2	19.3	46.5	

Percentage of people who trust political parties to a great/medium extent	Algeria	Palestine	Iraq	Jordan	Lebanon	Morocco	Tunisia	Egypt	Yemen
Wave 1 (2007)	17.5	46.9		32.5	22.1	18.0			20.1
Wave 2 (2011)	18.8	28.2	15.4	30.5	22.9		22.1	27.8	25.6
Wave 3 (2013)									
Wave 4 (2016)	14.0	17.9		5.9	14.2	10.1	11.7	20.2	

Source: Arab Barometer, 'Data Analysis Tool', 2007–2018, https://www.arabbarometer.org/survey-data/data-analysis-tool/.

indirect democratic power by bypassing the electoral system'.[2] Alternative political participation tends to take place outside formal political structures and associated behaviour such as joining a political party, voting or running for elected office. Engaging in alternative politics can be either a choice or a necessity. While ruling elites can easily manipulate political parties and elections, alternative political spaces are often more difficult to control. Furthermore, the average citizen does not have access to many of the levers of traditional politics. Thus, as Ellen Lust-Okar and Saloua Zerhouni note, when formal politics becomes meaningless, citizens turn to 'other avenues of popular political participation that are within the reach of the masses and often escape state control'.[3]

The post-Arab Spring period has seen a rise in alternative political participation, in part due to the growing gap in trust between people and their governments in the region (Table 1). According to the Arab Barometer, in Egypt, for example, 78.6% of people surveyed said that they trusted the government 'a great deal' or 'quite a lot' in 2011, compared to 64.8% in 2016; and in Tunisia, about half as many people (33.4%) said that they trusted the government 'a great deal' or 'quite a lot' in 2016 as did so in 2011 (62.2%). The 2016 numbers are even lower with regard to political parties, in which only 20.2% express 'a great deal' or 'quite a lot' of trust in Egypt, and only 11.7% in Tunisia.[4] Such low levels of trust do not mean, however, that the population has turned away from the idea of politics writ large. Rather, many people within the Arab world have become *more* engaged in politics since 2011 – albeit in new and alternative ways.

In Tunisia, for example, citizens continue to participate in demonstrations and protests. There, 16% of Arab Barometer survey respondents said that they themselves participated in the protests against Ben Ali between 17 December 2010 and 14 January 2011, and 45% that their friends or acquaintances had participated; and in the most recent wave of Arab Barometer data (2016), similar numbers (14%) said they had participated in a protest, march or sit-in during the past three years, and 11% that they had attended a meeting to discuss a subject or sign a petition, making it clear that while trust in formal institutions has decreased, similar numbers of people are taking to the street to make their voices heard. (See Table 2a). This is also clear from the large number of protests across the region

---

2 Peter Dahlgren, 'Social Media and Counter-Democracy: The Contingencies of Participation', *Electronic Participation*, Kristiansand 2102, p. 3.
3 Ellen Lust-Okar and Saloua Zerhouni, *Political Participation in the Middle East*, Boulder 2008, p. 34.
4 Arab Barometer, https://www.arabbarometer.org/survey-data/data-analysis-tool/.

Table 2a: Civic activism: citizen activism (%)

	Algeria	Palestine	Jordan	Lebanon	Morocco	Tunisia	Egypt	Yemen
Percentage of people who are members of a political party (2016)	2.4	13.4	0.4	11.6	3.2	2.1	0.8	
Percentage of people who are members of a charitable society (2013)	7.6	11.1	4.1	8.4	6.3	2.7	2.6	22.9
Percentage of people who are members of a youth, cultural or sports organisation (2013)	13.5	11.4	1.8	9.9	12.1	2.8	1.5	13.9
Percentage of people who have attended meetings or activities related to the last parliamentary campaign (2016)	12.3	21.9	22.6	13.8	12.9	11.2	7.0	31.9
Percentage of people who have attended a meeting to discuss a subject or sign a petition (2016)	13.1	24.2	4.5	17.4	13.1	10.9	3.2	
Percentage of people who have participated in a protest, march or sit-in (2016)	5.3	30.9	2.6	15.3	19.5	14.4	3.5	

Source: Arab Barometer, 'Data Analysis Tool', 2007–2018, https://www.arabbarometer.org/survey-data/data-analysis-tool/.

Table 2b: Civic activism: number of protests, 2009–2016

	2009	2010	2012	2014	2016	2019
Algeria	12	8	59	125	233	223
Bahrain					316	121
Egypt	17	45	218	463	220	27
Iraq					125	33
Jordan					43	65
Kuwait					6	1
Lebanon					120	42
Libya	3	1	59	185	85	29
Morocco	5	7	55	86	93	206
Oman						3
Saudi Arabia					6	0
Syria						61
Tunisia	1	22	187	126	488	427
Yemen					82	56

Source: ACLED (Armed Conflict Location & Event Data Project), 'Data Export Tool', https://www.acleddata.com/data/.

(Table 2b). According to the ACLED database,[5] in the first three months of 2019, North Africa (Morocco, Algeria, Tunisia, Libya and Egypt) saw 912 protests, more than the combined number for the years 2010 to 2014 (842).

Yet while these numbers can shed some light on political action taking place in the streets, it is nearly impossible to quantify the full picture of alternative politics, much of which happens outside formal structures and at an individual level. Furthermore, some alternative political participation is, at face value, apolitical, yet can 'carry considerable political meaning'.[6] As Asef Bayat has argued, 'the vehicles through which ordinary people change their societies are not simply audible mass protests or revolutions … rather, people resort more widely to … "non-

---

5 ACLED (Armed Conflict Location & Event Data Project), https://www.acleddata.com/data/.
6 Lust-Okar and Zerhouni, *Political Participation*, p. 36.

movements" – the collective endeavours of millions of non-collective actors, carried out in the main squares, back streets, court houses, or communities'.[7]

Why alternative politics?

There are three primary reasons why alternative political participation has flourished where traditional political participation has failed. First, there is no longer space for meaningful political action by citizens across the region. With few exceptions, Arab states have not opened up the space for political opposition in any real way. In Morocco, for example, a new constitution was one of the outcomes of the 2011 protests there, and on paper it devolved power to the elected parliament; but in reality the king retains the last word on all relevant political matters, including the power to dismiss the prime minister,[8] a power he exercised in March 2017. After Morocco's political parties were unable to form a governing coalition during five months of negotiations, King Mohammed VI issued a statement that Prime Minister Abdelilah Benkirane would be replaced. While the monarchy officially rejected claims of influence over the political sphere, the palace was uncomfortable with the increasing popularity and adversarial politics of Benkirane's Party of Justice and Development (PJD).[9] One analyst asserted that Benkirane's dismissal was 'seen as an attempt by the monarchy and its deep state network of elite allies – known as Makhzen – to regain political power'.[10]

In Morocco and elsewhere in the region, political parties, where they exist, have little chance of effecting change – either acting as straw men to the ruling parties to give the political system a veneer of legitimacy, or risking arrest should they dare to challenge the authoritarian leadership. Furthermore, in the eight years since the Arab Spring began, as societies became emboldened in their demands for change, many states in the region began to crack down on the public sphere,

---

7 Asef Bayat, *Life as Politics: How Ordinary People Change the Middle East*, Stanford 2103, p. ix.
8 Sarah E. Yerkes, 'Morocco: The Model for Reform?', *The Arab Awakening: America and the Transformation of the Middle East*, ed. Brookings Institution, Washington, DC 2011, pp. 196–205.
9 Vish Sakthivel, 'The Moroccan King Dismisses an Islamist Prime Minister', Washington Institute for Near East Policy, 17 March 2017, https://www.washingtoninstitute.org/policy-analysis/view/the-moroccan-king-dismisses-an-islamist-prime-minister.
10 Mohamed Daadaoui, 'Morocco's King Just Named a New Prime Minister, in Case You Forgot Who's in Charge', *The Washington Post* 20 March 2017, https://www.washingtonpost.com/news/monkey-cage/wp/2017/03/20/moroccos-king-just-named-a-new-prime-minister-in-case-you-forgot-whos-in-charge/.

whether by instituting harsh laws governing the NGO sector, jailing journalists or pushing through legal measures, as in President al-Sisi's successful attempt in Egypt to amend the constitution to make himself president for life, to further consolidate authoritarian rule.[11] In Egypt and elsewhere, social activists face intimidation and state-sponsored violence, as well as arbitrary detentions.[12] This leaves little space for formal political action.

Second, alternative political participation is cheaper and more accessible to the average person than is the traditional or formal equivalent. Even in the more permissive environments, such as Tunisia or Lebanon, starting a political party or running for office is a time-consuming and costly endeavour. Furthermore, public trust in political parties is low, resulting in a lack of respect for political leaders and institutions.[13] Engaging in a protest, or writing a Facebook post critical of the regime, is a much easier way to make one's voice heard. Individual-level activism requires little planning, and can have more results that are more immediately apparent than joining a political party, participating in a campaign or even voting.

Third, the large youth population in the region, where many countries have more than 40% of their population under the age of 25 (Table 3), has more experience with alternative political participation – particularly social media and street art – and has grown up in an environment where street activism is more effective than voting at changing political leadership. Art is one form of alterative politics that has been used by youth in the region to keep the revolutionary spirit alive after the Arab Spring. Music, poetry, photography, playwriting and graffiti have been used across the region as forms of self-expression, and can take on strong political messages. Mark LeVine notes that during the years after the uprisings, 'the form and content of the art produced by Arab activist artists has continuously changed … as conditions on the ground, the political situations, and the goals, dreams and expectations of the artists' change'. Each country that witnessed protests has experienced different, but no less energetic and creative, forms of artistic output and

---

11 Tamara Qiblawi, 'Egyptian Voters Back Constitutional Referendum That Could Extend Sisi's Rule – CNN', CNN 23 April 2019, https://edition.cnn.com/2019/04/23/middleeast/egypt-referendum-results-intl/index.html. The constitutional amendments were approved by 88.8% of voters in a national referendum in April 2019 and enacted into law.
12 Amr Hamzawy, 'Egypt's Resilient and Evolving Social Activism', Carnegie Endowment for International Peace, 5 April 2017, https://carnegieendowment.org/2017/04/05/egypt-s-resilient-and-evolving-social-activism-pub-68578.
13 Sarah Yerkes and Zeineb Ben Yahmed, 'Tunisia's Political System: From Stagnation to Competition', Carnegie Endowment for International Peace, 28 March 2109, https://carnegieendowment.org/2019/03/28/tunisia-s-political-system-from-stagnation-to-competition-pub-78717.

production. LeVine cites 'Tunisian rap, Libyan literature, Moroccan experimental theater, Yemeni protest music and Egyptian graffiti' as some of the types of artistic output that blossomed after the Arab Spring. He adds that these art forms 'have historically "thrived on conflict" while at the same time push[ing] the boundaries of moral, political and cultural freedom while giv[ing] vent to the frustrations of the people, especially the youth'.[14]

Table 3: Youth population (% aged 24 or under)

Algeria	44
Bahrain	34
Egypt	52
Iraq	58
Jordan	54
Kuwait	40
Lebanon	39
Libya	42
Morocco	42
Oman	48
Qatar	25
Saudi Arabia	41
Syria	51
Tunisia	39
UAE	22
Yemen	60
Canada	27
USA	32

Source: CIA *World Factbook*.

14 Mark LeVine, 'When Art Is the Weapon: Culture and Resistance Confronting Violence in the Post-Uprisings Arab World', *Religions* 6, 2015, p. 1282.

Protests as Politics

Since the Arab Spring, the region has seen, at a regular pace, protests of varying size and effectiveness. The success of protesters in bringing down both Ben Ali and Mubarak in 2011 inspired many smaller protest movements in the subsequent years. Two of the larger protest movements have taken place in North Africa: Morocco's Rif protests, and those that in 2019 brought down Abdelaziz Bouteflika, who had held the Algerian presidency since 1999. These two protest movements in neighbouring countries represent two different types of regime response, as well as different outcomes.

Protests are a low cost, low barrier-to-entry form of political activity. Organising a group of individuals to come on to the streets is often cheap, and requires little time. Protest demands are often simplistic in nature with clear, easy to follow slogans, requiring far less knowledge of complex political issues than does understanding political party platforms or participating in town hall meetings. Furthermore, even small protests can quickly turn into large movements. As Marc Lynch notes, 'protest by a small number of early movers signals to others in society, who are privately dissatisfied but less willing to take risks, that others share their grievances. If those early movers go unpunished, it raises their confidence about the riskiness of expressing their dissent'.[15]

Protests in the region have indeed proven to be an effective means for getting the attention of the regime. As Stephen Grand observes, 'the latent threat of citizens flooding the streets in protest can be a potent force in keeping political leaders in check. It can also give particular civic groups the legitimacy and influence to press elected leaders for greater transparency, accountability, and citizen participation, as these groups are understood to represent a far larger popular constituency.' Arab leaders need only look at the growing number of their colleagues whose regimes ended after masses flooded the streets demanding change. Thus protests can scare leaders into making concessions; or they can spur leaders to take action – sometimes violent – against their own people. There is no guarantee protests will result in a positive outcome or meet the demands and needs of the protesters. And even if they do, they are a 'very blunt instrument for effecting political change. They can be difficult to orchestrate, and they may have myriad unintended consequences'.[16]

---

15 Marc Lynch, 'Introduction', *The Arab Uprisings Explained: New Contentious Politics in the Middle East*, ed. Marc Lynch, New York 2014, p. 8.
16 Stephen Grand, *Understanding Tahrir Square*, Washington, DC 2103, p. 199.

Algeria's protests: peaceful yet uncertain

Protests in Algeria calling for the end to President Bouteflika's rule began in mid-February 2019, but took on a larger profile on 3 March, when Bouteflika (through an advisor) filed his candidacy for president for the 18 April elections. At that point, the protests shifted towards a unified slogan of 'no to a fifth term', with protesters focusing their anger on the fact that Bouteflika, who is severely incapacitated, would be allowed to participate in the upcoming elections. The protesters' demands have evolved with the situation on the ground, beginning with a call for Bouteflika to withdraw his candidacy for a fifth presidential term, evolving into a call for his resignation, and then growing into a demand for the dismantling of the entire political system (often referred to as *le pouvoir*).

While the protesters soon succeeded in persuading Bouteflika to withdraw his candidacy and instead extend his fourth mandate while a transitional government could be put in place, more remarkably, within a month, the ailing leader submitted his resignation. Nevertheless, the Friday after he resigned (5 April), hundreds of thousands of protesters again flooded the streets, demanding the removal of what they saw as an outdated and opaque political apparatus with a cadre of ruling party officials, army officers and businessmen pulling the strings of a leader who had not uttered a word in public since 2013.[17] As one protester, teacher Ahmed Badili said, 'We want to uproot the symbols of the system.'[18]

The protests were surprising, because Algeria had appeared largely immune from protest during the Arab Spring, in part because while it shared many of the underlying economic and social conditions of its North African neighbours, the Algerian people did not attribute their daily challenges to President Bouteflika. Thus, while protests, at times widespread, did occur in Algeria in January 2011, these avoided calls to unseat Bouteflika and were largely confined to specific demands that the regime was able to meet by, for example, lifting the state of emergency, increasing public sector spending and lowering food prices. As Frederic Volpi noted, 'not only did the regime survive this tumultuous period, but it hardly deviated from its habitual methods of authoritarian governance'.[19] While some smaller protests cropped up between 2011 and 2019, the Algerian state was largely untouched, or was able to meet protester's demands (such as by enacting presidential term limits in 2016). However, the drivers of the 2019 protests have

---

17 Lamine Chikhi and Hamid Ould Ahmed, 'Algeria Protesters Return to the Streets as Spy Boss Reported Sacked', Reuters 5 April 2019, https://af.reuters.com/article/topNews/idAFKCN1RH19W-OZATP.
18 France 24 2019.
19 Frederic Volpi, 'Algeria versus the Arab Spring', *Journal of Democracy* 24.3, 2013, p. 104.

been in place since Bouteflika became incapacitated by a stroke in 2013, along with the simultaneous decline in oil and gas revenue that made it more difficult for the state to satisfy public demand for goods and services. The protesters this time around also reflected a different demographic than in the past, when protests tended to be dominated by young men, and often turned violent. This time, the protesters represented people of all ages and walks of life, with a prominent showing by women, and including students as well as journalists, labour union members and youths as well as older Algerians.

While Bouteflika stepped down on 3 April 2019, the protests were still unfolding at the time of writing. Thus, it is not yet clear whether they can be classified as successful. The protesters did achieve their initial demands, but the military, which has the power to make or break the transition, seemed to be wavering as to how far it would let the country move towards a liberal and uncertain future.

Nevertheless, the fact that the people of Algeria succeeded in removing a leader who had been in power for two decades is meaningful, and has reminded activists throughout the Arab world that citizens have a voice and are able to enact change. This message rang loud and clear during the early days of the Arab Spring, but after it was clear that states were either cracking down on the public sphere, as in Egypt and Saudi Arabia, or descending into civil war, as in Libya, Syria and Yemen, protests largely lost their momentum in the region.

The protesters achieved their first two goals – having Bouteflika withdraw his candidacy for a fifth term and removing him from office – due to a variety of factors. In part, the non-stop nature of the protests made clear that the people were not going to go quietly back home. Following the initial demonstrations, each subsequent Friday saw larger crowds in the streets in Algeria's major population centres. The protesters generally relied on slogans that were short and refrained from using profanity or harsh language. Some of the most common slogans – 'Enough!', 'Leave Means Leave', and 'The people are united against the regime' – were easy for people of all ages and walks of life to rally around.[20]

Additionally, the protests remained peaceful, both physically and in the virtual realm. Protesters used slogans in support of the military – showing solidarity between the two groups that subsequently made it difficult for the army to engage in any sort of violence and eventually saw Army Chief of Staff Gaid Salah calling for Bouteflika to be removed from power. Social media posts also largely remained

20 Nabila Ramdani, 'The Fight for Freedom in Algeria Isn't Finished', *Foreign Policy* 13 March 2019, https://foreignpolicy.com/2019/03/13/
the-fight-for-freedom-in-algeria-isnt-finished-abdelaziz-bouteflika-arab-spring-protests/.

positive, even invoking humour at times, making it more difficult for the regime to attack the protesters online. For example, protesters created memes around iconic ad campaigns, such as playing on Marlboro with the slogan 'You are in bad shape [*mal barré*], your system is seriously damaging our health.' In another example, protesters pushed back against a fifth presidential term for Bouteflika with a play on a Chanel perfume ad, stating, 'Only Chanel can be No. 5.'[21]

Additionally, the protesters successfully relied on social media to draw attention to their cause. Hashtags such as 'Algeria rises up' and 'civil disobedience' have been a common tool of protesters, particularly the Active Youth Collective, a Facebook-based activist network made up of lawyers, journalists and students with members in Algeria and the diaspora.[22] Other influential social media accounts, such as DzWikileaks, the Algerian Youth Revolution and Bejaia City have been instrumental in helping to publicise protests, although much of the organisation is done through private Facebook groups as well as WhatsApp, Viber and Telegram to avoid regime surveillance.[23] Protesters have also circulated footage of the protests widely through Twitter, Facebook and Instagram, helping to expose people around the world to the situation on the ground.[24] The Algerian diaspora in Paris, Montreal, Geneva and elsewhere helped draw attention there to the movement. Solidarity protests were held in London and New York, as well as in Tunis.[25] And, perhaps more significantly, unlike in the past, protests this time have received domestic media coverage – particularly after journalists protested against Bouteflika's rule – both in mainstream newspapers and in private broadcasts.[26]

---

21 Nacima Ourahmoune, 'Algeria: How Millennials Used Humour and Creativity to Force Abdelalziz Bouteflika to Stand Aside', *The Conversation* 13 March 2019, http://theconversation.com/algeria-how-millennials-used-humour-and-creativity-to-force-abdelalziz-bouteflika-to-stand-aside-113417.
22 France 24 2019.
23 RFI (Radio France Internationale), 2 March 2019, 'Bouteflika Appoints New Campaign Manager as Algerian Protests Peak on Social Media', http://en.rfi.fr/africa/20190302-social-media-bouteflika-algeria-sacks-campaign-manager.
24 AFP 6 March 2019, 'Social Media Breaks "Wall of Fear" for Algeria Protesters', https://www.france24.com/en/20190306-social-media-breaks-wall-fear-algeria-protesters.
25 Omar Havana, '"This Is Our Time; It's the Time for Algerian People"', Al-Jazeera 11 March 2019, https://www.aljazeera.com/indepth/inpictures/time-time-algerian-people-190311061538682.html.
26 AFP 17 April 2019, 'Algeria Protests Loosen Stranglehold on Media', https://www.arabnews.com/node/1483716/media; Al-Jazeera 18 March 2019, 'Bouteflika Protests: Algeria's Shifting Media Space', https://www.aljazeera.com/programmes/listeningpost/2019/03/bouteflika-protests-algeria-shifting-media-space-190317083422948.html.

Morocco's Rif protests: *regional revolts and regime repression*

The protest movement in Morocco's Rif region began in October 2016 after the death of 31-year-old Mohsen Fikri, a fishmonger who was crushed inside a garbage truck while trying to recover fish confiscated by police in the northern city of Al-Hoceima. His death unleashed mounting anger over what was perceived as humiliation suffered by the Berbers in the historically neglected Rif region. Protests spread across rural Morocco, where many people identified with Fikri and his family. In December 2017, another series of protests erupted in the north-east (in the town of Jerada) after two brothers aged 23 and 30 died while illegally extracting coal from a defunct mine. Both incidents highlighted economic deprivation in the Rif and the long-standing marginalisation experienced by people there. Thus, protesters centred their demands on regional development and job creation, including calling for the establishment of a museum and university in Al-Hoceima, a new hospital and oncology ward and the completion of a long-promised highway.[27]

The Moroccan protests differed from the Algerian ones both as regards the response of the state and in their regional, rather than national, orientation. In Morocco, the government cracked down hard on the protesters, arresting hundreds of activists, beginning with prominent figure Nasser Zafzafi on 29 May 2017, following an earlier instruction to imams to preach sermons warning against dissent.[28] Zafzafi's arrest and the subsequent crackdown were spurred on by a statement he made during a sermon in a mosque, asking if the mosque was there to serve God or those in power.[29]

Since the beginning of the Rif protests, more than a thousand people have been arrested on politically motivated charges, including at least seven independent journalists. While those detained include prominent protesters, others are ordinary activists brought up on charges such as 'participating in an unregistered demonstration, insulting law enforcement officers and inciting others to commit

27 Ursula Lindsey, 'In Morocco, Protesters Organise against Repression with New and Traditional Tactics' MobLab 6 October 2017, https://mobilisationlab.org/stories/morocco-tactics-counter-repression/.

28 Amnesty International, 28 November 2017, 'Morocco: Protesters, Activists and Journalists Detained over Rif Protests Must Be Released', https://www.amnesty.org/en/latest/news/2017/11/morocco-protesters-activists-and-journalists-detained-over-rif-protests-must-be-released/.

29 Jasmin Lorch and Jonas Burkhard, 'Online and Traditional Forms of Protest Mobilization: Morocco's Rif Protests and Beyond', Middle East Institute, 22 August 2017, https://www.mei.edu/publications/online-and-traditional-forms-protest-mobilization-moroccos-rif-protests-and-beyond.

a criminal offense'.[30] Furthermore, as the Rif protests remained largely confined to that region, which has a long history of uprisings dating back to the 1920s, the Moroccan government was able to attempt to discredit the protesters by calling them separatists and questioning their loyalty to the state.[31]

King Mohammed VI played a mediating role, however, offering 'carrots' to the protesters in the form of much-needed development and infrastructure assistance, and criticising his own ministers for failing to implement a $63.5-million development programme for Al-Hoceima.[32] He repeatedly criticised the public administration there, but defended the police against allegations of misconduct and abuse. Furthermore, while 53 of the protesters were convicted in June 2018 on an array of charges including arson, rebellion, damaging public property, staging unauthorised protests and harming the state's internal security, and sentenced to prison on terms ranging from a year to 20 years, in August 2018 King Mohammed pardoned 184 activists, including 11 of those arrested in the June 2017 crackdown.

While the Algerian protests have been classified as largely leaderless, the Moroccan government targeted one particularly vocal protester, Zafzafi, who gained prominence through videos he posted to YouTube as one of the key protest leaders. While many Moroccans dispute that Zafzafi actually speaks for the protesters, using him as a symbol has benefited both the state, who punished the protesters by putting their leader in jail, and the protesters, by making a martyr out of one of their own. Zafzafi was eventually sentenced to 20 years in prison for his participation in the protests. In prison, he and other prominent protest figures have reportedly been held in solitary confinement for months at a time.[33]

Both sets of protests have relied on social media to help coordinate activists' actions and keep information flowing, and in the Moroccan case, the government tried to censor that activity by blocking internet connections during the November 2017 protests.[34] The media apparatus covering the Moroccan protests was impressive. Protests were broadcast live on social media and were covered by regional

---

30 Ilhem Rachidi, 'Morocco's Crackdown Won't Silence Dissent – Foreign Policy', *Foreign Policy* 16 January 2019, https://foreignpolicy.com/2019/01/16/moroccos-crackdown-wont-silence-dissent-maroc-hirak-amdh/.
31 Lorch and Burkhard, 'Online and Traditional Forms'.
32 RTS 26 June 2017, 'Le roi du Maroc mécontent du développement de la région du Rif', https://www.rts.ch/info/monde/8732110-le-roi-du-maroc-mecontent-du-developpement-de-la-region-du-rif.html.
33 Amnesty International, 'Morocco: Protesters'.
34 Carolyn Tackett and Emna Sayadi, 'Morocco: A Complete Blackout during Protests in Al-Hoceima', *Access Now* 30 November 2017, https://www.accessnow.org/morocco-complete-blackout-protests-al-hoceima/.

online media and dedicated channels such as Rifpress and Rif24. This allowed the Rif diaspora to have access to the protests in real time and disseminate them broadly. Independent and opposition media, such as the magazine *TelQuel* and the news sites Le Desk and Lakome also played a crucial role in the early months of the protests, by providing detailed and sympathetic accounts of demonstrations and clashes as well as updates on trials, allegations of torture and prison conditions.

Social Media

The role of social media during the Arab Spring

Many people have given social media significant credit for the success of the Tunisian and Egyptian revolutions. In the early days of the Tunisian protests that sparked the Arab Spring, cyber activists, bloggers and journalists were able to disseminate information about what was happening in Tunisia's interior, which was poorly connected to the rest of the country, to both Tunis and the world in general. The internet, combined with satellite television, thus became a platform to magnify the brutality of the regime. Facebook and other new media tools certainly helped spread information within each country about where protests would occur, and helped connect what would otherwise be disparate individuals and groups. As Rex Brynen and colleagues argue, 'Twitter and mobile phones turned every protester into a roaming reporter, allowing information-sharing and uploading of images to the Internet in real time.'[35] Yet one of the most effective tools of the Arab Spring was actually satellite television (and the television company Al-Jazeera in particular), which was able to raise awareness globally about the protests.

While Arab governments had engaged in varying levels of internet censorship prior to the Arab Spring, that censorship was not sufficient to prevent the spread of news about the ongoing protests. As Zeynep Tufecki notes, in 2011, 'many governments … were naïve about the power of the internet and dismissed "online" acts as frivolous and powerless'. Even when regimes tried to push back against the growing tide of social media, the move often backfired. In Tunisia, for example, Ben Ali had tried to ban Facebook, but 'Facebook had become too useful for too many in the general population to be easily outlawed, but also too

---

35 Rex Brynen, Pete W. Moore, Bassel F. Salloukh and Marie-Joëlle Zahar, *Beyond the Arab Spring: Authoritarianism and Democratization in the Arab World*, Boulder 2012, p. 239.

Table 4a: Population using the internet (%)

	2010	2011	2012	2013	2014	2015	2016
Algeria	12.50	14.90	18.20	22.50	29.50	38.20	42.95
Bahrain	55.00	77.00	88.00	90.00	90.50	93.50	98.00
Egypt	21.60	25.60	26.40	29.40	33.90	37.80	41.30
Iraq	2.50	5.00	7.10	9.20	13.20	17.20	21.20
Jordan	27.20	34.90	37.00	41.40	46.20	60.10	62.30
Kuwait	61.40	65.80	70.50	75.50	78.70	77.50	78.40
Lebanon	43.70	52.00	61.30	70.50	73.00	74.00	76.10
Libya	14.00	14.00	–	16.50	17.80	19.00	20.30
Morocco	52.00	46.10	55.40	56.00	56.80	57.10	58.30
Oman	35.80	48.00	60.00	66.50	70.20	73.50	76.90
Qatar	69.00	69.00	69.30	85.30	91.50	92.90	94.30
Saudi Arabia	41.00	47.50	54.00	60.50	64.70	69.60	74.90
Syria	20.70	22.50	24.30	26.20	28.10	30.00	31.90
Tunisia	36.80	39.10	41.40	43.80	46.20	46.50	49.60
UAE	68.00	78.00	85.00	88.00	90.40	90.50	90.60
Yemen	12.40	14.90	17.50	20.00	22.60	24.10	24.60

Source: World Bank Indicators, https://data.worldbank.org/indicator/IT.NET.USER.
ZS?end=2017&start=2009, sourced from International Telecommunication Union, World
Telecommunication/ICT Development Report and database.

politically potent to ignore'.[36] In the earliest days of the protests, Al-Jazeera was a crucial tool, in that it covered the protests across the region when governments banned national television from doing so.[37] The Mubarak government shut down Al-Jazeera's Cairo office and prevented its submission over the Nilesat network, yet Al-Jazeera was able to switch to a different bandwidth and continue reporting on the unfolding revolution in Egypt and protests across the region.

The importance of television (rather than social media) is clear from survey

---

36 Zeynep Tufekci, *Twitter and Teargas: The Power and Fragility of Networked Protest*, New Haven, CT 2017, p. 20.
37 Brynen et al., *Beyond the Arab Spring*, p. 236.

Table 4b: Mobile phone subscriptions (per 100 people)

	2010	2011	2012	2013	2014	2015	2016
Algeria	91	97	100	103	111	108	116
Bahrain	126	132	163	168	174	184	210
Egypt	84	97	110	111	104	100	102
Iraq	76	80	82	96	94	93	90
Jordan	92	99	112	123	126	151	104
Kuwait	133	155	150	178	201	149	133
Lebanon	66	75	76	74	78	80	81
Libya	177	161	155	165	137	156	122
Morocco	99	111	117	125	129	124	118
Oman	151	149	152	151	156	158	155
Qatar	123	118	123	147	139	151	142
Saudi Arabia	188	191	182	177	171	167	149
Syria	56	62	64	62	73	76	72
Tunisia	104	115	118	115	128	129	125
UAE	132	135	155	178	185	196	215
Yemen	47	48	56	66	65	56	60

Source: World Bank Indicators, https://data.worldbank.org/indicator/IT.CEL.SETS.
P2?end=2017&start=2009, sourced from International Telecommunication Union, World
Telecommunication/ICT Development Report and database.

data. According to the Arab Barometer, 95% of Egyptians and 83% of Tunisians got their information about the protests in 2011 from television. Thus, while 82% of Tunisians and 51% of Egyptians reported having a Facebook page in 2011, most of the citizens of these states did not see social media as a source for their information about the protests. Nevertheless, people in the Arab world remain relatively well connected to the internet and the percentage of the population that use the internet today has grown dramatically since 2010 (Table 4a). In Algeria, for example, according to the Arab Barometer, 43% of people surveyed in 2016 reported using the internet, compared to just 13% in 2010; and in the Gulf region, the vast majority of the population was connected in 2016, from 98% in Bahrain, to 94% in Qatar, to 91% in the UAE, compared to much lower numbers in 2010 (55%, 69% and 68%

respectively). Furthermore, mobile phone subscriptions in the region are quite high (Table 4b). Thus, even in remote areas of the region, where internet infrastructure is lacking, individuals tend to rely on SMS or cellular communication to transmit both political and non-political messages.

The importance of social media should not be overstated, however. During the Arab Spring, while states were initially slow to catch on to the importance of the internet in mobilising the public, eventually both the Egyptian and Tunisian governments 'completely shut down or severely curtailed' the internet, forcing the revolutionaries to turn to traditional media as well as offline societal networks and interpersonal communication to get their message out.[38] Thus, the question is whether Arab states can keep up with new media: are regimes able to absorb and adapt to new tools and techniques that proliferate, or will this realm grow too quickly for them, leaving them always to play catch-up?

Why social media work today...

The use of social media as a form of alternative politics did not begin with the Arab Spring. Social movements and civil society organisations had long existed in the region, and the proliferation of social media made it possible both for these groups to connect with each other across towns and oceans and, initially, allowed them to bypass the watchful eye of the state.

The Kifaya movement in Egypt that was launched in 2004, and played a major role in pushing for political reform during the 2005 elections, was one of the largest grassroots movements of the time. While Kifaya began with a physical meeting of Egyptian intellectuals in the home of al-Wasat party leader Abu al-Ila Madi, it soon grew in part through the use of SMS technology and blogs to gain momentum and spread its message. The group held a series of protests, including anti-Mubarak demonstrations in April 2005 that took place simultaneously across 14 cities in Egypt. While the movement itself was not widely successful, it set a 'new and important precedent by challenging the incumbent regime directly and by encouraging the formation of other groups' in Egypt. Kifaya was the first political movement to use social media as its primary source of communication, thereby setting the stage for the 2011 revolution.[39]

---

38 Mohamed Ben Moussa, 'From Arab Street to Social Movements: Re-Theorizing Collective Action and the Role of Social Media in the Arab Spring', *Westminster Papers in Communication and Culture* 9.2, 2013, p. 58.
39 Carnegie Endowment for International Peace, 'Kifaya', 22 September 2010, https://carnegieendowment.org/2010/09/22/kifaya-pub-54922.

The rise of protests as a tool for political action goes hand-in-hand with the continued use of social media. When organising for action, individuals or groups simply need to send out a Tweet or a Facebook post, or create a hashtag that will inspire others to join. Furthermore, by sharing one's message on a global platform, it is far easier to get media coverage and create international sentiment behind what might otherwise be a local issue. For example, the Saudi #Women2Drive campaign that started in the wake of the Arab Spring in 2011 was responsible, in part, for the lifting of the ban on Saudi women driving. While much of the work to make the campaign relevant took place offline, it eventually gained international attention, with solidarity protests in the United States that received high-level support from American figures, including Congresswoman Nancy Pelosi.[40] While some of the main activists have since been arrested and used by the Saudi regime in their broader crackdown on human rights, there is no question that the use of social media both to raise global awareness of the lack of women's rights in Saudi Arabia and to connect Saudi activists to each other was crucial to the campaign's initial success.

Social media work for activists for four primary reasons: they have much lower 'transaction costs' than traditional face-to-face activism; it is easy to transmit information widely through social media; regimes face a higher cost when they try to crack down on social media; and there are tremendous 'scale and diffusion effects' of using them.[41] Additionally, social media are a relatively affordable mechanism of communication, benefiting from their lack of structure and hierarchy, which enables everyday people to voice their opinions and to be heard.[42] The formation of horizontal ties – connecting people with each other on an equal level – can provide individuals with 'feelings of competence, such as a sense of empowerment'.[43] That empowerment is often more direct and stronger than participation in formal politics, which is hierarchical in nature and in which it is difficult for individuals to have a clear and direct impact.

Thus today, social media remain an effective tool for activists to both organise and highlight their struggles. Some bloggers who got their start in the early 2000s have developed into savvy activists. This development is most prevalent in Tunisia, where the open political environment allows cyber-activists to maintain

40 See her Twitter post, 17 June 2011, 3:05 pm, accessed 22 January 2020, https://twitter.com/SpeakerPelosi/status/81799658443251712.
41 Marc Lynch, 'Media, Old and New', *Arab Uprisings Explained*, ed. Lynch, p. 93.
42 Ben Moussa, 'From Arab Street'.
43 Peter Dahlgren, 'Do Social Media Enhance Democratic Participation?', Rosa Luxemburg Stiftung Policy Paper 04/2013, August 2013, https://www.rosalux.de/en/publication/id/7126/do-social-media-enhance-democratic-participation/.

the level of internet freedom necessary to continue using that space for political action. Matt Gordner notes that Tunisian cyber-activists have moved from being dissidents under the Ben Ali regime to being citizens of a new democracy. Originally spreading news about protests throughout Tunisia and to the international community, in the years after the revolution, many of the activists came to occupy leadership positions in Tunisia's social and political scenes. Gordner writes that 'despite initial attempts to mobilize with other organizations ... individual pursuits are regarded by these leading figures as more efficacious than collective action in the post-Ben Ali period'.[44]

... and why social media fail

While social media have many benefits of for activists, there are also several negative implications. While, in 2010–2011, the Ben Ali and Mubarak regimes (as well as others in the region) were caught off-guard by the ability of people to mobilise and the capacity for information to spread quickly across and between countries, today regimes have learned to use social media for their own interests. States like Egypt have established their own social media accounts to counter the opposition; and in the wake of the Arab Spring, regimes have developed a 'massive state capacity and experience in surveillance, repression, infiltration and control'.[45] Thus, social media can make it easier for the state to track critical voices and to manipulate protest activity, as activists are easier to spot on social media than in traditionally organised political activity.

Governments can also push back against activists more directly through social media – by threatening activists, arresting them or organising counter-protests and smear campaigns against them. In the era of 'fake news', it is not always easy for individuals to determine whether social media accounts belong to real activists or are government-devised fakes. Additionally, cyber-bullying and net harassment, whether by governments or citizens who side with the government, can lead as easily to silencing voices as to magnifying them. While social media represent just one part of the broader press landscape, the overall picture of press freedom in the region reflects this government pushback. According to the Reporters without Borders Press Freedom Index, the region as a whole is doing worse today than in 2010 (Table 5). Most states have seen a decline in their press freedom ratings,

44 Matt Gordner, 'Blogging Bouazizi: The Role of Tunisian Cyberactivists Before and After the Jasmine Revolution', *Middle East – Topics and Arguments* 6, 2016, pp. 61–62.
45 Marc Lynch, 'Media, Old and New', *Arab Uprisings Explained*, ed. Lynch, p. 96.

including Lebanon, whose rating went from 20.5 to 31.15 (on a scale of 100, where zero is the best score), the UAE, which went from 23.75 to 40.86, and Iraq, which went from 45.58 to 56.56 between 2010 and 2018.

Table 5: Press Freedom Index (0–100 scale, 0 is best)

	2010	2013	2014	2016	2017	2018
Algeria	47.33	36.54	36.26	41.69	42.83	43.13
Bahrain	51.38	62.75	58.26	54.86	58.88	60.85
Egypt	43.33	48.66	51.89	54.45	55.78	56.72
Iraq	45.58	44.67	45.44	54.35	54.03	56.56
Jordan	37.00	38.47	40.42	44.49	43.24	41.71
Kuwait	23.75	28.28	30.71	32.59	33.61	31.91
Lebanon	20.50	30.15	31.89	31.95	33.01	31.15
Libya	63.50	37.86	39.72	57.89	56.81	56.79
Morocco	47.40	39.04	39.19	42.64	42.42	43.13
Oman	40.25	41.51	38.69	40.43	40.46	40.67
Qatar	38.00	32.86	34.32	35.97	39.83	40.16
Saudi Arabia	61.50	56.88	58.30	59.72	66.02	63.13
Syria	91.50	78.53	77.04	81.35	81.49	79.22
Tunisia	72.50	39.93	38.15	31.60	32.22	30.91
UAE	23.75	33.49	36.03	36.73	39.39	40.86
Palestine	56.13	43.09	39.84	42.93	42.90	42.96
Yemen	82.13	69.22	67.26	67.07	65.80	62.23

Source: Reporters without Borders.

Another issue with regard to social media is that while they are effective in mobilising individuals, once those individuals return home, their activism often wanes. The horizontal ties created by social media have a downside: they are often weak and, as Lynch notes, 'do not necessarily translate into enduring movements or robust political parties capable of mounting a sustained challenge to entrenched regimes or becoming governing parties'.[46] Tufekci points out, furthermore, that

---

46 Marc Lynch, 'Media, Old and New', *Arab Uprisings Explained*, ed. Lynch, p. 94.

groups formed via social media often fall apart quickly, because they have 'side-stepped some of the traditional tasks of organizing' which 'helps create collective decision-making capabilities ... and builds a collective capacity among move-ment participants through shared experience and tribulation'.[47] Political activity via social media is often not sufficiently large to be effective. Social movements have three types of capacity: 'narrative capacity, disruptive capacity, and electoral and/or institutional capacity'.[48] While groups that have a virtual base but lack a traditional grassroots following might be effective in the first two categories – changing the narrative and creating disruption – they often falter when it comes to creating real electoral or institutional change.

Labour Unions

Another category of alternative political actor is labour unions. In much of the region, such unions, although technically separate from the state, have tradition-ally played a powerful role. One of the most influential is the General Tunisian Labour Union (UGTT). Labour unions have played an important political role in Tunisia since the foundation of the General Confederation of Tunisian Workers (CGTT) in 1924, including organising a general strike in 1952 that contributed significantly to Tunisia's achievement of independence from France in 1956.[49] Ian Hartshorn describes the UGTT as 'authentically a nationalist group', noting that '[i]ts cadres were at the vanguard, and many, including their early leader Farhat Heched, paid with their lives' (Heched was assassinated in 1952).[50]

While labour unions in Tunisia are not part of the formal political apparatus, they have consistently had a quasi-formal political role, with labour leaders from time to time taking positions within the political apparatus – either in political parties or in the administration itself. For example, in 1964, UGTT leader Habib Achour was appointed to the Political Bureau of then-president Habib Bourgui-ba's Néo-Destour party. The inclusion of labour leaders within the political estab-lishment has often been mutually beneficial – providing unions with a seat at the political table and a direct line of influence, and insulating the government from what has, at times, been disruptive and harmful action by the unions in pursuit of their interests. In the prelude to the 2019 presidential and parliamentary elections,

47 Tufekci, *Twitter and Teargas*, p. 23.
48 Tufekci, *Twitter and Teargas*, p. 192.
49 For a detailed explanation of labour unions in Tunisia, see Ian M. Hartshorn, *Labor Politics in North Africa: After the Uprisings in Egypt and Tunisia*, New York 2018.
50 Hartshorn, *Labor Politics*, pp. 124–25.

the UGTT stated that it would take on a political role, although it was not clear at the time of writing whether this meant that the union would present itself as a separate political party, or simply support certain parties and candidates during the campaign.[51]

The tool most commonly used by the UGTT to pressure the state to adopt policies in its favour is the general strike. These have tended to decrease in frequency during times of tighter union–regime cooperation and flare up during periods of government weakness, such as the 26 January 1978 strike that quickly turned into a violent revolt and was seen as the first major challenge to Bourguiba's rule in 22 years.[52] This event created a large rift between the UGTT leadership, which was subjected to house arrest following the strike, and the Bourguiba government. Bourguiba was able to push back strongly against the UGTT, and in softer ways, such as by co-opting union leaders and replacing the union leadership, that are not available to the post-revolutionary democratic government.

President Ben Ali took a different approach towards the UGTT, seeing them as a potential tool to bolster his regime, and therefore using top-down control over the organisation. Because of the sheer size of the UGTT's constituency (the public sector workers), however, and the lack of other credible and influential unions (let alone civil society organisations), it remained 'the only game in town', enabling it to consolidate support and manage to remain somewhat independent from the government even during the Ben Ali years.[53]

Today, the union has around 400,000 members and represents the nearly 670,000 public servants in the country; if it can manage to bring even half of its membership into the streets, it can bring the country to a standstill.[54] Nevertheless, the UGTT leadership stayed on the sidelines during both the 2008 Gafsa protests and in the early days of the 2010–2011 revolution, holding off from calling for a general strike until 14 January 2011. As the protests unfolded, the UGTT membership continued to take to the streets alongside unemployed youth, civil society activists, bloggers and others, while the leadership was more detached, balancing

51 *TRTWorld* 10 April 2019, 'The Political Debut of Tunisia's Only Labour Union, Explained', https://www.trtworld.com/magazine/the-political-debut-of-tunisia-s-only-labour-union-explained-25734.

52 *TRTWorld*, 'The Political Debut'.

53 Vickie Langohr, 'Labor Movements and Organizations', *Arab Uprisings Explained*, ed. Lynch, p. 186.

54 Reuters 17 January 2019, 'Tunisia's Powerful UGTT Workers Union Holds Nationwide Strike', available at https://www.aljazeera.com/news/2019/01/tunisia-powerful-ugtt-workers-union-holds-nationwide-strike-190117081348601.html.

the needs of members against the desire to maintain some ties to the regime. Eventually, as Hartshorn notes, the UGTT leaders took on a role in the revolution, as they 'could not ignore the revolutionary wave and moved to support their local cadres who had joined the protests'.[55] One member of the UGTT Administrative Commission identifies the police violence in the Kasserine protests as the 'tipping point', when 'unionists reached a consensus on the need to do everything in their power to force the UGTT leadership to end the mediation approach and seek to overthrow the government'.[56]

While the UGTT leadership may have been reluctant to side with the protesters at first, union members not only took part in the protests, but also served an important logistical role, allowing their facilities to be used as shelter for the protesters and offering them political and material support. As one union member from Bizerte said, 'The UGTT offices are sacred and have been since the colonial era. No authority dares touch those who take refuge at the UGTT – the police aren't authorised to lay a hand on the demonstrators.'[57] Following the revolution, the UGTT played a variety of overtly political roles, from approving governor appointments to holding minister-level positions. However, the UGTT membership did not always approve of the organisation's becoming a formal part of the system, and the three UGTT members serving in the first transitional government quit after protests by UGTT regional offices.

Despite its connection to the *ancien régime*, the UGTT managed to maintain its strength during Tunisia's transition. As Hartshorn describes, 'Through the revolutionary and transition process, the UGTT masterfully used one facet of its strength to enhance others. It built street power by reminding militant members of their long history, while actively creating a narrative around its own independence. It used those militant street activists to win concessions and support from political parties.'[58] Furthermore, the organisation has benefited from the rise of the Nidaa Tounes party, several of whose members (including President Beji Caid Essebsi) had themselves served in the Ben Ali and/or Bourguiba regimes. While the UGTT is not formally affiliated with Nidaa Tounes, 'there is broad overlap in identity … The affinities between the union and the party [are] clear, with Beji Caid Essebsi having been affiliated with the UGTT for years'.[59]

---

55 Hartshorn, *Labor Politics*, p. 120.
56 Hela Yousfi, *Trade Unions and Arab Revolutions: The Tunisian Case of UGTT*, New York 2018.
57 Yousfi, *Trade Unions*.
58 Hartshorn, *Labor Politics*, p. 159.
59 Hartshorn, *Labor Politics*, pp. 134–135.

Another important role of the UGTT has been in the consensus-building process that took place in the early years of the transition, particularly after the tumultuous period of 2012–2013 that saw the assassination of two leftist politicians and dwindling public support for the transitional government. The UGTT was the founding member of the National Dialogue Quartet, calling for a national dialogue in June 2012 to help ease the political chaos that was unfolding.[60] Along with the Tunisian Confederation of Industry, Trade and Handicrafts (UTICA), the Human Rights League and the Order of Lawyers, the UGTT oversaw a series of meetings from August 2013 to January 2014 that kept the country's political transition on track and netted the Quartet a Nobel peace prize in 2015.[61] The Quartet devised a roadmap to move the country forward, calling for political change via the resignation of the Troika government, to be replaced by a technocratic government with an independent prime minister, for the adoption of new constitution within four weeks and for the establishment of an independent electoral commission to oversee the upcoming presidential and parliamentary elections. The roadmap was signed by 21 political parties from across the spectrum, giving the document a legitimacy that the Quartet, as an unelected body, lacked at times. As noted by one of the members of the Quartet, the former president of UTICA Ouidad Bouchamaoui, although the UGTT and UTICA represented what were at times opposing forces (workers and business, respectively), they were able to overcome their differences for the good of the country.[62]

Conclusion: Will Alternative Politics Replace Formal Politics?

The trend in the region seems to be shifting away from formal, centralised politics towards alternative politics – be it through protest, social media, labour unions or other not officially organised forms of political engagement. Rather than joining a political party, running for office or even voting in an election, people in the MENA region are choosing to engage in political activism of a more personalised nature. This trend is neither unique to the MENA region, nor is it surprising. While the initial period after the 2011 revolutions led to a sense of euphoria and empowerment amongst the people of the region, that euphoria has faded into

---

60 Issandr el Amrani, 'Tunisia's National Dialogue Quartet Set a Powerful Example', International Crisis Group 10 October 2015, https://www.crisisgroup.org/middle-east-north-africa/north-africa/tunisia/tunisia-s-national-dialogue-quartet-set-powerful-example.
61 Ouidad Bouchamaoui, 'Roundtable with Ouidad Bouchamaoui', Atlantic Council, 10 April 2019.
62 Bouchamaoui, 'Roundtable'.

complacency at best and anger, frustration and violence at worst, as people see that their governments are unable or unwilling to uphold their end of the social contract. And governments, which saw their predecessors or their neighbours' regimes ousted by similar anger nine years ago, have responded with a mix of repression and appeasement that has only served to widen the gap in trust between the people and formal politics.

Thus, alternative political participation is an easier, and often more effective means of advocating for one's interests. The barriers to entry are lower than in formal politics, and certain forms, such as social media, are low-cost, meaning that virtually anyone, of any age or income group, can have a voice. Alternative political participation is also highly unpredictable, however: far more so than formal politics, under which at least the rules of the game tend to be codified or well known. While protests and social media are often regulated, outcomes can vary widely, from peaceful revolution to arrest or death. Furthermore, the leader-less and non-hierarchical nature of alternative political participation means that people with little to no training in politics are entering an arena in which certain skills are required to succeed. While orchestrating a protest or building a viral Twitter campaign require impressive organising abilities, these are not the same skills as are required to run for office, such as being able to develop or implement public policy.

Alternative political participation, particularly protests, can also engender a sense of false hope for the protesters. The alternative politics arena is far more 'black and white' than that of formal politics. As the recent Algerian protests have shown, slogans might bring down a government, but they cannot build a replace-ment. Thus, for politics in the Arab world to succeed requires a combination of the formal and the alternative – an outlet for citizens to have a voice, as well as a responsive apparatus to bring about the change that voice is calling for.

Bibliography

ACLED (Armed Conflict Location & Event Data Project), 'Data Export Tool', https://www.acleddata.com/data/.

AFP 17 April 2019, 'Algeria Protests Loosen Stranglehold on Media', https://www.arabnews.com/node/1483716/media.

AFP 6 March 2019, 'Social Media Breaks "Wall of Fear" for Algeria Protesters', https://www.france24.com/en/20190306-social-media-breaks-wall-fear-algeria-protesters.

Al-Jazeera 18 March 2019, 'Bouteflika Protests: Algeria's Shifting Media
    Space', https://www.aljazeera.com/programmes/listeningpost/2019/03/
    bouteflika-protests-algeria-shifting-media-space-190317083422948.html.
Amnesty International, 28 November 2017, 'Morocco: Protesters, Activists
    and Journalists Detained over Rif Protests Must Be Released', https://www.
    amnesty.org/en/latest/news/2017/11/morocco-protesters-activists-and-
    journalists-detained-over-rif-protests-must-be-released/.
Arab Barometer, 'Data Analysis Tool', 2007–2018, https://www.arabbarometer.
    org/survey-data/data-analysis-tool/.
Bayat, Asef, *Life as Politics: How Ordinary People Change the Middle East*,
    Stanford 2103.
Ben Moussa, Mohamed, 'From Arab Street to Social Movements:
    Re-Theorizing Collective Action and the Role of Social Media in the Arab
    Spring', *Westminster Papers in Communication and Culture* 9.2, 2013,
    pp. 47–68.
Bouchamaoui, Ouidad, 'Roundtable with Ouidad Bouchamaoui', Atlantic
    Council, 10 April 2019.
Brynen, Rex, Pete W. Moore, Bassel F. Salloukh and Marie-Joëlle Zahar,
    *Beyond the Arab Spring: Authoritarianism and Democratization in the Arab
    World*, Boulder 2012.
Carnegie Endowment for International Peace, 'Kifaya', 22 September 2010,
    https://carnegieendowment.org/2010/09/22/kifaya-pub-54922.
Chikhi, Lamine and Hamid Ould Ahmed, 'Algeria Protesters Return to the
    Streets as Spy Boss Reported Sacked', Reuters 5 April 2019, https://
    af.reuters.com/article/topNews/idAFKCN1RH19W-OZATP.
Daadaoui, Mohamed, 'Morocco's King Just Named a New Prime Minister, in
    Case You Forgot Who's in Charge', *The Washington Post* 20 March 2017,
    https://www.washingtonpost.com/news/monkey-cage/wp/2017/03/20/
    moroccos-king-just-named-a-new-prime-minister-in-case-you-forgot-whos-
    in-charge/.
Dahlgren, Peter, 'Do Social Media Enhance Democratic Participation?', Rosa
    Luxemburg Stiftung Policy Paper 04/2013, August 2013, https://www.
    rosalux.de/en/publication/id/7126/do-social-media-enhance-democratic-
    participation/.
Dahlgren, Peter, 'Social Media and Counter-Democracy: The Contingencies of
    Participation', *Electronic Participation*, Kristiansand 2102, pp. 1–12.
El-Amrani, Issandr, 'Tunisia's National Dialogue Quartet Set a Powerful
    Example', International Crisis Group 10 October 2015, https://www.

crisisgroup.org/middle-east-north-africa/north-africa/tunisia/tunisia-s-national-dialogue-quartet-set-powerful-example.

Gordner, Matt, 'Blogging Bouazizi: The Role of Tunisian Cyberactivists Before and After the Jasmine Revolution', *Middle East – Topics and Arguments* 6, 2016, pp. 54–63.

Grand, Stephen, *Understanding Tahrir Square*, Washington, DC 2103.

Hamzawy, Amr, 'Egypt's Resilient and Evolving Social Activism', Carnegie Endowment for International Peace, 5 April 2017, https://carnegieendowment.org/2017/04/05/egypt-s-resilient-and-evolving-social-activism-pub-68578.

Hartshorn, Ian M, *Labor Politics in North Africa: After the Uprisings in Egypt and Tunisia*, New York 2018.

Havana, Omar, '"This Is Our Time; It's the Time for Algerian People" ', Al-Jazeera 11 March 2019, https://www.aljazeera.com/indepth/inpictures/time-time-algerian-people-190311061538682.html.

Langohr, Vickie, 'Labor Movements and Organizations', *Arab Uprisings Explained*, ed. Marc Lynch, New York 2014, pp. 180–200.

LeVine, Mark, 'When Art Is the Weapon: Culture and Resistance Confronting Violence in the Post-Uprisings Arab World', *Religions* 6, 2015, pp. 1277–313.

Lindsey, Ursula, 'In Morocco, Protesters Organise against Repression with New and Traditional Tactics', MobLab 6 October 2017, https://mobilisationlab.org/stories/morocco-tactics-counter-repression/.

Lorch, Jasmin and Jonas Burkhard, 'Online and Traditional Forms of Protest Mobilization: Morocco's Rif Protests and Beyond', Middle East Institute, 22 August 2017, https://www.mei.edu/publications/online-and-traditional-forms-protest-mobilization-moroccos-rif-protests-and-beyond.

Lust-Okar, Ellen and Saloua Zerhouni, *Political Participation in the Middle East*, Boulder 2008.

Lynch, Marc, ed., *The Arab Uprisings Explained: New Contentious Politics in the Middle East*, New York 2014.

Ourahmoune, Nacima, 'Algeria: How Millennials Used Humour and Creativity to Force Abdelalziz Bouteflika to Stand Aside', *The Conversation* 13 March 2019, http://theconversation.com/algeria-how-millennials-used-humour-and-creativity-to-force-abdelalziz-bouteflika-to-stand-aside-113417.

Qiblawi, Tamara, 'Egyptian Voters Back Constitutional Referendum That Could Extend Sisi's Rule – CNN', CNN 23 April 2019, https://edition.cnn.com/2019/04/23/middleeast/egypt-referendum-results-intl/index.html.

Rachidi, Ilhem, 'Morocco's Crackdown Won't Silence Dissent – Foreign Policy', *Foreign Policy* 16 January 2019, https://foreignpolicy. com/2019/01/16/moroccos-crackdown-wont-silence-dissent-maroc-hirak-amdh/.

Ramdani, Nabila, 'The Fight for Freedom in Algeria Isn't Finished', *Foreign Policy* 13 March 2019, https://foreignpolicy.com/2019/03/13/the-fight-for-freedom-in-algeria-isnt-finished-abdelaziz-bouteflika-arab-spring-protests/.

Reuters 17 January 2019, 'Tunisia's Powerful UGTT Workers Union Holds Nationwide Strike', available at https://www.aljazeera.com/ news/2019/01/tunisia-powerful-ugtt-workers-union-holds-nationwide-strike-190117081348601.html.

RFI (Radio France Internationale), 2 March 2019, 'Bouteflika Appoints New Campaign Manager as Algerian Protests Peak on Social Media', http://en.rfi. fr/africa/20190302-social-media-bouteflika-algeria-sacks-campaign-manager.

RTS 26 June 2017, 'Le roi du Maroc mécontent du développement de la région du Rif', https://www.rts.ch/info/monde/8732110-le-roi-du-maroc-mecontent-du-developpement-de-la-region-du-rif.html.

Sakthivel, Vish, 'The Moroccan King Dismisses an Islamist Prime Minister', Washington Institute for Near East Policy, 17 March 2017, https://www. washingtoninstitute.org/policy-analysis/view/the-moroccan-king-dismisses-an-islamist-prime-minister.

Tackett, Carolyn and Emna Sayadi, 'Morocco: A Complete Blackout during Protests in Al-Hoceima', *Access Now* 30 November 2017, https://www. accessnow.org/morocco-complete-blackout-protests-al-hoceima/.

TRTWorld 10 April 2019, 'The Political Debut of Tunisia's Only Labour Union, Explained',https://www.trtworld.com/magazine/the-political-debut-of-tunisia-s-only-labour-union-explained-25734.

Tufekci, Zeynep, *Twitter and Teargas: The Power and Fragility of Networked Protest*, New Haven, CT 2017.

Volpi, Frederic, 'Algeria versus the Arab Spring', *Journal of Democracy* 24.3, 2013, pp. 104–15.

Yerkes, Sarah E., 'Morocco: The Model for Reform?', *The Arab Awakening: America and the Transformation of the Middle East*, ed. Brookings Institution, Washington, DC 2011, pp. 196–205.

Yerkes, Sarah E., *Where Have All the Revolutionaries Gone?*, Center for Middle East Policy at Brookings, Washington, DC, March 2017, https://www. brookings.edu/wp-content/uploads/2017/03/cmep_20160317_where_have_ revolutionaries_gone.pdf.

Yerkes, Sarah E. and Zeineb Ben Yahmed, 'Tunisia's Political System: From Stagnation to Competition', Carnegie Endowment for International Peace, 28 March 2109, https://carnegieendowment.org/2019/03/28/tunisia-s-political-system-from-stagnation-to-competition-pub-78717.

Yousfi, Hela, *Trade Unions and Arab Revolutions: The Tunisian Case of UGTT*, New York 2018.

10

Youth Activism and the Politics of 'Mediapreneurship': The Effects of Political Efficacy and Empowerment on Mediated Norm Conveyance in Tunisia and Morocco

Roxane Farmanfarmaian

Since 2011, the role of social media in the politics of the southern bank of the Mediterranean has changed substantially. Until then, uprisings and sustained social movements – the Cypress Revolution in Lebanon, the Green Revolution in Iran, the 'We are all Khaled Said' in Egypt – had utilised mobile phones, shared webpages and digital information exchange as the means of political activism, and new media use was undoubtedly gathering steam in popular abilities to mediate organisation, demonstration and change.[1] But it was when Tunisia triggered the 2011 Arab uprisings, which then found expression in demonstrations from Morocco to Yemen, that protestors, particularly younger people who were already skilled in using digital platforms and texting, took to using social media as a tool of local mobility and international strategic communication, broadcasting in real time their demands for work, government transparency and political change.[2] These

---

1 Suzi Mirgani, 'The State of the Arab Media in the Wake of the Arab Uprisings', *Bullets and Bulletins: Media and Politics in the Wake of the Arab Uprisings*, eds. Mohamed Zayani and Suzi Mirgani, London 2106, p. 5.
2 Jean-Pierre Filiu, *The Arab Revolution: Ten Lessons from the Democratic Uprisings*, London 2011.

movements, composed of a variety of ages and sectors, used traditional forms of activism – demonstrations, placards, speeches – as well as social media and citizen journalism to organise, but also to bypass government narratives, report directly from the streets, share photographs and videos of events captured on their mobile phones, tweet, blog and podcast and develop new media celebrities, showing up the self-censorship of the establishment media, and transmitting their messages across their own countries, their region and to the world at large.[3] As Creech noted, 'by giving a technological form to the protests that could be captured by [international] media, mobile recording technologies, alongside the distribution networks of YouTube, LiveLeak, Facebook, and Twitter, helped valorize the movement and articulate it'.[4]

The Arab uprisings were the training ground for young people, many new to the political sphere, whose use of social media on the streets blurred the lines between activism and journalism, and contributed to the compound terms 'citizen journalist', 'citizen media' and 'media activist', now in common use.[5] Lilie Chouliaraki describes this evolution clearly as a 'democratisation of technology' and, simultaneously, as a 'technologisation of democracy'.[6] For those protesting in 2011 in Tunisia and Morocco and throughout the Arab world, their collective success in gaining the international media attention they set out to achieve contributed to a

---

3 Anita Breuer, Todd Landman and Dorothea Farquhar, 'Social Media and Protest Mobilization: Evidence from the Tunisian Revolution', *Democratization* 22.4, 2015, pp. 764–92; Johanne Kuebler, 'Overcoming the Digital Divide: The Internet and Political Mobilization in Egypt and Tunisia', *CyberOrient* 5.1, http://www.cyberorient.net/article. do?articleId=6212; Marcin Lewiński and Dima Mohammed, 'Deliberate Design or Unintended Consequences? The Argumentative Uses of Facebook during the Arab Spring', *Journal of Public Deliberation* 8.1, 2012, pp. 1–11; Marc Lynch, 'After Egypt: The Limits and Promise of Online Challenges to the Authoritarian Arab State', *Perspectives on Politics* 9.1, 2011, pp. 301–10; Nevzat Soguk, 'Uprisings in "Arab Streets", Revolutions in "Arab minds"! A Provocation', *Globalizations* 8.5, 2011, pp. 595–99.
4 Brian Creech, 'Disciplines of truth: The "Arab Spring", American journalistic practice, and the production of public knowledge', *Journalism* 16.8, 2015, pp. 1010–1026.
5 Sami Ben Gharbia, October 2013, and Samia Errazzouki, January 2016, interviews with the author; see also Breuer, Landman and Farquhar, 'Social Media'.
6 Lilie Chouliaraki, 'Self-Mediation: New Media and Citizenship', *Critical Discourse Studies* 7.4, 2010, pp. 227–232. Chouliaraki goes on to explain: 'The "democratisation of technology" addresses self-mediation from the perspective of the empowering potential of new media technologies to invent novel discourses of counter-institutional subversion and collective activism; ... the "technologisation of democracy", addresses self-mediation from the perspective of the regulative potential of new media technologies to control the discourses and genres of ordinary participation and, in so doing, to reproduce the institutional power relations that such participation seeks to challenge.'

sense of empowerment, and a perception of their own ability to influence change in the social and political spheres.[7]

At the time, the movements were often described as 'youth led', with the young credited as bringing fresh dynamism to mass mobilisation through horizontal and leaderless linkages activated via social media. Subsequent academic assessment has offered a useful corrective, in highlighting the complex nature of the groups that contributed to the protests, and the pitfalls in homogenising even the 'youth' aspect of the demonstrators, which can erase class and income differences, both of which reflected significant variance in the demonstrators' motivations for joining the uprisings.[8] It is not the contention here that all young people utilising social media in Morocco and Tunisia benefited from the events of 2011, nor that 'youth', as a socially constructed category which at certain political junctures might be credited as an agent of change, describes the field under examination here. The focus of this study is on urban, educated youth and activists using new media.[9] Many of these were sidelined by the neo-liberal programmes that King Mohammed VI of Morocco and Tunisian ex-president Ben Ali set up despite their ostensible focus on the 'educated unemployed', who in turn became drivers in 'mediating' the uprisings through websites, blogs, Facebook postings and distributed Twitter feeds. Some, such as bloggers Dina Ben-Mhenni and Slim Amamou in Tunisia, burst on to the scene; others, often more seasoned journalists and media activists, developed or refashioned existing websites, including al-Nawat, Bawsala, Tunisia Live and I Watch in Tunisia, and Mamfakinch, Lakome, Ya Biladi and Le Mag in Morocco, to impact the uprisings and their aftermath.[10] The merging of new media coverage and political activism was a feature of the interpretation, by younger, tech-savvy contributors, of the forces of change both technologically and politically in communicating protest, organisation and new ideas of identity and meaning. Produced under the umbrella of I Am Vigilant (and since 2017, a branch of Transparency International in Tunisia), I Watch sums up the confluence in this way:

---

7 Anita Breuer and Jacob Groshek, 'Online Media and Offline Empowerment in Post-Rebellion Tunisia: An Analysis of Internet Use during Democratic Transition', *Journal of Information Technology & Politics* 11.1, 2014, pp. 25–44.

8 Maria Paciello and Daniela Pioppi, 'Youth as Actors of Change? The Cases of Morocco and Tunisia', *The International Spectator* 53.2, 2018, pp. 38–39.

9 'Youth' is itself a contested term in regards to its biological beginning and end, and is used widely here to refer to people ranging from teenagers to those in their early thirties.

10 At different times, many of these websites have been supported by NGOs, with varying degrees of NGO influence over their workings.

The organization was founded after the Tunisian revolution on March 21, 2011. The organization includes a number of young men and women active in various parts of the Republic and all of them are working to preserve the gains of the revolution. I am vigilant in the youthful potential of Tunisia. The young people who made the revolution have credentials that make them trustworthy. The organization works to include young people in the decision-making system and rejects guardianship in any way because of lack of expertise.[11]

This chapter considers how today's 'mediapreneurs' are exploring different ways to function as a responsible force of resistance within states still undergoing political transition. The term 'mediapreneur' engages with the multiple meanings ascribed to the interaction of media, journalism and activist communication that young people, as well as experienced activist journalists, have developed in challenging their existing political, social and communicative environments. I adopt John Downing's definition of media activism as 'collective communication practices that challenge the status quo, including established media'.[12] Berman and Pickard offer a useful elaboration, in noting that 'we conceive of the media both as a tool for political mobilization and as an object of political struggle as activists endeavour to reform, delegitimize, or build more democratic alternatives to the commercial mass media system'.[13] Citizen journalism is defined by John Hamilton as 'non-professionals practising journalism', with 'professional' connoting those having undergone 'a period of intensive training'.[14] In states with limited media freedom, such as Ben Ali's Tunisia and Mohammed VI's Morocco, media training has often lacked professional credibility, while greater scope for professionalisation is offered within the frame of citizen journalism and what Samia Errazzouki calls 'citizen media'.[15] As Hamilton observes, citizen journalism is 'enabling people outside of closed news organizations to gather, write and

---

11 I Watch, 2019, https://www.iwatch.tn/ar/.

12 John D.H. Downing, 'Social Movement Media and Media Activism', *Oxford Research Encyclopedias*, 'Communication', May 2018, DOI:10.1093/acrefore/9780190228613.013.574.

13 David E. Berman and Victor Pickard, 'Media Activism', March 2018, *Oxford Bibliographies*, DOI: 10.1093/obo/9780199756841-0201.

14 John Hamilton, 'Citizen Journalism', June 2015, *Oxford Bibliographies*, DOI: 10.1093/obo/9780199756841-0169.

15 Samia Errazzouki, 'Under Watchful Eyes: Internet Surveillance and Citizen Media in Morocco, the Case of Mamfakinch', *The Journal of North African Studies* 22.3, 2017, pp. 361–85; Roxane Farmanfarmaian, 'What Is Private, What Is Public, and Who Exercises Media Power in Tunisia? A Hybrid-Functional Perspective on Tunisia's Media Sector', *The Journal of North African Studies* 19.5, 2014, pp. 656–78.

distribute information globally; it also wreaks havoc on claims that only profes-
sionally trained journalists can write authoritative accounts, as well as that traditionally objective-style reporting is the only way to compose such accounts'[16].

In bringing these multiple forms and purposes of communicative expression
together in processes of resistance that are both political and performative, the
analysis presented here draws on media, social movement and political studies
literatures to understand the interaction and co-constitutive nature of mediapreneurship's trajectory in the years following the Arab uprisings. It is based on field
research in both Morocco and Tunisia between 2013 and 2016, and on interviews
with new media activists and bloggers. The period of analysis includes 2011, but
looks beyond that year to the present, to consider how new media activists have
capitalised on their experiences from that time to sustain a media presence, and
develop ongoing forms of communicative resistance. Within that timeframe, these
mediapreneurs have themselves become part of the social landscape, bringing to
their enterprise the next generations of young media activists committed to political change negotiated through digital communicative space. Three case studies
provide the empirical illustration of how specific forms of new media activism
translated into mediapreneurship, and how that has weathered increasing restrictions on media freedom in both Tunisia and Morocco, as practitioners developed
sustainable approaches to promoting norms and forms of news reporting consistent with those agitated for in 2011.

Norms, Mediapreneurship and Empowerment

Theoretically, the development of mediapreneurship as an activist process can be
understood at two levels. Firstly, in demanding new approaches to political and
human rights practices, young media activists began a process that Finnemore and
Sikkink describe as 'norm entrepreneurship'.[17] This is a three-step progression in
which alternative social behaviour is, first, introduced as appropriate, and second
(as expressed in the slogans and messaging mediated during the demonstrations of
the Arab uprisings), is adopted by different groups in what Finnemore and Sikkink
label 'norm cascades'. The third step, internalisation, was not generally achieved
by the Arab uprisings, in that governments and elite networks pushed back,
rejecting the norms of pluralism, and human rights including free expression, and

---

16 Hamilton, 'Citizen Journalism'.
17 Martha Finnemore and Kathryn Sikkink, 'International Norm Dynamics and Political
Change', *International Organization* 52.4, 1998, pp. 887–917.

reasserted instead narratives justifying central control and repression. Contesting authoritarian discourse, and promoting and practising instead the values projected during the freer days of the Arab uprisings, so as to sustain their vitality and legiti-macy and thereby spread the new norm internalisation within their communities, is the task that current activist mediatisation can be understood as pursuing.

The second theoretical level relates to the experiences that young media activists themselves underwent at the time, and the regional and international responses they elicited. The impact of this experience can be explained using the theoretical framework of internal political efficacy and, as will be elaborated in the next section, produced an ongoing commitment to the powers of new media technologies to promote alternative norm adoption for political and economic change. It will be argued here that this gave impetus to continuing engagement in mediapreneurship. Specifically, this encompasses the routing of the management and organisation of social movement activism through internet-based and social media communication ventures dedicated to norm conveyance and information provision in a process of risk taking (financial, economic and political) to attain a profit – that profit being the improvement of society for the benefit of those not currently in power.[18] The utilisation of digital mediation to forge social meaning and community continued, therefore, as the Arab Spring drew to an end and politi-cal opportunity narrowed. Bloggers and web-based citizen journalists developed communicative strategies through existing, as well as new online and social media outlets, so as to carve out ongoing spaces of political expression to preserve, and expand on, the achievements of the uprisings, recasting once again the relation-ship between new media use, authoritarian power, news dissemination and youth activism.[19]

The salience of this process has, however, been blurred by the retention of power by entrenched elite networks, and their ability to absorb the lessons around the opportunities and dangers inherent in the new uses of media technology.[20]

---

18 'Entrepreneurship' is here defined as '[t]he capacity and willingness to develop, organise and manage a business venture along with any of its risks in order to make a profit' (http://www.businessdictionary.com/definition/entrepreneurship.html).
19 Magdalena Karolak, 'Social Media in Democratic Transitions and Consolidations: What Can We Learn from the Case of Tunisia?', *The Journal of North African Studies* Online first, June 2018, DOI: 10.1080/13629387.2018.1482535; 'Democratic Transitions and Consolidations: What Can We Learn from the Case of Tunisia?', *The Journal of North African Studies* Online first, June 2018, DOI: 10.1080/13629387.2018.1482535.
20 Steven Heydemann and Reinoud Leenders, 'Authoritarian Learning and Counter-Revolution', *The Arab Uprisings Explained: New Contentious Politics in the Middle East*, ed. Marc Lynch, New York 2014, pp. 75–92; Mirgani, 'State of the Arab Media'.

Showing themselves to be as capable as the activists in generalising from circumstances elsewhere in the region during the uprisings, authoritarian governments
adapted a range of high-tech strategies to their own needs. This has enabled them
not only to push back against activist narratives by mediating their own in order
to connect with their publics, but to strengthen communicative cohesion across the
branches of government, the intelligence services and the military in the face of
social disruption.[21] Large cyber-control centres and broad social media capacities
were rapidly incorporated into the governments left standing after the Arab uprisings, while new or existing laws were rapidly configured to restrict or steer internet usage according to government diktat.[22] Further, the media linkage between
governments and large business interests was strengthened.[23] This has materially contributed to what Alina Mungiu-Pippidi describes as 'media capture': 'a
situation in which the media have not succeeded in becoming autonomous in
manifesting a will of their own, nor able to exercise their main function, notably
of informing people. Instead, they have persisted in an intermediate state, with
vested interests, and not just the government, using them for other purposes.'[24]

   Governments, however, including those that are authoritarian and tightly integrated with powerful business networks, have faced a stark reality in the aftermath
of the Arab uprisings: the citizens of the Arab world, if only briefly, expressed
their voice, experienced its power, and continue to have access to the technologies
and networks that enable private and social exchange.[25] Although government surveillance capacity now constrains activist expression online, and users are wary
of incursions into their privacy, this has not deterred the growth and sustainability
of a largely activist-driven sector within the internet-based web and social media

21 Heydemann and Leenders, 'Authoritarian Learning'; Marc Lynch, 'Media, Old and New',
Arab Uprisings Explained, ed. Lynch, p. 94.
22 Alexis Artaud de la Ferrière and Nareseo Vallina-Rodriguez, 'The Scissors and the
Magnifying Glass: Internet Governance in the Transitional Tunisian Context', *The Journal
of North African Studies* 19.5, 2014, pp. 639–55; Bouziane Zaid, 'The Authoritarian Trap in
State/Media Structures in Morocco's Political Transition', *The Journal of North African
Studies* 22.3, 2017, pp. 340–60.
23 Abdelfettah Benchenna, Driss Ksikes and Dominique Marchetti, 'The Media in Morocco:
A Highly Political Economy, the Case of the Paper and On-line-Press since the Early 1990s',
The Journal of North African Studies 22.3, 2017, pp. 386–410; Farmanfarmaian, 'What Is
Private'.
24 Alina Mungiu-Pippidi, 'Freedom without Impartiality: The Vicious Circle of Media
Capture', *Media Transformations in the Post-Communist World*, ed. Peter Gross and Karol
Jakubowicz, Plymouth 2013, p. 41.
25 Lynch, 'Media, Old and New'.

spheres.[26] States no longer hold narrative monopolies, and although the range of counter-narratives has shrunk, the threat they represent – of capturing the public mood and expanding rapidly across the public sphere – is a risk governments recognise they cannot entirely immunise themselves against.[27]

The following section will examine why this is the case, and how the younger generation of activists and new media journalists developed competencies and skills in the course of the uprisings that have driven mediapreneurship with two identifiable purposes: first, to ensure that facts and alternative interpretations of news and events are available and sustain the public sphere; and second, to serve as mechanisms of norm conveyance (such as transparency and watchdog reporting), as part of a long-term process to achieve social internalisation of alternative notions of what is politically appropriate and desirable in their communities.[28] In the third section, case studies drawn from Tunisia and Morocco will illustrate both conceptually and in practice how this development has contributed to broadening the discourse in each state, and forcing official tolerance in landscapes where strong government narratives dominate.

Evolution of Youth and Activist Mediapreneurship

The aspirations, and then disappointments, that accompanied the Arab uprisings have tended to focus on the lack of significant political gains achieved after the emergence of a broad popular movement that clearly expressed its demands. What is less well understood are the successes that were achieved, and their longer-term implications: in particular, the competencies developed by a number of those engaged in mediating the uprisings; the strategic experiences they gained in reconfiguring the social context and normative practices at the time; the transparency and monitoring they delivered during the post-2011 transition phases; and the empowerment that attended domestic, regional and international responses. Even as the political opportunities for structural change at the centre shrank in the face of government pushback, these successes translated into significant structural changes elsewhere, including in the communicative capacities of younger reporters and activist journalists, in the role of media in alternative norm promotion and in the complexity of the public sphere.

---

26 Erkan Saka, 'Social Media in Turkey as a Space for Political Battles: AKTrolls and Other Politically Motivated Trolling', *Middle East Critique* 27.2, 2018, pp. 161–77.
27 Errazzouki 'Under Watchful Eyes'; Lynch, 'Media, Old and New'.
28 Finnemore and Sikkink, 'International Norm Dynamics'.

What is more, in both Tunisia and Morocco, the decade preceding the uprisings had witnessed greater openness in media practices, leading to a rise in public
debate through radio call-in shows, laying the ground for ongoing expectations
on the part of both media practitioners and the public of a more vibrant, more
performative public sphere. In Tunisia, the privatisation of media prior to the
fall of Ben Ali had opened spaces for a limited degree of public engagement, as
explained in 2009 by Mosaïque Radio's Ouertan: 'Through our programs, lis-
teners begin to understand that people can be different, and by listening to the
debates in our programs they begin to accept that differences exist, that you have
to accept criticism ... [W]e, the young ones, dream of a career in Tunisia, so
we want to develop Tunisia. We want to teach people that there is not one sole
right opinion.'[29] In Morocco, the early years of the reign of Mohammed VI were
marked by a certain level of easing in both censorship and constraint on the media
sector, and the appearance of a variety of critical papers and magazines had led
to an opening of public debate on previously taboo subjects.[30] While these openings were limited, they contributed to new arenas of civic exchange and narrative
development, which found force in the ensuing uprisings, but likewise, remained
part of the public consciousness in the period that followed.

Internal political efficacy

The success experienced by citizen journalists, web managers, Twitter generators
and others who engaged actively in the uprising process through smart phones and
internet exchanges contributed to the mobilisation in a way that was understood
as a true feat. The very fact of holding demonstrations, the new manner of using
communicative technology to achieve their organisation, their repeated mobilisation, and as they evolved, their ability to provoke government responses and
engage international news and other media attention, were a triumph, particularly
in the face of regimes known to be censorious, repressive and often violent.

A standard predictor of conventional political participation is political efficacy.[31] 'External efficacy' reflects responsiveness by government leaders and
institutions to public participation through voting, for example. 'Internal efficacy'

---

29 Quoted in Rikke Haugbølle and Francesco Cavatorta, '"Vive la grande famille des médias
tunisiens" Media Reform, Authoritarian Resilience and Societal Responses in Tunisia', The
Journal of North African Studies 17.1, 2012, p. 107.
30 Benchenna, Ksikes and Marchetti, 'Media in Morocco'.
31 Stephen C. Craig and Michael A. Maggiotto, 'Measuring Political Efficacy', Political
Methodology 8.3, 1982, pp. 85–109; James Maddux, 'Self-Efficacy: The Power of Believing

describes the extent to which individuals or groups perceive themselves as able to influence politics.[32] The demonstrations of 2011, in combining particularist grievances with a universalist appeal to rights and dignity, developed a shared narrative that imbued the protesters with a sense that they were able to influence politics. Not only did their common slogans get picked up by Al-Jazeera as a regional story in which each location had a role and importance, but, as the rolling demonstrations broke through the 'wall of fear' and galvanised public participation, and eventually, incurred political responses, the successes in one place became the successes of those everywhere else, including among the demonstrators who appeared outside Arab embassies in response to tweets and social media messaging in locations throughout the world. The individual experience as part of a consolidated effort vis-à-vis the political system incurred feelings of reward and internal political efficacy – their contribution was understood to have cultural meaning, materially, as part of a movement, and symbolically, as having political voice.[33] In particular, as Breuer and Gorshek noted, media activists were at the forefront of the process, knowing that 'one of the most important functions of digital activist networks was helping to develop a new culture of public deliberation and to construct a national collective identity supportive of resistance'.[34]

Political empowerment

Associated with the concept of internal political efficacy is the developmental idea of empowerment, a process by which individuals become participants, rather than solely recipients, within the political process. Defined by the UN Research Institute for Social Development as 'the organised efforts to increase control over resources and regulative institutions on the part of groups and movements of those hitherto excluded from such control', political empowerment is characterised by collective organisation to enhance influence and bargaining power.[35] Further, it

You Can', *Handbook of Positive Psychology*, eds. Shane Lopez and C.R. Snyder, New York 2001, pp. 277–87.

32 Craig and Maggiotto, 'Measuring Political Efficacy'.

33 Gabriel Almond and Sidney Verba, *The Civic Culture. Political Attitudes and Democracy in Five Nations*, Princeton 1963.

34 Breuer and Groshek, 'Online Media'; see also Emma Murphy, 'Theorizing ICTs in the Arab World: Informational Capitalism and the Public Sphere', *International Studies Quarterly* 53.4, 2009, pp. 1131–53.

35 Peter Utting, 'The Challenge of Political Empowerment', UNRISD (United Nations Research Institute for Social Development), 23 March 2012, http://www.unrisd.org/news/utting-empowerment.

is a process whereby involvement in collective action enables the acquisition of complex political skills, as in strategising communicative distribution of ideas, norms and practices. This positively affects the perception of citizenship, and the individual's own role and capacity to influence political decision-making as well as the social and cultural systems in which they are located.[36] Thus, shifts in political culture reflect the aggregation of individuals' attitudes toward the political system, and reconfigure their perception of their position and power within that system.[37]

As the Arab uprisings coincided with an explosion in mobile phone ownership and social network use across the world, a trend in which the region was well represented, digital media leaders rode a wave of empowerment, in which tech and protest were tightly integrated, and worked together to overcome the silence and fear induced by authoritarianism, engineering instead mass political expression.[38] What is more, the arena of the local became coincident with the international, as both conveyed and accessed information across borders in real time. The political boundaries of internet activism on such a scale were being explored for the first time, and only later would scholars debate whether there was such a thing as a Facebook or Twitter revolution, and argue over whether protest and political structures had inherently changed with the advent of social media and the web.[39] In the camp that questions social media's transformative impact, Nabil Dajani states that 'social media can play an active role in organizing and informing the masses, but there is still no empirical evidence to support the position that social and other mass media are sufficient means for bringing about attitude change, let alone regime change'[40]. Even so, the experience of empowerment at the time was to prove significant, and contributed to a rapid accumulation of political and communicative competencies of tech acquisition and expectations within a mass popular movement for immediate, accurate reporting. Webmasters, Twitter commentators, bloggers and social media content-generators became the new newscasters and opinion setters, enjoying a credibility that regime broadcasters had

36 Breuer and Groshek, 'Online Media'.
37 Almond and Verba, *Civic Culture*.
38 Everette Dennis, Justin Mann and Robb Woods, *Media Use in the Middle East, 2013: An Eight-Nation Survey by Northwestern University in Qatar*, 2013, http://menamediasurvey.northwestern.edu.
39 Evgeny Morozov, *The Net Delusion: The Dark Side of Internet Freedom*, Public Affairs, New York 2012.
40 Nabil Dajani, 'Technology Cannot a Revolution Make: *Nas*-book not Facebook', *Arab Media & Society*, 5 March 2012, www.arabmediasociety.com/technology-cannot-a-revolution-make-nas-book-not-facebook/.

never experienced, and an international following, as well as collaboration and uptake by the international media. This cemented the sense of internal political efficacy, while at the same time placing those leading the mediation process at the forefront of the technology's new facilities, as they engaged in experimental and increasingly professionalised methods of collecting and analysing data, disseminating visuals and funding the enterprise of greater audience access.

As the doors of political opportunity began to close post-2011, with the Tunisian government exerting increased levels of control over protests in the wake of two political assassinations, and the Moroccan government shutting them down with conciliatory promises of constitutional change and economic payoffs, the dust began to settle, revealing a more complex public and media sphere, and significant shifts in popular political awareness, social media use and news consumption.[41] The importance of local news had risen and it had gained audience share, while popular suspicion of Al-Jazeera's political agenda and those of other regional satellite broadcasters had reduced their regional popularity, and the web was becoming increasingly important as a source of news for a larger audience, rivalling television in many states, including Morocco and Tunisia, especially among young people and women.[42] Meanwhile, a number of the new media leaders, and their sites, had faded away. These included Tunisia Live, e-observation.org – winner of the best website award in Tunisia in 2014 – and citizen-journalism site Mamfakinch in Morocco, as well as several Tunisian activists who had gained near celebrity status, such as bloggers Dina Ben-Mhenni and Slim Amamou.[43] What is more, trust in internet privacy, as well as in its utility as a source of political empowerment, was diminishing, even as more people throughout the region accessed it via their phones, rather than laptops or desktops, and more people were using WhatsApp than email.[44]

However, importantly, a number of the new media leaders at the time of the Arab uprisings, as well as new activists, further professionalised, building on the

---

41 Omair Anas, 'After the Uprisings: Critical Reception of Empowered Arab Audiences', *New Media Configurations and Socio-Cultural Dynamics in Asia and the Arab World*, eds. Nadja-Christina Schneider and Carola Richter, London 2015, pp. 110–33; Roxane Farmanfarmaian, 'Media and the Politics of the Sacral: Freedom of Expression in Tunisia after the Arab Uprisings', *Media, Culture and Society* 39.7, 2017, pp. 1043–62; David Romero and Arturo Molina, 'Collaborative Networked Organisations and Customer Communities: Value Co-Creation and Co-Innovation in the Networking Era', *Production Planning Control* 22, 2011, 447-472, https://doi.org/10.1080/09537287.2010.536619.
42 Benchenna, Ksikes and Marchetti, 'Media in Morocco'.
43 Errazzouki 'Under Watchful Eyes'; Karolak, 'Social Media'.
44 Northwestern University in Qatar 2013, 2014, 2015.

empowerment and competencies gained during the period of protests as well as in their immediate aftermath. They expanded their sites, and, in the face of closures due to new internet laws and repression, developed new sites when existing ones were shut down.

The motivation for the mediated activism had meanwhile shifted. Norms promoted during the uprisings had been broadly adopted as cascades of news and information had been disseminated through digitised media. Such norms had come to be recognised as critical to the transition and consolidation of community pluralism and stronger practices of human rights, whether through uncensored reporting or by holding the government to account. These norms, having resonated with the publics while in action, had not induced the freeing of government from the clasp of the ruling elites, and hence, it was clear, norm adoption had not moved into what Finnemore and Sikkink describe as the 'internalisation' phase.[45] Focused on promoting internalisation, digital media activists continued the process of change-making by producing sustainable outlets of professionalised media production, in order to serve as norm-conveyers to sustain and expand the process. This sense of efficacy – of being able to drive change through mediated political empowerment – has translated into multiple examples of mediapreneurship within the political sphere. The experience of taking part in the movements that brought about a period of dynamic political change has endowed these citizen-actors with a sense of 'ownership' over an ongoing transitional reform process, and increased their willingness to channel political action through new media. Unlike in the case of conventional media, where coverage can raise the cost of possible repression, new media opportunity costs are relatively low, and amplification of the message can be modulated according to political exigencies.[46] In the following section, three such cases are examined.

Mediapreneurs in Tunisia and Morocco

In Finnemore and Sikkink's analysis of norm dynamics, the emergence of new norms, or normative practices, rests on two elements: 'norm entrepreneurs', and 'organisational platforms from which entrepreneurs act'.[47] Although the authors do not define norm entrepreneurs, they describe them as agents that 'call attention to issues, or even "create" issues by using language that names, interprets, and

---

45 Finnemore and Sikkink, 'International Norm Dynamics', p. 895.
46 Breuer and Gorshek, 'Online Media'.
47 Finnemore and Sikkink, 'International Norm Dynamics', p. 896.

dramatizes them', as well as locating them in larger contexts of social meaning.[48] This is because new norms do not emerge in a vacuum, but must compete in an already populated field of norms and perceptions of interest. As existing norms describe behaviours and interests that are projected as 'appropriate' – through official discourse, for example – norm entrepreneurs must, in Finnemore and Sikkink's view, at times express activism through 'inappropriateness' – such as by revealing discomfiting facts through investigative reporting, or 'speaking truth to power'. In doing so, norm entrepreneurs who utilise media as their organisational platforms, and who disrupt social meanings through projections of new norms that contest old ones, can be understood as mediapreneurs.

In Tunisia, a range of media activists set up platforms and blogs at various times in the period leading up to the overthrow of President Ben Ali, and continued to do so after his departure. Two are examined here: al-Nawat, among the oldest surviving web-based platforms that has consistently described itself as an activist media site; and Inkyfada, an investigative magazine site set up in 2012, after the first wave of demonstrations and initial appointment of new government officials. In Morocco, where censorship has consistently deepened since the 2011 demonstrations, alternative news sites are closed regularly, with some reappearing with similar staff, but under different names. The opposition news site Lakome, today in its iteration as Lakome2, offers a useful example of mediapreneurship, having continued to dedicate itself to filling gaps in coverage by the conventional news and, so far, avoiding complete closure.

Al-Nawat

Founded by human rights lawyer Riadh Guerfali and tech journalist Sami Ben Gharbia, al-Nawat (The Core) was a political advocacy site from its inception in 2004. The platform, censored by Ben Ali's famous internet security apparatus, which filtered websites that published articles critical of the government or criticised Tunisia's human rights record – all of which al-Nawat did – was often inaccessible during those years; the address page simply blanked out with the standard 'File not Found' error message. Its current 'About' page notes that this stopped on 13 January 2011, and goes on to explain its mission:

> Our platform develops its content directly from contacts on-the-ground, and
> from contributions from activists, whistleblowers, and citizens involved

---

48 Finnemore and Sikkink, 'International Norm Dynamics', p. 897.

in public processes, particularly those suffering disfunction. We are very committed to the protection of privacy, the defense of free expression, OpenData and the right to access information and public documents.[49]

Leading up to the 2011 uprisings, Ben Gharbia, in his late twenties at the time, lived in the Netherlands, and from there curated information sent from all over Tunisia via Twitter, email or social media by demonstrators, citizen journalists and other activists. He compiled, edited and reposted the information on al-Nawat's site. In this way, he avoided the censors, and, with his partners in Tunis, he was able to call attention to issues as they arose, and broadcast much that was 'inappropriate' according to the guidelines set out by the regime. 'It was,' he said, 'an example of the media's new ability to transmit information quickly through different national nodes, so we could curate it in a form that addressed the needs of the public in Tunisia itself. We couldn't have done it if I hadn't been abroad – as then the information from within Tunisia couldn't have been collected, and yet what made it compelling was as a Tunisian, I could compile the news that meant something for Tunisians.'[50] As with classic entrepreneurship, the endeavour faced risks, but reaped returns in playing its part in the overthrow of the regime, which enabled Ben Gharbia to return to Tunis as the media environment opened up, freed from censorship and rid of the vast regime of online surveillance.[51]

Al-Nawat received a number of media prizes for its reporting and coverage of the uprising, including from Reporters Without Borders and Index on Censorship, and funding from international NGOs. Although it prided itself on attracting good journalists, in the years between 2011 and 2014 al-Nawat prioritised citizen journalism, advocacy and the promotion of its political norms, focusing on blogging rather than journalism per se in its coverage of democracy, transparency, good governance, justice, fundamental liberties and rights and full disclosure.[52] Yet, as the country regained stability, and the new media environment, previously content with scrappy websites reflecting their youthful founders, rapidly matured, al-Nawat professionalised. Its website began to produce stories simultaneously in French, Arabic and English. Visuals increased in number, and it added new sections, including one on leaks. It likewise began to focus more on

---

49 Al-Nawat, 2019, http://nawaat.org/portail/en/.
50 Ben Gharbia, interview.
51 Artaud de la Ferrière and Vallina-Rodriguez, 'The Scissors'.
52 Al-Nawat, 2019.

the professionalisation of journalism, conducting training sessions and hosting interns. Most recently, it has developed a video-making branch.

Critically, al-Nawat has continued to project its identity as a conveyor of norms that remain under-represented in the political and social practices of the country. It continues to publish text that names and dramatises issues that contest existing norms, such as a May 2019 story entitled 'Irregular Migration: In Tunisian Territorial Waters, the Army Kills',[53] or a profile in February 2019, which began as follows:

> As per the official request of prime minister Youssef Chahed, the name of Marouen Mabrouk was removed from the list of 48 Tunisians sanctioned by the European Union for misappropriation of state funds. Unlike other friends and relatives of deposed president Ben Ali who saw their money frozen by the EU, Mabrouk was able to find himself a new political shield to protect his wealth following the revolution that swept the country in 2011.[54]

In its role of mediapreneur, al-Nawat utilises its platform to sustain a discourse that privileges the norms it fought for in the uprising, and which it continues to promote in its efforts to inspire its readers to internalise them.

Inkyfada

Walid Mejeni and Sana Uwaey both studied journalism in France before returning to Tunisia a few years prior to the uprising. Both worked in regime media, and both worked at al-Nawat, before breaking away while still in their twenties to establish a venture called al-Khat (The Line). A company dedicated to freedom of the press and freedom of expression, it soon launched Inkyfada, an online magazine focused on high-quality investigative journalism. From the very outset, their approach was mediapreneurship – to develop an economically sound entity that would, in Mejeni's words, 'work in practical ways on the ground'. Through Inkyfada, they set out to ask – and answer – 'the real questions, offer transparency (a mirror of what happens in society), debates around what the public really

---

53 Sana Sbouaï, 'Irregular Migration: In Tunisian Territorial Waters, the Army Kills', Al-Nawat 5 May 2019, https://nawaat.org/portail/2019/05/05/irregular-migration-in-tunisian-territorial-waters-the-army-kills/.
54 Mohammed Samih Beji Okkez, 'Marouen Mabrouk, a Story of Impunity after the Revolution', Al-Nawat 25 February 2019, https://nawaat.org/portail/2019/02/25/marouen-mabrouk-a-story-of-impunity-after-the-revolution/.

finds important, so we can be of service'.[55] To develop a viable economic model, al-Khat launched a web platform for training, working with NGOs and media companies such as Heinrich Böll and Deutsche Welle and building skills through blogs of young people, 'so journalism is expressed in their voices', according to Uwaey.[56] It likewise launched a production section for bespoke editing, and Le Lab for customised web design; all to ensure the enterprise would survive financially. Unlike at al-Nawat, it was decided to accept advertising. According to its mission page,

> Inkyfada's objective is to reveal, make visible and render accessible that which is hidden, and offer a better understanding of the world through investigation, fact-based journalism and the publication of deep reportage, portraits, and articles that explain through contextualisation. Inkyfada assumes openly its role of opposition and counter-weight, with real impact on public debate, in its struggle against the impunity and opacity of those in power, and all forms of injustice that emanate from them.[57]

Though many of the norms being projected and conveyed chime with those openly promoted by al-Nawat, the focus and approach of Inkyfada could not be in greater contrast. The articles are long, and designed to offer a full picture through high-calibre investigative reporting. It is visually rich, filling the webpage with colour and arresting graphics. Inkyfada's first significant piece of reporting, and one which placed it on the map and had considerable impact, was an interactive terrorism map that tracked, for the first time, where and when incidents were occurring as Tunisia entered a period of frequent terrorist attacks, and how many people (both civilians and military) were killed, providing background details and comments on each occurrence. Their main focus, however, has been on stories with social impact: the state of homelessness, the plight of single mothers returning from ISIS camps, trafficking of minors, harmful neglect of trains and other infrastructure, the migrant crisis and growing problems in accessing clean water.

As it has matured, Inkyfada has expanded its selection of coverage, adding sections on Witness accounts, Portraits of the Voiceless, and Plain Speaking, all shorter pieces that highlight an injustice, a specific area of neglect (such as the Plain Speaking piece on Tunisia's pollution problem) or a public struggle.

---

55 Walid Mejeni, June 2014, interview with author.
56 Sana Uwaey, June 2014, interview with author.
57 Inkyfada, 2019, https://inkyfada.com/fr/.

Through quality coverage of such topics, accompanied by photographs, graphics, maps and survey data, the Inkyfada mediapreneurs are naming and drawing attention to the iniquities and normative failures of the social structure, and using the site for meaning-making to draw in readers. In capturing their attention, the staff at Inkyfada project the norms their enterprise is designed to promote. As Majeni explained, 'We can carry things the society doesn't recognise, or accept, or wish to hear. We can publish on issues that wouldn't normally be accepted by mainstream editors. And we will provide the whole documentation of an event – pictures of the terrain, descriptions of who was where and when and who said what at all times; we provide full historical records that can serve in the future for research.'[58] Although the site has recently undergone a change in management, the staff and established goals of mediapreneurship have continued seamlessly, engaging serious young reporters in publishing new work to expand the social internalisation of values linked to investigative reporting that holds the government to account.

Lakome and Lakome2

Lakome was founded during a period of media transition in Morocco which preceded the political turmoil of 2011 and the rise of the protest movement referred to there as 'Le Mouvement du 20 Février' (20 February Movement). In the 1990s and early 2000s, Arabic-language weeklies had proliferated as laws had shifted, enabling for the first time more open political, and particularly economic, reporting. Furthermore, market adjustments made it possible for the press to be designed and run according to entrepreneurial principles.[59] However, in a cycle common in Morocco, repression gradually followed, and the result was that many of the alternative political voices that had flourished in the Arabic-language weeklies and dailies, which tended to be highly professional and politically liberal, moved towards establishing web news sites as safer havens. Among these were two well-known mediapreneurs, Aboubakr Jamai and Ali Anouzla, who launched the news website Lakome, running editions in both French and Arabic. Jamai had made his name as a co-founder of *Le Journal*, a weekly magazine that became well known for challenging the institutional and political context in which Morocco found itself at the time, and was finally closed down by the monarchy. Anouzla, founder of several weeklies including *al-Jarida al-Oukhra* and *al-Jarida al-Oula*, was

---

58 Majeni, interview.
59 Benchenna, Ksikes and Marchetti, 'Media in Morocco'.

equally recognisable as a sharp journalist and resourceful entrepreneur with powerful connections, despite being politically critical of the establishment. The 2011
turmoil furthered the expansion of alternative news portals by younger members
of the media community, with the appearance of Ya Biladi, Goud, Badil and Le
Mag, the more mainstream Hespress and Hibapress – whose editors publish material that often comes close to, but never goes over, the line of official tolerance
– the bilingual strongly pro-government news portal Le360, and the open website
DemaineOnline, linked to Ali Lambrabet, a journalist with an extensive record of
being critical of the Moroccan state, which had led to his serving several prison
sentences, and to a ten-year ban on working as a journalist.

Digitally delivered news thereby was turned into a vibrant new location within
the public sphere, a place for activist journalism and critical opinion to convey
alternative discourses and project norms at odds with the prevailing official discourse. What is more, it was at the time seen as a terrain where there was less risk
of reprisal due to the plethora of ventures and competition among them for audience buy-in; the sense of 'safety in numbers' was bolstered after 2011 in light of
the changes to the constitution adopted to appease protestor demands. All of this
was meanwhile complemented by the Moroccan Twitter community, commonly
referred to as 'Twittoma', which often mobilised around stories that questioned
the official coverage of the news, and the rigid red lines that reduced media leverage. The combination of a large supportive Twitter community projecting the
values promoted by the online opposition websites created a 'norm cascade', in
which alternative interpretations of issues and ideas were mediated and popularly
espoused within the Moroccan public sphere. However, as the internet became the
locus of activism, the government began erecting firewalls to contain it.[60] Several
legal battles against webmasters followed, and in 2013, Ali Anouzla, editor of
the Arabic edition of Lakome, was jailed after publishing a link to a propaganda
video from al-Qaeda in the Islamic Maghreb. He was accused of offering 'material
support' and 'inciting others to carry out terrorist acts'.[61] According to Benchenna,
Ksikes and Marchetti, 'a political and legal reshuffle of the nature of news coverage via a complete overhaul of the Press Code, and a strengthening of monitoring
measures took place in 2016'.[62] Unable to keep Lakome alive without Anouzla,
Jamai was forced to let it close. Lakome's audience, however, soon made it clear

60 Errazzouki, 'Under Watchful Eyes'.
61 Benchenna, Ksikes and Marchetti, 'Media in Morocco'; Fatima el-Issawi, *Moroccan
National Media: Between Change and Status Quo*, London School of Economics Middle
East Centre Report, April 2106.
62 Benchenna, Ksikes and Marchetti, 'Media in Morocco', p. 390.

that a gap had opened in the market, and in 2015, a new version, Lakome2, now only available in Arabic, was launched, with many of the old staff, although some had migrated to another new entity, Le Desk, now a rival to Lakome2, and only available via subscription.

The return of Lakome, which claimed it would stick to the editorial line of its predecessor, echoed throughout Moroccan media, particularly as the fate of Anouzla's legal case remained uncertain, and he continued to be under official probation.[63] Due to his legal precarity, Anouzla had opted to bear personally the financial burden of the re-launch, and went live with large blank spots throughout the website, which he argued were ad space that would be filled once legal obstacles no longer posed risks for potential investors and shareholders.[64] This constitutes a clear illustration of the economic as well as political risks mediapreneurs face in their endeavours to carve out spaces for norm conveyance and news dissemination. Further, as repression has increased, editors and reporters have continued to scale back their aspirations, as it has become clear that Morocco's regime makes it impossible for them to produce uncensored copy and stories critical of the Court, including stories about corruption and nepotism and other breaches of norm dynamics projected during the uprisings. As long as the readership is contained and small in number, the powers that be are willing to tolerate these online sites. But the leeway for mediapreneurship, even for seasoned professionals who command considerable respect within the community, has narrowed significantly. The impact of the regime's activities to counter dissent is not limited to the alternative online press, but affects Twittoma activities as well. Although Lakome2 continues to publish, it does so largely at the discretion of the authorities. For young reporters, however, it offers, along with its peers such as Goud, Febrayer and Le Desk, and the highly popular middle-of-the road sites such as Hespress and Hibapress, the only real opportunity to practise ethical journalism without significant government interference.

Conclusion

In sum, the three cases described above reflect very different approaches to mediapreneurship, although all share in the practice of a journalism that fills gaps in

---

63 Nizar Bennamate, 'Ali Anouzla: "Lakome2 gardera la meme ligne editorial que son predecesseur"', *TelQuel* 5 August 2015, http://telquel.ma/2015/08/05/compte-rebours-lancement-lakome2_1458644.

64 Ali Anouzla, 'Rajiin', Lakome2.com, 9 August 2015, http://lakome2.com/index.php/permalink/3071.html#.VcogaJNVikp.

official information coverage, and commitments to editorial independence and norm-conveyance as a long-term project. They likewise reflect the maturing output, and accumulated business acumen, of new media activists whose period of greatest prominence occurred in the years surrounding the 2011 uprisings, but who have survived rising censorship, and the drifting away of a public previously loud in its support of their normative goals. Their sustained ability to utilise new media for activist purposes reflects the empowerment and sense of internal political efficacy nurtured during the uprisings, as their work contributed significantly to processes of political change. Today, each is confronting a climate in which political norms have shifted back towards those predating the uprisings by some margin; and yet, one in which the mediascape itself has been altered. The niche which media entrepreneurs currently inhabit makes the public sphere more complex, enabling contestation and public engagement an ongoing discursive venture, albeit one both politically and economically risky. Nevertheless, their unwavering messaging is tolerated by regimes wary of closing in too tightly on sites that express alternative norms, as long as their audiences remain relatively confined, gambling that this defuses discontent via internet communication, rather than seeding protests in the future. For the mediapreneurs themselves, projecting and sustaining conversations of resistance, and norms that the public embraced and in fact demanded at one time, ensures that the projection of alternative behavioural appropriateness continues to be vital, and over time, will increasingly be internalised as an alternative to official practice.

Bibliography

Almond, Gabriel and Sidney Verba, *The Civic Culture. Political Attitudes and Democracy in Five Nations*, Princeton 1963.

Al-Nawat, 2019 http://nawaat.org/portail/en/.

Anas, Omair, 'After the Uprisings: Critical Reception of Empowered Arab Audiences', *New Media Configurations and Socio-Cultural Dynamics in Asia and the Arab World*, eds. Nadja-Christina Schneider and Carola Richter, London 2015, pp. 110–33.

Anouzla, Ali, 'Rajiin', Lakome2.com, 9 August 2015, http://lakome2.com/index.php/permalink/3071.html#.VcogaJNVikp.

Artaud de la Ferrière, Alexis and Nareseo Vallina-Rodriguez, 'The Scissors and the Magnifying Glass: Internet Governance in the Transitional Tunisian Context', *The Journal of North African Studies* 19.5, 2014, pp. 639–55.

Beji Okkez, Mohammed Samih, 'Marouen Mabrouk, a Story of Impunity after the Revolution', al-Nawat 25 February 2019, https://nawaat.org/portail/2019/02/25/marouen-mabrouk-a-story-of-impunity-after-the-revolution/.

Benchenna, Abdelfettah, Driss Ksikes and Dominique Marchetti, 'The Media in Morocco: A Highly Political Economy, the Case of the Paper and On-line-Press since the Early 1990s', *The Journal of North African Studies* 22.3, 2017, pp. 386–410.

Bennamate, Nizar, 'Ali Anouzla: "Lakome2 gardera la même ligne editorial que son predecesseur"', *TelQuel* 5 August 2015, http://telquel.ma/2015/08/05/compte-rebours-lancement-lakome2_1458644.

Berman, David E. and Victor Pickard, 'Media Activism', 28 March 2018, *Oxford Bibliographies*, DOI: 10.1093/obo/9780199756841-0201.

Breuer, Anita and Jacob Groshek, 'Online Media and Offline Empowerment in Post-Rebellion Tunisia: An Analysis of Internet Use during Democratic Transition', *Journal of Information Technology & Politics* 11.1, 2014, pp. 25–44.

Breuer, Anita, Todd Landman and Dorothea Farquhar, 'Social Media and Protest Mobilization: Evidence from the Tunisian Revolution', *Democratization* 22.4, 2015, pp. 764–92.

Chouliaraki, Lilie, 'Self-Mediation: New Media and Citizenship', *Critical Discourse Studies* 7.4, 2010, pp. 227–232.

Craig, Stephen C. and Michael A. Maggiotto, 'Measuring Political Efficacy', *Political Methodology* 8.3, 1982, pp. 85–109.

Creech, Brian, 'Disciplines of truth: The "Arab Spring", American journalistic practice, and the production of public knowledge', *Journalism* 16.8, 2015, pp. 1010–1026.

Dajani, Nabil, 'Technology Cannot a Revolution Make: *Nas*-book not Facebook', *Arab Media & Society*, 5 March 2012, www.arabmediasociety.com/technology-cannot-a-revolution-make-nas-book-not-facebook/.

Dennis, Everette, Justin Mann and Robb Woods, *Media Use in the Middle East, 2013: An Eight-Nation Survey by Northwestern University in Qatar*, 2013, http://menamediasurvey.northwestern.edu.

Downing, John D.H., 'Social Movement Media and Media Activism', *Oxford Research Encyclopedias*, 'Communication', May 2018, DOI: 10.1093/acrefore/9780190228613.013.574.

El-Issawi, Fatima, *Moroccan National Media: Between Change and Status Quo*, London School of Economics Middle East Centre Report, April 2106.

Errazzouki, Samia, 'Under Watchful Eyes: Internet Surveillance and Citizen Media in Morocco, the Case of Mamfakinch', *The Journal of North African Studies* 22.3, 2017, pp. 361–85.

Farmanfarmaian, Roxane, 'Media and the Politics of the Sacral: Freedom of Expression in Tunisia after the Arab Uprisings', *Media, Culture and Society* 39.7, 2017, pp. 1043–62.

Farmanfarmaian, Roxane, 'What Is Private, What Is Public, and Who Exercises Media Power in Tunisia? A Hybrid-Functional Perspective on Tunisia's Media Sector', *The Journal of North African Studies* 19.5, 2014, pp. 656–78.

Filiu, Jean-Pierre, *The Arab Revolution: Ten Lessons from the Democratic Uprisings*, London 2011.

Finnemore, Martha and Kathryn Sikkink, 'International Norm Dynamics and Political Change', *International Organization* 52.4, 1998, pp. 887–917.

Haugbølle, Rikke and Francesco Cavatorta, ' *"Vive la grande famille des médias tunisiens"* Media Reform, Authoritarian Resilience and Societal Responses in Tunisia', *The Journal of North African Studies* 17.1, 2012, pp. 97–112.

Hamilton, John, 'Citizen Journalism', 29 June 2015, *Oxford Bibliographies*, DOI: 10.1093/obo/9780199756841-0169.

Heydemann, Steven and Reinoud Leenders, 'Authoritarian Learning and Counter-Revolution', *The Arab Uprisings Explained: New Contentious Politics in the Middle East*, ed. Marc Lynch, New York 2014, pp. 75–92.

I Watch 2019, https://www.iwatch.tn/ar/.

Inkyfada, 2019, https://inkyfada.com/fr/.

Karolak, Magdalena, 'Social Media in Democratic Transitions and Consolidations: What Can We Learn from the Case of Tunisia?', *The Journal of North African Studies* Online first, June 2018, DOI: 10.1080/13629387.2018.1482535.

Kuebler, Johanne, 'Overcoming the Digital Divide: The Internet and Political Mobilization in Egypt and Tunisia', *CyberOrient* 5.1, http://www.cyberorient.net/article.do?articleId=6212.

Lakome2, https://lakome2.com/.

Lewiński, Marcin and Dima Mohammed, 'Deliberate Design or Unintended Consequences? The Argumentative Uses of Facebook during the Arab Spring', *Journal of Public Deliberation* 8.1, 2012, pp. 1–11.

Lynch, Marc, 'After Egypt: The Limits and Promise of Online Challenges to the Authoritarian Arab State', *Perspectives on Politics* 9.1, 2011, pp. 301–10.

Lynch, Marc, 'Media, Old and New', *The Arab Uprisings Explained: New Contentious Politics in the Middle East*, ed. Marc Lynch, New York 2014, pp. 93–109.

Maddux, James, 'Self-Efficacy: The Power of Believing You Can', *Handbook of Positive Psychology*, eds. Shane Lopez and C.R. Snyder, New York 2001, pp. 277–87.

Mirgani, Suzi, 'The State of the Arab Media in the Wake of the Arab Uprisings', *Bullets and Bulletins: Media and Politics in the Wake of the Arab Uprisings*, eds. Mohamed Zayani and Suzi Mirgani, London 2016, pp. 1–22.

Morozov, Evgeny, *The Net Delusion: The Dark Side of Internet Freedom*, Public Affairs, New York 2012.

Mungiu-Pippidi, Alina, 'Freedom without Impartiality: The Vicious Circle of Media Capture', *Media Transformations in the Post-Communist World*, ed. Peter Gross and Karol Jakubowicz, Plymouth 2013, pp. 33–48.

Murphy, Emma, 'Theorizing ICTs in the Arab World: Informational Capitalism and the Public Sphere', *International Studies Quarterly* 53.4, 2009, pp. 1131–53.

Paciello, Maria and Daniela Pioppi, 'Youth as Actors of Change? The Cases of Morocco and Tunisia', *The International Spectator* 53.2, 2018, pp. 38–51.

Romero, David and Arturo Molina, 'Collaborative Networked Organisations and Customer Communities: Value Co-Creation and Co-Innovation in the Networking Era', *Production Planning Control* 22, 2011, pp. 447–472, https://doi.org/10.1080/09537287.2010.536619.

Saka, Erkan, 'Social Media in Turkey as a Space for Political Battles: AKTrolls and Other Politically Motivated Trolling', *Middle East Critique* 27.2, 2018, pp. 161–77.

Sbouaï, Sana, 'Irregular Migration: In Tunisian Territorial Waters, the Army Kills', al-Nawat 5 May 2019, https://nawaat.org/portail/2019/05/05/irregular-migration-in-tunisian-territorial-waters-the-army-kills/.

Soguk, Nevzat, 'Uprisings in "Arab Streets", Revolutions in "Arab minds"! A Provocation', *Globalizations* 8.5, 2011, pp. 595–99.

Utting, Peter, 'The Challenge of Political Empowerment', UNRISD (United Nations Research Institute for Social Development), 23 March 2012, http://www.unrisd.org/news/utting-empowerment.

Zaid, Bouziane, 'The Authoritarian Trap in State/Media Structures in Morocco's Political Transition', *The Journal of North African Studies* 22.3, 2017, pp. 340–60.

Author Interviews

Sami Ben Gharbia, founder al-Nawat, October 2013, Tunis.
Samia Errazzouki, journalist, Mamfakinch, January 2016, Rabat.
Walid Mejeni, co-founder and publisher, Inkyfada (al-Khat), June 2014, Tunis.
Sana Uwaey, co-founder and editor, Inkyfada (al-Khat), June 2014, Tunis.

11

Judicial Activism, Women's Rights and Cultural Change in Post-Uprising Tunisia

Amel Mili

The objective of this chapter is to explore the relation between gender activism and institutional and cultural change in Tunisia after the revolution. Specifically, the chapter looks at the extent to which the legal strides that women are achieving in terms of formal equality are changing the cultural environment in which they are happening, and transforming the notion of citizenship in Tunisia. This study is based on an exploration of the interactions between the institutions promulgating laws and the institutions implementing them. It focuses mainly on the process that led to the promulgation of the 2014 constitution, and on the institutional implementation of the principles enshrined in it, through the examination of legal cases dealing with some of the constitutional principles. To this end, the chapter analyses how the principles of equality, freedom of belief, separation between secular law and sharia (religion-inspired) law and separation between religion and state are being implemented.

Institutional Change and Continuity in Tunisia, 2011–2019

The courts as a source of institutional stability

Richard McAdam argues that institutional change is hard to achieve, as it presupposes a process of social learning.[1] Political institutions are built and designed to last, so that continuity can be assured. However, there are moments in the history of a country when opportunities open up for new social learning that precipitates the need for institutional change. For Tunisia, such a moment arose in 2011–2013, when the country was in the throes of a momentous political transition, and had to decide, through its constitutional assembly, whether to adapt its 1959 constitution to the modern era, or draft a new constitution from scratch. While the desire for a clean break from the autocratic past favoured drafting a new constitution, the make-up of the constitutional assembly (where the religious party Ennahdha held a relative majority of seats) was perceived by many as a potential threat to the secular principles that were enshrined in the 1959 constitution. Of course, one could argue that to the extent that the 2011 elections of the constitutional assembly were free and fair, they were a reflection of the will of the people; but the democratic process in Tunisia opened up so quickly in 2011 (January to October of that year) that the secular political forces did not have time to organise, and were badly fragmented. For its part, Ennahdha was quick on its feet, having existed for decades, mostly underground, through the network of mosques. Thus, one can view the election result as a reflection of a difference in organisational readiness, rather than as a faithful reflection of the political preferences of the Tunisian public at large.

Of course, the practice of law does not depend exclusively on the constitution, but also to a large extent on the body of laws that are enacted under that constitution, and, most critically, on the jurisprudence that the courts build as they interpret and apply the law. Courts in general are conservative institutions; their mission is to preserve order and assure continuity. Furthermore, during political transitions, courts act as guarantors of continuity and institutional stability; and that was certainly the case for the Tunisian judicial system during the country's political transition, when the executive and the legislative branches were experiencing rapid change.

Gender standards as a barometer of socio-political progress

When the decision was made to draft a new constitution rather than revising the existing one, the country came face to face with a momentous choice: drafting a new constitution carries with it the potential for radical progress, but also the risk

---

1 Richard McAdams, 'The Origin, Development, and Regulation of Norms', *Michigan Law Review* 96.2, 1997, https://repository.law.umich.edu/mlr/vol96/iss2/4/.

of significant loss, depending on who gains the upper hand in the constitutional assembly. The 1959 constitution was drafted at a time when Tunisian society was a traditional one, governed by centuries-old religiously inspired rules and traditions; modern secular principles were totally alien to such a society, and it is conceivable that President Habib Bourguiba, who was the main architect of the constitution, had to make many concessions in his effort to gain acceptance; such concessions were not necessary in 2011. The constitution was later modified, moreover, to accommodate Bourguiba (president until 1987) and Zine el-Abidine Ben Ali (president from 1987 to 2011) in their wish to be presidents for life; in 2011, that was out of the question. The potential for significant process after the revolution was therefore evident. At the same time it should be recognised that the 1959 constitution enshrined many principles of a modern state, to which Tunisians had grown attached, and many feared that if the constitutional debate were to be too open, these might be under threat.

At the centre of the constitutional debate was the question of what kind of state the people of Tunisia wanted; options varied between two extremes: either a secular state built according to international standards of universal human rights and the rule of law, and continuing the tradition of secularism started in the 1959 constitution, or a religious-inspired model of the state, intended to resurrect the glory of the caliphate. The debate involves two intertwined aspects of public life. It is not merely a political debate, as to what form of polity Tunisia should institute. It is also to a large extent a societal debate, dealing with national identity.

Very quickly, women's rights and the role of women in society came to be among the central questions of this debate, and a focus of contention between the opposing parties. Women's rights have always been at the intersection between human rights on the one hand and cultural and state identity and Islamic heritage on the other.[2] Claims for women's rights have been tied to the fight for state identity and the wish to ensure a secular identity for the state. Claims for women's rights have also been tied to claims for minority rights, such as those of the LGBTQ community. It is the contention of feminists that women's rights flourish better in societies that refer to a set of values based on human rights and international law, rather than on Islamic law. These values were endorsed by feminists of the Maghreb, from differing backgrounds, who convened in 1995 in preparation for the UN Fourth World Conference on Women in Beijing and produced a document

---

2 Amel Mili, 'Exploring the Relationships between Gender Politics and Representative Government in the Maghreb: Analytical and Empirical Observations', Ph.D. thesis, Rutgers University 2009.

entitled 'One Hundred Measures for Equality'.[3] We can classify these values into the following broad categories: the separation of Islam from Islamic law; the right of women to full access to citizenship; women's autonomy within the household; the prevention of gender-based violence; control over sexuality; and control over reproduction.

These values are the same as those proposed by Ronald Inglehart and Christian Welzel, who, drawing on a considerable body of evidence from societies spanning 85% of the world's population, illustrate the convergence of value systems with gender equality and democracy, and develop a model of social change that predicts how value systems are likely to evolve and to impact the processes of modernisation and democratisation.[4] Gender equality is at the heart of the process that would foster democracy, and is supported by those who themselves hold a set of values based on secularism, sexual freedom and acceptance of difference.

Background

In this section, I review in turn some major milestones in the course of the Tunisian revolution that led to the opening-up of a new space for 'social learning' and the negotiation of new concepts of state identity, citizenship and institutional change.

The political transition, a tug-of-war between continuity and change

One of the most crucial questions that Tunisia faced after the flight of Ben Ali was how to fill the void his departure had left. From January 2011 to October 2011, different political forces in the country (including civil society organisations, labour unions, political parties that had been underground, remnants of Ben Ali's party and new parties) competed to fill this void. Among them were forces that wanted to ensure continuity, and others that wanted a clean break from the past. On 14 January 2011, upon the departure of Ben Ali, the prime minister, Mohamed Ghannouchi, declared himself interim president by virtue of the constitution of 1959, which provided for appointing the prime minister as interim president when the president is temporarily unable to fulfil his duties. When it became clear that Ben

---

3 Dorra Mahfoudh, 'Le Collectif Maghreb-Égalité 95: pour un mouvement féministe maghrébin', *Nouvelles Questions Féministes* 2.33, 2014, pp. 132–35.
4 Ronald Inglehart and Christian Welzel, *Modernization, Cultural Change and Democracy: The Human Development Sequence*, Cambridge 2005.

Ali had left the country indefinitely, it was determined that a different article of the constitution applied: that providing for the appointment of a temporary president until new elections were held. Consequently, and in accordance with the constitution, the chair of the Tunisian legislative assembly, Foued Mbazaa, was appointed interim president. Apart from this transition, little changed in the composition of the government.

Sensing that their wish to break with the past was being thwarted, protesters resolved to gather in the Kasbah square in Tunis, the site of government. The protest movement launched a social media campaign to attract more supporters, and many who wanted to see a break with the old regime joined the march. Thousands of people from across the country walked together to express their reappropriation of the public space and the need to take into consideration the will of the people. This came to be known as the movement of 'al-Kasbah I', and it forced the prime minister to reshuffle his cabinet. The prime minister and the leading figures of the Ben Ali regime attempted once more to reposition themselves to lay claim to the revolution and play a role within it: in an attempt to co-opt the revolution and normalise the situation, members of Ben Ali's party formed a new government, which included figures from opposition parties and some independents. Civil society groups were meanwhile growing stronger, however, and staged a second protest – 'al-Kasbah II' – demanding that all the figures of the Ben Ali regime be excluded from any future political role. This time, the protest movement forced the prime minister himself to step down. On 3 March 2011, a caretaker government was formed, made up exclusively of new figures. All members of the Ben Ali regime were removed, and Ben Ali's political party was officially dismantled. The agreement reached between the new interim president and the political forces in place represented by different associations and labour unions called for the suspension of the 1959 constitution, the dissolution of parliament, the formation of a time-limited technocratic government and elections for a Constitutional National Assembly whose main mission would be to draft a new constitution. Accordingly, an electoral commission was set up to prepare a new electoral law for the upcoming free elections. Around 150 personalities, drawn from unions, associations, political parties and civil society organisations, including women's associations, became members of the commission. Its creation constituted a bold move, which signalled a clean break with the past.

It was clear, however, that all these simultaneous 'transitions' involved considerable risks, as they left the country facing three 'voids'. First, there was an institutional void, as the government fell under pressure from protesters demanding a clean break with the Ben Ali state apparatus. The effect was mitigated by the

infrastructure of transitional institutions, but there was a general sense of permis-
siveness or licence with respect to institutional authority. Second there was a legal
void, which stemmed from the decision to suspend the 1959 constitution, thereby
creating a legal vacuum, in which nothing is taken for granted and everything is
subject to debate. Finally, there was a social void, or what is defined as 'a void in
legitimacy, competence, obligation, accountability, representation and moral and
legal restraints' created by what is referred to as 'the total state'.[5]

By opening the possibility of drafting a new constitution, the commission raised
the stakes of the political debate to extraordinary levels, and this in turn shaped
and put into focus the sharp divisions in Tunisian society between two political
trends: those who wanted a modern state inspired by the Western model of liberal
democracy, and those who view the Western model of liberal democracy as an
alien political system whose adoption is a betrayal of Tunisia's authentic identity.

First free elections: the clash of law and culture

The 1959 Tunisian constitution allowed the founding of associations and provided
for their right to assemble, but these rights were contingent upon the approval of
the minister of interior. The intent behind this was to ensure that the activities
and assemblies of associations did not disturb public order. In practice, however,
the executive branch used its power to silence critics. With the overthrow of the
Ben Ali regime, several organisations that had been operating 'under the radar'
emerged into the open and claimed their right to speak and participate in the
national debate. This revealed an extraordinary level of political energy in the
country. Among the organisations taking part in the national debate about Tunisia's future, women's groups proved to be a formidable force, able to affect the
direction of the debate and the political and social decisions that the country
would make.

The first issue that women's organisations aimed to address was that of gender
parity in the electoral law, to ensure the presence of women in the National
Constitutional Assembly. To this end, they used multiple strategies to mobilise
civil society actors and gain support for their cause. At the narrative level, some
feminist groups developed a rhetoric of 'justice': women who participated in the
uprising and were very active during the events of al-Kasbah I and II deserved

---

5 Fatima Sadiqi, 'Women's NGOs and the Struggle for Democracy in Morocco', *Non-State
Actors in the Middle East: Factors for Peace and Democracy*, eds. Galia Golan and Walid
Salem, London 2013, pp. 325–337.

to be represented in the assembly and take part in drafting the constitution, an important and decisive step in the design of the future of all Tunisian citizens. Women emphasised the direct causal relation between parity and fair elections, and between parity and the safeguarding of revolutionary gains. Independent women's organisations such as the ATFD (Association Tunisienne des Femmes Democrates: that is, Tunisian Association of Democratic Women) made sure that women were present in all the electoral proceedings: participating in designing the electoral process; participating as candidates; ensuring equal opportunity with respect to candidacies; and ensuring equal access to voting rights. They also organised seminars and meetings with international women's networks and international NGOs to learn from similar international experiences. The commission charged with protecting the objectives of the revolution, an institution established shortly after January 2011 to be the voice of the revolution and to ensure that the gains of the revolutionary movement were not diverted, also supported their efforts. A quotation from the president of the commission, the professor of law Yadh Ben Achour, reflects a broadly held view of gender parity in political institutions: 'This is an initiative brought forth by democratic political parties, civil society and independent women and men, that has been approved democratically.' Echoing his view, Rachida Bel Haj Zekri, president of the Association of Tunisian Women for Research and Development, declared:

The principle of parity enshrined in the new electoral guidelines has a symbolic significance. It is a measure of positive discrimination that recognises the right of women to gain access to political office and to the public space; this measure will certainly have a positive impact in the medium term on discriminatory practices within political parties. Its ultimate impact will be contingent upon the struggle that Tunisian women are pursuing at different levels within political parties to ensure that women be given prominent positions in electoral lists. The success of this measure is also contingent upon the dedication and political commitment of women in this critical phase, and of the effort of leaders of women's organisations to raise awareness of gender issues.[6]

In an effort to accommodate the wishes of women's organisations, the electoral commission agreed to mandate that all party lists alternate between men

---

6 Lilia Labidi, *Electoral Practice of Tunisian Women in the Context of Democratic Transition*, Washington, DC 2015.

and women. This failed to produce the desired results, however. The elections, held on Sunday 23 October 2011, were universally hailed as a great success in terms of voter participation, poll management and transparency. According to the independent election commission, turnout among registered voters was 86.1%; but this has to be set against the fact that the level of voter registration was low, perhaps due to the short period of time that potential voters had to register, against a background of decades of political inactivity. The first observation we can make about the results is that, despite the efforts of women's organisations and the goodwill of the electoral commission, the proportion of women elected to the constitutional assembly stood at 'only' 27.19%. The second observation is that the party with the highest female representation was the religious party, Ennahdha. These two outcomes stem from the way seats were assigned to parties, and from the level of organisational readiness of the various parties on the eve of the electoral campaign. When it drew the electoral map, the electoral commission delineated electoral districts across the country, and assigned a number of seats available for each district, on the basis of the latest population census. All the lists of candidates in a given electoral district had to have the assigned number of candidates. In each district, lists of party candidates were ranked from 1 to n, where n is the number of seats in that district. When the votes in that district were tallied, each list was granted a number of seats proportional to the number of votes it had obtained, and these seats were automatically assigned to the first candidates on the list. Very few lists had a woman at the head; since most party lists were headed by men, women tended to occupy positions two, four, six and so on, decreasing their chance of being elected when the party won only one seat in any given district. This is precisely what happened.

Of the eleven parties who fielded candidates, only Ennahdha, the PDP, the POCT and the MDS had existed prior to the revolution. All of these had been ruthlessly silenced under the the Bourguiba and Ben Ali regimes, and had been active only during the few past periods of relative liberalisation. Of these parties, the most successful survivor was Ennahdha. A possible explanation for Ennahdha's resilience may be that, unlike all other opposition parties, it possessed, in the network of mosques across the country, an organisational infrastructure wherein its ideology could be maintained under the guise of routine religious discourse. Given the importance of religion in Tunisian society, any move of the Bourguiba or of the Ben Ali regime against religious activities would have encountered strong opposition. Ennahdha was, moreover, able to use the infrastructure of mosques across the country as an organisational tool to mobilise its base and remain active. When the electoral process was opened up, and political activity was again legal, the party was quick on its feet, unlike other, older parties that had for a long time been dormant. As the election results show, these resuscitated parties did no better than brand new ones that had sprung up in the post-revolution period. Some, such as the POCT (Communists) and the MDS (Socialists), adopted slogans that had been meaningful in the 1960s and 1970s, but have long since been discredited. Because of the multitude of parties competing in the elections, most lists could only gather enough votes for one seat, sometimes two. The only party that tended to garner enough votes to win more than one seat in each electoral district was Ennahdha, which explains why the majority of women in the assembly belonged to it.

Taken together, these factors explain why, even though gender parity was scrupulously observed in the election process, it did not translate into gender parity in the composition of the constitutional assembly. Furthermore, it in itself led to the greatest proportion of women who were elected being in the ranks of the religious party.

The law was in fact undermined by the social belief that men make better leaders than women, such that political parties placed only men at the head of their lists. On the morning after the elections, women's organisations were shocked by the result, to the extent that they felt trapped by the decision to draft a new constitution, rather than amend the existing one, wishing they had opposed it. Even though the elections were held with the greatest transparency, they do not appear to reflect the true political orientations of the majority of Tunisians, as is noted further below. Indeed, the dominance of Ennahdha in these elections can be explained by a number of factors that are incidental and fortuitous. First, throughout the regimes of Bourguiba and Ben Ali, religious opposition to their regime was the only viable one: when all other parties vanished under the weight of political oppression, religious opposition endured, exploiting the network of mosques around the country as its default infrastructure. As a result, as soon as the political process opened up, it was quick to emerge and resume activity. Second, in the elections to the National Constitutional Assembly of 2011, Ennahdha was competing with a fragmented array of brand new parties struggling to define their platforms and to gain some name recognition. Third, the average Tunisian voter could easily tell what Ennahdha stood for: adherence to the Arab/Islamic identity of Tunisia; adherence to an Islamic model of the state, albeit in a modern form; adherence to an Islamic social order. The typical voter had, by contrast, a limited understanding of the platforms of the multitude of other parties, and little understanding of how they differed from each other. As a result, Ennahdha appeared as a default option for many. Finally, Ennahdha had significant financial assets, which it used strategically to support its campaign.

The decision to draft a new constitution was driven more by a desire to break from the past than by the need to make profound changes to the 1959 constitution. Yet, by committing to the drafting of a new constitution, and by electing a constitutional assembly in which Ennahdha held the greatest number of seats, the country has exposed itself to the possibility of heading in a direction totally different from the trajectory it has followed for the last six decades. For gender activists, this is a very serious situation. Not surprisingly, Ennahdha, emboldened by its success at the polls, felt empowered to question many of the founding principles of the 1959 constitution, and this caused a great deal of panic within the secular camp, which had never comtemplated that such principles would ever be called into question.

Issues in Debate at the National Assembly

The fight for the soul of the new republic

Religion and politics remain intertwined, and this is a central feature of all Arab governments, even those that are considered most secular. While the three states of the Maghreb proclaim Islam as a state religion in their constitutions, they all show a mixture of secular and religious aspects in their conduct of state affairs. At times of political upheaval, the quest for legitimacy is usually negotiated though the infusion of Islam into politics. Two major schools of thought compete in the debate on the separation of state from religion in Islam.[7] The first school, represented by secular Arabs, proclaims that a division between the state and religion is possible in Islam, sees it as a prerequisite for the advancement of democracy in the Arab world and strives to separate spiritual life (a personal experience) from civil life (a public experience).[8] The second school of thought argues that Islam is more than simply a spiritual commitment. Indeed, the Quran does not merely address the spiritual needs of believers, but also provides detailed recommendations pertaining to civil, penal and constitutional law; hence it is not possible to separate religion from the state in Islam, because Islam encompasses the state.

After the Tunisian revolution and the return of the leader of the Islamist party to Tunisia, new behaviours and narratives began to emerge; while these behaviours

7 Mohamed Charfi, *Islam and Liberty: The Historical Misunderstanding*, London 2005; John L. Esposito, *Islam: The Straight Path*, Oxford 1998; David L. Gellner, 'Studying Secularism, Practicing Secularism, Anthropological Imperative', *Social Anthropology* 9.3, 2001, pp. 337–240.
8 Charfi, *Islam and Liberty.*

cannot necessarily be attributed to Ennahdha and its leaders, it is plausible to maintain that its dominance in the power structure of Tunisia emboldened certain extremist elements. From daycare centres where little girls are veiled, to preachers extolling the virtues of modest dress and long beards, to public lectures delivered by preachers invited from Egypt and Gulf countries and calling for female circumcision: all of this is completely alien to the vast majority of Tunisians, who have grown accustomed to decades of public life under a constitution wherein religion plays a very minor role. Yet, in addition to the features just mentioned, the practice of polygamy and traditional forms of marriage have also started to emerge. According to a report produced by the news network France 24, the first cases of traditional marriage were recorded in some Tunisian popular neighbourhoods, and then spread to a number of universities, giving Tunisians a foretaste of what to expect if religious parties were given the opportunity to impose their version of a constitution and effectively to rule the country. As mentioned above, the country witnessed an influx of radical preachers from Egypt, Bahrain, Kuwait or Saudi Arabia, known to the Tunisian public thanks to religious satellite channels: these present themselves as agents of change, calling for the adoption of sharia law and proclaiming the need for a radical social change affecting behaviour, relationships and politics.[9] In addition, Salafi groups threatened women on account of their dress, used violence to prevent the sale of alcohol, and mounted an organised attack on establishments serving alcohol, cultural institutions and cinemas; they also attacked artists and intellectuals, and intervened against establishments being open during Ramadan. While these developments were not necessarily the work of Ennahdha per se, many observers felt that they were facilitated by the fact that Ennahdha was in power (much in the way that some observers believe that the current administration in the US emboldens many right-wing groups).

In the National Constitutional Assembly, debate raged on the relation between politics and religion. Two competing projects were under discussion. On one side was the view espoused by various gender-oriented organisations, civil society groups and many parties represented in the constitutional assembly, which envisages a separation between state and religion, referencing the international human rights framework and emphasising the distinction between citizenship and religious affiliation. With regard to gender issues, organisations such as the Association of Democratic Women and the Association of Women for Research and Development demanded the removal of all limitations imposed by the Tunisian

---

9 Amel Grami, 'The Debate on Religion, Law and Gender in Post-Revolution Tunisia', *Philosophy and Social Criticism* 40.4–5, 2014, pp. 391–400.

state on the UN Convention on the Elimination of All Forms of Discrimination against Women (CEDAW). On the other side was the view supported by the most powerful party in the constitutional assembly, which calls for the application of certain aspects of Islamic law, considers religious affiliation a part of citizenship and argues in favour of a principle of complementarity, rather than of equality, between the sexes. A number of conservative associations and political parties indeed organised protests involving thousands of demonstrators gathered on the steps of the national assembly in Bardo, urging members to adopt sharia as the fundamental source of legislation for Tunisia's new constitution – the first time that such a thing had happened in the history of Tunisia. Meanwhile, copies of an unofficial constitution were being leaked, with sharia cited as the only or the main source of law. This would mean abandoning many of the women's rights granted by the 1956 family law and the 1959 constitution. In the view of fundamentalists, secular laws such as those concerning adoption and single mothers who give their own surnames to their children conflict with some interpretations of sharia; according to conservative Islamist activists, family law contravenes sharia particularly when it comes to polygamy, adoption, and child custody. A strict application of sharia law would mean, furthermore, a return to harsh and inhumane punishments such as lapidation or amputation. It should be noted, finally, that Muslim fundamentalists (represented on the right wing of Ennahdha) view sharia law as being mandated by God, and hence not subject to debate, interpretation or amendment.

Sensing the danger to women's rights, women's organisations moved to launch a large-scale campaign intended to draw attention to the debate taking place in the constitutional assembly, and to the possibility that the nation stood to lose many of the social advances it achieved in the past few decades. Many Tunisians were very receptive to this campaign, as most recognised the role that these gains have played in making the country what it is, and would never willingly permit them to slip away. Interestingly, Tunisians from all walks of life, including men and women, young and old, women dressed in Western style and women wearing hijabs, found themselves walking side by side, calling on the constitutional assembly to maintain the gender gains enshrined in Tunisia's code of personal status.

Bridging the political divide

While the initial plan was for the National Consitutional Assembly to take one year to draft the new constitution, the complexity of the issues being debated and the extent of disagreement between the parties kept it in session for over two years. All the while, Ennahdha, which held the majority in the assembly, was also the dominant party responsible for running an interim government. Four factors in relation to this two-year period that may have helped convince Ennahdha to take a conciliatory position on constitutional matters. First, they were actually in power for the first time in their existence, and learned to their cost that it is easier to be in the opposition and criticise than it is to be in power and govern; and second, flowing from this, their tenure exposed their incompetence and the hollowness of their promises, which they were unable to fulfil.[10] Third, they were taken by surprise by the enthusiasm and energy of the opposition to the plan they had in mind for Tunisia. Fourth, they may have understood that if they were inflexible in dealing with the constitution, they might win the constitutional fight, but would very probably lose the first post-constitution elections.

As a result, the constitution of the second Tunisian Republic, enacted in January 2014 after two years of bitter debate and negotiations, is balanced, and reflects the conciliatory tone of the parties that were represented in the assembly. Article 1 of the constitution declares Tunisia to be an Islamic, Arab country. This is an interesting article, because it could mean different things to different parties. On the one hand, Ennahdha saw it as a vindication of their position on the identity of the country, and on the potential for future legislative measures to their liking. Secular parties, for their part, saw it simply as the verbatim repetition of article 1 of the 1959 constitution, and hence a continuation of the spirit of that constitution. Having that article in the 1959 constitution had not precluded previous governments (Bourguiba's from 1959 to 1987 and Ben Ali's from 1987 to 2011) from pursuing aggressively secular policies. They may moreover see it as a descriptive, rather than a prescriptive, statement: according to Monia Ben Jemia, analysis of the successive versions of article 1 shows that the intent was not to make Islam the official religion of the state.[11] Indeed, several articles of previous drafts stipulated that the designation of Islam as the state religion could not be altered by constitutional amendment. The fact that these versions of the constitution were not adopted is evidence that the constitutional assembly did not intend to designate a state religion for Tunisia; hence article 1 is to be viewed as a mere descriptive observation. Finally, if there is any doubt as to the meaning of this article, article 2 of the same constitution dispels it. Article 2 highlights the civil nature of the state: it specifies Tunisia to be a state with a civil character, based on citizenship,

---

10 Laura Guazzone, 'Ennahda Islamists and the Test of Government in Tunisia', *The International Spectator* 48.4, 2013, pp. 30–50.
11 Monia Ben Jemia, http://leaders.com.tn/article/16864-monia-ben-jemia.

the will of the people and the supremacy of the law. It further stipulates that this article is not subject to amendment.

The 2014 constitution of Tunisia also includes a preamble of five paragraphs that reflects the spirit in which the document is written. The first paragraph cites the assembly's aspiration to break with a past characterised by injustice, corruption and tyranny. The second cites the characteristics of the historical and spiritual identity of the country – which include Islamic teachings of openness and moderation, universal human rights and human values. It also cites the principles that inspire the constitution: the historical and cultural heritage of Tunisia, the reformist movement based on the country's Arab-Islamic identity, the universal gains of human civilisation, and those achieved by the people of Tunisia. The third paragraph pertains to the nature of the political system, encompassing the civil nature of the state, the rule of law, the sovereignty of the people, free and fair elections, the separation and the balance of powers, the preservation by the state of individual liberties, human rights, judicial independence, equality between male and female citizens and equality between social classes and geographic regions. The fourth paragraph addresses international law, reaffirming the affiliation of Tunisia to the Arab/Muslim world, and inferring therefrom its support for the Arab Maghreb Union countries, for the Arab nation and the complementarity of African nations, for the self-determination of all the peoples, notably the Palestinianians and for the struggle against racism and discrimination. The fifth paragraph, finally, proclaims the need to protect the environment and to aspire to achieve sustainability in our use of natural resources; it also challenges the people of Tunisia to make a commensurate contribution to human civilisation.

In summary, this preamble promotes principles of positive law that may be the foundation for a constitutional court: the civil nature of the state; the principle of equality; the aspiration to the sustainability of natural resources; adherence to principles of human rights. The principles of political and judicial organisation are usually perceived, furthermore, as the foundations of a democratic system of governance, implying the sovereignty of the people, the rule of law and the separation and balance of powers, consistent with the three organisational pillars of the Council of Europe: human rights, democracy and the rule of law.

This constitution nevertheless reflects the sharp divisions that characterised its incubation. While the preamble declares that the constitution is based on the teachings of Islam, it does not refer to sharia law, but does refer to the 'noble human values and the universal principles of human rights'. Also, it praises the virtues of pluralism, administrative neutrality and respect for freedoms and human rights. As mentioned above, article 1 declares Islam to be the religion of the country (though not of the state), and article 2 declares Tunisia to be a civil state based on citizenship; article 141 goes on to declare that articles 1 and 2 (which appear to be incompatible) are both immutable (not subject to amendment). Whereas article 1 and 2 contradict each other (since the first suggests that Tunisia has an official religion and the second implies that its religion is immaterial), article 6 contradicts itself. It starts out by saying that the state is the protector of religion (presumably Islam), but adds that it is also the guarantor of the freedom of conscience, of belief and of worship (in effect protecting religious diversity, not the country's specific official religion). This article also declares that the state is the protector of religious symbols, but that it ensures the neutrality of mosques and other places of worship with respect to any political activities (a clear reference to Ennahdha's use of mosques for political/ electoral ends). Article 20, meanwhile, declares that all citizens (both male and female) have the same rights and the same duties, and that they are equal before the law. Article 14 mandates that the public administration be responsible to uphold principles of neutrality and equality; but article 73 mandates that the president be a Muslim. The oath of office that members of parliament (article 58), the president (article 76) and members of the government must take is of a decidedly religious nature. Article 77 provides that the president appoint the top religious authority of the nation, the mufti, which is hardly consistent with the principle of the separation of state and religion. Finally, the Arabic version of the constitution starts and ends with a religious formula, invoking God.

These tensions between two incompatible visions of the state may be viewed as irreconcilable differences, or more charitably as sensible compromises between diverse parties in the constitutional assembly. Either way, they make it difficult to view the constitution as a harmonious whole, as claimed in article 144. In the following sections we review some of the issues of contention that were the focus of the constitutional debate.

Points of Contention

Gender equality vs gender complementarity

According to Grami,[12] the concept of gender complementarity is a common view among religious groups, especially from the Abrahamic faiths, who believe that God created humankind in pairs and assigned a specific role to each gender. The Turkish president Rejeb Tayib Erdoğan, who has said that gender equality is

---

12 Grami, 'Debate on Religion'.

unnatural, is one of many political figures subscribing to this view. The idea is shared by the Muslim Brotherhood and Islamist groups in Egypt, Jordan, Palestine and Morocco.[13] Even though it sounds fairly innocent, the concept of complementarity, as opposed to equality, could lead to the seclusion of women inside the home and limit them to housework and child-rearing. As a document governing the rights and duties of citizens in a free country, the constitution ought not to make any distinction on the basis of gender, which could be used later (in subsequent articles, or by subsequent amendments or judicial interpretation) to justify many inequalities. Women's organisations in Tunisia were afraid of hidden agendas behind the notion of complementarity, and fought vigorously to enshrine gender equality in the constitution. They used various tools, from legal instruments to cultural images and frames. The collective Tunisian for Women's Rights, Equality, Citizenship organised countless seminars and discussions to raise public awareness. They created a Facebook page to post events or provide details about meetings. They published a *Manifesto of Women for Equality and Citizenship*, in which they expressed their commitment to upholding the social and legal gains women had made, and their commitment as feminists to fight against all forms of discrimination and violence against women. They reiterated their determination to stand against any attempt to violate the rights acquired by women under the pretext of religious and cultural specificities, or any view that enclosed identity in a fixed and prescribed vision. The collective Hrayer Tounes (Free Women of Tunisia), composed of various feminist and other associations such as Mousawat (Equality), Destourna (Our Constitution), the Women and Leadership Association, the Association for the Promotion of Arab Women and Amnesty International, organised an event to celebrate International Women's Day, involving a huge march through the main streets of Tunisia. Many people from all walks of life, women and men, joined in to support Hrayer Tounes. Some of the women were wearing the Tunisian flag, while others wore traditional Tunisian costumes. To most observers, this event reflected the extent to which a vast segment of the Tunisian population rally around the goals of gender equality and the realisation of feminist ideals.

Apostasy vs freedom of worship

Apostasy is a complex and controversial issue within the Muslim community. While Islam recognises freedom of worship for non-Muslims, the same freedom

---

13 Grami, 'Debate on Religion'.

does not apply to Muslims themselves. 'Apostasy' refers to the condition of people who embraced Islam during its early times but tried to leave the faith after the death of the prophet Muhammad. On account of the fear that this would weaken the faith, it came to be considered a crime punishable by death. The sentence was extended to apply to any Muslim considered an apostate. In twenty-first century Tunisia, apostasy remains a significant issue, and relevant to gender, because it reflects the extent to which the country wishes (or does not wish) to be defined by religion. The debate over apostasy took on considerable importance precisely because it opposes two visions (secular vs religious) of Tunisian society, with considerable implications for gender policies.

This issue arose in the constitutional assembly when one deputy accused another of apostasy, provoking a vigorous outcry from secular parties, who feared the potential abuse of such language, and the possibility that it might lead to inquisition-like 'witch-hunts'. It was felt that unless the constitution explicitly forbade accusations against citizens of apostasy, there would be a risk of damaging the social fabric of the country. While all parties in Tunisia recognise freedom of religious practice, the Islamist party wanted to control the worship of the Muslim population; Tunisians had a foretaste of what this might mean when youthful mobs started harassing women whose dress they considered inappropriate, or establishments that served alcohol, or restaurants that were open during Ramadan, or TV broadcasters that showed movies they disapproved of. While Ennahdha cannot be held responsible for this behaviour, one can make the case that its electoral success emboldened extremist groups (as mentioned above, in the same way as the election of President Trump in the US emboldened several marginal groups there). Secular parties vigorously opposed Ennahdha's plan to control freedom of worship in Tunisia, because such control might give rise to such abusive institutions as a Taliban-or ISIS- or al-Qaeda-like Ministry of Virtue and a morality police.

Culture and law in Tunisian courts

In a constitutional system, executive power and legislative power are customarily granted on a limited-term basis. Judicial power, by contrast, is generally granted indefinitely. Hence, in periods of political transition, when the executive and legislative branches might experience power vacuums, the judicial branch can often provide much-needed continuity. At a time when political forces compete for power, the existence of the judiciary helps to recast the conflicting interests in terms of cases that can be resolved peacefully through law. The judiciary meanwhile perceives the power vacuum that arises in times of political transition as an opportunity to reassert itself in the emerging political landscape.

Despite a history of authoritarianism in the region, there have been several instances when the judicial power engaged in a tug-of-war with the executive branch, and tried to uphold the rule of law in politically sensitive cases. However, while some judges engage in judicial activism to carve out a space for citizens to use their political rights, we find other judges playing a different, much more conservative, part when it comes to family matters and gender roles. Hence, the new gains women achieved by virtue of Tunisia's 2014 constitution are being offset in practice by reactionary judicial practice, as we illustrate through a landmark court case below.

The Judicial System in Practice

All the uplifting, high-minded rhetoric of the constitution notwithstanding, the citizens of Tunisia must deal in practice with the law as it is understood, interpreted and applied by judges. This section considers a concrete post-constitution court case, and analyses the way in which court handled it by drawing on the constitution, sharia law and the code of personal status. The jurisprudence that this case creates is also analysed. The case pertains to the principle of equality enshrined in the Tunisian constitution, and to the role of religion in court proceedings.

Article 1 on trial: the case of interfaith marriages

Although the constitution was enacted in January 2014, it took several weeks for the first court case to arise to challenge its first article. Article 1 of the new Tunisian constitution came into focus when the Tunisian Court of Appeal considered its first case in reference to state identity, and to the main source of law. In a decision rendered on 26 June 2014, dealing with case number 36737, the court had to make a ruling with regard to how it interprets the declaration of article 1 to the effect that Tunisia is an Islamic state. The facts of the case are these: a Tunisian woman married to a non-Muslim husband died, and when her husband claimed a share of her inheritance, her family denied it on the grounds that he was not a Muslim.

This was not the first time that the issue of the marriage of a Tunisian woman to a non-Muslim man, and its implication in terms of inheritance law, had arisen in the Tunisian courts. Under the Tunisian constitution of 1959, the Supreme Court of Tunisia set a precedent for the question in 1982, in the famous 'Huriya case':

Huriya, a Tunisian citizen, married a Frenchman and acquired French citizenship. When her mother passed away, one of her brothers submitted a claim that she was not entitled to her share of the inheritance because she was an apostate, having married a non-Muslim. In its decision, the Supreme Court found that marrying a non-Muslim was not in itself grounds for the imputation of apostasy, but obtaining a 'non-Muslim' citizenship through marriage was. The court further ruled that the marriage was actually null, by virtue of article 5 of the family code. Its reasoning was the following: article 5 of the Tunisian family law allows marriage except in the case of a legal obstacle. This is labelled in Arabic *mawaanee shariya*, referring to legal impediments, but the court interpreted it as meaning 'sharia-related impediment'. Because she was an apostate, and because inheritance law refers to sharia clauses, Huriya lost her right to her inheritance from her mother. In this case, the court placed religious law above the secular laws of the country and considered sharia law to be the extra-referential authority in cases of 'ambiguity' of the legal text. It is an example of what is called 'judicial activism by extra-legal referentials'.

The Court of Appeal, in dealing with the case number 36737 under the new Tunisian constitution of 2014, followed the same reasoning, using two arguments. First, the court found that the marriage was null and void, on the grounds that the Tunisian woman in the case was a Muslim and her husband a non-Muslim. The court cited the sharia clause that forbids a Muslim woman from marrying a non-Muslim man. The court then cited article 88 of the code of personal status, which prohibits inheritance under two circumstances: if the claimant is found guilty of murdering the person she or he is inheriting from; and if the claimant is a non-Muslim.

In her editorial dated 20 April 2015 in the news magazine *Leaders*, Monia Ben Jemia, president of the Association of Democratic Women, lamented the court's decision, pointing out that with their ruling, the judges of the Court of Appeal made sharia law the source of the code of personal status, and asserted the claim that this code was inspired by Malekite jurisprudence (referring to an Islamic school of legal thought that dates back to the eighth century CE). Ben Jemia pointed out that the court's ruling was in violation of Tunisia's adherence to the CEDAW (see above), which Tunisia ratified in 1985, and lifted all reservations put in family matters on 23 April 2014.[14] Instead of referring directly to the 2014

---

14 Monia Ben Jemia, 'L'article 1 de la constitution devant la Cour d'appel de Tunis: (A propos de l'arrêt n°36737 du 26.6.2014)', *Leaders* 20 April 2015, https://www.leaders.com.tn/article/16864-monia-ben-jemia.

constitution, and ruling according to the egalitarian principles upheld therein, the court used the 1956 code of personal status, subverting it by means of an ambiguity that arises in the Arabic text, to interpret the meaning of article 1 of the constitution in a way that departs significantly from the principles it embodies and from the lawmakers' intent.

For even although article 1 of the 2014 constitution is an exact copy of article 1 of the 1959 constitution, its intended interpretation is radically different. The 1959 constitution was written shortly after Tunisia obtained its independence from France, at a time when it was important for Tunisians to affirm their identity in distinction from that of the colonial power they had just driven out of their country. In declaring in their first article that Tunisia now an Islamic, Arab country, Tunisian lawmakers were reclaiming their country from the colonial power and returning it to what was felt to be its rightful, authentic character. The context in which the National Constitutional Assembly wrote the 2014 constitution is markedly different from that of 1959. After 55 years of independence, Tunisia has had ample time to develop and nurture a unique identity, not as a negative reaction to a colonial experience, as was the case in 1959, but rather as a positive effort to acknowledge its rich, diverse history and its willingness to embrace openness, modernity and cultural diversity. Many Tunisians, moreover, and especially the younger generation, do not view an Arab/Islamic identity as central to their Tunisian one; rather, they view it as one among many components. There is ample empirical evidence of this, in young people's interest in Western music, for example, or their fluency in foreign languages (French, English), or lack of observance of Islamic rituals (prayer, fasting, etc.). History bears out this view, since Tunisia has been at the crossroads of many migrations and invasions, including those of the Phoenicians, Romans, Byzantines, Arabs, Turks and French. It follows that when the constitutional assembly decided to adopt the same article 1 as in the 1959 constitution, it did so on behalf of a confident nation that celebrates its cultural heritage but is resolutely forward-looking. Unlike the 1959 constitution, furthermore, and as exemplified above, the 2014 constitution follows article 1 with several articles that qualify the declaration contained in article 1, and in some cases can even be seen as contradicting or challenging it.

By considering article 1 in isolation, and interpreting it to mean that sharia law had some bearing upon the case before it, the Court of Appeal made a selective reading of the constitution. The fact of the matter is that article 2 declares Tunisia to be a civil state based on citizenship and the rule of law, and several subsequent articles stress equality between citizens, without discrimination. Article 146 declares moreover that the constitution is a cohesive whole, with no hierarchy of articles, and that articles cannot be invoked in isolation. Article 141 declares as immutable a number of constitutional premises, including the civil nature of the state, the adoption of a republican regime, the protection of human rights and (to prevent repetition of abuses of the past) term limits for presidents.

In justifying its decision, the Court of Appeal upheld the argument submitted by the family of the deceased woman, to the effect that article 6 of the 2014 constitution, which protects freedom of belief and freedom of worship, had no bearing on the matter of inheritance, since beliefs were not the subject of the court case. Yet this position is in clear contradiction of the constitution's pervasive emphasis on equality and opposition to discrimination on the basis of religion and other criteria, as cited for example in article 21. Thus, despite these new constitutional dispositions, the courts resort still to extra-legal references to motivate their decisions, and remain bound by constraints that stem from long-standing jurisprudence developed under the constitution of 1959. While the adoption of a progressive constitution is a necessary condition for progress, it is clearly not a sufficient condition; the interpretation of the constitution, and of subsequent legislation, is subject to much cultural bias, and is slow to evolve.

By reading the constitution selectively, and by asserting that in cases of ambiguity they should refer to sharia law as their general extra-legal support to interpret the law, the judges of the Court of Appeal demonstrated that the fight over legitimacy, national identity and gender roles is an ongoing one. A comparison between the Huriya case of 1984 and the 2014 case we have examined shows that the dynamics and the power struggle present under the authoritarian rule of the Ben Ali regime and the constitution of 1959 persist under a democratically elected government and a newly enacted constitution. The existence of two parallel reference systems, sharia law on one side and human rights on the other, and the unresolved tension between a perceived glorious past (when Islam was equated with progress and prosperity) and a painful present (when Tunisia, along with the Arab/Islamic world of which it is a part, finds itself left behind), continue, notwithstanding a democratic polity and despite three years of negotiations and attempts to 'bridge the gap'.

Conclusion

In this chapter, I reviewed the process of political transition that Tunisia has experienced since 2011, surveying the forces that drive this transition and analysing the choices that the country made under the influence of these forces. I attempted to analyse what has changed and what remains static in the course of this transition, and observed that, of the three branches of constitutional government, the judicial system reflects continuity: it is the branch that best ensures stability in the midst of the chaos caused by the changes in the other two branches; but it is also the branch that weighs against rapid progress, since it does not react immediately to changes in the other branches. Perhaps we cannot have one without the other: slow response time is the price we have to pay to ensure institutional stability in the midst of a transition.

Indeed, Tunisia's judicial branch, most notably the administrative tribunal, has played an important role in ensuring an orderly political transition, since it often served as a legal reference point, and was called upon to arbitrate in many conflicts between contenders in the legislative or executive branches. Tunisia's administrative tribunal is modelled on France's Conseil d'État (Council of State), whose primary role is to provide legal counsel to the other branches of government; when the other branches are in transition, as they were in Tunisia in the period of interest, the judicial branch refers to existing legislation and existing precedent, which are by definition are rooted in the past.

Be that as it may, I argue that the constitution enacted by Tunisia in 2014 is a great source of pride for the country, on account not only of its progressive tone, but also of the conciliatory process that gave rise to it through national consensus. As far as gender issues are concerned, the constitution is surprisingly progressive, especially in light of the make-up of the constitutional assembly that authored it. Still, it is perhaps unreasonable to expect the constitution to effect change immediately; a constitution is only the framework within which future legislation is drafted, and legislation is only the framework within which future court rulings are issued. We need patience, to let the spirit of the new constitution flow through the system, and perhaps to permit a new generation of judges to take the reigns of the judicial branch.

By comparison with other political transitions (such as the French, Russian or Iranian revolutions), the Tunisian revolution has been very peaceful whilst nevertheless achieving great strides forward. A little patience is a small price to pay for such a return on investment.

Bibliography

Ben Jemia, Monia, 'L'article 1 de la constitution devant la Cour d'appel de Tunis: (A propos de l'arrêt n°36737 du 26.6.2014)', *Leaders* 20 April 2015, https://www.leaders.com.tn/article/16864-monia-ben-jemia.

Charfi, Mohamed, *Islam and Liberty: The Historical Misunderstanding*, London 2005.

Esposito, John L., Islam: *The Straight Path*, Oxford 1998

Gellner, David L., 'Studying Secularism, Practicing Secularism, Anthropological Imperative', *Social Anthropology* 9.3, 2001, pp. 337–240.

Grami, Amel, 'The Debate on Religion, Law and Gender in Post-Revolution Tunisia', *Philosophy and Social Criticism* 40.4–5, 2014, pp. 391–400.

Guazzone, Laura, 'Ennahda Islamists and the Test of Government in Tunisia', *The International Spectator* 48.4, 2013, pp. 30–50.

Inglehart, Ronald and Christian Welzel, *Modernization, Cultural Change and Democracy: The Human Development Sequence*, Cambridge 2005.

Labidi, Lilia, *Electoral Practice of Tunisian Women in the Context of Democratic Transition*, Washington, DC 2015.

Mahfoudh, Dorra, 'Le Collectif Maghreb-Égalité 95: pour un mouvement féministe maghrébin', *Nouvelles Questions Féministes* 2.33, 2014, pp. 132–35.

McAdams, Richard, 'The Origin, Development, and Regulation of Norms', *Michigan Law Review* 96.2, 1997, https://repository.law.umich.edu/mlr/vol96/iss2/4/.

Mili, Amel, 'Exploring the Relationships between Gender Politics and Representative Government in the Maghreb: Analytical and Empirical Observations', Ph.D. thesis, Rutgers University 2009.

Sadiqi, Fatima, 'Women's NGOs and the Struggle for Democracy in Morocco', *Non-State Actors in the Middle East: Factors for Peace and Democracy*, eds. Galia Golan and Walid Salem, London 2013, pp. 42–53.

12

The Secular–Islamist Divide in Tunisia: Myth or Reality?

Alessandra Bonci

This chapter examines the secular–Islamist divide in Tunisia by presenting narratives which we can find at the opposite poles of a spectrum. At one pole are scholars and political and social actors who claim that the divide is a present and problematic reality in the country; at the opposite pole, many others argue that such a divide does not really exist. This study presents narratives of polarisation in Tunisia, taking the opposing positions of Brandon Gorman and Abdelkarim Harouni to contextualise the debate. Gorman maintains that the divide is a myth, and that it does not influence people's lives. Harouni,[1] by contrast, a prominent member of the Islamist party Ennahdha, considers post-revolutionary Tunisia to be a deeply divided country. In his view, there is a profound 'Islamists versus seculars' cleavage, which he has explicitly labelled a 'double extremism': a clash between radical Islamists and radical seculars.

These antithetical positions are complex, and it would be erroneous to consider the divide purely from the secular–Islamist angle, as the struggle between the two by no means exhausts the debate on polarisation. Indeed, historically, a secular–Islamist divide has existed in Tunisia since the 1940s, when Habib Bourguiba and Salah Ben Youssef mobilised in accordance with two opposing visions for their country, the former secular and the latter more linked to Arab–Islamic values. Notwithstanding

---

1 Brandon Gorman, 'The Myth of the Secular–Islamist Divide in Muslim Politics: Evidence from Tunisia', *Current Sociology* 66.1, 2017, DOI: 10.1177/0011392117697460; Abdelkarim Harouni, interview with the author, Québec City, February 2017.

Tunisia's history, the divide today does not permeate the entire society; this chapter observes the impact of the divide upon Tunisian politics, and analyses how the 'narrative of the divide' has shaped and informed this field in particular.

The theoretical frame of this study draws from the classical theories of democratisation, authoritarianism and the concept of 'twin tolerations',[2] but is also informed by the theory of class struggle,[3] the 'moderation through inclusion' hypothesis,[4] and theories of institution-building and modernisation.[5] In addition, the concepts of Islamism, polarisation and secularism need to be explored. If, traditionally, secularism and religion have been competing concepts in Western politics, and can easily be associated with opposing political trends, in Tunisia the parameters change. In this North African country, in fact, religious and secular values characterise simultaneously both secular and religious parties.[6] Thus, the crystallisation observable in Tunisia between opposing political positions does not necessarily match political orientations. This validates Gorman's point concerning the absence of polarisation at the level of individual citizens; but it does not prove the absence, as he claims, of polarisation *tout court*.

This is most evident when it comes to the societal and political debate about individual civil rights. The two sides of this particular argument represent the opposite poles of the wider debate; the report of the COLIBE (La Commission des libertés individuelles et de l'égalité: in English, Commission for Individual Freedoms and Equality), set up by the president of the Tunisian republic, Beji Caid Essebsi, on 13 August 2017 to update Bourguiba's 1956 family and personal code, therefore seems useful as an empirical case study to shed light on the discussion. The COLIBE case study presented here is an attempt to observe the divide

---

2 Alfred Stepan, 'Religion, Democracy and the "Twin Tolerations"', *Journal of Democracy* 11.4, 2000, pp. 37–57.

3 Fabio Merone and Francesco Cavatorta, 'Post-Islamism, ideological evolution and "la Tunisianité" of the Tunisian Islamist party al-Nahda', *Journal of Political Ideologies* 20.1, 2015, pp. 27–42.

4 Francesco Cavatorta and Fabio Merone, 'Moderation through Exclusion? The Journey of the Tunisian Ennahda', *Democratization* 20.5, 2013, pp. 857–75; Jillian Schwedler, 'Democratization, Inclusion and the Moderation of Islamist Parties', *Development* 50.1, 2007, pp. 56–61.

5 Alaya Allani, 'The Islamists in Tunisia between Confrontation and Participation: 1980–2008', *The Journal of North African Studies* 14.2, 2009, pp. 257–72; Sami Zemni, 'From Revolution to Tunisianité: Who is the Tunisian People?: Creating Hegemony through Compromise', *Middle East Law and Governance* 8.2–3, 2016, pp. 131–150; Larbi Sadiki, 'The Search for Citizenship in Bin Ali's Tunisia: Democracy versus Unity', *Political Studies* 50.3, pp. 497–513.

6 Anne Wolf, *Political Islam in Tunisia: A History of Ennahdha*, London 2017, p. 6.

between seculars and Islamists from a cultural and historical, rather than from a 'conservative versus Western-style progressive' perspective.

The focus here upon a single case study stems from a specific empirical choice: the debate around the COLIBE and individual rights was broad, and exacerbated the secular–Islamist division, while also showing interesting contradictions. A similar intensity of polarisation had already been evident in Tunisia after Nessma TV broadcast the controversial film *Persepolis* in 2012, and after the murders of leftist members of parliament Chokri Belaid and Mohamed Brahmi in 2013. What is especially interesting about the heated debate concerning the COLIBE, however, is the fact that it did not arise during a state of emergency, or because of external factors. Changing the inheritance law was a clear and lucid political initiative of Beji Caid Essebsi as head of state. Thus, it seems apt to explore the COLIBE debate as a discrete case study, and to analyse how the secular–Islamist divide is framed politically.

Methodologically, this study combines a critical analysis of the existing literature on secularism, Islamism and polarisation with first-hand interviews of members of parliament from the main political parties in Tunisia, carried out during extensive fieldwork between 2018 and 2019. My fieldwork reveals clearly that a sort of double extremism in Tunisia is alive and well in people's narratives about their country and in political rhetoric; and it should be noted that while Gorman and Anne Wolf unveil the manipulative logic of the divide as a political tool,[7] this chapter focuses rather on the narrative and the perception of it, which are sufficient in themselves to trigger political and social conflicts. It is relevant, on the one hand, to examine Harouni's position, because Ennahdha is the most popular Tunisian party, and it can therefore be inferred that many Tunisians share Harouni's view. On the other hand, the prevailing academic discourse with regard to a secular–Islamist cleavage does not accord with Harouni's view: the consensus seems to be, indeed, that no such cleavage exists in Tunisia.[8] So, what is at stake in terms of the secular–Islamist debate? And how can we make sense of these opposed positions?

---

7 Gorman, *The Myth*; Anne Wolf, 'What Are "Secular" Parties in the Maghreb? Comparing Tunisia's Nidaa Tounes and Morocco's PAM', *Political Parties in the Arab World: Continuity and Change*, eds. Francesco Cavatorta and Lise Storm, Edinburgh 2018, p. 49.
8 Zemni, 'From Revolution to Tunisianité', pp. 131–150.

Islamism, Secularism, Polarisation and *Tunisianité*

As mentioned above, this study is grounded on the notions of Islamism, polarisation and secularism. Broadly speaking, 'Islamism' refers to the building of a political project according to religion and Islamic law. However, many different Islamist trends have developed over time within different Arab societies. Asef Bayat explains that 'Islamism has seen many kinds of representations ... The term "Islamic fundamentalism" has now been superseded by others, including "Islamic movements", "political Islam", "Islamic activism", "Islamic revivalism" or "resurgence" and "new religious politics"'.[9] As Bayat highlights, Islamism has been explained as a reactionary drive against 'the West' *tout court*, or it is considered a reaction to post-modernity. Olivier Roy contends that Islamist parties have become detached ideologically from the notion of *umma* (Islamic 'nation' or community) and the Ikhwanist concept of brotherhood: they have 'Islamonationalised' instead, becoming standard political parties.[10] For Roy, the crisis of Islamism is visible in the loss of its revolutionary, anti-imperialist and social message, in favour of the implementation of sharia law. He focuses, therefore, on the phenomenon of 'post-Islamism'. Since Islamists cannot change politics through religion, because of political repression, Islamism ends up as an identitarian trait: the post-Islamist narrative structures itself specifically on its alterity vis-à-vis the West, instead of building on its own original drive. In Roy's assessment, a distinction is to be drawn between nationalist Islamists and Jihadist groups, who, conversely, are still fighting for the internationalised, de-territorialised Islamist idea of the *umma*.[11]

Another key concept in the complex history of Tunisia and of the Arab world more broadly is that of secularism, traditionally opposed to religion. As the Iranian intellectual Abdelkarim Soroush explains, in the Western–Christian tradition, the incarnation of God in Jesus superimposed, in the philosophical terms, the material over the transcendent and the immanent.[12] In addition, the omnipresence of theocracy during the Middle Ages distanced philosophers from religion, creating the intellectual space for a strict division between the secular and the religious. Today, according to Roy, the main division between Islamists and secular people is reflected in identitarian practices. With regard to Western

---

9 Asef Bayat, 'Islamism and Social Movement Theory', *Third World Quarterly* 26.6, 2005, pp. 891–908.
10 Olivier Roy, 'Le post-Islamisme', *Revue du monde musulman et de la Méditerranée* 85/86, 1999, pp. 11–30.
11 Olivier Roy, 'Islamisme et nationalisme', *Pouvoirs* 104, 2003, pp. 45–53.
12 Roy, 'Le post-Islamisme', pp. 85–86.

tradition, Charles Taylor asserts that 'secularity consists in the falling off of religious belief and practice, in people turning away from God, and no longer going to Church';[13] but Taylor's categories are crucial only to a Western-centred understanding of secularism. Katerina Dalacoura claims, conversely, that the phenomenon of Muslim Brotherhood in 1970's Egypt was born from nationalism and was not simply a matter of religion. For her, 'secularity, like other features of modernity, finds different expressions in different civilizations', and the nineteenth-century introduction of the nation state generated a new conception of authority: namely, a secular one, which excised traditional religious authority.[14] This can be read as a traumatic development for Arab countries, since it involved a radical change in their way of conceiving power. Dalacoura thus argues that the Muslim Brotherhood phenomenon is in fact a product of modernity, and, surprisingly, deeply rooted in secularism. In Tunisia, however, the colonial rulers imposed secularism, and violently enforced a separation between the secular state and the traditional religious background of the nation. This practice of secularism continued after independence and remains bound up with memories of colonialism and repression.

The third basic notion of this study is that of polarisation, which expresses itself through the secular–Islamist cleavage. In her study of polarisation in the US, Lilliana Mason suggests that 'the effect of sorting on bias and anger are significantly stronger than its effect on issue extremity, leading to an electorate whose members are more biased and angry than their issue positions alone would explain'.[15] This is to say that polarisation has the power to exacerbate political choices and embitter the political debate – a phenomenon that is at play in Tunisia. Moreover, political polarisation does not only reflect ideological tension; it also represents the frustration derived from deep regional inequalities, as is observable in Tunisia as between the northern and coastal regions and the southern, interior ones.[16] Polarisation is also framed around the concept of identity. Zemni explains that, after the fall of Zine el-Abidine Ben Ali, polarisation concerned how Tunisians perceived themselves. The political debate started focusing on who

---

13 Charles Taylor, *A Secular Age*, Cambridge, MA 2007, p. 2.
14 Katerina Dalacoura, 'The Secular in Non-Western Societies', SSRC (Social Science Research Council), 11 February 2014, https://tif.ssrc.org/2014/02/11/the-secular-in-non-western-societies/, quotation at p. 2.
15 Lilliana Mason, '"I Disrespectfully Agree": The Differential Effects of Partisan Sorting on Social Issue Polarization', *Midwest Political Science Association* 59.1, 2015, p. 142.
16 Maha Yahya, 'Great Expectations in Tunisia', Carnegie Middle East Center, 31 March 2016, https://carnegie-mec.org/2016/03/31/great-expectations-in-tunisia-pub-63138.

Tunisians *are*, rather than what the state should *do* in terms of political economy or institutions. Thus, the identity question became essential to political actors, to frame public debate: 'In a phase of extraordinary politics, the question of the legitimacy of the people refers to the way "the people" has come to rethink itself in relation to its history and to the newly emerging institutions.'[17]

Crucially, as Zemni points out, it is impossible to talk about polarisation without exploring the concept of *tunisianité*. The revolution of 2011 was not only a phase of regime change, but also a moment when Tunisians' identity and expectations were redefined and reframed. The notion of *tunisianité* was framed under the 'Troika',[18] eliding the 'idea of dissidence', to be presented as *the only* identity that Tunisians possess. In the process, non-orthodox identities and dissidents have thus been marginalised, and *tunisianité* has become an 'authoritarian' ideology. According to Zemni, the concept became a 'hegemonic discourse, making possible a complex configuration of class dominance (linking urban elites, middle classes and parts of the lower classes), in which a negotiated compromise (more than a consensus) replaced the polarisation of irreconcilable interests'.[19] This suggests that both Islamists and seculars can be reconciled to the concept of *tunisianité*.

There is thus no consensus in the academic literature concerning the secular–Islamist divide. Gorman observes that polarisation between Islamists and seculars does not seem to occur at the individual level, claiming on this basis that a secular–Islamist divide does not exist in Tunisia.[20] Moreover, in his view, such a divide cannot possibly exist there, because members of both groups often adopt elements of the opposing group's ideology. Thus, social progressivism or conservatism are decoupled from any secular or Islamic allegiance. To prove his point, Gorman argues that not all Islamists hold conservative visions of politics and society, and that progressive parties are not necessarily liberal with regard to human rights: they support, for instance, article 230 of the penal code, concerning the criminalisation of homosexuality. Wolf shares Gorman's view;[21] she notes, however, that reality is too complex to be reduced to labels. From her research on the so-called 'secular and liberal' party Nidaa Tounes, she infers that after the 2011 uprising, the party needed new legitimation from its voters. Building trust

17 Zemni, 'From Revolution to Tunisianité', p. 132.
18 The three-party Ennahdha-dominated government that took power following the 2011 constituent assembly election.
19 Zemni, 'From Revolution to Tunisianité', p. 132.
20 Gorman, *The Myth*.
21 Wolf, 'What Are "Secular" Parties in the Maghreb?'.

meant reassuring voters with regard to the party's values, such as conservatism, which of course encompasses religion and the rebranding of Islam: 'far from being secular ... Nidaa Tounes activists see themselves as the guardian of their countries' "true" Islamic heritage, promote their own brand of Islam, and increasingly resort to religious speech to further their political aims.'[22]

Despite the persuasive arguments presented by Gorman, his claim about the absence of a divide is not fully convincing. He equates classical ideologies – left and right – with the liberal/illiberal level of analysis. In fact, his argument shifts the debate from the presence or absence of the divide to one regarding degree of 'openness' on specific social policies. As he also highlights, however, that the secular–Islamist cleavage does not reflect a Western liberal–illiberal opposition. The secular–religious cleavage in Tunisia seems to be ideological, therefore oriented at finding a popular scapegoat upon which to pin the failures of the democratic transition.

The COLIBE, or, How Polarisation Emerges in Tunisia

The Commission

The COLIBE – The Commission for Individual Rights and Equality – composed of lawyers, religious and secular professors and human rights activists, was very diverse. As mentioned above, it was formed on 13 August 2017 by President Beji Caid Essebsi, to reform the Tunisian code of personal status (Code de Statut Personnel, or CSP) first promulgated on 13 August 1956. Essebsi's choice to appoint the COLIBE commission on the anniversary of the promulgation of Bourguiba's CSP is not coincidental: it has a strong symbolic meaning, with Essebsi presenting himself as the new Bourguiba, the wise man and father of the country who brings modernity to his people.

The presidential initiative was greeted with enthusiasm by secular Tunisian elites, intellectuals and human rights activists. The COLIBE was supported by civil society groups and activists who condemned the intimidations coming from 'religious extremists';[23] Bochra Bel Haj Hmida, the president of the Commission, had even received insults from radical Islamists on her Facebook page. As she later declared, she expected reactions from some religious members of society, but she

---

22 Wolf, 'What Are "Secular" Parties in the Maghreb?'.
23 See, for example, https://www.webmanagercenter.com/2018/07/02/421773/satisfecit-des-organisations-de-la-societe-civile-a-propos-du-rapport-de-la-colibe/.

THE SECULAR–ISLAMIST DIVIDE IN TUNISIA: MYTH OR REALITY? 271

was shocked at the denigration and the open threats she received, especially from imams.[24] Gradually, however, criticism grew, exploding after the report, which focused on multiple aspects of civil rights deemed controversial, was released in June 2018. Only a few days later, the online journal *Kapitalis* stated that it 'was ambitious but lacked in courage', as it should have been more structured, with feasible solutions for the lack of civil rights implementation.[25] Following publication, many street demonstrations took place across the country, as the report had a profound impact on public opinion. On 13 August 2018, members of secular civil society associations and activists assembled in Avenue Habib Bourguiba to express their support for the new civil rights code. The demonstration was expected to be large and well organised, but the main avenue of the city capital was only half full and few of those present were young activists. By contrast, the demonstrations opposing the COLIBE suggestion on inheritance law – one of the report's most controversial points – were huge. On 3 August in Sfax, a huge march against the COLIBE was held, and on 11 August the National Coordination for the Defence of the Quran, the Constitution and Equitable Growth organised a demonstration in Bardo (Tunis) rallying thousands of people to protect 'the Tunisian family'. The following day, another demonstration took place in the capital to denounce the violation of Quranic law.

From a whole two-hundred page report on civil rights, however, only two issues heated the summer of 2018 in Tunisia: the decriminalisation of homosexuality, and the issue of men's and women's equality in inheritance. Ultimately, the work of the ad hoc commission was reduced in the public arena to a discouraging and Manichean simplicity. The report became the object of an intense media campaign, which succeeded in dividing the political parties and public opinion, showing how, despite the politics of consensus, polarisation had emerged. In addition, both sets of demonstrations protested against the Islamist party, Ennahdha.

Secular parties and members of civil society organisations were against Ennahdha for two main reasons: ideological, since they clearly did not share Ennahdha's socially conservative positions, labelled as backward and repressive; and fearful of conspiracy, as many liberals claimed that the threats and the violent insults

---

24 Yassine Bellamine, 'Une prière de rue à l'Avenue Habib Bourguiba en représailles au rapport de la COLIBE' , *Huffpost Maghreb* 6 August 2018, https://www.huffpostmaghreb. com/entry/une-priere-collective-a-lavenue-habib-bourguiba-en-represailles-au-rapport-de-la-colibe_mg_5b64bfe7e4b0de86f4a166d9.
25 Farhat Othman, 'Colibe: Un rapport ambitieux, mais manquant de courage', *Kapitalis* 13 June 2018, http://kapitalis.com/tunisie/2018/06/13/colibe-un-rapport-ambitieux-mais-manquant-de-courage/.

against Bochra Bel Haj Hmida were orchestrated by Ennahdha itself. However, the real danger to Ennahdha's public image was represented by its own support- ers, disillusioned by the party's stalling on controversial issues, and hoping for a stronger verdict on the content of the report. As Human Rights Watch reported, the Shura Council of the party finally stated, on 26 August, 'The council reaffirms its position that not only does the initiative calling for equality in inheritance contradicts the religious teachings and the texts of the constitution and the per- sonal status code, but also invokes fears related to the stability of the Tunisian family and the traditions of society.'[26] The chairman of Ennahdha's Shura Council, Abdelkarim Harouni, said his party would 'oppose any law that goes against the Quran and the Constitution'.[27] And by so doing, Ennahdha repositioned itself in the grey area in between liberal democracy and the rule of religion, stressing the priority of Tunisia's stability without making a definitive choice.

As Merone explains, the protest against the COLIBE report led by Islamists close to Ennahdha complicated the already heated debate. In fact, Ennahdha set out no clear position for or against the content of the report until the end of summer 2018: 'Ennahdha claimed to have abandoned Islamic activism. To some observers, this suggested that Ennahdha was not fully committed to its break with religious engagement and was merely projecting an image that would appease Tunisian secularists and their allies in the West.'[28] In addition, as Sharan Grewal points out, the debate aroused by the COLIBE report tended to strengthen the image of President Essebsi as the 'new Bourguiba', forcing Islamists on the defensive.[29] Indeed, its content forced Rached Ghannouchi, Ennahdha's leader, to choose 'between pleasing [the party's] conservative base and cultivating its pro- gressive image abroad'.[30] This explains why Ennahdha struggled for some time to reach a definitive position in opposition to the report.

Explaining the criticism from Ennahdha' popular base, Rory McCarthy writes

---

26 'Tunisia: Ennahdha Rejects Inheritance Equality', Human Rights Watch, 2018, https:// www.hrw.org/news/2018/09/06/tunisia-ennahda-rejects-inheritance-equality.
27 'Tunisia's Ennahda rejects proposal to enshrine secular inheritance into law', Middle East Eye,2018,https://www.middleeasteye.net/news/tunisias-ennahda-rejects-proposal-enshrine-secular- inheritance-law.
28 Fabio Merone, 'Politicians or Preachers? What Ennahda's Transformation Means for Tunisia', Carnegie Middle East Centre, 31 January 2019, https://carnegie-mec.org/2019/01/31/ politicians-or-preachers-what-ennahda-s-transformation-means-for-tunisia-pub-78253.
29 Sharan Grewal, 'Can Tunisia Find a Compromise on Equal Inheritance?', The Brookings Institution, 25 September 2018, https://www.brookings.edu/blog/order-from-chaos/2018/09/ 25/can-tunisia-find-a-compromise-on-equal-inheritance/.
30 See above note.

that the party's internal tensions have been present for a while, due to its bipolar political and religious objective and its constant adaptation to the political landscape: 'the tension was ... described as the problem of "double belonging", the longstanding ambiguity of acting like a political party while also operating as a religious social movement invested in preaching and social outreach.'[31] In addition, as Merone explains, dissatisfaction with Ennahdha also stems from a larger ideological conflict between modernists and reformists: 'On the one hand, there is the decades-long national debate on secularism and modernity. On the other, there is the more recent – for some quite controversial – political framework of including moderate Islamists in the process of democracy building.'[32] In addition, especially in 2019, when socio-economic conditions in Tunisia deteriorated, 'there [were] no assurances that secular forces would accept Ennahdha's participation in government ... Tunisia [continued] to face the contradiction of having political elites that call for democracy without having fully accepted a strong Islamist party'.[33] This was a crucial moment in the contemporary history of the country, with secular and religious forces struggling against each other and within their own electoral bases to gain social and electoral primacy.

Finally, during the demonstrations of summer 2018 in the capital, Tunis, slogans against Ennahdha were chanted in between the national anthem and other patriotic chants, while banners were held aloft declaring '*Ennahdha dégage!*' ('Get lost, Ennahdha!'). As noted above, the necessity for a scapegoat, for both the pro- and the anti-COLIBE demonstrations, seems emblematic of a real ideological battle. This battle is also visible from the partisan headlines of some online newspapers: for example, 'The old Islamic demons resurged again to fight the COLIBE report.'[34] Such a headline is ideologically biased and clearly targets Ennahdha. The article goes on clearly to address Ennahdha as the force behind the demonstrations.

---

31 Rory McCarthy, 'When Islamists Lose: The Politicization of Tunisia's Ennahda Movement', *The Middle East Journal* 72.3, 2018, p. 376.
32 Fabio Merone, 'Inheritance Reform Could Threaten Tunisia's Democratization Process', *The Globe Post* 16 September 2018, https://theglobepost.com/2018/09/16/inheritance-reform-tunisia/.
33 Merone, 'Politicians or Preachers?'.
34 'Tunisie – Les anciens démons des islamistes refont surface pour combattre le rapport de la COLIBE', Ramsis, tunisienumerique.com, https://www.tunisienumerique.com/tunisie-les-anciens-demons-des-islamistes-refont-surface-pour-combattre-le-rapport-de-la-colibe/.

Polarisation through the symbolism of presidential speeches

Polarisation in Tunisia, which was deemed latent until the debate around the COLIBE report, can also be seen by analysing of the symbolic narrative in presidential speeches. For example, the speech delivered by Beji Caid Essebsi on Women's Day in 2017 was much less polemical than that of 2018, when his rhetoric radically changed. In 2017, Essebsi said that 'going towards equality does not mean fighting religion', and emphasised that despite the state being based on civil law, Tunisians are Muslim, and whoever rules must therefore consider this 'religious and cultural specificity'. In other words, the president's strategy in 2017 still seemed to be framed in a logic of inclusion and consensus. However, on 13 August 2018, he deliberately overlooked the 'specificity' he had talked about the previous year, and strongly advocated for civil rights.

Such a profound symbolic change is indicative of the growing secular–Islamist divide in Tunisia. Essebsi had clearly judged that it was time to implement gender equality, and recommended equality of rights be accepted across the whole political spectrum in Tunisia. As reported in the independent weekly newspaper *Réalités*, the debate on the COLIBE started with very sharp positions from the beginning, but became polarised still further in the aftermath of the president's speech.[35] Although presenting himself as Bourguiba's natural heir in both Women's Day speeches, Essebsi had clearly decided to tackle religious conservatism head-on in that of 2018. He declared that civil rights and religion should be kept separate, and that religion should not influence the building of a civil society. In speaking thus, the Tunisian president chose to draw a line between modernists and Islamists, clearly exploiting the old oppositional scheme that many others had used successfully before him. Anouar Boukhars argues that thanks to his confrontational posture, Beji Caid Essebsi became the symbol of resistance against Islamism, and 'the true carrier of the Bourguiban spirit of modernity and nationalism'.[36]

In the first two weeks after the presentation of the COLIBE report, the political positions were already highly polarised, between absolute rejection and total agreement. For the most widely read francophone pan-African weekly *Jeune Afrique*, the reactions provoked by the COLIBE recommendations in the Tunisian political arena resembled a 'battle' more than a debate.[37] Moreover, in his last

---

35 'Journée de la Femme: BCE sur les pas de Habib Bourguiba?', Réalités.com, 2018, https://www.realites.com.tn/2018/08/journee-de-la-femme-bce-sur-les-pas-de-habib-bourguiba/.
36 Anouar Boukhars, 'The Fragility of Elite Settlements in Tunisia', *African Security Review* 26.3, 2017, pp. 257–70.
37 Syrine Attia, 'Tunisie: pro et anti loi sur les libertés et l'égalité s'apprêtent à croiser le fer',

speech Essebsi attacked Ennahdha on its reputation, at a time of profoundly polarised positions. His argument was that since the *nahdaween* (Ennahdha membership) voted for the new constitution, they should be aware that Tunisia is governed by civil and not by Islamic law. By this he implied that such debates on civil rights should not concern Islamists, who tend to confuse religion and the civil code. This seems to amount to a political strategy to delegitimise Ennahdha in voters' eyes. According to Sharan Grewal, 'By elevating "culture war" issues and reactivating the secular–Islamist cleavage, Essebsi is able to distract attention … from the poor economic situation and help re-unify the "secular" or "modernist" forces ahead [of] the 2019 elections.'[38] Moreover, Essebsi's strategy of creating opposition on civil rights could be instrumental in pushing Ennahdha to take a false step and undermine its international credibility. The seculars, on the other hand, expected Essebsi's discourse to be sharper, as Yassine Brahim, leader of the Afek Tounes party, and Hama Hammami, leader of the Popular Front, made clear, with Brahim stating that Afek was against the compromise between Nidaa Tounes and Ennahdha, and that such an alliance is a 'danger for Tunisia', and Hammami arguing that the president should have been less accommodating and more confrontational towards the Islamists: Essebsi was hesitant and confused, in Hammami's view, because he felt obliged to maintain a political balance.[39]

Slim Laghmani, a constitutional lawyer and member of the COLIBE, declared that he had expected the report to produce violent reactions, since it tackles a number of taboos, but that the cleavage is problematic, because the near absence of nuanced positions reveals that the debate has become a purely ideological confrontation. The argument has shifted from the juridical to the political: ideological dispute has usurped the place of discussion of the report's content. Moreover, the fact that the document is known as the 'Bochra Belhaj Hmida report' only compounds the problem: on the one hand, Belhaj Hmida became the target of multiple threats *ad personam*, and on the other, the report was to an extent delegitimised by being identified with a single person. Thus, Laghmani complained, ideologisation

---

Jeune Afrique, 2018, https://www.jeuneafrique.com/614372/societe/tunisie-pro-et-anti-loi-sur-les-libertes-et-legalite-sappretent-a-croiser-le-fer/.

38 Quoted by Rami Allahoum, 'Tunisia's President Vows to Give Women Equal Inheritance Rights', Al-Jazeera, 13 August 2018, https://www.aljazeera.com/news/2018/08/tunisia-president-vows-give-women-equal-inheritance-rights-180813172138132.html.

39 Yassine Bellamine, 'Une prière de rue à l'Avenue Habib Bourguiba en représailles au rapport de la COLIBE', *Huffpost Maghreb* 6 August 2018, https://www.huffpostmaghreb.com/entry/une-priere-collective-a-lavenue-habib-bourguiba-en-represailles-au-rapport-de-la-colibe_mg_5b64bfe7e4b0de86f4a166d9.

and personalisation had profoundly impaired debate on the outcome of the COLIBE's work.[40]

Polarised actors

In Tunisia, the ruling parties are Ennahdha and Nidaa Tounes, while Afek Tounes, Machru Tounes, the Popular Front and the Free Patriotic Union constitute the opposition. Compounding the problem of the national divide, some of these progressive and leftist political parties are in fact more 'fundamentalist' than Ennahdha. For example, Jabha Chaabia (the Popular Front) and Machru Tounes, self-declared secular parties, are adamant in framing Ennahdha as the enemy of the country, rather than recognising the latter's contribution to the success of the Tunisian transition. While Nidaa's discourse is more ambiguous vis-à-vis Ennahdha, the rhetoric of the leftist party Jabha Chaabia maintains that Ennahdha is responsible for women's oppression in the country, and for young women wearing the hijab. According to one member of the party, 'Ennahdha contributed to the worsening of the situation for women in Tunisia. Ennahdha does not look at women in a progressive way when it comes to civil rights.'[41] Machru Tounes members go even further, declaring that Ennahdha is socially regressive. Many Machru members maintain that Ghannouchi warned Tunisians who would not vote for him that they would go to hell, and even encouraged many to join Daesh (ISIS). Since Machru Tounes interpreted the consensus arrangement between Nidaa and Ennahdha as treason, the party focused on taking on anti-Ennahdha positions. When asked to define whether Ennahdha is a backward party, members of Machru in the city of Sfax responded, 'Can the Taliban ever become a democratic party?! People like Ennahdha act like they have democratic values but they don't really believe in democratic values.'[42]

Accusations were thrown at the Islamist party also in the aftermath of the violence of the last few years: since Tunisians are not used to public violence, many seculars attributed it to the 'evil hand' of Ghannouchi. It indeed seems difficult, in such a context, not to consider the environment as polarised; the secular–Islamist divide appears to be entrenched and amenable to exploitation for political ends. As Cavatorta and Haugbølle have argued, Ennahdha was considered a

---

40 Businessnews.com.tn, 'Slim Laghmani : Le rapport de la Colibe a relevé nos contradictionsculturelles', https://www.businessnews.com.tn/Slim-Laghmani--Le-rapport-de-la-Colibe-a-relevé-nos-contradictions-culturelles,520,82112,3.

41 Interview with the author, member of Jabha Chaabiya, Gafsa, 2018.

42 Interview with the author, member of Machru Tounes, Sfax, 2018.

plague, a true danger for the country, since the time of Ben Ali. It was for this reason that there was no real challenge to Ben Ali's power, since the opposition forces were deeply divided along the lines of the Islamist–secular cleavage. As these authors state, 'indeed, many of Tunisia's more secular dissidents perceived Ben Ali as a lesser evil than Ennahdha'.[43] The democratic transition did not seem to assuage the fears of many in the modernist and self-labelled secular camp.

Secular-*Laïque* Fundamentalist–Islamist Divide and Democracy

Secularism in the Arab world

What do Tunisian polarisation and the secular–Islamist divide tell us about the notion of secularism? This section aims at shedding light on the myth of secularism, the 'must' for democracy. Secularism is also considered the guarantor for freedom of expression and the only tool to protect the state from the interference of religion. However, the reality on the ground shows that secularism is not the only political model whereby to govern a society through political pluralism, especially in non-Western societies. There are two interlinked aspects of Taylor's conceptualisation of secularism that deserve greater attention. It is crucial to ask, first, whether secularisation is a Western specificity, and second, whether it can be considered a type of extremism (as Harouni, for instance, claims[44]). This is particularly important in non-Western contexts, where the notion of secularism is bound up with memories of colonialism and power differentials. As John Keane observes, the concept of secularism became 'an insult' to many Muslims.[45] Building on a stereotyped division between a secular, modernised West and a religious and backward Islamic world, the twenty-first century view of Muslim societies has endorsed the belief that the latter are hopelessly opposed to the secular. This stark juxtaposition overlooks the fact that the West also 'endures the weight' of religion. Scholars have for instance highlighted the US paradox, to the effect that the supposed land of freedoms is not in fact so very secular: the influence of religious lobbies (especially evangelical Christians) and an American rhetoric deeply steeped in religion serve to demonstrate the point.[46] Be that as it may, Taylor and

---

43 Rikke Hostrup Haugbølle and Francesco Cavatorta, 'Will the Real Tunisian Opposition Please Stand Up? Opposition Coordination Failures under Authoritarian Constraints', *British Journal of Middle East Studies* 38.3, 2011, pp. 323–341.
44 Harouni, interview with author.
45 John Keane, 'Secularism?', *The Political Quarterly* 71.1, pp. 5–19.
46 Elizabeth Bernstein and Janet R. Jakobsen, 'Sex, Secularism and Religious Influence in

many others analyse secularism from a Western perspective, where its conception is intimately linked to liberal values; but this does not apply in many other parts of the world, where the link dissolves. In relation to the different possible ways to understand secularism, Saba Mahmood goes so far as to argue that 'instead of regarding the secular state as the solution to discrimination against religious minorities, it must itself be understood as part of the problem'.[47]

In a recent contribution to the literature, Wolf writes: 'the immediate aftermath of the 2010/11 popular uprisings in the Middle East and North Africa saw the rise and electoral victories of Islamist parties. Their surge has led an increasing number of scholars to analyse political developments in the region through the binary lens of "Islamists versus secularists".'[48] This builds on Talal Asad's argument that the purported division is fictive, as 'secular is not the opposite of religious and some-times even overlaps with it'.[49] The aim here is to nuance the concept of secular-ism in the Arab world. According to Wolf, the Ben Ali government put in place a threefold mechanism to get rid of Islamists: firstly by marginalising them as terrorists and extremists; secondly by promulgating a state-sponsored Islam; and thirdly by focusing on the Westernisation of Tunisian culture. Wolf postulates that secular parties 'have themselves a religious constituency. In both Morocco and Tunisia increased liberties following the 2010/11 uprisings forced secular parties to become more accountable to the people and to reflect their religious sensibili-ties'.[50] Thus, since Nidaa Tounes's conservatism must be formally different from Ennahdha's, people think there is an *actual* difference between the parties. To better understand the philosophical and political problem this chapter deals with, it might be useful to recall the history of certain ideas, especially of secularism and religion, in Tunisia.

Birol Baskan points out that the way in which religion and religious affairs interact with the state depends on the state-building process.[51] The modern state-building process in North Africa is the result of colonialism, which explains the oppressive control of the state over the religious sphere. Colonialism and

US Politics', *Third World Quarterly* 31.6, 2010, pp. 1023–39.

47 Saba Mahmood, *Politics of Piety*, Princeton 2105.

48 Wolf, *Political Islam*, p. 163.

49 Talal Asad, 'Secularism, hegemony and fullness', Colloquium SSRC Social Science Research Council, https://tif.ssrc.org/2007/11/17/secularism-hegemony-and-fullness/.

50 Anne Wolf, 'What are "Secular" Parties in the Maghreb? Comparing Tunisia's Nidaa Tounes and Morocco's PAM', *Political Parties in the Arab World: Continuity and Change*, eds. Francesco Cavatorta and Lise Storm, Edinburgh 2018, p. 103.

51 Birol Baskan, 'The State in the Pulpit: State Incorporation of Religious Institutions in the Middle East', *Politics and Religion* 4.1, 2011, pp. 13–53.

secularism thus became synonymous in people's perception, with secularism being associated with the marginalisation of religion within the public sphere and with an illiberal and despotic ideology. In other words, secularism became the authoritarian tool to repress religion and maintain the status quo. It is indeed perceived as the legacy of colonialism in many Arab countries, and this is why the notion attracts such virulent criticism in many political and intellectual circles: secularism is perceived as oppressive, rather than as emancipatory. We are faced in fact with a paradox of liberalism, in that while the actual policies to the imple- mentation of which secularism leads might indeed be progressive (in a norma- tive sense), the way in which they are implemented is profoundly coercive. As Dalmasso and Cavatorta explain, 'the need for context is paramount and when this institutional context is taken into account, the simplistic distinction between authoritarian Islamists and democratic seculars is no longer convincing.'[52]

Asad, for his part, focuses on non-Western conceptions of secularism by observ- ing its relation to modernity. He suggests, provocatively, that instead of defining the deep meaning of 'secular', it would be more fruitful to focus on 'an inquiry into what is involved when "the secular" is invoked – who tries to define it, in what context, how and why'.[53] By analysing Mahmood's writings on secularism, Asad under- stands secularism as a 'mode of international hegemony'.[54] In a famous passage, he explained that religion 'is not the locus of "the sacred" ... but the normative process of defining what is integral and excluding what is marginal to the modern state'. He focuses on the nineteenth-century modernisation process as the channel of convey- ance of Western liberal ideas. Thus, 'secularism has meant something more than a simple separation of religion and the state. It has involved the coercive universaliza- tion of modern morality, knowledge, law and nation-statehood'.[55]

For Asad 'it is important from the very beginning to grasp the salience of non- European and non-Western peoples' histories for the construction of the project of modernity'.[56] If Taylor is interested in the conditions of belief and in people's

---

52 Emanuela Dalmasso and Francesco Cavatorta, 'Reforming the Family Code in Tunisia and Morocco – the Struggle between Religion, Globalisation and Democracy', *Totalitarian Movements and Political Religions* 11.2, 2010, p. 218.
53 Talal Asad, 'Thinking about the Secular Body, Pain and Liberal Politics', *Cultural Anthropology* 6.4, 2011, p. 673.
54 Talal Asad, 'Secularism, Hegemony and Fullness', SSRC (Social Science Research Council) colloquium, 7 November 2007, https://tif.ssrc.org/2007/11/17/secularism- hegemony-and-fullness/.
55 Talal Asad, 'Religion and Politics: An Introduction', *Social Research* 59.1, 1992, pp. 3–16.
56 Ayşe Polat, 'A Comparison of Charles Taylor and Talal Asad on the Issue of Secularity', *Human and Society*, p. 225, https://pdfs.semanticscholar.org/787a/39b65664a5d91ce4f9b676

capacity of choosing and worshipping, Asad equates secularism with modernity and modernisation. He points to the problematic value of secularism, as the
implicit invitation for people to conform to modernity. Ashley Lebner observes
that 'for Asad, secularization is the institution of a secular domain of concepts distinguished from religion, while secularism is a political doctrine that attempts to
govern the relationship between religion and the secular';[57] while Stepan reminds
us that many leaders in post-independent Muslim countries, 'like Egypt's Gamal
Abdel Nasser, Algeria's Ahmed Ben Bella, or Tunisia's Habib Bourguiba, were
secular nationalists who (like Turkey's Atatürk) used authoritarian measures
to control and repress many religious leaders in the name of modernity'.[58] The
problem, again, is that the conflation of secularism with modernity does not eliminate the authoritarian nature of these nationalist leaders' project, which, in turn,
reflects badly on the notion of secularism, particularly, for some political and
social movements at least, in post-authoritarian societies.

As repeatedly suggested above, the existence of a secular–Islamic divide in
Tunisia can hardly be dismissed as a myth. For Malika Zeghal, for instance, and
for McCarthy, it is undoubtedly present, and is a reality to be contended with.[59]
Interestingly, however, the divide is not over institutional issues, as we know that
long ago the Islamists entered and accepted the democratic game.[60] According to
Zeghal, the debate is rather about people's different ways of life, and, more specifically, seculars' concerns about threats to their privileges and their Westernised
lifestyles.[61] During the revolution, there was a moment when the secular–Islamist
divide seemed to fade away, and Tunisians saw themselves as 'one people'; but
after a first moment of enthusiasm, a second phase followed, when differences

---

5728202c62172e.pdf?_ga=2.17155769.1024764541.1570802986-168579641.1570802986.
57 Ashley B. Lebner, 'The Anthropology of Secularity beyond Secularism', *Religion and
Society: Advances in Research* 6, 2015, p. 65.
58 Alfred Stepan, 'The Multiple Secularisms of Modern Democratic and Non-Democratic
Regimes', *Rethinking Secularism*, eds. Craig Calhoun, Mark Juergensmeyer and Jonathan
VanAntwerpen, Oxford 2011, p. 127.
59 Malika Zeghal, 'Competing Ways of Life: Islamism, Secularism and Public Order in the
Tunisian Transition', *Constellations* 20.2, 2013, pp. 254–74; Rory McCarthy, 'Re-Thinking
Secularism in Post-Independence Tunisia', *The Journal of North African Studies* 19.5, 2014,
pp. 733–50.
60 Allani 'Islamists in Tunisia'; Cavatorta and Merone, 'Moderation through Exclusion?';
McCarthy, 'When Islamists Lose'; Fabio Merone and Francesco Cavatorta, 'Post-Islamism,
Ideological Evolution and "la Tunisianité" of the Tunisian Islamist Party al-Nahda', *Journal
of Political Ideologies* 20.1, 2015, pp. 27–42; Wolf, 'What Are "Secular" Parties in the
Maghreb?'.
61 Zeghal, 'Competing Ways of Life', p. 254.

emerged once more. 'This overwhelming re-entry of "Islam2" and "secularism" into the arena of electoral politics and of deliberative public expressions turned out to be complicated by the history of these concepts in Tunisia before the uprisings.'[62] Zeghal argues that during the Ben Ali era, the concepts of Islam and secularism were politically charged, and responded to specific political aims; she explains, interestingly, that Islamists and secularists both took advantage of post-revolutionary freedom of expression and 'competed on their different conceptions of ways of life'.[63] The resurgence of the secular–Islamist debate after the revolution is in fact mostly due to the political desire to divert attention towards identity issues: after the revolution the public debate never seriously faced the crucial concerns of the economic crisis or youth unemployment. Conversely, the place of religion in politics became one of the most-debated issues in post-revolutionary Tunisia.[64]

Laïque *fundamentalism and its effects on democracy*

In Tunisia – the only success story of democratisation in the MENA region after the Arab uprisings – the presence of a social cleavage in such a fragile context makes one wonder whether political polarisation affects the entire society and the new-born democratic institutions. Stepan's 'twin tolerations' – 'the freedom for democratically elected government and freedom for religious organization in civil and political society' – seem the perfect recipe for the existence of any democracy.[65] Yet, it is a long process, within which the Western rhetoric of peaceful secularism needs to be problematised. Stepan indeed shows that truly Western democracies themselves struggled – and still struggle – to build and apply the twin toleration paradigm. Since the secular–Islamist cleavage seems to be the main obstacle to such twin toleration, it is legitimate to ask whether such a process could harm the fragile democratic institutions in Tunisia. What if the divide is not only real, but part of the twin toleration process itself? To make sense of this, it is crucial to focus on the specific kind of secularism which has most influenced Tunisian politics: French *laïcité* (laicism).

The French model of secularism deserves attention here, on account of the French colonial domination of Tunisia and the intellectual legacy it left there. As

---

62 Zeghal, 'Competing Ways of Life', p. 255.
63 Zeghal, 'Competing Ways of Life', p. 256.
64 Nadia Chaabani, *Tunisie, deuxième République: chronique d'une constituante (2011–2014)*, Tunis 2018; Selma Mabrouk, *2011–2014, Le bras de fer*, Tunis 2018.
65 Stepan, 'Religion, Democracy', p. 39.

already mentioned, secularism is not a neutral or a natural concept. The French form of it is *laïcité*. For Robert Zaretsky '*laïcité* … today has acquired so much mystique as to be practically an ideology, a timeless norm that defines Frenchness'. Zaretsky took his cue from a *Charlie Hebdo* polemical article about the Islamic veil. The main argument of the French magazine was that Muslims were attacking French values and culture, especially that pillar of the French system, *laïcité*. Zaretsky explains that in the early 1900s, the concept of *laïcité* regarded purely the separation of state and church: 'as in the United States, French secularism initially sought to ensure religious pluralism in the public and private spheres – nothing more, nothing less.' A different discourse and practice of *laïcité* arose during the 1980s and the 1990s, however, when the number of Muslim immigrants to France grew and the battle over costume began. According to Zaretsky, the term *laïcité* lost its former meaning and became a nationalistic slogan.[66]

Indeed, the concept of *laïcité* is misused and misrepresented by new political actors who decided to co-opt it, as did Jean Marie Le Pen's Front National. Zaretsky claims that the party 'has weaponized *laïcité*' and that the concept became a tool to separate the world into French, or French-behaving, people, and others.[67] Thus, *laïcité* consists today of an aggressive and fundamentalist set of ideas, because it adheres to an identity: 'Frenchness'. 'Conventional wisdom suggests that the antidote to religious fundamentalism is more secularism. But that is a very big mistake. The best response to bad religion is better religion, not secularism.'[68] Is there a link, then, between the French *laïcité* and so-called secular fundamentalism?

Given the proximity of intellectual circles in France and in Tunisia, the discussion as to what constitutes a genuine form of secularism has informed the debate about the separation of mosque and state there too, as it has in the other former French colonies in North Africa. To appreciate the degree of polarisation in contemporary Tunisia, we therefore need to look more closely at 'secular fundamentalism', because the concept seems largely to be ignored as a social and political phenomenon, and religion to be the only institution tarnished with taint of extremism. A number of scholars have nevertheless attempted to illustrate how secular fundamentalism works. Vincent Geisser coined the term 'secular Salafism' to

---

66 Robert Zaretsky, 'How French Secularism Became Fundamentalist', *Foreign Policy* 7 April 2016, https://foreignpolicy.com/2016/04/07/the-battle-for-the-french-secular-soul-laicite-charlie-hebdo/.
67 Zaretsky, 'How French Secularism'.
68 Jim Wallis, *God's Politics: Why the Right Gets It Wrong and the Left Doesn't Get It*, New York 2009, p. 66.

denote the Manichean, identity-based approach of the French satirical magazine *Charlie Hebdo*, for instance. In 2012, directly after its publication of images of the prophet Muhammad, Geisser declared that the magazine was trying to 'impose its secular purity by considering the others fanatics'.[69] What is of interest here is the extremity of a secular–religious opposition whereby religion is denied a presence in the public space.

Secular extremism in fact involves the intention to abolish religion entirely not only from the political sphere, but from the public social sphere as well. This is to be contrasted with more mainstream understandings of secularism, as indicated above. In the social sciences, secularisation is described as 'the process by which sacred beliefs are weakened over time, religion becomes less influential in social life, and scientific and other rationalist worldviews come to dominate both the understanding of nature and social life'.[70] The National Secular Society proposes a notion of secularism that surpasses the mere separation of religion from the state, and is intrinsically linked to democracy and fairness. In other words, secularism stands for religious freedom, and guarantees freedom of speech and expression.[71]

As already indicated, this view is in stark contrast to the more fundamentalist discourses and practices that Geisser has highlighted in France, and that find, to a degree, their echo in the Tunisian public and institutional debate, as in the case of the public debates over the COLIBE report during the summer of 2018. At that time, observers in Tunisia focused on the sharp contrast between those who, on the one hand, maintained that modifying inheritance legislation was *haram* (forbidden by God), and those who, on the other hand, attacked Ennahdha as 'terrorists and backward', arguing that religion should be kept out of politics. The effect of such a deep polarisation of the public debate was to block discussion of the inheritance law *tout court*.

According to Daniel Conkle, the notion of secular fundamentalism needs to be nuanced to encompass a historical, an academic and an economic dimension. He assures us that there is no reason to think that religion cannot help a society to advance by its inclusion in a healthy social and political debate. By excluding religion from public life, we automatically demote it to the status of a 'second-class

69 Alexandra Schwartzbrod, 'Le piège d'un débat idéntitaire et binaire. Entrevue à Vincent Geisser', *Libération* 19 September 2012, https://www.liberation.fr/planete/2012/09/19/le-piege-d-un-debat-identitaire-et-binaire_847472.
70 Craig Calhoun, Mark Juergensmeyer and Jonathan VanAntwerpen, *Rethinking Secularism*, Oxford 2011.
71 National Secular Society, 'What is secularism?', https://www.secularism.org.uk/what-is-secularism.html.

source of truth'.[72] In fact, the political choice to divide citizens between the secular and modern and the religious and backward would necessarily give rise to social tensions. Nowadays, among Western countries, as observed by Richard Ekins, there is effectively a tacit agreement that states should be secular; accompanied, however, by a fear that the admission of religion would endanger secularism and damage the structure of the state itself: 'secular fundamentalism is taken to require and justify particular aspects of a democratic regime.'[73] Ekins explains that the overvaluation of the Enlightenment leads us to forget about the very conditions under which secularism was born: namely, a Christian context; on this account, for Ekins, 'regimes that entrench secularism and exclude religious groups from participation in politics are not truly democratic'. Indeed, 'civil authorities must be prepared to tolerate religious persons' or groups' organizing politically and participating in the democratic process'.[74]

Ekins's position is rooted in the argument of Stepan, who criticises the general assumption according to which a separation between the religious and political spheres must be a feature not only of Western, but of all democracies.[75] To address the issue of the relation between Western democracies and religion, Stepan decided to analyse more closely EU member states. He observes that most European countries have a long-standing established church: Lutheran, Protestant or Roman Catholic. In fact, as he explains, 'virtually no Western European democracy now has a rigid or hostile separation of church and state'.[76] Stepan's point concerns not only the separation of religious from secular power, but implies too the need for more respect and mutual acknowledgement from both the religious and the secular sides.

However, Stepan's conception of Western Europe as a model of twin toleration can be challenged by observing the social tensions that have emerged across Europe following '9/11', the emergence of Islamic terror, the Arab Spring and the Syrian civil war. In the last two decades, in fact, we have witnessed a spike in radicalisation and in tension between state institutions and religions. For all that secularism remains a vital component of democracy and an aspiration central to contemporary societies, it can easily drift to extreme positions. If, on

---

72 Daniel Conkle, 'Secular Fundamentalism, Religious Fundamentalism and the Search for Truth in Contemporary America', *Journal of Law and Religion* 12.2, 1996, p. 358.
73 Richard Ekins, 'Secular Fundamentalism and Democracy', *Journal of Markets and Morality* 8.1, 2005, p. 84.
74 Ekins, 'Secular Fundamentalism', p. 89.
75 Stepan, 'Religion, Democracy', p. 41.
76 Stepan, 'Religion, Democracy', p. 41.

the one hand, in a healthy political system, secularism guarantees the protection of religion, in a fragile political environment, where secularism fears for its very existence, it can shift from being a protector to an oppressor of religion. When secularism is under threat, it aims at dominating religion through the institutions of the state.

Notions of extreme secularism and religiosity have characterised intellectual and public debates for quite some time in the Arab world, revolving around concepts of democracy, civil society and individual rights.[77] The Tunisian political environment is no exception, with the processes of democratisation placing such debates openly on the public and political stage. The process of designing new political and social institutions, together with the drafting of a new constitutional text and an array of legislative initiatives to substitute those implemented by the authoritarian regime, is particularly prone to exposure to such debates about secularism and religion. In Tunisia, the politics of consensus is merely rhetoric. In reality, intolerance seems to be spreading within and between parties. As the case of the COLIBE shows, there is a genuine ideological battle between radically different worldviews, although this is framed within the institutions and discourse of democracy, which would seem to underpin Gorman's argument about the absence of a real divide. As noted above, at the individual level, Tunisians do not differ much from one another in terms of expressed attitudes, confirming the idea that the divide does not exist or is very narrow.[78] However, public debate and political parties or social movements present a radically different picture, of a Tunisia in which religious and secular extremism are aggregators of preferences and support. A culture of forceful debate is surely healthy in a newly established democracy; yet at the same time stubborn confrontation can damage the stability of a country. In many ways, it is not surprising that Tunisia is experiencing this paradox, as secularism in non-Western contexts is particularly complex.

Conclusion

To sum up, this study has focused on the secular–Islamist debate in Tunisia in order to understand its underlying narratives and to make sense of its actors' positions. The debate on the COLIBE is linked to a much wider debate, about notions

77 Michaelle L. Browers, *Democracy and Civil Society in Arab Political Thought: Transcultural Possibilities*, Syracuse, NY 2006.
78 Eva Wegner and Francesco Cavatorta, 'Revisiting the Islamist–Secular Divide: Parties and Voters in the Arab World', *International Political Science Review* 40.4, 2019, pp. 558–75.

of secularism and religion. This chapter started from the opposed positions of Abdelkarim Harouni and Brandon Gorman. If the former asserts that Tunisia today is characterised by a deep secular–Islamist divide, the latter claims that there is no such thing at the individual level. We then examined the phenomenon of secular fundamentalism, by focusing on the problematic concept of French *laïcité* and its legacy in Tunisia. It seems, in the final analysis, that despite Tunisia's democratic transition, the secular–Islamist divide is still present, and still influences political debate there.

Polarisation in Tunisia is of particular interest, in so far as it seems integral to an explanation of similar dynamics elsewhere in the Arab world, and to the illumination of the challenges a new-born democracy must face. First, it is important to understand whether such a divide in Tunisia is a physiological juncture or an inhibiting factor for democratisation. Second, the political scenario in North Africa changed deeply after 2011. In Morocco in 2017, protesters explicitly demanded democracy to combat *hogra* – the humiliation faced by the poor – and were brutally repressed.[79] While Algeria is still struggling against the old regime despite the departure of Abdelaziz Bouteflika in 2019, Libya is at war, and the al-Sisi regime in Egypt is spreading terror over its people: a Human Rights Watch assessment reports that 'under Sisi, Egypt's use of the death penalty has soared, with thousands of death sentences ordered since 2013'.[80] Tunisia seems to be the only 'success story'. But nine years after the uprisings, it is surely time to look at the 'Tunisian exception'[81] in a more critical manner.[82] As Daniel Brumberg worryingly puts it, 'Despite the remarkable achievement represented by Tunisia's 2014 National Dialogue, the country remains profoundly polarized.'[83] Of interest here

79 Christoph H. Schwarz, 'Morocco's Social Protests across Time and Space', *openDemocracy* 13 June 2018, https://www.opendemocracy.net/en/north-africa-west-asia/moroccos-social-protests-across-time-and-space/.

80 Amr Magdi, 'Why Executions in Egypt are Skyrocketing and Why They Should End', Human Rights Watch, 25 March 2109, https://www.hrw.org/news/2019/03/25/why-executions-egypt-are-skyrocketing-and-why-they-should-end.

81 Laura De Rouck, 'Tunisie postrévolutionnaire: de l'effervescence démocratique à la désillusion ? L'"exception tunisienne" vue par les Tunisiens', M.A. dissertation, Université Catholique, Louvain 2018; Safwan Masri and Lisa Anderson, *Tunisia: An Arab Anomaly*, New York 2017.

82 Amin Allal and Vincent Geisser, *Tunisie. Une démocratisation au-dessus de tout soupçon?*, Paris 2018; Michel Camau, *L'exception tunisienne. Variations sur un mythe*, Paris/Tunis 2018.

83 Daniel Brumberg, 'Tunisia's Fragmented and Polarized Political Landscape', Arab Center Washington DC, 2019, http://arabcenterdc.org/policy_analyses/tunisias-fragmented-and-polarized-political-landscape/.

is that polarisation exists in forms both actual and narrated, such that it becomes an arduous task indeed to deconstruct the phenomenon. According to Mahmood, 'modern secular governance has played a crucial role in exacerbating religious tensions in the region, hardening interfaith boundaries and polarizing religious differences'.[84] Mahmood's critical work aims at problematising and analysing two dimensions of secularism: 'political secularism', and 'secularity'. If the former concerns relations between state and religion, the latter instead pertains to the 'values' of secularism in a secular society. Mahmood criticises secularism on the grounds that the principle of separation between religion and state is itself more an illusion than a reality: the sacrosanct freedom of worship in private does not equate to freedom of practice, regarding which it is the secular state that decides. As Mahmood's case studies on the Bahais, the crucifix and the hijab illustrate, different rationales are applied to similar cases in the name of the secular notions of 'public order', 'risk of proselytism' and 'gender inequality'. As she notes: 'I have analyzed it [secularism] as an enormously generative feature of political secularism that constantly undercuts a substantive critique of its structured violence by resurrecting its own terms as the solution to that violence.'[85]

The case of the COLIBE clearly shows how a polarisation between seculars and Islamists is present in Tunisia, despite not being traceable, as Gorman argues, to the level of the individual citizen. This chapter has shown, through this empirical case, how the divide is alive and well in Tunisia, and nourished by the simplistic and Manichean imaginary of the double. Zemni explains that the secular–Islamist divide has operated as a powerful imaginary whereby Islamism was for some a threat to the new nation, and for others represented the hope of being rid of an imposed 'secularism'. Thus, 'Islamist imaginary … structured more and more the political debates'.[86] But why divide political appeal between threat and hope? Central to the issue, as Hannah Pfeifer explains, are certain underlying assumptions concerning Islamists and power; that is, that Islamists would take over a state which is unarguably secular; that the Islamists would then build an Islamic state; and that the religious and political spheres are strictly divided. Pfeifer, citing Ennahdha's Rached Ghannouchi, asserts: 'the French model of "comprehensive secularity", i.e., laicism, with its total exclusion of religion from public life, is considered as a form of state imposition of a secular lifestyle on its people.'[87]

---

84 Saba Mahmood, 'Secularism, Sovereignty, and Religious Difference: A Global Genealogy?', *Environment and Planning: Society and Space* 35.2, 2107, p. 197.
85 Mahmood, 'Secularism, Sovereignty', pp. 179–209, quotation at p. 207.
86 Zemni, 'From Revolution to Tunisianité', p. 139.
87 Hannah Pfeifer, 'The Normative Power of Secularism. Tunisian Ennahdha's Discourse on

Therefore, secularism can be considered a normative standard which, in recent times, has shaped even the Islamists' politics in Tunisia. It is crucial to ask, furthermore, whether a new-born democracy should reframe its own standards.

Bibliography

Allahoum, Rami, 'Tunisia's President Vows to Give Women Equal Inheritance Rights', Al-Jazeera, 13 August 2018, https://www.aljazeera.com/news/2018/08/tunisia-president-vows-give-women-equal-inheritance-rights-180813172138132.html.

Allal, Amin and Vincent Geisser, *Tunisie. Une démocratisation au-dessus de tout soupçon?*, Paris 2018.

Allani, Alaya, 'The Islamists in Tunisia between Confrontation and Participation: 1980–2008', *The Journal of North African Studies* 14.2, 2009, pp. 257–72.

Asad, Talal, 'Religion and Politics: An Introduction', *Social Research* 59.1, 1992, pp. 3–16.

Asad, Talal, 'Secularism, Hegemony and Fullness', SSRC (Social Science Research Council) colloquium, 7 November 2007, https://tif.ssrc.org/2007/11/17/secularism-hegemony-and-fullness/.

Asad, Talal, 'Thinking about the Secular Body, Pain and Liberal Politics', *Cultural Anthropology* 6.4, 2011, pp. 657–75.

Baskan, Birol, 'The State in the Pulpit: State Incorporation of Religious Institutions in the Middle East', *Politics and Religion* 4.1, 2011, pp. 13–53.

Bayat, Asef, 'Islamism and Social Movement Theory', *Third World Quarterly* 26.6, 2005, pp. 891–908.

Bellamine, Yassine, 'Hamma Hammami regrette la demi-mésure de Béji Caïd Essebsi et tire à boulets rouges sur Ennahdha', *Huffpost Maghreb* 3 August 2018,https://www.huffpostmaghreb.com/entry/hamma-hammami-regrette-la-demi-mesure-de-beji-caid-essebsi-et-tire-a-boulets-rouge-sur-ennahdha_mg_5b72a041e4b0bdd0620c8c6c.

Bellamine, Yassine, 'Une prière de rue à l'Avenue Habib Bourguiba en représailles au rapport de la COLIBE', *Huffpost Maghreb* 6 August 2018, https://www.huffpostmaghreb.com/entry/une-priere-collective-a-lavenue-

---

Religion, Politics and the State (2011–2016)', *Politics and Religion* 12.3, 2019, pp. 478–500, quotation at p. 14.

habib-bourguiba-en-represailles-au-rapport-de-la-colibe_mg_
5b64bfe7e4b0de86f4a166d9.

Bernstein, Elizabeth and Janet R. Jakobsen, 'Sex, Secularism and Religious
Influence in US Politics', *Third World Quarterly* 31.6, 2010, pp. 1023–39.

Boukhars, Anouar, 'The Fragility of Elite Settlements in Tunisia', *African
Security Review* 26.3, 2017, pp. 257–70.

Browers, Michaelle L., *Democracy and Civil Society in Arab Political Thought:
Transcultural Possibilities.* Syracuse, NY 2006.

Brumberg, Daniel, 'Tunisia's Fragmented and Polarized Political Landscape',
Arab Center Washington DC, 2019, http://arabcenterdc.org/policy_analyses/
tunisias-fragmented-and-polarized-political-landscape/.

Calhoun, Craig, Mark Juergensmeyer and Jonathan VanAntwerpen, *Rethinking
Secularism*, Oxford 2011.

Camau, Michel, *L'exception tunisienne. Variations sur un mythe*, Paris/Tunis
2018.

Cavatorta, Francesco and Rikke Hostrup Haugbølle, 'The End of Authoritarian
Rule and the Mythology of Tunisia under Ben Ali', *Mediterranean Politics*
17.2, 2012, pp. 179–95.

Cavatorta, Francesco and Fabio Merone, 'Moderation through Exclusion? The
Journey of the Tunisian Ennahdha', *Democratization* 20.5, 2013, pp. 857–75.

Chaabani, Nadia, *Tunisie, deuxième République: chronique d'une constituante
(2011–2014)*, Tunis 2018.

Conkle, Daniel, 'Secular Fundamentalism, Religious Fundamentalism and the
Search for Truth in Contemporary America', *Journal of Law and Religion*
12.2, 1996, pp. 337–70.

Dalacoura, Katerina, 'The Secular in Non-Western Societies', SSRC (Social
Science Research Council), 11 February 2014, https://tif.ssrc.org/2014/02/11/
the-secular-in-non-western-societies/.

Dalmasso, Emanuela and Francesco Cavatorta, 'Reforming the Family Code
in Tunisia and Morocco – the Struggle between Religion, Globalisation and
Democracy', *Totalitarian Movements and Political Religions* 11.2, 2010,
pp. 213–28.

De Rouck, Laura, 'Tunisie postrévolutionnaire: de l'effervescence démocratique
à la désillusion? L'"exception tunisienne" vue par les Tunisiens', M.A.
dissertation, Université Catholique, Louvain 2018, https://www.academia.
edu/36754247/Tunisie_post-r%C3%A9volutionnaire_de_leffervescence_
d%C3%A9mocratique_%C3%A0_la_d%C3%A9sillusion_L_exception_
tunisienne_vue_par_les_Tunisiens.

Ekins, Richard, 'Secular Fundamentalism and Democracy', *Journal of Markets and Morality* 8.1, 2005, pp. 81–93.

Gorman, Brandon, 'The Myth of the Secular–Islamist Divide in Muslim Politics: Evidence from Tunisia', *Current Sociology* 66.1, 2017, DOI: 10.1177/0011392117697460.

Grewal, Sharan, 'Can Tunisia Find a Compromise on Equal Inheritance?', The Brookings Institution, 25 September 2018, https://www.brookings.edu/blog/order-from-chaos/2018/09/25/can-tunisia-find-a-compromise-on-equal-inheritance/.

Keane, John, 'Secularism?', *The Political Quarterly* 71.1, pp. 5–19.

Lebner, Ashley B., 'The Anthropology of Secularity beyond Secularism', *Religion and Society: Advances in Research* 6, 2015, pp. 62–74.

Mabrouk, Selma, *2011–2014, Le bras de fer*, Tunis 2018.

Magdi, Amr, 'Why Executions in Egypt are Skyrocketing and Why They Should End', Human Rights Watch, 25 March 2109, https://www.hrw.org/news/2019/03/25/why-executions-egypt-are-skyrocketing-and-why-they-should-end.

Mahmood, Saba, *Politics of Piety*, Princeton 2105.

Mahmood, Saba, 'Secularism, Sovereignty, and Religious Difference: A Global Genealogy?', *Environment and Planning: Society and Space* 35.2, 2107, pp.179–209.

Mason, Lilliana, '"I Disrespectfully Agree": The Differential Effects of Partisan Sorting on Social Issue Polarization', *Midwest Political Science Association* 59.1, 2015, pp. 128–45.

Masri, Safwan and Lisa Anderson, *Tunisia: An Arab Anomaly*, New York 2017.

McCarthy, Rory, 'Re-Thinking Secularism in Post-Independence Tunisia', *The Journal of North African Studies* 19.5, 2014, pp. 733–50.

McCarthy, Rory, 'When Islamists Lose: The Politicization of Tunisia's Ennahda Movement', *The Middle East Journal* 72.3, 2018, pp. 366–84.

Merone, Fabio, 'Inheritance Reform Could Threaten Tunisia's Democratization Process', *The Globe Post* 16 September 2018, https://theglobepost.com/2018/09/16/inheritance-reform-tunisia/.

Merone, Fabio, 'Politicians or Preachers? What Ennahda's Transformation Means for Tunisia', Carnegie Middle East Centre, 31 January 2019, https://carnegie-mec.org/2019/01/31/politicians-or-preachers-what-ennahda-s-transformation-means-for-tunisia-pub-78253.

Merone, Fabio and Francesco Cavatorta, 'Post-Islamism, Ideological Evolution and "la Tunisianité" of the Tunisian Islamist Party al-Nahda', *Journal of Political Ideologies* 20.1, 2015, pp. 27–42.

Othman, Farhat, 'Colibe: Un rapport ambitieux, mais manquant de courage', *Kapitalis* 13 June 2018, http://kapitalis.com/tunisie/2018/06/13/colibe-un-rapport-ambitieux-mais-manquant-de-courage/.

Pfeifer, Hannah, 'The Normative Power of Secularism. Tunisian Ennahda's Discourse on Religion, Politics and the State (2011–2016)', *Politics and Religion* 12.3, 2019, pp. 478–500.

Polat, Ayşe, 'A Comparison of Charles Taylor and Talal Asad on the Issue of Secularity', *Human and Society*, https://pdfs.semanticscholar.org/787a/39b65 664a5d91ce4f9b6765728202c62172e.pdf?_ga=2.17155769.1024764541. 1570802986-168579641.1570802986.

Roy, Olivier, 'Islamisme et nationalisme', *Pouvoirs* 104, 2003, pp. 45–53.

Roy, Olivier, 'Le post-Islamisme', *Revue du monde musulman et de la Méditerranée* 85/86, 1999, pp. 11–30.

Sadiki, Larbi, 'The Search for Citizenship in Bin Ali's Tunisia: Democracy versus Unity', *Political Studies* 50.3, pp. 497–513.

Schwartzbrod, Alexandra, 'Le piège d'un débat idéntitaire et binaire. Entrevue à Vincent Geisser', *Libération* 19 September 2012, https://www.liberation.fr/ planete/2012/09/19/le-piege-d-un-debat-identitaire-et-binaire_847472.

Schwarz, Christoph H., 'Morocco's Social Protests across Time and Space', *openDemocracy* 13 June 2018, https://www.opendemocracy.net/en/ north-africa-west-asia/moroccos-social-protests-across-time-and-space/.

Schwedler, Jillian, 'Democratization, Inclusion and the Moderation of Islamist Parties', *Development* 50.1, 2007, pp. 56–61.

Stepan, Alfred, 'The Multiple Secularisms of Modern Democratic and Non-Democratic Regimes', *Rethinking Secularism*, eds. Craig Calhoun, Mark Juergensmeyer and Jonathan VanAntwerpen, Oxford 2011, pp. 114–44.

Stepan, Alfred, 'Religion, Democracy and the "Twin Tolerations"', *Journal of Democracy* 11.4, 2000, pp. 37–57.

Taylor, Charles, *A Secular Age*, Cambridge, MA 2007.

Wallis, Jim, *God's Politics: Why the Right Gets It Wrong and the Left Doesn't Get It*, New York 2009.

Wegner, Eva and Francesco Cavatorta, 'Revisiting the Islamist–Secular Divide: Parties and Voters in the Arab World', *International Political Science Review* 40.4, 2019, pp. 558–75.

Wolf, Anne, *Political Islam in Tunisia: A History of Ennahdha*, London 2017.

Wolf, Anne, 'What are "Secular" Parties in the Maghreb? Comparing Tunisia's Nidaa Tounes and Morocco's PAM', *Political Parties in the Arab World: Continuity and Change*, eds. Francesco Cavatorta and Lise Storm, Edinburgh 2018.

Yahya, Maha, 'Great Expectations in Tunisia', Carnegie Middle East Center, 31 March 2016, https://carnegie-mec.org/2016/03/31/great-expectations-in-tunisia-pub-63138.

Zaretsky, Robert, 'How French Secularism Became Fundamentalist', *Foreign Policy* 7 April 2016, https://foreignpolicy.com/2016/04/07/the-battle-for-the-french-secular-soul-laicite-charlie-hebdo/.

Zeghal, Malika, 'Competing Ways of Life: Islamism, Secularism and Public Order in the Tunisian Transition', *Constellations* 20.2, 2013, pp. 254–74.

Zemni, Sami, 'From Revolution to Tunisianité: Who is the Tunisian People?: Creating Hegemony through Compromise', *Middle East Law and Governance* 8.2/3, 2016, pp. 131–150.

Contributors

Alessandra Bonci is a PhD Candidate in Political Science at Laval University, Québec, Canada. She's currently working on a dissertation on Salafism in Tunisia with a gender perspective. She is interested in gender studies and politics in Tunisia and the MENA region. Bonci is also working on the secular–Islamist divide in Tunisia and the role of the Tunisian diaspora in France and Italy in the 2011 revolution. She recently published the article 'Salafi fuel for ISIS tanks? The ideological relationship between Salafism and the Islamic State' in *Mediterranean Politics*.

Amel Mili holds a JD in law and a master's degree in Public Administration from the University of Tunis, Tunisia. She holds a master's degree and a doctorate in Global Affairs from Rutgers University. From April 1991 to December 2000 Amel served as a Judge in the Administrative Court of Tunisia. From January 2010 to May 2017 Amel served as Programme Director for the Arabic Language and Culture Programme at the Lauder Institute, University of Pennsylvania. From September 2018 to present Amel works as an Assistant Teaching Professor in the Department of Global Studies and Modern Languages at Drexel University. Since 2011, Amel has been closely following, researching and writing on the political transition taking place in the MENA region. Her recent co-edited book is titled *Arab Women's Activism and Socio-Political Transformation: Unfinished Gendered Revolutions*, London. 2018

Amir Magdy Kamel is a Lecturer (Assistant Professor equivalent) in the Defence Studies Department and a Fellow in the Institute of Middle Eastern Studies, both at King's College London, UK. His research interests lie in the overlap between economics and politics, and particularly how different perspectives inform this relationship. This has led to two research projects. The first focuses on foreign policy (EU and US) and political economy issues in the Middle East and North Africa. Amir took up the role of a Visiting Scholar at Georgetown University in 2017 to carry out research for this project. The second more recent project explores how cryptocurrencies impact states and their capabilities. These research projects have resulted in various books, chapters, and articles published in peer-reviewed journals, as well as conference presentations and comments in the media. Amir holds a PhD from King's College London (2013), an MSc in International Relations (2009), and a BSc in Economics with Management Systems (2008). He also has over six years combined experience of providing advice to various government and humanitarian agencies, working as an analyst for an international economic consultancy organisation, and as a member of the steering committee for a nuclear policy focused NGO.

Amr Hamzawy is a senior research scholar at Stanford University's Center for Democracy, Development, and the Rule of Law. From September 2018 to June 2019, he was in an award year at the German Wissenschaftskolleg zu Berlin. Hamzawy was a member of Egypt's People's Assembly in 2012, having won office in the first election after the 2011 revolution. His book *On the Habits of Neo-authoritarianism: Politics in Egypt from 2013 to 2019* appeared in Arabic in September 2019.

Fatima El-Issawi is Reader in Journalism and Media Studies at the University of Essex. She is a Visiting Senior Fellow at LSE Centre for Africa and King's College Institute of Middle Eastern Studies. She is currently the Principal Investigator of the project 'Media and Transitions to Democracy: Journalistic Practices in Communicating Conflicts – The Arab Spring', funded by the British Academy Sustainable Development Programme. The project examines the interplay between news media and political conflicts in post-2011 uprisings in North Africa. Her expertise in the media industry with a specific focus on Middle East and North Africa (MENA) crosses journalism, public communication, policy and academia. She has over fifteen years of experience as international correspondent in conflict zones in the MENA region.

Francesco Cavatorta is Professor of Political Science and Director of the *Centre Interdisciplinaire de Recherche sur l'Afrique et le Moyen Orient* (CIRAM) at Laval University, Quebec, Canada. His research focuses on the dynamics of authoritarianism and democratisation in the Middle East and North Africa. His current research projects deal with party politics and the role of political parties in the region. He has published numerous journal articles and books.

Until June 2017, **George Joffé** lectured on the international relations of the Middle East and North Africa in the Department of Politics and International Studies at the University of Cambridge. He had previously been attached to the School of Oriental and African Studies and to Kings College at London University. Between 1997 and 2000, he was also Deputy Director and Acting Director of the Royal Institute of International Affairs in London. He is also the Founding Editor of the *Journal of North African Studies*.

Lahouari Addi is Professor of Sociology at the Institute of Political Studies at the University of Lyon 2 in France. He is a Research Fellow at the CERIEP (*Centre d'études et de recherches de l'Institut d'études politiques*) and at the GREMMO (*Groupe de recherches et d'études sur la Méditerranée et le Moyen-Orient*). He is also a member of the research lab CNRS Triangle. He is the author of *L'Algérie et la démocratie* (1994) and *Les Mutations de la société algérienne* (1999) published by La Decouverte. He has published *Radical Arab Nationalism and Political Islam* in 2017 with Georgetown University Press, and his latest book is titled *La crise du discours religieux musulman: le nécessaire passage de Platon à Kant*, Louvain 2019.

Maati Monjib is a Professor of Political History at the Mohammed V University in Rabat. Born in Morocco, he holds two doctorates. His first is in North African Politics obtained at Montpellier III University (France). His second is in African Political History obtained at Dakar University (Senegal). He has taught at Moroccan, Senegal, and US universities. He has authored numerous books on the Middle East, North Africa and Africa, including: *The Moroccan Monarchy and the Struggle for Power*, Paris 1992; and with Z. Daoud, *A Political Biography of Mehdi Ben Barka*, Paris 1996–2000; *Islamists Versus Secularists in Morocco*, Amsterdam 2009; *The National Movement in Northern Morocco*, Rabat 2014; and *The Press Between Information and Defamation in Morocco and Comparative Cases*, Rabat 2019. He is a former Fulbright Scholar in the United States (2005–2006) and was the 2009 Patkin Visiting Fellow at the Brookings Institution's Center for Middle East Policy. He is a human rights defender and has spent several years in political exile outside his native country (1992–2000).

Nidhal Mekki is a PhD candidate at Laval University, Canada. He holds a master's degree in Public and Financial Law from the Faculty of Juridical, Political and Social Sciences of Tunis (FSJPST). Former legal advisor at the Tunisian National Constituent Assembly, Nidhal also writes on human rights issues and democratic transition in Tunisia and Arab countries.

Roxane Farmanfarmaian is Director of International Relations and Global Studies at the University of Cambridge's Institute of Continuing Education, and Affiliated Lecturer of Modern Middle East Politics at the Department of Political and International Studies (POLIS). Awarded a 4-year, £630,000 grant from Al-Jazeera Media Corp. in 2013, she was Principal Investigator of the University of Cambridge–Al-Jazeera Media Project researching 'Media in Political Transition in Turkey, Tunisia, and Morocco'. A founding member of the Centre of International Relations of the Middle East and North Africa based at POLIS, she was also Editor of the *Cambridge Review of International Affairs* from 2002–2005. She obtained her PhD and MPhil from Cambridge, and BA from Princeton. Her publications include *Blood and Oil: A Prince's Memoir of Iran, From the Shah to the Ayatollah*; *War and Peace in Qajar Persia: Implications Past and Present,* and numerous journal articles, including two special issues of the *Journal of North African Studies* on 'Media in Tunisia' and 'Moroccan Medias' and a special issue of *Middle East Critique* on 'Media in Turkey'. A compiled volume, *Media in Political Transition in the Southern Mediterranean* is forthcoming from Routledge.

Salam Kawakibi is the Director of the Arab Center for Resaerch and Policy Studies, Paris, France. Between 2007 and 2017 he was Deputy Director and Research Director in Arab Reform Initiative. He is also the president of Initiative for a New Syria, president of board of trustees of Ettijahat – Independent culture (www.ettijahat.org), president of board of The Day After association (www.tda-sy.org), and a member of the Consultative Council of the Mediterranean Citizens' Assembly (www.acimedit.net). Salam Kawakibi is also a member of the Advisory Committee of the UNU Institute on Globalization, Culture and Mobility (UNU-GCM). He teaches in the Masters programme on Development and Migration at Université Paris 1 Panthéon-Sorbonne. Between 2009 and 2011, he was Principal Researcher at the Faculty of Political Science of the University of Amsterdam and between 2000 and 2006 he was director of the *Institut Français du Proche Orient* (IFPO) in Aleppo, Syria. He holds a DEA in Political Sciences from l'Institut d'Etudes Politiques, Aix-En-Provence, a DEA in International Relations from Aleppo University and a BA in Economics from Aleppo University.

Sarah Yerkes is a Fellow in Carnegie's Middle East Program, where her research focuses on Tunisia's political, economic, and security developments as well as state–society relations in the Middle East and North Africa. She has been a Visiting Fellow at the Brookings Institution and a Council on Foreign Relations International Affairs Fellow and has taught in the Security Studies Program at Georgetown University and at the Elliott School of International Affairs at the George Washington University. She is a former member of the State Department's policy planning staff, where she focused on North Africa. Previously, she was a foreign affairs officer in the State's Department's Office of Israel and Palestinian affairs. She also served as a geopolitical research analyst for the US military's Joint Staff Strategic Plans and Policy Directorate (J5) at the Pentagon, advising the Joint Staff leadership on foreign policy and national security issues.